Employment Law: The Essentials

12th edition

David Lewis and Malcolm Sargeant

David Lewis is Professor of Employment Law at Middlesex University Law School and a member of the CIPD. Apart from teaching on a range of degree courses and being a regular contributor to specialist commercial seminars, he has considerable experience as a consultant. He is a member of the editorial committee of the *Industrial Law Journal* and was appointed an ACAS arbitrator in 1999.

Malcolm Sargeant is Professor of Labour Law at Middlesex University Business School. He has written widely on employment law subjects, especially on issues related to transfers of undertakings, discrimination in employment and age discrimination. Prior to becoming an academic he was personnel manager of a large financial services company and director of a recruitment and management consultancy. He teaches Discrimination Law and Employment Law at Middlesex University and is an Academic Fellow of the CIPD.

The Chartered Institute of Personnel and Development is the leading publisher of books and reports for personnel and training professionals, students, and all those concerned with the effective management and development of people at work. For details of all our titles, please contact the publishing department:

tel: 020 8612 6204

e-mail: publishing@cipd.co.uk

The catalogue of all CIPD titles can be viewed on the CIPD website: www.cipd.co.uk/bookstore

Employment Law: The Essentials

12th edition

David Lewis and Malcolm Sargeant

Chartered Institute of Personnel and Development

Published by the Chartered Institute of Personnel and Development,
151, The Broadway, London, SW19 1JQ
This edition first published 2013
First edition published 1983
Second edition published 1986
Third edition published 1990
Fourth edition published 1994
Fifth edition published 1997
Sixth edition published 2000
Seventh edition published 2002
Eighth edition published 2004
Ninth edition published 2007
10th edition published 2009
11th edition published 2011

Designed by Exeter Premedia, India
Printed in Great Britain by Bell & Bain, Glasgow

British Library Cataloguing in Publication Data

A catalogue of this publication is available from the British Library

ISBN 978 1 84398 315 6

Chartered Institute of Personnel and Development, CIPD House,
151, The Broadway, London, SW19 1JQ
Tel: 020 8612 6200
E-mail: cipd@cipd.co.uk
Website: www.cipd.co.uk
Incorporated by Royal Charter.
Registered Charity No. 1079797

Contents

	Abbreviations	x
	List of cases cited	xiii
	Preface to the 12th edition	xxxii
	Walkthrough of textbook features and online resources	xxxv
Chapter 1	The Sources and Institutions of Employment Law	1
	Civil and criminal law	1
	Legislation and codes of practice	2
	Common law and the court hierarchy	3
	European Union law	5
	The key institutions	7
	Key learning points	12
	Explore further	14
Chapter 2	Formation of the Contract of Employment (1): The sources of terms	15
	Contracts of employment	15
	Express terms and statutory statements	17
	Collective agreements	22
	Workforce agreements	24
	Works rules and policy guidance	25
	Custom and practice	26
	Terms implied by statute and regulations	26
	Terms implied by the common law	27
	Key learning points	27
	Explore further	30
Chapter 3	Formation of the Contract of Employment (2): Implied terms of law	31
	Duties of the employer	31
	Duties of the employee	39
	Public interest disclosures	43
	The law governing inventions and copyright	46
	Key learning points	48
	Explore further	51
Chapter 4	Recruitment and Selection	53
	Employment status	53
	Outsourcing	57
	Fixed-term or indefinite contract?	57
	Part-time or full-time?	59
	Should temporary employees or agency staff be hired?	62

	Should a probationary period be imposed?	67
	Regulatory constraints	67
	Key learning points	69
	Explore further	72
Chapter 5	Pay Issues	73
	The duty to pay wages	73
	The national minimum wage	76
	Pay statements	80
	Guarantee payments	80
	Pay and sickness	82
	Statutory sick pay	84
	Suspension on medical grounds	85
	Key learning points	86
	Explore further	89
Chapter 6	Discrimination Against Employees (1)	91
	Equality law	91
	The protected characteristics	93
	Prohibited conduct	102
	Harassment and victimisation	110
	Like for like comparison	112
	Discrimination at work	113
	Key learning points	114
	Explore further	117
Chapter 7	Discrimination (2): Lawful Discrimination, Vicarious Liability, Burden of Proof, Enforcement and Equality of Terms	119
	Lawful discrimination: the exceptions	119
	An employer's vicarious liability for discrimination by employees	129
	The burden of proof in discrimination claims	132
	Enforcement	134
	The Equality and Human Rights Commission	135
	Public sector equality duty	136
	Key learning points	146
	Explore further	150
Chapter 8	Parental Rights	151
	Time off for antenatal care	151
	Maternity leave	152
	Statutory maternity pay	157
	Parental leave	159
	Ordinary paternity leave	162
	Additional paternity leave	164
	Adoption leave	166

	Time off for dependants	168
	Flexible working	170
	Risk assessment	173
	Key learning points	175
	Explore further	178
Chapter 9	Health and Safety at Work	179
	Injury prevention and injury compensation	179
	The Health and Safety at Work Act 1974	181
	Regulations	184
	Inspection and enforcement	191
	Offences	194
	Key learning points	196
	Explore further	200
Chapter 10	The Regulation of Working Time	201
	The Working Time Regulations 1998	201
	Time off for trade union duties and activities	213
	Time off for employee representatives and employee trustees of pension funds	218
	Time off for study or training	219
	Time off to look for work	219
	Key learning points	220
	Explore further	224
Chapter 11	Variation, Breach and Termination of the Contract of Employment at Common Law	225
	Variation	225
	Breach of contract	226
	Automatic termination: frustration	229
	Termination without notice: summary dismissal	230
	Termination with notice	231
	Remedies for wrongful dismissal	232
	Key learning points	233
	Explore further	236
Chapter 12	Unfair Dismissal (1): Exclusions and the Meaning of Dismissal	237
	Exclusions and qualifications	237
	The meaning of dismissal	238
	Constructive dismissal	240
	The effective and relevant date of termination	244
	Key learning points	246
	Explore further	249

Chapter 13	Unfair Dismissal (2): Potentially Fair Reasons and the Concept of Reasonableness	251
	Giving a reason for dismissal	251
	Automatically unfair dismissal	253
	Potentially fair reasons for dismissal	255
	Industrial action and lack of jurisdiction	262
	Reasonableness in the circumstances	263
	The Code of Practice and procedural fairness	265
	Key learning points	269
	Explore further	273
Chapter 14	Redundancy	275
	Qualifications and exclusions	275
	The definition of redundancy	276
	Offers of alternative employment	278
	Unfair redundancy	279
	Consultation	282
	Key learning points	283
	Explore further	286
Chapter 15	Unfair Dismissal and Redundancy Claims	287
	Making a claim	287
	Conciliation and compromise agreements	290
	Arbitration	291
	The remedies for unfair dismissal	292
	Awards of compensation	294
	Calculating a redundancy payment	299
	Employee rights on insolvency	300
	Key learning points	301
	Explore further	305
Chapter 16	Continuity of Employment and Transfers of Undertakings	307
	Continuity of employment	307
	A week's pay	313
	Transfers of undertakings	315
	Key learning points	325
	Explore further	328
Chapter 17	Information and Consultation	329
	Introduction: duties to inform and consult	329
	Transnational information and consultation	330
	Information and consultation requirements in the United Kingdom	334
	The Information and Consultation Regulations 2004	334
	Confidentiality	339
	Penalties and protection	339

	Collective redundancies	340
	Transfers of undertakings	347
	Health and safety	349
	Key learning points	355
	Explore further	359
Chapter 18	Trade Unions and Collective Bargaining	361
	Trade unions and Certificates of Independence	361
	Recognition	364
	Statutory recognition procedures	365
	Disclosure of information for collective bargaining	367
	The legal enforceability of collective agreements	370
	Discrimination on the grounds of trade union membership or activities	370
	Industrial action	374
	Picketing	379
	Union responsibility for the acts of its members and officials	381
	Remedies	382
	Industrial action that affects the supply of goods or services to an individual	383
	Key learning points	384
	Explore further	387
	Glossary	**389**
	Index	**393**

Abbreviations

AC Appeal Cases

ACAS Advisory, Conciliation and Arbitration Service

ACOP Approved Code of Practice

All ER All England Law Reports

CA Court of Appeal

CAC Central Arbitration Committee

CBI Confederation of British Industry

Ch Chancery Division

CJEU Court of Justice of the European Union, formerly the European Court of Justice (ECJ)

CMLR Common Market Law Reports

CO Certification Officer

COSHH Control of Substances Hazardous to Health Regulations 2002

DPA Data Protection Act 1998

EA Employment Act 2002

EA 2010 Equality Act 2010

EADR Regulations Employment Act 2002 (Dispute Resolution) Regulations 2004

EAT Employment Appeal Tribunal

EC European Community

ECA European Communities Act 1972

ECHR European Court of Human Rights

ECJ – *see* CJEU

ECR European Court Reports

EHRC Equality and Human Rights Commission

EHRR European Human Rights Reports

ERA Employment Rights Act 1996

ERel Act Employment Relations Act 1999

ETA Employment Tribunals Act 1996

EU European Union

EWC Expected Week of Confinement

EWC Directive European Works Council Directive 1994

EWCA England and Wales Court of Appeal

HASAWA Health and Safety at Work Act 1974

HMRC Her Majesty's Revenue and Customs

HRA Human Rights Act 1998

HSCE Regulations Health and Safety (Consultation with Employees) Regulations 1996

HSE Health and Safety Executive

ICR Industrial Cases Reports

IRLIB Industrial Relations Legal Information Bulletin

IRLR Industrial Relations Law Reports

LBPIC Regulations Telecommunications (Lawful Business Practice) (Interception of Communications) Regulations 2000

LWTL Lawtel

MA Maternity Allowance

MHSW Regulations Management of Health and Safety at Work Regulations 1999

MPL Regulations Maternity and Parental Leave etc Regulations 1999

NMW National Minimum Wage

NRA Normal retirement age

PAL Regulations Paternity and Adoption Leave Regulations 2002

PPE Personal Protective Equipment

PTW Regulations Part-time Workers (Prevention of Less Favourable Treatment) Regulations 2000

QB Queen's Bench Division

RIDDOR Reporting of Injuries, Diseases and Dangerous Occurrences Regulations 1995

RIP Regulation of Investigatory Powers Act 2000

RTOST Regulations Right to Time off for Study or Training Regulations 2001

SAP Statutory Adoption Pay

SC Supreme Court

SI Statutory Instrument

SMP Statutory Maternity Pay

SNB Special Negotiating Body

SRSC Regulations Safety Representatives and Safety Committee Regulations 1977

SSCBA Social Security and Benefits Act 1992

SSP Statutory Sick Pay

TFEU Treaty on the Functioning of the European Union

TICE Regulations Transnational Information and Consultation of Employees Regulations 1999

TUC Trades Union Congress

TULRCA Trade Union and Labour Relations (Consolidation) Act 1992

TUPE Regulations Transfer of Undertakings (Protection of Employment) Regulations 2006

TURERA Trade Union Reform and Employment Rights Act 1993

UKHL United Kingdom House of Lords

WLR Weekly Law Reports

WT Working Time

WT Regulations Working Time Regulations 1998

List of cases cited

***Abernethy v Mott, Hay and Anderson* (1974) IRLR 213** **239**
Abrahams v Performing Rights Society (1995) IRLR 486 236
Adamas Ltd v Cheung (2011) IRLR 1014 234
Adams v British Airways (1996) IRLR 574 29
Adams v Lancashire County Council (1996) IRLR 154 327
Adamson v B&L Cleaning Ltd (1995) IRLR 193 ..... 50, 270
Addison v Ashby (2003) IRLR 211 203
Adeneler v Ellinikos Organismos Galaktos Case C-212/04 (2006) IRLR 716 70
Adin v Sedco Forex International (1997) IRLR 280 82
Affleck v Newcastle Mind (1999) IRLR 405 28
Airbus Ltd v Webb (2008) IRLR 309 268
Airlie v City of Edinburgh District Council (1996) IRLR 516 29
Alabaster v Barclays Bank (No.2) (2005) IRLR 576 149
Alamo Group (Europe) Ltd v Tucker (2003) IRLR 266 348
Alboni v Ind Coope Retail Ltd (1998) IRLR 131 271
Alcan Extrusions v Yates (1996) IRLR 327 247
Alexander v STC Ltd (1991) IRLR 286 234
Ali v Christian Salvesen Food Services Ltd (1997) IRLR 17 ..... 18–19, 312
Alidair Ltd v Taylor (1978) IRLR 82 272
Allders International v Parkins (1981) IRLR 68 ..... 228, 230
Allonby v Accrington and Rossendale College (2004) IRLR 224 148
Alma Ltd v Bonner (2011) IRLR 204 302
Alonso v Osakidetza-Servicio (2007) IRLR 911 70
Amicus v City Building (2009) IRLR 253 358
Amicus v Macmillan Publishers Ltd (2007) IRLR 885 356
Amministrazione delle Finanze v Simmenthal Case 106/77 (1978) ECR 629 13
Amnesty International v Ahmed (2009) IRLR 884 ..... 104, 120
Anglian Homes Ltd v Kelly (2004) IRLR 793 272
Annabel's (Berkeley Square) Ltd v HM Revenue and Customs Commissioners (2009) ICR 1123 ..... 315, 327
Annandale Engineering v Samson (1994) IRLR 59 28
APAC v Kirwin (1978) IRLR 318 357
Aparau v Iceland Frozen Foods (1996) IRLR 119 ..... 29, 234, 248, 285
Archibald v Fife Council (2004) IRLR 651 129
Armour v Skeen (1977) IRLR 310 194
Armstrong v Newcastle NHS Trust (2006) IRLR 124 148
Artisan Press v Strawley (1986) IRLR 126 303
Ashley v Ministry of Defence (1984) IRLR 57 222
ASLEF v Brady (2006) IRLR 76 269
Asociación Nacional de Grandes Empresas de Distribución v Federación De Asociaciones Sindicales Case C-78/11 (2012) IRLR 779 209
Aspden v Webbs Poultry Group (1996) IRLR 521 83
Attorney-General v Blake (2001) IRLR 37 234

Attorney General's reference (No.1 of 1983) 1 All ER 369 87
AUT v Newcastle University (1987) ICR 317 285
Autoclenz Ltd v Belcher (2011) IRLR 820 55
Avon and Somerset Police Authority v Emery (1981) ICR 229 149
Avon County Council v Howlett (1993) 1 All ER 1073 87
Awotana v South Tyneside NHS Trust (2005) IRLR 958 303
Azmi v Kirklees M B.C. (2007) IRLR 484 .... 108, 109

***B v A* (2007) IRLR 576 .... 102**
B v BAA (2005) IRLR 927 247
Babula v Waltham Forest College (2007) IRLR 346 51
BAC v Austin (1978) IRLR 332 48
Bacica v Muir (2006) IRLR 35 .... 203, 220
Bainbridge v Circuit Foil UK Ltd (1997) IRLR 305 88
Bakers' Union v Clark's of Hove (1978) IRLR 366 342
Balfour Kilpatrick Ltd v Acheson (2003) IRLR 683 .... 270, 271, 387
Balgobin and Francis v London Borough of Tower Hamlets (1987) IRLR 401 130
Bank of Credit and Commerce SA v Ali (No.3)(1999) IRLR 508 .... 48, 234
Barber v RJB Mining (UK) Ltd (1999) IRLR 308 204
Barnsley M.B.C. v Prest (1996) ICR 85 304
Bass Leisure v Thomas (1994) IRLR 104 285
Baxter v Harland & Wolff (1990) IRLR 516 49
BCCI v Ali (No.3)(1999) IRLR 508 .... 48, 234
Beneviste v University of Southampton (1989) IRLR 122 149
Benson v Secretary of State (2003) IRLR 748 304
Benton v Sanderson Kayser (1989) IRLR 299 285
Bevan Ashford v Malin (1995) IRLR 360 272
Birch and Humber v University of Liverpool (1985) IRLR 165 239
Blackburn v Chief Constable of West Midlands Police (2009) IRLR 135 143
Bliss v South East Thames Regional Health Authority (1985) IRLR 308 .... 234, 248
Blue Star Ltd v Williams (1979) IRLR 16 255
Blyth v Scottish Liberal Club (1983) IRLR 245 235
Bolton Roadways Ltd v Edwards (1987) IRLR 392 271
Bolton School v Evans (2006) IRLR 500 51
Boorman v Allmakes Ltd (1995) IRLR 553 303
Booth v United States of America (1999) IRLR 16 308
Boots plc v Lees (1986) IRLR 485 293
Borders Regional Council v Maule (1993) IRLR 199 223
Bosworth v A Jowett (1977) IRLR 341 48
Botel's case [*Arbeiterwohlfahrt der Stadt Berlin v Botel*] (1992) IRLR 423 148
Botzen v Rotterdamsche Droogdok Maatschappij BV Case 186/83 (1986) 2 CMLR 50 .... 319, 337
Bouchaala v Trust House Forte (1980) IRLR 382 260
Bowden v Tuffnel Parcels Express Ltd (2001) IRLR 838 202
Boxfoldia Ltd v NGA (1988) IRLR 383 387
Boyo v Lambeth Borough Council (1995) IRLR 50 .... 234, 235
Brandon v Murphy Bros (1983) IRLR 54 272

Brasserie du Pêcheur SA v Federal Republic of Germany (1996) ECR 1029 13
Braund Ltd v Murray (1991) IRLR 100 304
British Airways v Henderson (1979) ICR 77 220
British Airways v Moore and Botterill (2000) IRLR 296 174
British Airways v UNITE the Union (No.2)(2010) IRLR 809 378–9
British Airways plc v Williams Case C-155/10 (2011) IRLR 948 221
British Bakeries v Adlington (1989) IRLR 218 222
British Coal v Cheesebrough (1990) IRLR 148 313
British Home Stores v Burchell (1978) IRLR 379 258–9
British Leyland v Powell (1978) IRLR 57 149
British Nursing Association v Inland Revenue (2002) IRLR 480 77–8
British Telecom v Sheridan (1990) IRLR 27 13
British Telecommunications v Roberts and Longstaffe (1996) IRLR 601 106–7
Britool Ltd v Roberts (1993) IRLR 481 304
Bromley v Quick Ltd (1988) IRLR 249 149
Bromsgrove v Eagle Alexander (1981) IRLR 127 262
Brown v JBD Engineering Ltd (1993) IRLR 568 248
Brownbill v St Helens & Knowsley NHS Trust (2011) IRLR 128 139
Brunnhofer v Bank der Österreichischen Postsparkasse AG (2001) IRLR 571 148
Buckland v Bournemouth University (2010) IRLR 445 248
Burlo v Langley (2007) IRLR 145 304
Burns v Santander UK plc (2011) IRLR 639 75–6
Byrne v BOC Ltd (1992) IRLR 505 272
Byrne v City of Birmingham D.C. (1987) IRLR 191 326
Byrne Brothers (Formwork) Ltd v Baird (2002) IRLR 96 220

***Cable & Wireless v Muscat* (2006) IRLR 355** **71**
Cadman v Health and Safety Executive (2006) IRLR 969 149
Cadoux v Central Regional Council (1986) IRLR 131 29
Calder v Rowntree Mackintosh (1993) IRLR 212 149
Caledonian Mining Ltd v Bassett (1987) IRLR 165 248
Cambridge and District Co-op v Ruse (1993) IRLR 156 285
Cambridge and Peterborough NHS Trust v Crouchman (2009) ICR 306 301
Camden and Islington NHS Trust v Kennedy (1996) IRLR 381 302
Canniffe v East Riding Council (2000) IRLR 555 131
Cantor Fitzgerald v Bird (2002) IRLR 867 248
Cantor Fitzgerald International v Callaghan (1999) IRLR 234 .... 50, 248
Capek v Lincolnshire County Council (2000) IRLR 590 234
Capital Hartshead Ltd v Byard (2012) IRLR 814 286
Capita Health Solutions Ltd v McLean (2008) IRLR 595 .... 322, 327
Capper Pass Ltd v Lowton (1976) IRLR 366 148
Carl v University of Sheffield (2009) IRLR 616 70
Carlson v Post Office (1981) IRLR 158 .... 372, 385
Carmichael v National Power plc (2000) IRLR 43 .... 55–6, 64, 69, 71
Cartwright v Clancey Ltd (1983) IRLR 355 88
Catamaran Cruisers v Williams (1994) IRLR 386 271
Caterpillar Logistics Services (UK) Ltd v Huesca de Crean (2012) IRLR 410 50

Cavenagh v Evans Ltd (2012) IRLR 679 235
Cavendish Munro Professional Risks Management Ltd v Geduld (2010) IRLR 38 51
Cawley v South Wales Electricity Board (1985) IRLR 89 248
Cerberus Ltd v Rowley (2001) IRLR 160 235
Cereal Packaging Ltd v Lynock (1998) IRLR 510 256
Certification Officer v Squibb UK Staff Association(1979) IRLR 75 364
Chapman v Letheby & Christopher Ltd (1981) IRLR 440 248
Chief Adjudication Officer v Rhodes (1999) IRLR 103 35
Chief Constable of Lincolnshire Police v Stubbs (1999) IRLR 81 130
Chief Constable of West Yorkshire Police v Vento (2001) IRLR 124 113
Christie v Haith Ltd (2003) IRLR 670 149
Churchill v Yeates Ltd (1983) IRLR 187 288
Clark v BET plc (1997) IRLR 348 235
Clark v Nomura plc (2000) IRLR 766 235
Clark v Oxfordshire Health Authority (1998) IRLR 125 69
Clarke v Redcar and Cleveland Borough Council. (2006) IRLR 324 302
Cleveland County Council v Springett (1985) IRLR 131 .... 358, 385
Clwyd C.C. v Leverton (1985) IRLR 197 149
Cole Ltd v Sheridan (2003) IRLR 52 248
Colen and another v Cebrian (UK) Ltd (2004) IRLR 210 16
Colley v Corkindale (1995) ICR 965 311
Collison v BBC (1998) IRLR 239 325
Commerzbank AG v Keen (2007) IRLR 132 28
Commission v UK (1994) IRLR 292 13
Commission v UK [2007] IRLR 721 197
Commission for Racial Equality v Dutton (1989) IRLR 8 115
Commissioners of Inland Revenue v Post Office Ltd (2003) IRLR 199 203
Commissioner of Police of the Metropolis v Shaw (2012) IRLR 291 51
Commotion Ltd v Rutty (2006) IRLR 172 173
Consignia plc v Sealy (2002) IRLR 624 302
Consistent Group Ltd v Kalwak (2008) IRLR 505 71
Constantine v Cory Ltd (2000) ICR 939 302
Converform Ltd v Bell (1981) IRLR 195 234
Cook v Square D Ltd (1992) IRLR 34 49
Coors Ltd v Adcock (2007) IRLR 440 87
Corner v Buckinghamshire Council (1978) IRLR 320 228
Cornwall County Council v Prater (2006) IRLR 362 310
Corps of Commissionaires Ltd v Hughes (2009) IRLR 122 221
Corr v IBC Ltd (2008) ICR 372 35
Cox v Sun Alliance Ltd (2001) IRLR 448 50
Coxall v Goodyear Great Britain Ltd (2002) IRLR 742 .... 37, 49
CPS Recruitment Ltd v Bowen (1982) IRLR 54 .... 274, 284
Crawford v Suffolk Mental Health Partnership NHS Trust (2012) IRLR 402 49
Credit Suisse Ltd v Armstrong (1996) IRLR 450 50
Croke v Hydro Aluminium Worcester Ltd (2007) ICR 1303 51
Cross v Highlands and Islands Enterprise (2001) IRLR 336 49
Crossley v Faithful & Gould Ltd (2004) IRLR 377 48
Crosville Wales Ltd v Tracey and another (No.2) (1996) IRLR 691 303

Crosville Motor Services Ltd v Ashfield (1986) IRLR 475 386
Crouch v British Rail Engineering Ltd (1988) IRLR 404 37
Crowson Fabrics Ltd v Rider (2008) IRLR 288 50
Curling v Securicor (1992) IRLR 549 285
Curr v Marks & Spencer plc (2003) IRLR 75 311

***Da'Bell v NSPCC* (2010) IRLR 19 .... 134**
Dacas v Brook Street Bureau (UK) Ltd (2004) IRLR 358 65
Dattani v Trio Supermarkets Ltd (1998) IRLR 240 86
Davies v HSE (2003) IRLR 170 .... 195, 200
Davies v M J Wyatt (Decorators) Ltd (2000) IRLR 759 221
Davies v Neath Port Talbot Borough Council (1999) IRLR 769 214
Dawkins v Department of the Environment sub nom Crown Suppliers PSA (1993) IRLR 284 115
Dawnay, Day & Co. v de Bracconier d'Alphen (1997) IRLR 285 50
Deakin v Kuehne & Nagel Drinks Logistics Services Ltd (2012) IRLR 513 221
Deary v Mansion Hide Upholstery Ltd (1983) IRLR 195 200
Deeley v British Rail Engineering Ltd (1980) IRLR 147 28
Degnan v Redcar B.C. (2005) IRLR 615 148
De Grasse v Stockwell Tools (1992) IRLR 269 286
Delaney v Staples (1992) IRLR 191 75
Delaney v Staples t/a De Montfort Recruitment (1991) IRLR 112 87
Dench v Flynn & Partners (1998) IRLR 653 295
Dentmaster (UK) Ltd v Kent (1997) IRLR 636 50
Department for Work and Pensions v Thompson (2004) IRLR 348 101
Department for Work and Pensions v Webley (2005) IRLR 288 58–9
Department of Constitutional Affairs v Jones (2008) IRLR 128 134
Devis & Sons Ltd v Atkins (1977) IRLR 314 269
Devonshire v Trico-Folberth (1989) IRLR 397 303
Dietman v London Borough of Brent (1988) IRLR 299 235
Digital Equipment Co Ltd v Clements (No.2) (1998) ICR 258 304
Dines v Initial Health Care Services and Pall Mall Services Group Ltd (1994) IRLR 336 327
Discount Tobacco v Williams (1993) IRLR 327 86
DJM International Ltd v Nicholas (1996) IRLR 76 .... 70, 315
Dobie v Burns International (1984) IRLR 329 271
Doble v Firestone Tyre and Rubber Co. Ltd (1981) IRLR 300 247
Dominguez v Centre Informatique de Centre Ouest Atlantique Case C-282/10 (2012) IRLR 321 .... 209, 221
Drage v Governors of Greenford High School (2000) IRLR 314 249
Driver v Air India (2011) IRLR 992 48
Dryden v Greater Glasgow Health Board (1992) IRLR 469 248
Dudley Bower Building Services Ltd v Lowe (2003) IRLR 260 327
Dugdale v Kraft Foods (1976) IRLR 368 140
Dugmore v Swansea NHS Trust (2003) IRLR 164 190
Duncombe and others v Secretary of State for Children, Schools and Families (2011) IRLR 498 70

Dunlop Tyres Ltd v Blows (2001) IRLR 629 29
Dunnachie v Hull City Council (2004) IRLR 727 297–8
Duport Steels Ltd v Sirs (1980) IRLR 116 377
Dutton v Hawker Siddeley Aviation Ltd (1978) IRLR 390 219–20

***Eagland v British Telecom plc* (1992) IRLR 323 .... 29**
Eastwood v Magnox plc (2004) IRLR 733 48
Eaton v Nuttall (1977) IRLR 71 148
EBR Attridge Law v Coleman (No.2) (2010) IRLR 10 102–3
ECM (Vehicle Delivery Services) Ltd v Cox (1999) IRLR 559 70
Edinburgh Council v Brown (1999) IRLR 208/243 385
Edwards v Chesterfield Royal Hospital NHS Foundation Trust (2012) IRLR 129 235
EETPU v Times Newspapers (1980) 1 All ER 1097 232 362
E Green Ltd v ASTMS and AUEW (1984) IRLR 135 357
Elkouil v Coney Island Ltd (2003) IRLR 174 .... 283, 286
Elizabeth Claire Ltd v Francis (2005) IRLR 858 270
Ely v YKK Ltd (1993) IRLR 500 .... 269, 271
Enderby v Frenchay Health Authority (1993) IRLR 591 .... 142, 149
Enessy Co. v Minoprio (1978) IRLR 489 303
Enfield Technical Services Ltd v Payne (2008) IRLR 500 28
English v Thomas Sanderson Blinds Ltd (2008) IRLR 342 103
Eurobrokers Ltd v Rabey (1995) IRLR 206 50
Evans v Malley Organisation Ltd (2003) IRLR 156 314
Evesham v North Hertfordshire Health Authority (1999) IRLR 155 139
Eversheds Legal Services v De Belin (2011) IRLR 448 154
Express and Echo Publications v Tanton (1999) IRLR 367 56
Eweida v British Airways (2010) IRLR 322 109

***Faccenda Chicken Ltd v Fowler* (1986) IRLR 69 .... 42**
Fairfield Ltd v Skinner (1993) IRLR 3 87
Farnsworth Ltd v McCoid (1999) IRLR 626 385
Farrant v The Woodroffe School (1998) IRLR 176 .... 50, 262
Farrell, Matthews & Weir v Hansen (2005) IRLR 160 86
Fecitt v NHS Manchester (2012) IRLR 64 51
Federatie Nederlandse Vakbeweging v Staat der Nederlanden Case C-124/05 (2006) IRLR 561 221
Fentiman v Fluid Engineering Ltd (1991) IRLR 150 304
First West Yorkshire Ltd v Haigh (2008) IRLR 182 270
Fitzgerald v University of Kent (2004) IRLR 300 248
Flack v Kodak Ltd (1986) IRLR 255 310
Flett v Matheson (2006) IRLR 277 .... 28, 235
Ford v Warwickshire County Council (1983) IRLR 126 326
Ford Motor Co. v Hudson (1978) IRLR 66 269
Foreningen af Arbejdsledere i Danmark v Daddy's Dance Hall A/S (1988) IRLR 315 .... 321, 327
Frames Snooker v Boyce (1992) IRLR 472 271

Fraser v HLMAD Ltd (2006) IRLR 687 234
Fraser v South West London St George's Mental Health Trust (2012) IRLR 100 .... 48, 221
Freeman v Sovereign Chicken Ltd (1991) IRLR 408 302
Fyfe v Scientific Furnishings Ltd (1989) IRLR 331 303

***Gallacher v Department of Transport* (1994) IRLR 231 .... 385**
Gallagher v Alpha Catering Services Ltd (2005) IRLR 102 .... 208, 221
Gardner Ltd v Beresford (1978) IRLR 63 243
Garside & Laycock Ltd v Booth (2011) IRLR 735 271
Gascol Conversions v Mercer (1974) IRLR 155 29
Gate Gourmet Ltd v TGWU (2005) IRLR 881 .... 382–3, 386, 387
Gaviero v Galicia (2011) IRLR 504 70
GCSF v Certification Officer (1993) IRLR 260 364
General of the Salvation Army v Dewsbury (1984) IRLR 222 325
G F Sharp & Co. Ltd v McMillan (1998) IRLR 632 234
Gibbons v Associated British Ports (1985) IRLR 376 29
Gilbert v Kembridge Fibres Ltd (1984) IRLR 52 302
Gilham v Kent County Council (1985) IRLR 16 252
Gisda Cyf v Barratt (2009) IRLR 933 249
Glitz v Watford Electrical (1978) IRLR 89 28
GMB v Man Truck and Bus UK Ltd (2000) IRLR 636 341
GMB v Rankin (1992) IRLR 514 357
GMB and AMICUS v Beloit Walmsley Ltd (2004) IRLR 18 357
Gogay v Hertfordshire County Council (2000) IRLR 703 227–8
Goodwin v Cabletel (1997) IRLR 665 355
Goold Ltd v McConnell (1995) IRLR 516 49
Grainger v Nicholson (2010) IRLR 4 99
Greenhof v Barnsley M.B.C. (2006) IRLR 98 49
Gregory v Wallace (1998) IRLR 387 236
Gryf-Lowczowski v Hinchingbroke Healthcare NHS Trust (2006) IRLR 100 234
Guinness Ltd v Green (1989) IRLR 289 304
Gunton v London Borough of Richmond (1980) IRLR 321 230

***Hairsine v Kingston-upon-Hull City Council* (1992) IRLR 211 .... 222**
Hamilton v Argyll and Clyde Health Authority (1993) IRLR 99 270
Hamilton v Futura Floors (1990) IRLR 478 29
Hanson v Fashion Industries (1980) IRLR 393 326
Harding v London Underground (2003) IRLR 252 272
Hardy v Tourism South East (2005) IRLR 243 357
Harlow v Artemis Ltd (2008) IRLR 629 234
Harper v Virgin Net Ltd (2004) IRLR 390 234
Harris v Courage Ltd (1982) IRLR 509 271
Harris & Russell Ltd v Slingsby (1973) IRLR 221 235
Harrison v Norwest Holst (1985) IRLR 240 248
Hart v Marshall & Sons (1977) IRLR 61 229
Hartmann v South Essex NHS Trust (2005) IRLR 293 49

Harvard Securities v Younghusband (1990) IRLR 17 269
Haseltine Lake & Co. v Dowler (1981) IRLR 25 239
Hayward v Cammell Laird (1988) IRLR 257 .... 138, 142, 148
Heasmans v Clarity Cleaning (1987) IRLR 286 69
Heathmill Ltd v Jones (2003) IRLR 865 272
Heggie v Uniroyal Englebert Tyres Ltd (1998) IRLR 425 303
Hellyer Bros v Atkinson (1994) IRLR 88 239
Hempell v W H Smith & Sons Ltd (1986) IRLR 95 285
Henderson v Connect Ltd (2010) IRLR 466 271
Hennessy v Craigmyle Ltd (1985) IRLR 446 302
Henry v LGTS Ltd (2002) IRLR 472 29
Hewcastle Catering v Ahmed (1991) IRLR 473 16
Hewett v Brown Ltd (1992) ICR 530 49
Hibbins v Hester Way Neighbourhood Project (2008) UKEAT/0275/08 51
High Table Ltd v Horst (1997) IRLR 514 285
Hill v C A Parsons & Co. Ltd (1971) 3 WLR 995 231
Hill v Chapell (2002) IRLR 19 221
Hill v General Accident (1998) IRLR 641 83–4
Hilton v Shiner Ltd (2001) IRLR 727 48
Hilton Hotels v Protopapa (1990) IRLR 316 247
Hindes v Supersine Ltd (1979) IRLR 343 285
Hinton v University of East London (2005) IRLR 552 .... 291, 302
HM Revenue and Customs v Leisure Management Ltd (2007) IRLR 450 87
Holis Metal Industries Ltd v GMB (2008) IRLR 187 327
Hollister v National Farmers Union (1979) IRLR 238 .... 234, 261
Homan v A1 Bacon Ltd (1996) ICR 846 304
Home Office v Bailey (2005) IRLR 757 144
Homer v Chief Constable of West Yorkshire Police (2010) IRLR 619 104
Hone v Six Continents Retail Ltd (2006) IRLR 49 .... 38, 49
Hough v Leyland DAF Ltd (1991) IRLR 194 285
Hounslow L.B.C. v Klusova (2008) ICR 396 271
Howlett Marine Services Ltd v Bowlam (2001) IRLR 201 357
Howman & Sons v Blyth (1983) IRLR 139 82
Huet v Université de Bretagne Occidentale (2012) IRLR 703 70
Hughes v Corps of Commissionaires Management Ltd (2011) IRLR 915 208
Hughes v London Borough of Southwark (1988) IRLR 55 234
Huntley v Thornton (1957) 1 WLR 321 386
Hussman Manufacturing Ltd v Weir (1998) IRLR 288 86
Hyland v J. Barker Ltd (1985) IRLR 403 325
Hynd v Armstrong (2007) IRLR 338 321

***Ibekwe v LGTS Ltd* (2003) IRLR 697 .... 49**
ICL v Kennedy (1981) IRLR 28 235
Igbo v Johnson Matthey (1986) IRLR 215 247
Industrious Ltd v Horizon Ltd (2010) IRLR 204 302
Inspector of Factories v Austin Rover (1989) IRLR 404 198

Institution of Professional Civil Servants v Secretary of State for Defence (1987) IRLR 373 347
Intel Corporation Ltd v Daw (2007) IRLR 355 49
International Paint Co. v Cameron (1979) IRLR 62 286
IPC Ltd v Balfour (2003) IRLR 11 74
Item Software v Fassihi (2004) IRLR 928 50

***Jackson v Liverpool City Council* (2011) IRLR 1019 .... 50**
James v London Borough of Greenwich (2008) IRLR 302 71
Janata Bank v Ahmed (1981) IRLR 457 51
Jeetle v Elster (1985) IRLR 227 326
John Brown Engineering Ltd v Brown (1997) IRLR 90 286
John Lewis plc v Coyne (2001) IRLR 139 257
Johnson v Nottingham Police Authority (1974) ICR 170 285
Johnson v Peabody Trust (1996) IRLR 387 285
Johnson v Unisys Ltd (2001) IRLR 716 236
Johnson v Unisys Ltd (2002) IRLR 271 48
Jones v Associated Tunnelling Co. (1981) IRLR 477 21
Jones v Aston Cabinet Co. Ltd (1973) ICR 292 285
Jones v Gwent County Council (1992) IRLR 521 235
Jones v Tower Boot Co. Ltd (1997) IRLR 168 129–30
Jouini v Princess Personal Service GmbH (2007) IRLR 1005 327
Judge v Crown Leisure Ltd (2005) IRLR 823 .... 228, 234
Julio v Jose (2012) IRLR 180 .... 77, 87
Junk v Kühnel Case C-188/03 (2005) IRLR 310 .... 342, 343, 356

***Katsikas v Konstantidis* (1992) ECR 6577 .... 321**
Katskikas v Konstantidis (1993) IRLR 179 327
Keeley v Fosroc Ltd (2006) IRLR 961 .... 24, 28
Kells v Pilkington plc (2002) IRLR 693 149
Kenny v South Manchester College (1993) IRLR 265 316
Kent Management Services v Butterfield (1992) IRLR 394 87
Kerr v The Sweater Shop (1996) IRLR 424 86
Kerry Foods Ltd v Lynch (2005) IRLR 680 247
Keywest Club v Choudhury (1988) IRLR 51 326
Khatri v Cooperatieve Centrale Raiffeisen-Boerenleenbank BA (2010) IRLR 715 234
KHS AG v Schulte Case C-214/10 (2012) IRLR 156 222
Kimberley Group Housing Ltd v Hambley (2008) IRLR 682 320
King v Eaton Ltd (1996) IRLR 199 286
King v Eaton Ltd (No.2) (1998) IRLR 686 286
King v Great Britain-China Centre (1991) IRLR 513 .... 132–3, 134
Kingston v British Rail (1984) IRLR 146 271
Kingston upon Hull City Council v Dunnachie (No.3) (2003) IRLR 843 304
Kirklees MBC v Radecki (2009) IRLR 555 248
Knapton v ECC Clothing Ltd (2006) ICR 1084 304

Korashi v Abertawe Bro Morgannwg University Local Health Board (2012) IRLR 4 51
Kulkarni v Milton Keynes Hospital NHS Trust (2009) IRLR 829 272
Kuzel v Roche Products Ltd (2008) IRLR 530 51
Kwik-Fit v Lineham (1992) IRLR 156 247

***Ladbroke Racing v Arnott* (1983) IRLR 154** **271**
Ladele v London Borough of Isligton (2010) IRLR 211 .... 99, 108
Laing v Manchester City Council (2006) IRLR 748 133
Laird v A K Stoddart Ltd (2001) IRLR 591 87
Lakshmi v Mid Cheshire Hospitals NHS Trust (2008) IRLR 956 29
Lancashire Fires Ltd v SA Lyons & Co. Ltd (1997) IRLR 113 50
Lancaster University v University and College Union (2011) IRLR 4 344
Land Securities v Thornley (2005) IRLR 765 248
Landeshauptstadt Kiel v Jaeger (2003) IRLR 804 221
Landmark Brickwork Ltd v Sutcliffe (2011) IRLR 976 50
Lange v Schünemann GmbH (2001) IRLR 244 17
Langston v AUEW (1974) ICR 180 48
Lanton Leisure v White (1987) IRLR 119 247
Lassman v De Vere University Arms Hotel (2002) ICR 44 247
Lassman v Secretary of State (1999) ICR 416 304
Latimer v AEC Ltd (1953) AC 643 36
Laughton v Bapp Industrial Ltd (1986) IRLR 245 .... 50, 270
Laws v Keane (1982) IRLR 500 200
Leech v Preston B.C. (1985) IRLR 337 248
Leicestershire County Council v UNISON (2005) IRLR 920 343
Leisure Leagues Ltd v Maconnachie (2002) IRLR 600 .... 28, 221
Lesney Products Ltd v Nolan (1977) IRLR 77 277
Leyland Vehicles Ltd v Reston (1981) IRLR 19 304
List Design Group Ltd v Douglas, Catley and others (2003) IRLR 14 87
Lister v Hedley Hall Ltd (2001) IRLR 472 54
Litster v Forth Dry Dock Engineering Co Ltd (1989) IRLR 161 .... 13, 327
Lock v Cardiff Railway Co. Ltd (1998) IRLR 358 .... 257, 272
Logan Salton v Durham C.C. (1989) IRLR 99 247
London Ambulance Service v Charlton (1992) IRLR 510 222
London Borough of Harrow v Cunningham (1996) IRLR 256 272
London Borough of Islington v Ladele (2010) IRLR 211 ....
London Borough of Newham v Skingle (2003) IRLR 72 ....
London Borough of Newham v Ward (1985) IRLR 509 248
London Borough of Southwark v O'Brien (1996) IRLR 240 86
London Borough of Waltham Forest v Omilaju (2005) IRLR 35 .... 242, 248
London Probation Board v Kirkpatrick (2005) IRLR 443 .... 308, 311
London Underground Ltd v Associated Society of Locomotive Engineers and Firemen (2012) IRLR 196 .... 378, 386
London Underground v Noel (1999) IRLR 621 301
Lovett v Biotrace International Ltd (1999) IRLR 375 235
Lovie Ltd v Anderson (1999) IRLR 164 271

Luke v Stoke on Trent City Council (2007) IRLR 305 50
Lyddon v Englefield Brickwork Ltd (2008) IRLR 198 222

***Macari v Celtic F.C.* (1999) IRLR 787** **234**
MacCartney v Oversley House Management (2006) IRLR 514 207–8
MacFarlane v Glasgow City Council (2000) IRLR 7 69
Macmillan Inc v Bishopsgate Investment (1993) IRLR 393 50
MacShane and Ashton v Express Newspapers (1980) IRLR 35 376–7
Maidment v Cooper & Co. (1978) IRLR 462 149
Mailway (Southern) Ltd v Willsher (1978) IRLR 322 88
Malik v Bank of Credit and Commerce (1997) IRLR 462 .... 48, 234
Mandla v Dowell Lee (1983) IRLR 209 97
Mangold v Helm Case C-144/04 (2006) IRLR 143 6
Marleasing SA v La Comercial Internacional de Alimentacion SA (1990) ECR 4135 13
Marley Ltd v Anderson (1996) IRLR 163 301
Marshall v Industrial Systems Ltd (1992) IRLR 294 258
Marshall v NM Financial Management (1996) IRLR 20 51
Marshall v Southampton and SW Hampshire A.H.A. (1986) IRLR 140 13
Martin v MBS Fastenings (1983) IRLR 198 248
Matthews v Kent & Medway Fire Authority (2006) ICR 365 60
Maund v Penwith District Council (1984) IRLR 24 386
Mayr v Bäckerei und Konditorei Gerhard Flöckner Case C-506/06 (2008) IRLR 387 96
McAdie v Royal Bank of Scotland (2007) IRLR 895 270
McBride v Falkirk FC (2012) IRLR 22 48
McCarthys Ltd v Smith (1980) IRLR 208 6
McClintock v Department of Constitutional Affairs (2008) IRLR 29 99–100
McDermid v Nash Dredging (1987) IRLR 334 49
McDowell v Eastern BRS Ltd (1981) IRLR 482 285
McFarlane v Relate Avon (2010) IRLR 872 116
McKie v Swindon College (2011) IRLR 575 39
McKindley v W Hill Ltd (1985) IRLR 492 285
McLaren v Home Office (1990) IRLR 338 235
McLean v Rainbow Homeloans Ltd (2007) IRLR 15 270
McMeechan v Secretary of State for Employment (1997) IRLR 353 63
McNeil v Crimin Ltd (1984) IRLR 179 248
Mears v Safecar Security Ltd (1982) IRLR 501 88
Mennell v Newell & Wright Ltd (1997) IRLR 519 270
Methuen v Cow Industrial Polymers (1980) IRLR 289 149
Metroline Travel v UNITE the Union (2012) IRLR 749 .... 378, 386
Metropolitan Resources Ltd v Churchill Dulwich Ltd (2009) IRLR 700 319
Middlesbrough B.C. v TGWU (2002) IRLR 332 357
Mihlenstedt v Barclays Bank (1989) IRLR 522 28
Miklaszewicz v Stolt Offshore Ltd (2002) IRLR 344 51
Millbrook Furnishing Ltd v McIntosh (1981) IRLR 309 243
Ministry of Defence v Crook (1982) IRLR 488 222

Modern Injection Moulds Ltd v Price (1976) IRLR 172 285
Monk Staff Association v CO and ASTMS (1980) IRLR 431 363
Montgomery v Johnson Underwood Ltd (2001) IRLR 269 64
Moore v Duport Furniture (1982) IRLR 31 290
Morgan v West Glamorgan County Council (1995) IRLR 68 86
Morgans v Alpha Plus Ltd (2005) IRLR 234 304
Morris v Secretary of State (1985) IRLR 297 304
Morris v Walsh Western UK Ltd (1997) IRLR 562 308
Morris Angel v Hollande (1993) IRLR 169 50
Morrison v ATGWU (1989) IRLR 361 303
Morrow v Safeway Stores (2002) IRLR 9 .... 49, 247, 248
Motherwell Railway Club v McQueen (1989) ICR 419 303
Motorola Ltd v (1) Davidson and (2) Melville Craig Group Ltd (2001) IRLR 4 ....64, 71
Mowlem Northern Ltd v Watson (1990) IRLR 500 248
Moyhing v Barts and London NHS Trust (2006) IRLR 860 104
Mugford v Midland Bank plc (1997) IRLR 208 282
Murco Petroleum Ltd v Forge (1987) IRLR 50 248
Murray v Foyle Meats Ltd (1999) IRLR 562 .... 276, 277

***NAAFI v Varley* (1976) IRLR 408** **149**
Nagarajan v London Regional Transport (1999) IRLR 572 112
NCB v NUM (1986) IRLR 439 29
Nelson v BBC (No.2) (1979) IRLR 304 303
Nerva v UK (2002) IRLR 815 327
New Century Cleaning v Church (2000) IRLR 27 86
New ISG Ltd v Vernon (2008) IRLR 115 322–3
Nicoll v Nocorrode Ltd (1981) IRLR 163 325
Northamptonshire County Council v Entwhistle (2010) IRLR 740 302
Northgate HR Ltd v Mercy (2008) IRLR 222 286
Nottcutt v Universal Equipment Ltd (1986) I WLR 641 235
Nova Plastics Ltd v Froggatt (1982) IRLR 146 40–1
NUGSAT v Albury Bros (1978) IRLR 504 385
NURMTW v Serco Ltd (2011) IRLR 399 386
Nyazi v Rymans Ltd (1988) IRLIB 367 115

***OBG Ltd v Allan* (2007) IRLR 608** **386**
O'Brien v Sim-Chem Ltd (1980) IRLR 373 149
Octavius Atkinson Ltd v Morris (1989) IRLR 158 244
O'Kelly v Trust House Forte (1983) IRLR 286 71
O'Neill v Buckinghamshire County Council (2010) IRLR 384 178
Optare Group plc v TGWU (2007) IRLR 931 340
Owen & Briggs v James (1982) IRLR 502 132

***P v Nottingham County Council* (1992) IRLR 362** **271**
Paggetti v Cobb (2002) IRLR 861 .... 304, 326
Palmer v Southend B.C. (1984) IRLR 119 301

Panama v London Borough of Hackney (2003) IRLR 278 270
Pape v Cumbria County Council (1991) IRLR 404 37
Paris v Stepney Borough Council (1951) AC 376 49
Parker Foundry Ltd v Slack (1992) IRLR 11 303
Parkinson v March Consulting (1997) IRLR 308 269
Parkwood Leisure Ltd v Alemo-Herron (2011) IRLR 696 324
Parr v Whitbread plc (1990) IRLR 39 271
Parry v National Westminster Bank (2005) IRLR 193 303
Patel v Nagesan (1995) IRLR 370 301
Patel v RCMS Ltd (1999) IRLR 161 234
Patsystems v Neilly (2012) IRLR 979 50
Payne e v Secretary of State (1989) IRLR 352 326
Pearson v Kent County Council (1993) IRLR 165 326
Peninsula Business Services Ltd v Sweeney (2004) IRLR 49 86
PennWell Publishing (UK) Ltd v Ornstein and others (2007) IRLR 700 50
Pentney v Anglian Water Authority (1983) ICR 463 49
Pereda v Madrid Movilidad SA (2009) IRLR 959 222
Perkin v St Georges NHS Trust (2005) IRLR 934 271
Pfaffinger v City of Liverpool Community College (1996) IRLR 508 .... 276, 285
Pfeiffer and others v Deutsches Rotes Kreuz, Kreisverband Waldshut eV (2005) IRLR 137 221
Pickford v ICI (1998) IRLR 435 198
Pickford v Imperial Chemical Industries (1996) IRLR 622 49
Pickstone v Freemans plc (1988) IRLR 357 .... 13, 149
Pinewood Repro Ltd v Page (2011) ICR 508 286
Polentarutti v Autokraft Ltd (1991) IRLR 457 303
Port of London Authority v Payne (1992) IRLR 447 .... 292, 303
Port of Tilbury v Birch (2005) IRLR 92 304
Post Office v Sanhotra (2000) IRLR 866 248
Potter v Secretary of State for Employment (1997) IRLR 21 305
Powers and Villiers v A Clarke & Co. (1981) IRLR 483 285
Pressure Coolers Ltd v Molloy (2011) IRLR 630 327
Protectacoat Ltd v Szilagi (2009) IRLR 365 69
Pruden v Cunard Ltd (1993) IRLR 317 302
PSM International v McKechnie (1992) IRLR 279 51

***Qua v John Ford Morrison Solicitors* (2003) IRLR 184** **169–70**
Quashie v Stringfellows Restaurants Ltd (2012) IRLR 536 69
Quinn v Calder (1996) IRLR 126 29

***R v Associated Octel* (1997) IRLR 123** **183**
R v Attorney General for Northern Ireland (1999) IRLR 315 .... 205–6, 221
R v Boal (1992) IRLR 420 200
R v Bradford Teaching Hospital (2011) IRLR 582 272
R v British Steel (1995) IRLR 310 198
R v Broxtowe Borough Council ex parte Bradford (2000) IRLR 329 235
R v CAC (2006) IRLR 53 .... 367, 385

R v CAC ex parte BTP Tioxide (1982) IRLR 61 368
R v CAC ex parte Hy-Mac Ltd (1979) IRLR 461 14
R v CAC (on the application of the BBC) (2003) IRLR 460 14
R (on the application of Ultraframe) v Central Arbitration Committee (2005) IRLR 641 .... 336–7, 385
R v Chargot (2008) UKHL 73 .... 198, 200
R v Chief Constable of Merseyside Police ex parte Calveley (1986) 2 WLR 144 .. 235
R v Davies (2002) EWCA Crim. 2949 197
R v East Berkshire Health Authority ex parte Walsh (1984) IRLR 278 235
R v HTM Ltd (2006) EWCA Crim. 1156 .... 197, 198
R v F Howe & Son (1999) IRLR 434 200
R v Gateway Foodmarkets Ltd (1997) IRLR 189 181
R v Governing Body of Jewish Free School (2010) IRLR 136 97–8
R v Liverpool City Corporation (1985) IRLR 501 86
R v Nelson Group Services (Maintenance) Ltd (1998) 4 All ER 331 198
R v Rollco Screw Co Ltd (1999) IRLR 439 200
R (on the application of Age UK) v Secretary of State for Business, Innovation and Skills (2009) IRLR 1017 147
R v Secretary of State ex parte Factortame (1996) ECR 1029 13
R v Swan Hunter Shipbuilders Ltd and Telemeter Installations Ltd 183
R v Trustees of the Science Museum (1993) 3 All ER 853 198
R Cort & Son Ltd v Charman (1981) IRLR 437 248
Rainey v Greater Glasgow Health Board (1987) IRLR 26 .... 143, 149
Ramsey v Walkers Snack Foods Ltd (2004) IRLR 754 272
Rank Nemo (DMS) v Coutinho (2009) IRLR 672 112
Rank Xerox v Stryczek (1995) IRLR 568 302
Ranson v Customer Systems (2012) IRLR 769 50
Rao v Civil Aviation Authority (1994) IRLR 240 303
Ravat v Halliburton Manufacturing and Services Ltd (2012) IRLR 315 247
Ready Case Ltd v Jackson (1981) IRLR 312 247
Ready Mixed Concrete (South East) Ltd v Minister of Pensions and National Insurance (1968) 1 All ER 433 71
Redfearn v Serco Ltd (2006) IRLR 623 116
Reiss Engineering v Harris (1985) IRLR 23 47
Rentokil Ltd v Mackin (1989) IRLR 286 272
Revenue and Customs Commissioners v Annabel's Ltd (2008) ICR 1076 87
Rhondda Cynon Taf County Borough Council v Close (2008) IRLR 868 271
Richmond Pharmacology v Dhaliwal (2009) IRLR 336 111
Ridgway v NCB (1987) IRLR 80 385
Rigby v Ferodo Ltd (1997) IRLR 516 248
RMT v Midland Mainline Ltd (2001) IRLR 813 386
Robb v London Borough of Hammersmith (1991) IRLR 72 234
Robertson v Blackstone Franks Investment Management Ltd (1998) IRLR 376 ... 86
Robertson v British Gas (1983) IRLR 302 21
Robins UK v Triggs (2007) IRLR 857 .... 242, 248
Robinson v Crompton Parkinson (1978) IRLR 61 49
Robinson v Tescom Corporation (2008) IRLR 408 258
Robinson-Steele v RD Retail Services Ltd Case C-131/04 (2006) IRLR 386 211, 222

Rock Refrigeration Ltd v Jones (1996) IRLR 675 50
Rock-It Cargo Ltd v Green (1997) IRLR 582 302
Rockfon case [*Rockfon A/S v Specialarbejderforbundet i Danmark acting on behalf of Nielsen and others*] (1996) IRLR 168 357
Rodway v South Central Trains (2005) IRLR 583 160–1
Rogers v Chloride Systems (1992) ICR 198 271
Rolls-Royce Ltd v Price (1993) IRLR 203 286
Rolls-Royce plc v UNITE the Union (2009) IRLR 49 124–5
Rose v Dodd (2005) IRLR 977 234
Rowe v Radio Rentals (1982) IRLR 177 268
Royal Bank of Scotland v Harrison (2009) IRLR 28 .... 168–9, 177
Royal Mail Group v Communication Workers Union (2009) IRLR 1046 358
RSPCA v Cruden (1986) IRLR 83 303
Rummler v Dato-Druck GmbH (1987) IRLR 32 149
Russell v Transocean International Resources Ltd (2012) IRLR 149 210
Rutten v Cross Medical Ltd (1997) IRLR 249 28
Ryford Ltd v Drinkwater (1995) IRLR 16 222

***Sagar v Ridehalgh* (1931) Ch 310 .... 29**
St John of God Ltd v Brooks (1992) IRLR 546 271
Safeway Stores v Burrell (1997) IRLR 200 285
Sainsburys Ltd v Hitt (2003) IRLR 23 270
Salford Royal NHS Trust v Roldan (2010) IRLR 721 272
Saunders v National Scottish Camps Association (1981) IRLR 277 271
Savage v Saxena (1998) IRLR 182 296
SBJ Stephenson v Mandy (2000) IRLR 233 50
SCA Packaging Ltd v Boyle (2009) IRLR 54 115
Scally v Southern Health Board (1991) IRLR 522 49
Schmidt v Austicks Bookshops (1977) IRLR 360 101
Schmidt v Spar- und Leihkasse der Früheren Ämter Bordesholm, Kiel und Cronshagen (1994) IRLR 302 .... 316, 317, 327
Schultz v Esso Petroleum Co. Ltd (1999) IRLR 488 301
Scott v Coalite (1988) IRLR 131 247
Scottbridge Ltd v Wright (2003) IRLR 21 77
Scottish Midland Co-op v Cullion (1991) IRLR 261 270
Secretary of State v ASLEF (1972) QB 443 40
Secretary of State v Banks (1983) ICR 48 302
Secretary of State v Bearman (1998) IRLR 431 28
Secretary of State for Trade and Industry v Bottrill (1999) IRLR 326 284
Secretary of State v Campbell (1992) IRLR 263 271
Secretary of State v Cohen (1987) IRLR 169 325
Secretary of State v Crane (1988) IRLR 238 326
Secretary of State v Globe Elastic Ltd (1979) IRLR 327 .... 304, 326
Secretary of State v Lassman (2000) IRLR 411 326
Secretary of State v Stone (1994) ICR 761 304
Secretary of State v Walden (2001) IRLR 168 304
Secretary of State v Woodrow (1983) IRLR 11 304

Securicor Guarding Ltd v Fraser Security Services (1996) IRLR 552 70
Securicor Ltd v Smith (1989) IRLR 356 273
Seldon v Clarkson Wright and Jakes (2012) IRLR 591 123
SG&R Valuation Service Co. v Boudrais and others (2008) IRLR 770 32
Sharma v Manchester City Council (2008) IRLR 336 70
Shaw v CCL Ltd (2008) IRLR 284 ....
Shawkat v Nottingham City Hospital NHS Trust (No.2) (2001) IRLR 559 285
Sheet Metal Components Ltd v Plumridge (1979) IRLR 86 234
Sheffield City Council v Norouzi (2011) IRLR 897 131–2
Shepherd Ltd v Jerrom (1986) IRLR 358 235
Shillito v Van Leer (1997) IRLR 495 355
Shook v London Borough of Ealing (1986) IRLR 46 270
Sidhu v Aerospace Composite Technology (2000) IRLR 602 130
Sillars v Charrington Ltd (1989) IRLR 152 326
Silvey v Pendragon plc (2001) IRLR 685 235
Sim v Rotherham M.B.C. (1986) IRLR 391 50
Sime v Sutcliffe Catering Ltd (1990) IRLR 228 69
Singer Co. v Ferrier (1980) IRLR 300 285
Singh v British Steel (1974) IRLR 478 29
SIP Ltd v Swinn (1994) IRLR 323 87
Skiggs v South West Trains Ltd (2005) IRLR 459 .... 222, 272
Slaughter v Brewer Ltd (1990) IRLR 426 303
Smith v Cherry Lewis Ltd (2005) IRLR 86 357
Smith v City of Glasgow D.C. (1987) IRLR 326 271
Smith v London Metropolitan University (2011) IRLR 884 50
Smith v Safeway (1996) IRLR 456 101
Smith v Scot Bowyers Ltd (1986) IRLR 315 49
Snoxell v Vauxhall Motors (1997) IRLR 123 149
Société Générale (London Branch) v Geys (2011) IRLR 482 247
Sothern v Franks Charlesly (1981) IRLR 278 240
South Ayrshire Council v Morton (2002) IRLR 256 148
Southern Cross Ltd v Perkins (2011) IRLR 247 29
Southwark London Borough Council v Whillier (2001) ICR 142 385
Spaceright Europe Ltd v Baillavoine (2012) IRLR 111 321
Spackman v London Metropolitan University (2007) IRLR 744 234
Spence v Department of Agriculture and Rural Development (DARD) (2011) IRLR 806 277
Spencer v Gloucestershire County Council (1985) IRLR 393 278
Spijkers v Gebroeders Benedik Abattoir CV (1986) ECR 1119 .... 315, 318, 327
Spring v Guardian Assurance plc (1994) IRLR 460 38–9
Springboard Trust v Robson (1992) IRLR 261 141
Stacey v Babcock Power Ltd (1986) IRLR 3 272
Staffordshire C.C. v Secretary of State (1989) IRLR 117 247
Staffordshire County.Cpuncil. v Donovan (1981) IRLR 108 240
Stapp v Shaftesbury Society (1982) IRLR 326 248
Stephens & Sons v Fish (1989) ICR 324 326
Stewart v Moray Council (2006) IRLR 592 337–8
Stratford v Lindley (1965) AC 307 386

Street v Derbyshire Unemployed Worker Centre (2004) IRLR 687 51
Stringer v HM Revenue & Customs (2009) IRLR 214 210
Strouthos v London Underground Ltd (2004) IRLR 636 272
Sun Printers Ltd v Westminster Press Ltd (1982) IRLR 92 51
Sunderland Polytechnic v Evans (1993) ICR 196 87
Susie Radin v GMB (2004) IRLR 400 345–6
Sutherland v Hatton (2002) IRLR 263 .... 49, 198
Sutherland v Network Appliance (2001) IRLR 12 302
Süzen v Zehnacker Gebäudereinigung (1997) IRLR 255 327
Swainston v Hetton Victory Club (1983) IRLR 164 .... 301, 302
Sweeney v J & S Henderson Ltd (1999) IRLR 306 309
Sweetin v Coral Racing (2006) IRLR 252 358
Systems Floors (UK) Ltd v Daniel (1981) IRLR 475 29

***Tanner v Kean* (1978) IRLR 110 .... 240**
Taplin v C. Shippam Ltd (1978) IRLR 450 386
Tarbuck v Sainsburys Ltd (2006) IRLR 664 273
Tasci v Pekalp of London Ltd (2001) ICR 633 186
Taylor v Kent County Council (1969) 2 QB 560 285
Taylor v OCS Ltd (2006) IRLR 613 273
Taylor v Parsons Peebles Ltd (1981) IRLR 199 270
TBA Industrial Products Ltd v Morland (1982) IRLR 331 248
Tele Danmark [*Tele Danmark A/S v Handels- og Kontorfunktionærernesforbund i Danmark*] (2001) IRLR 853 .... 106, 116
Tele-trading Ltd v Jenkins (1990) IRLR 430 204
ten Oever's case [*ten Oever v Stichting Bedrijfspensioenfonds voor het Glazenwassers- en Schoonmaakbedrijf*] (1993) IRLR 601 148
TFS Derivatives Ltd v Morgan (2005) IRLR 246 50
TGWU v Howard (1992) IRLR 170 304
Thomas v Farr Plc (2007) IRLR 419 50
Thomas v NCB (1987) IRLR 451 149
Thomas v NUM (South Wales) (1985) IRLR 136 380
Thompson v GEC Avionics (1991) IRLR 448 248
Thomson v Alloa Motor Co. (1983) IRLR 403 271
Tice v Cartwright (1999) ICR 769 326
Ticehurst v British Telecom (1992) IRLR 219 234
Tower Hamlets Health Authority v Anthony (1989) IRLR 394 272
Tradewind Airways Ltd v Fletcher (1981) IRLR 272 298
Transco plc v O'Brien (2002) IRLR 444 49
Tullett Prebon PLC v BGC Brokers LP (2010) IRLR 648 .... 49, 241
Tyne & Wear Autistic Society v Smith (2005) IRLR 336 302

***UBS Ltd v Vestra LLP* (2008) IRLR 965 .... 50**
UCATT v Brain (1981) IRLR 224 270
UCATT v Rooke & Son Ltd (1978) IRLR 204 357
UK v Council of the European Union (1997) ICR 443 220
UK Coal Mining Ltd v National Union of Mineworkers (2008) IRLR 4 357

Unison v UK (2002) IRLR 497 386
United Bank v Akhtar (1989) IRLR 507 29
United Distillers v Conlin (1992) IRLR 503 270
University College London Hospital NHS Trust v Unison (1999) IRLR 31 376
University of Nottingham v Eyett (1999) IRLR 87 33

***Vakante v Governors of Stanhope School (No.2)* (2005) ICR 231** **28**
Vento v Chief Constable of West Yorkshire Police (No.2) (2003) IRLR 102 134
Viasystems v Thermal Transfer Ltd (2005) IRLR 953 49
Virgo Fidelis School v Boyle (2004) IRLR 268 51
Visa v Paul (2004) IRLR 42 49

***WAC Ltd v Whillock* (1990) IRLR 23** **51**
Wadley v Eager Electrical (1986) IRLR 93 261
Walker v J Wedgewood Ltd (1978) IRLR 105 49
Walker v Northumberland County Council (1995) IRLR 35 49
Wall v STC (1990) IRLR 55 235
Wall's Meat Co. Ltd v Khan (1978) IRLR 499 288
Walton v Independent Living Organisation (2003) IRLR 469 87
Walton Centre for Neurology v Bewley (2008) IRLR 588 149
Wandsworth London Borough Council v D'Silva (1998) IRLR 193 25
Wang v University of Keele (2011) IRLR 542 248
Wardle v Credit Agricole Bank (2011) IRLR 604 304
Warrilow v Walker Ltd (1984) IRLR 304 303
Weddall v Barchester Health Care (2012) IRLR 307 69
Werhof v Freeway Traffic Systems GmbH & Co. (2006) IRLR 400 28
West Bromwich Building Society v Townsend (1983) IRLR 147 .... 197, 200
West Midlands Co-op Ltd v Tipton (1986) IRLR 112 .... 249, 272
Weston v Vega Space Ltd (1989) IRLR 509 325
Westwood v Secretary of State (1984) IRLR 209 236
Whiffen v Milham Ford Girls School (2001) IRLR 468 281
Whitbread plc v Hall (2001) IRLR 275 272
White v Holbrook Ltd (1985) IRLR 215 49
White v Pressed Steel Fisher (1980) IRLR 176 354
White v Reflecting Roadstuds (1991) IRLR 332 248
Wignall v British Gas (1984) IRLR 493 216
Wilcox v Hastings (1987) IRLR 299 285
Wilding v BT plc (2002) IRLR 524 303
William Hill Organisation Ltd v Tucker (1998) IRLR 313 32
Williams v Compair Maxam Ltd (1982) IRLR 83 280
Williams v Watsons Ltd (1990) IRLR 164 235
Willoughby v CF Capital plc (2012) IRLR 985 247
Willow Oak Ltd v Silverwood (2006) IRLR 607 .... 265, 271, 272
Wilson v Post Office (2000) IRLR 834 269
Wilson & Bros Ltd v USDAW (1978) IRLR 20 344
Wilton v Cornwall Health Authority (1993) IRLR 482 247
Wiluszynski v London Borough of Tower Hamlets (1989) IRLR 279 227

Wood v Coverage Care Ltd (1996) IRLR 264 270
Wood Group Heavy Industrial Turbines Ltd v Crossan (1998) IRLR 680 293
Woods v WM Car Services (1982) IRLR 413 49
Woodward v Abbey National plc (2006) IRLR 677 51
WPM Retail v Lang (1978) IRLR 343 226
Wren v Eastbourne Borough Council (1993) IRLR 425 .... 70, 327

***X v Y* (2004) IRLR 625 .... 272**

***Yemm v British Steel* (1994) IRLR 117 .... 86**

***Zaman v Kozee Sleep Products Ltd (trading as Dorlux Beds UK)* (2011) IRLR 196 .... 348**

Preface to the 12th edition

There have been many changes to employment law since the previous edition was published and, at the time of writing, there is an Enterprise and Regulatory Reform Bill in Parliament. Major adjustments are planned in relation to dispute resolution, in particular by offering alternatives to employment tribunal adjudication and charging fees for hearings. Some of the measures are politically and economically contentious, but we hope that students will find that this enhances their interest in the subject.

Last but not least, we wish to draw attention to the fact that this book was originally published in 1983. We are grateful to the CIPD, its editors and production staff for ensuring that it has remained continuously in print over this 30-year period and look forward to many more editions.

David Lewis and Malcolm Sargeant

November 2012

Learning outcomes of the CIPD advanced level module Employment Law are covered in the text as follows:

Employment Law learning outcome	**Indicative module content**	***Employment Law* chapters**
1 Explain the core principles that underpin employment law as it applies in the UK, including common law, their purpose, origin and practical implications.	• accessing employment rights: employment status, worker status, continuity of employment, immigration regulations	Chapters 4 and 16
	• contracts of employment: establishing and changing contracts, express and implied terms, written statements of major terms and conditions	Chapters 2 and 3
	• discrimination law: the law as it relates to discrimination under the Equality Act 2010 because of the eight *protected characteristics*, namely Age, Disability, Gender Reassignment, Marriage and Civil Partnership, Race, Religion or Belief, Sex and Sexual Orientation, plus Pregnancy or Maternity, and also protection given to part-time workers, fixed-term employees and ex-offenders	Chapters 4, 6 and 7
	• dismissal law: unfair dismissal, constructive dismissal, wrongful dismissal, redundancy payments	Chapters 11–14
	• health and safety: criminal sanctions and their enforcement, personal injury law as it relates to the workplace, Working Time regulations	Chapters 3, 9 and 10
	• wages and salaries: unlawful deductions, the National Minimum Wage regulations, law on equality of terms, the payment of Statutory Sick Pay (SSP)	Chapters 5 and 7
	• transfer of undertakings law: rights relating to dismissal, terms and conditions of employment, consultation and continuity of employment in transfer situations	Chapter 16 and 17
	• family-friendly employment law: rights for primary carers; maternity, paternity and adoption pay and leave entitlements; the law relating to ante-natal care; the health and safety of pregnant workers; parental leave; time off for family emergencies; the right to request flexible working	Chapter 8
	• confidentiality issues: data protection law, interception of communications, the protection of trade secrets, the law on 'whistle-blowing'	Chapter 3
	• collective employment law: freedom of association, rights of trade union officials, industrial action, collective bargaining, right to be accompanied by a trade union representative, consultation rights	Chapters 10, 13, 17 and 18

Employment Law learning outcome	Indicative module content	*Employment Law* chapters
2 Advise colleagues about significant legal implications of decisions, plans or proposals in the employment field.	• The practical impact of the above body of law on day-to-day management activities and decision-making in organisations; the level and nature of risk associated with acting unlawfully, particularly where significant change is contemplated or planned.	Chapters 2–17
3 Advise about the appropriate action that should be taken in workplace scenarios where employment regulation applies.	• Approaches to recommend that are both lawful and effective in fields such as recruitment and selection, establishing terms and conditions, maintaining the working environment, managing performance, communication and involvement, discipline, pay and reward, training and development, allocating work and managing retirement.	Chapters 2–5, 6, 7, 9–15 and 17
4 Play a leading role in determining the appropriate organisational response when legal action on the part of a worker or employee is anticipated, threatened or taken	• Managing disciplinary and grievance procedures, undertaking disciplinary investigations, taking witness statements; sources of information on the expectations of the law, employer defences and on case law precedents.	Chapters 1 and 11–15
5 Participate in the preparation, presentation and settling of employment tribunal cases.	• Employment tribunals and other courts with jurisdiction to hear employmentrelated matters, tribunal procedures, rules of evidence, remedies; assessing the risks and potential costs associated with defending or settling claims in practice; alternative means of resolving disputes through mediation and arbitration.	Chapters 1, 7 and 15
6 Know how to keep their knowledge of developments in employment law up to date and advise about the impact of these developments on employment policy and practice in their organisations.	• Sources of information about the employment law and its evolution, including ACAS and the CIPD; key current and anticipated future developments and their practical significance for organisations.	Chapter 1

Walkthrough of textbook features and online resources

Abbreviations

AC Appeal Cases
ACAS Advisory, Conciliation and Arbitration Service
ACOP Approved Code of Practice
All ER All England Law Reports
CA Court of Appeal
HSE Health and Safety Executive
HMRC Her Majesty's Revenue and Customs
ICR Industrial Cases Reports
IRLB Industrial Relations Law Bulletin

ABBREVIATIONS

This text contains a number of abbreviations which you may not have come across before. An alphabetical list of abbreviations at the front of the book explains each one.

List of cases cited

Airbus Ltd v Webb (2008) IRLR 309 253
Airlie v City of Edinburgh District Council (1996) IRLR 516 28
Alabaster v Barclays Bank (No.2) (2005) IRLR 576 142
Alamo Group (Europe) Ltd v Tucker (2003) IRLR 266 328
Alboni v Ind Coope Retail Ltd (1998) IRLR 131 256
Alcan Extrusions v Yates (1996) IRLR 327 230

LIST OF CASES CITED

A fully indexed list of the cases cited within the book is provided at the front of the book to help you quickly find cases of particular interest. Leading cases are highlighted in bold.

CHAPTER OVERVIEW

This chapter will introduce you to both the way in which employment law is made and the institutions that develop, supervise and enforce it. We start with the distinction between civil and criminal law and a basic introduction to the legal system. Employment law is created by primary and secondary legislation which is then interpreted by the courts, especially by employment tribunals and the Employment Appeal Tribunal. They are influenced by Codes of Practice and, importantly, by EU

CHAPTER OVERVIEW

Each chapter opens with an overview outlining the purpose and content of the chapter.

LEARNING OUTCOMES

After studying this chapter you will be able to:

- understand and explain the main sources of UK and EU law, and describe the court system that applies to employment cases
- advise colleagues about the practical application of employment tribunals and the merits of

LEARNING OUTCOMES

A bulleted set of learning outcomes summarises what you can expect to learn from the chapter, helping you to track your progress.

REFLECTIVE QUESTION

Could a manager who understands how the shop floor operates and is familiar with the types of argument that may be raised during the disciplinary process prove more effective than a lawyer from outside?

REFLECTIVE QUESTION

A number of reflective questions in each chapter will test your understanding of key points and get you thinking about how to apply what you have learnt in practice.

CASE STUDY

MANGOLD V HELM

In the case of *Mangold v Helm*[5] the Munich Labour Court referred questions to the ECJ about whether the German law on fixed-term working was compatible with Community law on age discrimination. Although the implementation date for the age provisions of Directive 2000/78 was December 2003, Member States were allowed to delay implementation until December 2006 'to take account of particular conditions'.

In a decision which has significant ramifications, the ECJ held that national courts must guarantee the full effectiveness of the general principle of non-discrimination by setting aside any provision of national law which conflicts with Community law even where the period prescribed for transposition has not expired.

Discussion point

Do you think judges will be reluctant to set aside national laws?

CASE STUDIES

Particularly high profile or interesting cases have been highlighted in each chapter to demonstrate how employment law works in practice. Accompanying discussion points will challenge and engage you.

KEY LEARNING POINTS

- The most important source of law governing industrial relations is legislation enacted by Parliament.
- Legislation sometimes allows for a Minister or a statutory body to issue Codes of Practice.
- The most relevant Codes of Practice for employment law are issued by ACAS, the CEHR, the Information Commissioner and the Secretary of State.
- The case-law approach of the courts means that they are bound by the decisions of judges in higher courts.
- National courts must follow the decisions and guidance given by the European Court of Justice.

KEY LEARNING POINTS

At the end of each chapter, a bulleted list of key learning points summarises the chapter and pulls out the most important points for you to remember.

REFERENCES

1 On apprenticeship contracts see *Flett v Matheson* (2006) IRLR 277
2 On the relevance of the Unfair Contract Terms Act 1977 see *Commerzbank AG v Keen* (2007) IRLR 132
3 Although tribunal jurisdiction in anti-discrimination cases may not depend on the existence of an enforceable contract of employment; see *Vakante v Governors of Stanhope School (No.2)* (2005)

REFERENCES

Find original sources of information by using the reference lists at the end of each chapter.

EXPLORE FURTHER

Reading

- Davies, A. (2009) *Perspectives on Labour Law*. Oxford University Press, Part 1
- Deakin, S. and Morris, G. (2009) *Labour Law*. Hart, Chapters 1 and 2
- Smith, I. and Thomas, G. (2010) *Smith & Wood's Employment Law*. Butterworths, Chapter 2

Websites

- Advisory, Conciliation and Arbitration Service www.acas.org.uk
- Chartered Institute of Personnel and Development www.cipd.co.uk
- Department for Work and Pensions www.dwp.gov.uk/dfwp
- Department for Business Innovation and Skills www.bis.gov.uk

EXPLORE FURTHER

Explore further boxes contain suggestions for further reading and useful websites, so that you can develop your understanding of the issues and debates raised in each chapter.

Glossary

Additional maternity leave This commences on the day after the last day of the ordinary maternity leave period and continues for 26 weeks from the day on which it commenced.

Certification Officer Nominal head of the official organisation that holds the list of *independent trade unions* and adjudicates as to their independence or not.

GLOSSARY

Key legal terms are highlighted in bold when they first appear in the text. Find each term and its definition in the glossary at the back of the book.

ONLINE RESOURCES FOR STUDENTS

- Monthly updates from HR–Inform, the CIPD's employment law subscription service – view these resources to see what's changed in employment law.
- Student hints – quick tips for assessment on employment law courses.
- Annotated web links – access a wealth of useful information sources in order to develop your understanding of employment law issues.

Visit **www.cipd.co.uk/sss**

ONLINE RESOURCES FOR TUTORS

- Lecturer's guide – advice on how to teach using this text, including guidance on questions and discussion points raised in the book.
- PowerPoint slides – design your programme around these ready-made lectures.
- Additional case studies – ready-made activities test your student's knowledge in practical situations.

Visit **www.cipd.co.uk/sss**

CHAPTER 1

The Sources and Institutions of Employment Law

CHAPTER OVERVIEW

This chapter will introduce you to both the way in which employment law is made and the institutions that develop, supervise and enforce it. We start with the distinction between civil and criminal law and a basic introduction to the legal system. Employment law is created by primary and secondary legislation, which is then interpreted by the courts, especially by employment tribunals and the Employment Appeal Tribunal. They are influenced by Codes of Practice and, importantly, by EU law and the decisions of the Court of Justice of the European Union. Finally, we look at those organisations set up by Parliament to regulate industrial relations and dispute resolution.

LEARNING OUTCOMES

After studying this chapter you will be able to:

- understand and explain the main sources of UK and EU law, and describe the court system that applies to employment cases
- advise colleagues about the practical application of employment tribunals and the merits of using the alternative dispute resolution methods provided by ACAS and the CAC.

CIVIL AND CRIMINAL LAW

Criminal law is concerned with offences against the state and, apart from private prosecutions, it is the state which enforces this branch of the law. The sanctions typically imposed on convicted persons are fines and/or imprisonment. Civil law deals with the situations where a private person who has suffered harm brings an action against (ie sues) the person who committed the wrongful act which caused the harm. Normally, the purpose of suing is to recover damages or compensation. Criminal and civil matters are normally dealt with in separate courts which have their own distinct procedures.

In this book we shall be concentrating largely on civil law but we shall be describing the criminal law in so far as it imposes duties in relation to health and safety. In employment law the two most important civil actions are those based on the law of contract and the law of tort (delict in Scotland). The essential feature of a contract is a binding agreement in which an offer by one person (for example, an employer) is accepted by someone else (for example, a person seeking work). This involves an exchange of promises. Thus, in a **contract of employment** there is a promise to pay wages in exchange for an undertaking to be available for work. As we shall see later, the parties to a contract are not entirely free to negotiate their own terms because Parliament imposes certain restrictions and minimum requirements. The law of tort (delict) places a duty on everyone not to behave in a way that is likely to cause harm to others, and in the employment field the tort of negligence has been applied so as to impose a duty on employers to take reasonable care of their **employees** during the course of their employment. Various torts have also been created by the judiciary in order to impose legal liability for industrial action – for example, the tort of interfering with trade or business – but Parliament has intervened to provide immunities in certain circumstances (see Chapter 18).

LEGISLATION AND CODES OF PRACTICE

In this country the most important source of law governing industrial relations is legislation enacted by Parliament. Often the government will precede legislation by issuing Green Papers or White Papers. Traditionally, the Green Paper is a consultative document and the White Paper is a statement of the government's policy and intentions, although this distinction does not always seem to be adhered to. The government will announce its legislative programme for the forthcoming session in the Queen's Speech. A Bill is then introduced into the House of Commons (sometimes this process can begin in the House of Lords) and is examined at a number of sessions (readings) in both the House of Commons and the House of Lords. The agreed Bill becomes an Act (or statute) when it receives the Royal Assent. It is then referred to (cited) by its name and year, which constitutes its 'short title' (eg Equality Act 2010).

The provisions of an Act may not be brought into operation immediately because the government may wish to implement it in stages. Nevertheless, once the procedure is completed, the legislation is valid. The main provisions of a statute are to be found in its numbered sections, whereas administrative details, repeals and amendments of previous legislation tend to be contained in the schedules at the back. Statutes sometimes give the relevant Secretary of State the power to make rules (regulations) to supplement those laid down in the Act itself. These regulations, which are normally subject to parliamentary approval, are referred to as statutory instruments (SI) and this process of making law is known as delegated or subordinate legislation. Statutory instruments are cited by their name, year and number (eg the Employment Tribunal (Constitution and Procedure) Amendment Regulations 2010, SI No.131).

CODES OF PRACTICE

Legislation sometimes allows for an appropriate Minister or a statutory body to issue Codes of Practice. The primary function of these codes is to educate managers and **workers** by publicising the practices and procedures which the government believes are conducive to good industrial relations. Under section 199 of the Trade Union and Labour Relations (Consolidation) Act 1992 (TULRCA 1992) the Advisory, Conciliation and Arbitration Service (ACAS) has a general power to issue codes 'containing such practical guidance as [ACAS] thinks fit for the purpose of promoting the improvement of industrial relations'. Following representations by interested parties ACAS submits a draft code to the Secretary of State for approval before it is laid before Parliament. At the time of writing, ACAS Codes of Practice exist on the following topics: *Disciplinary and Grievance Procedures*; *Disclosure of Information to Trade Unions for Collective Bargaining Purposes*; and *Time Off for Trade Union Duties and Activities*. By virtue of section 14 of the Equality Act 2006, the Commission for Equal and Human Rights (EHRC can issue codes of the same standing as those of ACAS, and section 16 of the Health and Safety at Work Act 1974 (HASAWA 1974) gives the Health and Safety Executive (HSE) the power to approve Codes of Practice provided it obtains the consent of the Secretary of State on each occasion. The Information Commissioner also has powers to produce Codes of Practice for data controllers. Finally, sections 203–6 TULRCA 1992 entitle the Secretary of State to issue codes but before publishing a draft he or she is obliged to consult ACAS. However, no such duty exists if a code is merely being revised to bring it into conformity with subsequent statutory provisions.[1] Although emerging by different means, all these codes have the same legal standing – ie nobody can be sued or prosecuted for breaching a code – but in any proceedings before a tribunal, court (if the code was issued under TULRCA 1992 or HASAWA 1974) or the Central Arbitration Committee (CAC) a failure to adhere to a recommendation 'shall be taken into account'.[2]

COMMON LAW AND THE COURT HIERARCHY

The feature which distinguishes the English legal system from non-common-law systems is that in this country judicial decisions have been built up to form a series of binding precedents. This is known as the case-law approach. In practice this means that tribunals and judges are bound by the decisions of judges in higher courts. Thus employment tribunals, which are at the bottom of the English court hierarchy, are required to follow the decisions of the Employment Appeal Tribunal (EAT or Appeal Tribunal), the Court of Appeal and the Supreme Court (formerly the Appeal Committee of the House of Lords).[3] However, they are not bound by other employment tribunal decisions. The Employment Appeal Tribunal is bound by the decisions of the Court of Appeal and the Supreme Court and normally follows its own previous decisions. The Court of Appeal has a civil and criminal division and, while both are bound by the Supreme Court's decisions, only the civil division is constrained by its own previous decisions. The Supreme Court has stated that it will regard its own earlier decisions as binding unless in the circumstances of a particular case it is thought just to depart from them. In addition, all English and Scottish courts must follow the decisions of the Court of Justice of the European Union (CJEU).[4] When a court or tribunal needs clarification of European Union law in order to make a decision, it will refer the matter to the CJEU under Article 267 of the Treaty on the Functioning of the European Union (TFEU) (see below).

What constitutes the binding element of a judicial decision is for a judge or tribunal in a subsequent case to determine. Theoretically, what has to be followed is the legal principle or principles which are relied on in reaching the decision in the earlier case. In practice, judges and tribunals have a certain amount of discretion, for they can take a broad or narrow view of the principles which are binding upon them. If they do not like the principles that have emerged, they can refuse to apply them so long as they are prepared to conclude that the facts of the case before them are sufficiently different from the facts in the previous decision. Not surprisingly, this technique is known as 'distinguishing'. Thus, while it is correct to argue that the doctrine of precedent imports an element of certainty, it is wrong to assume that there is no scope for innovation in the lower courts.

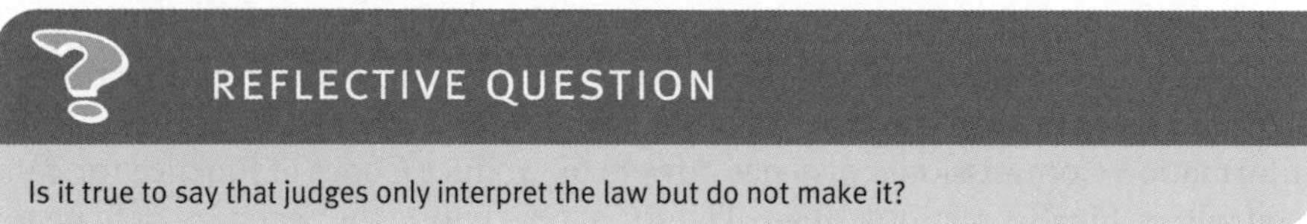

Is it true to say that judges only interpret the law but do not make it?

THE COURT HIERARCHY

The court structure in England and Wales is shown in diagrammatic form in Figure 1 (below).

Figure 1 Court structure in England and Wales

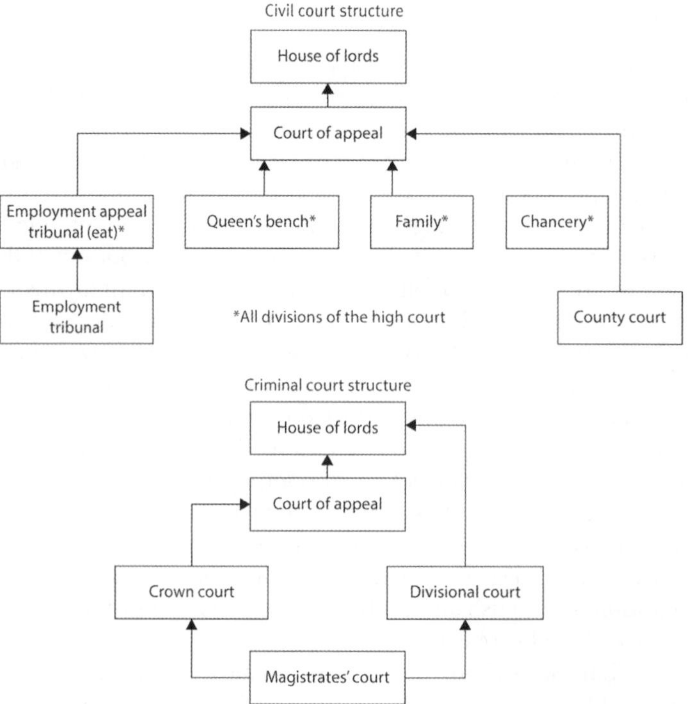

Most proceedings involving individual employment rights are commenced at employment tribunals, and appeals against an employment tribunal decision can normally be heard by the EAT only if there has been an error of law. An error of law occurs when a tribunal has misdirected itself as to the applicable law, when there is no evidence to support a particular finding of fact, or when the tribunal has reached a perverse conclusion – ie one which cannot be justified on the evidence presented.[5] Further appeals can be made on a point of law to the Court of Appeal and the Supreme Court, but only if permission is granted by either the body which made the decision or the court which would hear the appeal. Other civil actions can be started in the County Court or High Court. Appeals on a point of law against a decision made by either court can be lodged with the Court of Appeal and, if permission is granted, further appeal lies to the Supreme Court. There is also a 'leapfrog procedure' which enables an appeal against a decision of the High Court to go directly to the Supreme Court so long as all the parties involved give their consent.

Criminal proceedings are normally commenced in magistrates' courts – for example, if pickets are charged with obstructing police officers in the execution of their duty. The defence can launch an appeal on fact which goes to the Crown Court, but it is also possible for either party to appeal on a point of law to the Divisional Court of the Queen's Bench and then on to the Supreme Court. Prosecutions for serious offences – for example, under section 33 of HASAWA 1974 – are dealt with in the Crown Court, and appeals on a point of law go to the Court of Appeal and the Supreme Court in the usual way.

EUROPEAN UNION LAW

The United Kingdom joined the European Economic Community in 1973. Since then there have been a number of Treaties by which the Member States have agreed to develop the scope of the law of the European Union (EU). As from December 2009 the two principal sources of EU law are the Treaty on the Functioning of the European Union and the Treaty on European Union.

Article 288–292 of the TFEU allows the EU to introduce different types of legislation, the most important ones being regulations and Directives. Regulations tend to be of a broad nature and are directly applicable in all Member States. Most EU legislation that affects employment law is introduced, however, in the form of Directives. Directives are legislative instruments that require a Member State to translate (transpose) the contents of the Directive into national law. Member States are usually given a period of two to three years to carry this out.

CASE STUDY

MANGOLD v HELM

In the case of *Mangold v Helm*[6] the Munich Labour Court referred questions to the ECJ about whether the German law on fixed-term working was compatible with Community law on age discrimination. Although the implementation date for the age provisions of Directive 2000/78 was December 2003, Member States were allowed to delay implementation until December 2006 'to take account of particular conditions'.

In a decision which has significant ramifications, the CJEU held that national courts must guarantee the full effectiveness of the general principle of non-discrimination by setting aside any provision of national law which conflicts with Community law even where the period prescribed for transposition has not expired.

Discussion point

Do you think judges will be reluctant to set aside national laws?

If a Member State fails to transpose a Directive, a citizen may, in certain circumstances, rely on the EU law rather than on existing national laws. The Directive is then said to have direct effect. This can be the result of the Member State's either failing to transpose the Directive or inadequately transposing it. Direct effect is, however, usually only vertically effective – ie it can only be relied upon against the state or 'emanations' of the state.[7] This concept of direct effect has proved an important tool in the enforcement of Community law, especially with respect to Article 157 TFEU on equal pay.

Early cases in the Court of Justice of the European Union established the supremacy of Community law over national law.[8] National courts also have an obligation to interpret national law so that it gives effect to EU law.[9] This means that national legislation should be interpreted in a way that is consistent with the objects of the Treaty, the provisions of any relevant Directives and the rulings of the Court of Justice of the European Union.[10] In relation to the interpretation of Directives, this principle applies whether the national legislation came after or preceded the particular Directive.[11]

It is the European Communities Act 1972 (ECA 1972) which gives effect to the UK's membership of the EU. First, section 2(1) enables directly effective EU obligations to be enforced as free-standing rights. Thus in *McCarthys Ltd v Smith*[12] Article 157 TFEU on equal pay was applied following a reference to the European Court of Justice. Second, section 2(2) facilitates the introduction of subordinate legislation to achieve compliance with EU obligations – eg the Fixed-term Employees (Prevention of Less Favourable Treatment) Regulations 2002.[13] Articles 258 and 260 TFEU enable the European Commission to take steps to ensure that the UK complies with its obligations to give effect to Directives.[14] In addition, an individual may be able to obtain damages as a result of a Member State's failure to carry out its obligations under European Union law.[15]

THE KEY INSTITUTIONS

EMPLOYMENT TRIBUNALS

Industrial tribunals were first established under the Industrial Training Act 1964 but their jurisdiction has been greatly extended. Their name was changed to 'employment tribunals' by section 1 of the Employment Rights (Dispute Resolution) Act 1998. In this book they are always referred to by this newer name, even though some of the older cases cited still refer to them as industrial tribunals.

The Employment Tribunal Service was established in 1997 to provide administrative and organisational support for employment tribunals and the Employment Appeal Tribunal. There are 28 local tribunal offices in England, Wales and Scotland. The President of these tribunals is a barrister or solicitor of seven years' standing who is appointed by the Lord Chancellor for a five-year term. Normally tribunal cases are heard by legally qualified chairpersons and two other people who are known as lay members.[16] Tribunal appointments are for five years initially, and whereas the chairpersons are appointed by the Lord Chancellor and are subject to the same qualification requirements as the President, the lay members are appointed by the Secretary of State. They are drawn from two panels; one is formed as a result of nominations made by employer organisations, and the other consists of nominees from organisations of workers. Since 1999 the government has also advertised in the press so that individuals may nominate themselves for one of the panels. However, although lay members are expected to have an understanding of workplace practices and how people work together, they are not supposed to act as representatives of their nominating organisations.

Representation at hearings

Hearings at employment tribunals are relatively informal.[17] The parties may represent themselves or be represented by a legal practitioner, a trade union official, a representative from an employers' association or any other person. In practice, employers tend to be legally represented more often than employees, one reason being the unavailability of legal aid. Human resource managers should give very serious thought to the question of representation.

REFLECTIVE QUESTION

Could a manager who understands how the shop floor operates and is familiar with the types of argument that may be raised during the disciplinary process prove more effective than a lawyer from outside?

Costs and fees

Apart from appeals against improvement or prohibition notices issued under HASAWA 1974, costs are not normally awarded unless either party (or their representative) is deemed to have acted vexatiously, abusively, disruptively, or otherwise unreasonably, or the bringing or conducting of the proceedings was misconceived.[18]

The Government intends to introduce fees in the second half of 2013. These will be charged at two stages: on the issue of the claim, and prior to a hearing. It is envisaged that there will be two levels of fees. Level-1 claims will be for defined sums – for example, redundancy payments and unauthorised deductions from wages. Level-2 claims are those involving more complex issues, including discrimination and unfair dismissal. There will also be arrangements for multiple claims, a remission system for those on low incomes, and fees for appeals to the Employment Appeal Tribunal (see below).

Challenging tribunal decisions

Tribunal decisions can be challenged either by review or by appeal. The power of review, which enables the whole or part of a case to be re-heard and set aside or the original decision to be varied, may be exercised only on one of the following grounds:

- the decision was wrongly made as a result of error on the part of tribunal staff
- a party did not receive notice of the proceedings
- the decision was made in the absence of a person entitled to be heard
- new evidence has become available since the making of the decision and its existence could not have been reasonably known of or foreseen
- the interests of justice require a review.[19]

An appeal to the Employment Appeal Tribunal can only be made on a point of law and must be lodged within 42 days.[20]

THE EMPLOYMENT APPEAL TRIBUNAL (EAT)

The EAT, which was established in 1976, is serviced by Employment Tribunal Service offices in London and Edinburgh. It can sit anywhere in England, Wales or Scotland and consists of High Court judges nominated by the Lord Chancellor (one of whom serves as President) and a panel of lay members who are appointed on the joint recommendation of the Lord Chancellor and the Secretary of State. This panel consists of nominees from employers' and workers' organisations. Appeals are heard by a judge and either two or four lay persons, all of whom have equal voting rights. However, a judge can sit alone where the appeal arises from proceedings before an employment tribunal consisting of the chair alone.

Parties can be represented by whomsoever they please, and costs will be awarded only where the proceedings are deemed to have been unnecessary, improper, or vexatious or where there has been unreasonable conduct in bringing or conducting the proceedings.[21] Finally, the Appeal Tribunal may adjourn proceedings where there is a reasonable prospect of a conciliated settlement being reached.[22]

THE ADVISORY, CONCILIATION AND ARBITRATION SERVICE (ACAS)

ACAS has been in existence since 1974. Its work is directed by a council consisting of a chairperson and between nine and 15 members appointed by the Secretary of State. Three or four members are appointed after consultation with trade unions, the same number following consultation with employers' organisations, and the remainder are independent. The Service is divided into 13 regions which perform most of the day-to-day work – for example, handling direct enquiries from the public. Although ACAS is financed by the government, section 247(3) TULRCA 1992 states that it shall not be 'subject to directions of any kind from any Minister of the Crown as to the manner in which it is to exercise its functions'.

ACAS has the general duty of promoting the improvement of industrial relations, in particular by exercising its functions in relation to the settlement of trade disputes.[23] It also has specific functions which merit separate consideration.

Advice

ACAS may, on request or on its own initiative, provide employers, their associations, workers and trade unions with advice on any matter concerned with or affecting industrial relations.[24] In practice the forms of advice range from telephone inquiries to in-depth projects, diagnostic surveys and training exercises.

Conciliation

Where a trade dispute exists or is likely to arise, ACAS may, on request or of its own volition, offer assistance to the parties with a view to bringing about a settlement. This may be achieved by conciliation or other means – for example, the appointment of an independent person to render assistance. Before attempting to conciliate in collective trade disputes, ACAS is required to 'have regard to the desirability of encouraging the parties to a dispute to use any appropriate agreed procedures'.[25] According to its Annual Report for 20011/12, 830 collective cases were completed and conciliation was successful in 754 of them.

In addition to collective matters, ACAS has the task of conciliating in employment tribunal cases. When a complaint is presented to an employment tribunal, a copy of it is sent to a conciliation officer who has the duty to promote a settlement without the matter having to go to a hearing. Conciliation officers can intervene if requested to do so by the parties or where they believe they could act with a reasonable prospect of success. At the instigation of either party the officer may act before a complaint has been presented in respect of a matter which could be the subject of tribunal proceedings (for the conciliation officer's particular duty in unfair dismissal cases, see Chapter 15). So as not to undermine the conciliation process it is stipulated that anything communicated to an officer in connection with the performance of his or her functions shall not be admissible in evidence in any proceedings before an employment tribunal without the consent of the person who communicated it.

The ACAS Annual Report for 20011/12 reveals that 73,949 applications to employment tribunal were dealt with. Of these 43.4% were settled, 23.9 % were withdrawn and 20.8% went to a hearing.

REFLECTIVE QUESTION

What are the advantages to the parties of achieving a conciliated settlement?

Arbitration

At the request of one party but with the consent of all the parties to a collective dispute (or potential dispute), ACAS may appoint an arbitrator or arbitration panel from outside the Service or refer the matter to be heard by the Central Arbitration Committee (CAC). According to the ACAS Annual Report for 2010/12, 21 cases were referred to collective arbitration and dispute mediation. In performing this function ACAS is obliged to consider whether the dispute could be resolved by conciliation, and arbitration is not to be offered unless agreed procedures for the negotiation and settlement of disputes have been exhausted (save where there is a special reason which justifies arbitration as an alternative to those procedures).[26] CAC awards can be published only with the consent of all parties involved.

In addition, ACAS operates a voluntary arbitration scheme which provides an alternative to employment tribunals for the resolution of disputes over unfair dismissal. Where the parties agree to use the scheme, they must waive the rights they would otherwise have in relation to an unfair dismissal claim. Arbitrators are appointed from the ACAS Arbitration Panel, and hearings, which are held in private, are intended to be relatively speedy, cost-efficient and non-legalistic. The parties can reach an agreement settling their dispute at any stage. However, where an arbitrator makes an award, the parties cannot appeal on a point of law except where the Human Rights Act 1998 or EC law is relevant.[27]

REFLECTIVE QUESTION

Suggest reasons why the voluntary arbitration scheme for unfair dismissal has not been widely used.

Inquiry

ACAS may inquire into any question relating to industrial relations generally, in a particular industry or in a particular undertaking. Any advice or findings that emerge may be published so long as the views of all concerned parties have been taken into account.[28]

Other duties

Apart from the general power to issue codes of practice, ACAS has an important conciliation role to play in statutory recognition claims and in those situations where a recognised union has lodged a complaint that an employer has failed to disclose information which it requires for collective bargaining purposes (see Chapter 18).

THE CENTRAL ARBITRATION COMMITTEE (CAC)

The CAC consists of a chairperson, deputy chairpersons and other members, all of whom are appointed by the Secretary of State after consultation with ACAS. The members must have experience as employer or worker representatives, while the deputy chairpersons tend to be lawyers or academic experts in industrial relations. Like ACAS, the CAC is not subject to directions from a Minister. Apart from receiving requests to arbitrate directly from parties to a dispute, the CAC receives arbitration requests from ACAS (see above). Additionally, the CAC is required to make determinations under sections 183–5 TULRCA 1992 (dealing with complaints arising from a failure to disclose information). CAC awards are published and take effect as part of the contracts of employees covered by the award. Unless it can be shown that the CAC exceeded its jurisdiction,[29] breached the rules of natural justice or committed an error of law,[30] no court can overturn its decisions.

The CAC is also required to resolve disputes under the Information and Consultation of Employees Regulations 2004,[31] and the Annual Report 2011/12 reveals that four applications were received in this period. The Employment Relations Act 1999 (ERel Act) added an important new role in relation to the recognition and de-recognition of trade unions. The CAC receives the application for recognition and supervises the process, including the holding of a ballot amongst the affected employees, leading to a decision on whether recognition or de-recognition should be granted (see Chapter 18). It is required to establish a panel consisting of an independent chair and an experienced representative of employers and an experienced representative of workers to fulfil these functions. In dealing with these cases the Act requires the CAC to have regard to the object of encouraging and promoting fair and efficient practices in the workplace (so far as is consistent with its other obligations). According to the CAC Annual Report for 2011/12, trade unions submitted 43 applications for statutory recognition, and four complaints about disclosure of information were received.

THE CERTIFICATION OFFICER

The **Certification Officer** is also appointed by the Secretary of State after consultation with ACAS and is required to produce an annual report for them. He or she is responsible for maintaining a list of trade unions and employers' associations and, if an application is submitted, has to determine whether or not a listed union qualifies for a certificate of independence. The Certification Officer also handles:

- disputes which arise from trade union amalgamations and mergers and the administration of political funds
- complaints that the provisions of Chapter IV TULRCA 1992, concerning trade union elections, have been infringed and can determine the procedure to be followed on any application or complaint received[32]
- complaints by a member of breach of a trade union's own rules relating to a union office, disciplinary proceedings, ballots (on any issue other than industrial action) and the constitution and proceedings of the executive committee or of any decision-making meeting.[33]

In relation to all these jurisdictions an appeal can only be lodged if a point of law is involved.

Under the Trade Union and Labour Relations (Consolidation) Act 1992, the Certification Officer can direct a trade union to produce documents relating to its financial affairs. Where there appears to have been impropriety, the Certification Officer can appoint inspectors to investigate.[34]

The Information Commissioner

This officer replaced the Data Protection Commissioner in 2001. The Information Commissioner has a number of general duties, including the preparation and dissemination of codes of practice for guidance.[35]

KEY LEARNING POINTS

- The most important source of law governing industrial relations is legislation enacted by Parliament.
- Legislation sometimes allows for a Minister or a statutory body to issue Codes of Practice.
- The most relevant Codes of Practice for employment law are issued by ACAS, the CEHR, the Information Commissioner and the Secretary of State.
- The case-law approach of the courts means that they are bound by the decisions of judges in higher courts.
- National courts must follow the decisions and guidance given by the Court of Justice of the European Union.
- European laws take precedence and are directly effective against the state or emanations of the state, if not transposed correctly.
- Employment tribunals are specialist bodies, whose decisions can be appealed against, on points of law, to the Employment Appeal Tribunal.
- ACAS has the general duty of improving industrial relations and provides advice, individual and collective conciliation and arbitration services.
- The Central Arbitration Committee deals with complaints about failure to disclose information for the purposes of collective bargaining.
- The Central Arbitration Committee also has an important role to play in the procedure for the statutory recognition of trade unions.
- The Certification Officer maintains lists of employers' associations and trade unions and issues certificates of independence.

REFERENCES

1 See section 205 TULRCA 1992

2 Section 207A TULRCA 1992 provides for tribunal awards to be adjusted in certain circumstances where there has been a failure to comply with a Code.

3 In this book references to the decisions of the Supreme Court include cases decided by its predecessor.

4 The CJEU is the renamed European Court of Justice. In this book decisions of the European Court of Justice will be treated as those of the CJEU.

5 *British Telecom v Sheridan* (1990) IRLR 27

6 (2006) IRLR 143

7 See *Marshall v Southampton and South West Hampshire Area Health Authority* Case 152/85 (1986) IRLR 140

8 See *Amministrazione delle Finanze v Simmenthal* Case 106/77 (1978) ECR 629

9 See *Litster v Forth Dry Dock Engineering Co Ltd* (1989) IRLR 161

10 *Pickstone v Freemans plc* (1988) IRLR 357

11 See *Marleasing SA v La Comercial Internacional de Alimentacion SA* Case 106/89 (1990) ECR 4135

12 (1980) IRLR 208

13 SI 2002/2034

14 See *Commission v UK* (1994) IRLR 292

15 See Cases 46/93 and 48/93 *Brasserie du Pêcheur SA v Federal Republic of Germany* and *R v Secretary of State for Transport ex parte Factortame* (1996) ECR 1029

16 Certain claims can be heard by a chair sitting alone.

17 On tribunal practice and procedures see specialist texts.

18 Rule 40 Schedule 1 Employment Tribunal (Constitution and Rules of Procedure) Regulations 2004 SI No.1861

19 Rule 34 (see note 17)

20 Rule 3 Employment Appeal Tribunal Rules 1993 SI No.2854

21 Rule 34A Employment Appeal Tribunal Rules 1993 SI No.2854

22 Rule 36 (see note 17)

23 Section 209 TULRCA 1992

24 Section 213 TULRCA 1992

25 Section 210(3) TULRCA 1992

26 See section 212(3) TULRCA 1992

27 See ACAS Arbitration Scheme (Great Britain) Order 2004 SI No.753 and *The ACAS arbitration scheme for the resolution of unfair dismissal disputes: a guide to the scheme.*

28 See section 214 TULRCA 1992

29 See *R v CAC ex parte Hy-Mac Ltd* (1979) IRLR 461

30 See *R v CAC (on the application of the BBC)* (2003) IRLR 460

31 SI No.3426

32 See section 256 TULRCA 1992

33 Section 108A TULRCA 1992

34 See sections 37A–E TULRCA 1992

35 See section 51 Data Protection Act 1998

EXPLORE FURTHER

Reading

- Davies, A. (2009) *Perspectives on Labour Law.* Oxford University Press, Part 1
- Deakin, S. and Morris, G. (2012) *Labour Law.* Hart, Chapters 1 and 2
- Smith, I. and Thomas, G. (2010) *Smith & Wood's Employment Law.* Butterworths, Chapter 2

Websites

- Advisory, Conciliation and Arbitration Service www.acas.org.uk
- Chartered Institute of Personnel and Development www.cipd.co.uk
- Commission for Equality and Human Rights www.cehr.org.uk
- Court of Justice of the European Union www.curia.eu.int
- Department for Work and Pensions www.dwp.gov.uk/dfwp
- Department for Business Innovation and Skills www.bis.gov.uk
- Employment Appeal Tribunal www.employmentappeals.gov.uk
- HMSO www.hmso.gov.uk
- House of Lords www.parliament.uk/parliament/sitemap.htm
- International Labour Organisation www.ilo.org
- Trades Union Congress www.tuc.org.uk
- online journals
- http://www.xperthr.co.uk/

Xpert HR is an excellent source of information for **all** the chapters in this book. It contains case law reports, articles and much else, and is updated very frequently. Some colleges have a subscription to it, and parts of the website are free to use.

CHAPTER 2

Formation of the Contract of Employment (1): The sources of terms

CHAPTER OVERVIEW

This chapter and the next one are concerned with the contract of employment and how it comes into existence. We consider the influences that contribute to establishing the contents of the contract. Express terms agreed between the employer and the employee, or the employee's representatives, normally take precedence over all other terms. There is a statutory requirement for the employer to issue written particulars of employment to new employees within two months of their start date. These particulars are considered in detail here, as is the influence of collective agreements, workforce agreements, works rules, and custom and practice.

LEARNING OUTCOMES

After studying this chapter you will be able to:

- understand and explain the importance of the contract of employment to the conduct of human resource management
- advise colleagues about the status and content of written statements of employment terms and participate in their preparation
- understand the potential impact of statutory and common law implied terms.

CONTRACTS OF EMPLOYMENT

Apart from those of apprentices and merchant seamen, who can only be employed under written deeds and articles respectively, contracts of employment may be oral or in writing.[1] A contract of employment is like any other contract in the sense that it is subject to the general principles of law. In theory this means that the parties are free to negotiate the terms and conditions that suit them so long as they remain within the constraints imposed by statute and the common law.[2] In practice the majority of the workforce do not negotiate on an individual basis. An important proportion are engaged on such terms and conditions as are laid down in currently operative **collective agreements**. However, these agreements are confined to the minority of employers because about two-thirds of workplaces in the UK do not have any employees covered by collective agreements.

ILLEGAL CONTRACTS

One aspect of the common law which has been relied on, particularly in unfair dismissal cases, is the principle that courts will not enforce an illegal contract.[3] Thus, if employees receive additional payments which are not taxed, they may be debarred from exercising statutory rights on the ground that they were not employed under valid contracts of employment. However, an occasional payment by an employer to an employee without deduction of tax does not render the contract of employment unenforceable.[4]

CASE STUDIES

COLEN v CEBRIAN LTD

In *Colen v Cebrian Ltd*[5] the Court of Appeal held that when illegality is alleged, the burden of proof is on the party making the allegation to show that the contract had been entered into with the object of committing an illegal act or had been performed with that objective. If the contract was unlawful at formation or the intention was to perform it unlawfully, the contract will be unenforceable. However, if at the time of formation the contract was perfectly lawful and it was intended to be performed lawfully, the effect of some act of illegal performance is not automatically to make the contract unenforceable. If the contract is performed illegally and the person seeking to enforce it takes part in the illegality, that may render the contract unenforceable at his or her instigation. Yet not every illegal act participated in by the enforcer will have that effect. Where the enforcer has to rely on his or her own illegal action, the court will not assist. However, if he or she does not have to do so, the question is whether the method of performance and the degree of participation in the illegality is such as to make the contract illegal.

HEWCASTLE CATERING v AHMED

In *Hewcastle Catering v Ahmed*[6] the employee's involvement in a VAT fraud devised by the employer, and from which only the employer benefited, did not preclude a claim of unfair dismissal. According to the Court of Appeal, the general principle that a contract is unenforceable on grounds of illegality applies if in all the circumstances the court would appear to encourage illegal conduct. However, the defence of illegality will not succeed where the employer's conduct in participating in the illegal contract is so reprehensible in comparison with that of the employee that it would be wrong to allow the employer to rely on its being unenforceable.

Discussion point

Is the Court of Appeal's approach likely to benefit employees more than employers?

Subsequently, it has been accepted that if a contract has the effect of depriving HM Revenue and Customs of tax to which it is entitled, this does not necessarily make it unlawful: 'There must be some form of misrepresentation, some attempt to conceal the true facts of the relationship, before the contract is rendered illegal.'[7]

Although a contract of employment can be entered into quite informally, because of the consequences of having an employee on the books (see Chapter 4) a considerable degree of formality is desirable.

Figure 2 The sources of contractual terms

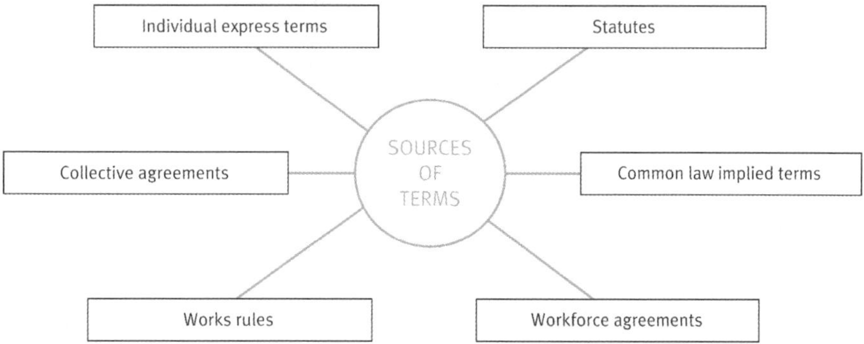

EXPRESS TERMS AND STATUTORY STATEMENTS

Express terms are those which are expressly stated to form part of the contract and they are binding irrespective of whether they differ from those contained in a job advertisement.[8] Apart from statutorily implied terms, which cannot be undermined, express terms normally take precedence over all other sources – ie common law implied terms and custom and practice. Not later than two months after the start of employment of a person whose employment continues for a month or more, the employer must supply written particulars of key terms of employment.[9] Indeed, in *Lange v Schünemann GmbH* [10] the European Court of Justice indicated that Article 2(1) of Directive 91/53 (on proof of the employment relationship) obliged an employer to notify an employee of any term which must be considered an essential element of the contract.

REFLECTIVE QUESTION

What practical and legal difficulties might arise if workers do not understand all the relevant terms and conditions at the time employment commences?

STATEMENT OF PARTICULARS

The following information must be given to employees individually, although in relation to the matters mentioned in items 6, 7, 9 and 15 below it is sufficient to make the information reasonably accessible to them by means of a document to which they are referred.[11]

1 *The identity of the parties*
Sometimes the identity of the employer can be in dispute – eg where people are 'hired out' to other organisations[12] or where the employer consists of a management committee running a charity.[13]

2 *The date on which the employee's period of continuous employment began (taking into account any employment with a previous employer which counts towards that period)*
Section 211 ERA 1996 defines the meaning of 'continuous employment' (see Chapter 16). It begins with the day that a person starts work for an organisation, but periods spent taking part in a strike do not count towards length of service.[14] The period of continuous employment is important because certain statutory rights are associated with length of service – for example, the right not to be unfairly dismissed and the right to a redundancy payment. Section 218 ERA 1996 preserves continuity of employment in certain circumstances, as do the Transfer of Undertakings (Protection of Employment) Regulations 2006[15] (Transfer Regulations). If continuity is not preserved, for whatever reason, qualified employees are entitled to redundancy payments from their previous employer. According to Regulation 4(1) of the Transfer Regulations, where there is a transfer of an undertaking (or part of an undertaking), employees who are transferred are to be treated as if they had originally made contracts with the **transferee employer**. (On the scope of the Transfer Regulations see Chapter 16.)

3 *The scale or rate of remuneration, or the method of calculating remuneration, and the intervals at which remuneration is paid*
The word 'remuneration' is not defined in the statute and ought to be regarded as including all financial benefits (see Chapter 5 on the National Minimum Wage Act 1998).

4 *Any terms and conditions relating to hours of work and normal working hours*
The concept of normal working hours is crucial, so in order to avoid confusion, employers should specify whether or not overtime is mandatory – ie forms part of the normal working hours. Care is especially needed when considering annualised hours contracts, where it may still be advisable to define the working week for the purpose of calculating holiday entitlement and any overtime payments owed to people who leave during the working year. The courts or tribunals will not necessarily be prepared to fill gaps left by agreements that are not comprehensive.

CASE STUDY

ALI v CHRISTIAN SALVESEN

In *Ali v Christian Salvesen*[16] the Court of Appeal concluded that the parties to a collective agreement, which was expressly incorporated into a contract of employment, might deliberately have omitted provisions dealing with termination of employment during the calculation period on the grounds that it was too complicated or too controversial to include.

Discussion point

What does this case tell us about the general willingness of courts to fill in gaps left by the parties to collective agreements?

Working hours are usually a matter for the parties to determine, but see Chapter 10 on the impact of the Working Time Regulations.[17]

5 *Any terms and conditions relating to holidays and holiday pay*
Employees are entitled to be paid if holidays are taken in accordance with the terms of their employment during their period of notice.[18] According to the EAT, the daily rate of pay for the purposes of accrued holiday entitlement should be calculated by dividing the annual salary by the number of working days.[19] Those employees protected by the Working Time Regulations are entitled to a minimum of 5.6 weeks' paid holiday per leave year (Regulation 13). The leave year can be the subject of agreement or, if there is no such agreement, it will commence on the day employment began and each subsequent anniversary thereafter (see Chapter 10).

6 *Any terms and conditions relating to incapacity for work due to sickness or injury*
This includes any provision for sick pay (see Chapter 5).

7 *Any terms and conditions relating to pensions and pension schemes*
This book does not generally address the complex issues of pension entitlement. However, it should be noted that, unless they opt out, workers over the age of 22 who earn more than £8,105 per annum have to be automatically enrolled in a workplace pension scheme. This currently applies to large employers but staging dates have been set so that all employers to be covered by 2017.

8 *A note stating whether a contracting-out certificate is in force*
Where it is a contractual term that employees are entitled to benefits under a pension scheme, employers must discharge their functions under such a scheme in good faith and, so far as it is within their power, procure the benefits to which the employees are entitled.[20]

9 *The length of notice which the employee is entitled to receive and is obliged to give*
See Chapter 11.

10 *The title of the job or a brief description of the employee's work*
If, in the interests of flexibility, a job description is widely drawn, it should be pointed out to employees that the ambit of their contractual obligations may be wider than the particular duties upon which they are normally engaged.[21]

11 *Where the employment is temporary, the period for which it is expected to continue or, if it is for a fixed term, the date when it is to end*
On fixed-term contracts see Chapter 4.

12 *The place of work or, if the employee is required or permitted to work at various places, an indication of the employer's address*
If an employee works in a number of different countries, the place of work has been defined by the Court of Justice of the European Union as the place where the employee habitually carries out his or her work.[22]

13 *Any collective agreements which directly affect the terms and conditions of employment, including, where the employer is not a party, the person by whom they were made*
Such agreements can be incorporated into a contract of employment (see below) and may even be transferred to a new employer by the Transfer Regulations.[23]

14 *Where the employee is required to work outside the UK for more than a month*
The period of work outside the UK, the currency in which payment will be made, any additional pay and benefits to be provided by reason of the work being outside the UK, any terms and conditions relating to the employee's return to the UK.

The Posted Workers Directive[24] provides added protection for people working in a Member State other than that in which they normally work. Any rules in force concerning terms and conditions of employment, as a result of law, regulation, administrative provision or by collective agreements in the state to which the employee is posted are to be guaranteed. These rules can include maximum work periods; rest periods; paid holidays; minimum rates of pay (although not supplementary occupational pensions); conditions for hiring out temporary workers; health and safety; protective measures for pregnant women and those that have recently given birth; and equal treatment between men and women.

15 *Any disciplinary rules applicable to the employee and any procedure applicable to the taking of disciplinary decisions (including dismissal) relating to the employee* [25]

16 *The name or description of the person to whom employees can apply if they are dissatisfied with any disciplinary decision or seek to redress a grievance*
The statement must indicate the manner in which any such application should be made.

17 *Any further steps consequent upon an application expressing dissatisfaction over a disciplinary decision (including dismissal) or grievance*
Two points should be noted here. First, although ERA 1996 does not state that employers must have disciplinary rules, the Code of Practice on Disciplinary and Grievance Procedures emphasises their desirability (see Chapter 13). Second, rules, disciplinary decisions (including dismissals), grievances and procedures relating to health and safety at work are exempted because separate rules and procedures are thought to be appropriate in this area and should be referred to in the information provided by employers under section 2 HASAWA 1974 (see Chapter 9).

If there are no particulars to be entered under any of the above headings, that fact must be mentioned in the written statement. It should also be noted that information relating to items 8, 11, 13, 14 and 16 may be given in instalments within the two-month period. The other items must be dealt with in a single document called a 'principal statement'. The information required can be supplied in the form of a written statement, a contract of employment or a letter of engagement.[26]

Changes cannot be made to a contract of employment without the consent of the employee, but where there is a change in any of the details required by section 1, written notification must be given to the employee within one month.[27] The nature of the changes must be set out in full, although the employer may refer to other documents for the same matters and in the same manner as for the original provision of particulars. There is no provision for the changes to be notified in instalments.

THE STATUS OF THE STATEMENT OF PARTICULARS

It is important to understand that the statement issued does not constitute a contract or even conclusive evidence of its terms, but is merely the employer's version of what has been agreed.[28] Indeed, in *Robertson v British Gas* [29] the Court of Appeal decided that a statutory statement could not even be used as an aid to the interpretation of the contract. If agreement has not been reached in a key area, management may choose to include in that statement what it considers to be reasonable arrangements. Technically, the statement will be inaccurate (because the terms were on offer rather than agreed at the time they were issued), but if the employee accepts the arrangements or acquiesces in them – ie by not challenging them – the employer's proposals may be deemed to have contractual effect. However, the EAT has suggested that a distinction might be drawn between a matter which has immediate practical application and one which does not. In *Jones v Associated Tunnelling Co.* [30] it was thought that it would be asking too much of ordinary employees to require them to object to erroneous statements of terms which had no immediate practical impact on them. The law does not oblige employees to sign the written particulars or even acknowledge their receipt, but if they confirm that what has been issued is an accurate summary of the main employment terms, the particulars may be treated by the courts as having contractual status.[31]

'Mandatory' and 'non-mandatory' terms

Where an employee is given a complete but incorrect statement – ie some of the particulars are wrong in that they do not reproduce what was agreed between the parties – the employee can complain to an employment tribunal, which has the power to confirm, amend or replace the particulars. However, unless the employment has terminated, the tribunal has no jurisdiction to interpret the statement.[32] If there is no written statement or an incomplete one is issued, the tribunal must determine what the missing particulars are.[33] According to the Court of Appeal,[34] the particulars required under 1, 2, 3, 9 and 10 above are 'mandatory' terms in that actual particulars must be given under those headings. On the other hand, the particulars required under 4–7 above are viewed as 'non-mandatory' in the sense that no particulars need to be inserted if none has been agreed. As regards 'non-mandatory' terms, the Court of Appeal held that an employment tribunal could not invent a term if nothing had been agreed by the parties. However, where a 'mandatory' term was omitted from a statement a tribunal would probably have to infer one. When the tribunal has decided what particulars should have been included, the employer is deemed to have provided the employee with a statement containing those particulars.[35] The sanction on an employer who fails to supply a suitable statement is that, in any of the proceedings listed in Schedule 5 EA 2002, a tribunal is obliged to make or increase an award by a minimum of two weeks' pay (or a maximum of four weeks' pay if that is considered just and equitable).[36]

COLLECTIVE AGREEMENTS

Terms may be derived from collective agreements as well as being individually negotiated. Such agreements tend to be classed as being of either a procedural or a substantive nature. A procedural agreement aims to govern the relationship between the signatories (employers and trade unions) by establishing methods of handling disputes, whereas a substantive agreement is intended to regulate the terms and conditions of employment of those who are covered by it. Like any other agreement, collective agreements will be construed by giving meaning to the words used in the factual context known to the parties at the time.[37] It is possible to conclude a collective agreement which is legally enforceable, although this is not normally the wish of either party.

REFLECTIVE QUESTION

What are the advantages and disadvantages of having a legally enforceable collective agreement?

By what mechanism, then, do individual employees derive the legal right to claim the terms and conditions which have been negotiated on their behalf? The answer lies in the process of incorporation, for by this device collectively agreed terms become legally binding as part of the individual contract of employment.[38] The simplest way of ensuring that substantive terms are incorporated into an employee's contract is by an express provision to this effect. Thus, workers may be employed on the basis of 'terms and conditions of employment which are covered by existing collective agreements negotiated and agreed with specific trade unions or unions recognised … for collective bargaining purposes'.[39] Commonly, collective agreements will be expressly incorporated because they are referred to in a section 1 ERA 1996 statement of particulars.

In relation to the matters specified in section 2(2) ERA 1996 employers can refer to 'some other document which is reasonably accessible', and this document may be a copy of the currently operative collective agreement. Equally, it is possible for terms to be incorporated from a collective agreement by implication or custom and practice.[40]

REFLECTIVE QUESTION

Why is it undesirable to rely on implication and custom and practice as sources of terms?

Implied incorporation occurs when employees have specific knowledge of the collective agreement and there is conduct which demonstrates that they accept the agreement and are willing to work under it. While this might be relatively straightforward in the case of union members, difficulties can arise in establishing the legal position of non-members. If such employees have habitually accepted and abided by the terms negotiated by the union, an implication arises that they will be bound by future agreements. However, if at any stage non-members declare that they are no longer willing to be bound by such agreements, that implication is no longer valid.[41]

NO-STRIKE CLAUSES AND COLLECTIVE AGREEMENTS

It is not always easy to decide which terms of a collective agreement are appropriate for incorporation into an individual contract of employment. Substantive terms are relatively straightforward (eg wages, hours, etc) but procedural requirements may also be binding as a result of an express obligation or the employer's implied duty to act in good faith.[42] Particular difficulties have been experienced in relation to no-strike clauses. An undertaking by the union not to call a strike before relevant procedures have been exhausted imposes an obligation on the union alone, but the following clause is clearly capable of being incorporated into individual contracts of employment: 'Employees will not engage in a strike or other industrial action until the grievance procedure has been exhausted.' The situation has been clarified by section 180 TULRCA 1992 which provides that no-strike clauses are binding only if the collective agreement:

- is in writing and contains a provision stating that the clause may be incorporated into a contract of employment
- is reasonably accessible to the employees concerned
- is concluded by an **independent trade union** and the individual contract of employment expressly or impliedly incorporates the no-strike clause.

Such clauses can be useful in drawing an employee's attention to the illegality of industrial action but strictly speaking they are unnecessary because most forms of industrial action are likely to breach an obligation imposed on all employees by the common law – ie the duty not to impede the employer's business (see Chapter 3).

CASE STUDY

KEELEY v FOSROC LTD

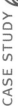

Christopher Keeley's contract of employment consisted of a written statement of employment terms which incorporated by reference the employer's staff handbook. Under the heading *Employee benefits and rights* there was a section on redundancy which dealt with certain procedural aspects. It also contained provisions giving those made redundant the right to time off to look for alternative work and the right to appeal against dismissal. Under the heading *Compensation* it provided that 'Those employees with two or more years' continuous service are entitled to receive an enhanced redundancy payment from the company, which is paid tax-free to a limit of £30,000. Details will be discussed during both collective and individual consultation.'

Following his dismissal on grounds of redundancy Mr Keeley claimed that he was contractually entitled to receive an enhanced redundancy payment. His claim was rejected in the High Court but allowed on appeal. According to the Court of Appeal, the fundamental starting point is the wording of the provision itself and the aptness of the provision in its own right to be a contractual term. The importance of the provision to the overall bargain is also highly relevant. A provision which is part of the employee's remuneration package may still be apt for construction as a term of the contract even if couched in terms of explanation or expressed in discretionary terms.[43]

Discussion point

What are the implications for employers of the Court of Appeal's approach to the status of staff handbooks in this case?

Subsequently, the Court of Appeal has stated that the touchstone for incorporation is whether a provision impacts on working conditions.[44]

WORKFORCE AGREEMENTS

The Working Time Regulations 1998 and the Maternity and Parental Leave Regulations 1999 are examples of where it is possible for 'relevant' agreements to be reached which enable employers to agree variations to the Regulations directly with their employees or with their representatives. These 'relevant' agreements can be concluded via a process of bargaining. Where there are no collective agreements, employers can reach **workforce agreement**s with their employees or their representatives. For example, Regulation 23 of the Working Time Regulations allows a workforce agreement to modify or exclude Regulation 4(3) concerning the reference period for calculating the 48-hour average, Regulations 6(1) to (3) and (7) regulating night work, Regulation 10(1) dealing with the entitlement to an 11-hour break in each 24 hours, Regulations 11(1) and (2) providing a weekly or fortnightly break and Regulation 12(1) concerning rest breaks, provided certain conditions are met. These conditions are contained in Schedule 1.

An agreement is a workforce agreement where:

- it is in writing
- it has effect for a specified period not exceeding five years
- it applies to all the relevant members of a workforce or all the relevant members who belong to a particular group
- it is signed by the representatives of the group[45]
- copies of the agreement are readily available for reading prior to the signing.

WORKS RULES AND POLICY GUIDANCE

The essential difference between collective agreements and works rules lies not so much in their subject matter but in the fact that the contents of the latter are unilaterally determined by the employer. While both can be expressly or impliedly incorporated into individual contracts of employment (using the mechanisms described above), works rules offer one great advantage to the employer: whereas a collective agreement can be altered only with the consent of the parties to it, management can lawfully change the content of works rules at any time. A refusal to adhere to the revised rules would amount to a breach of contract (ie a failure to obey lawful and reasonable orders). Thus a contractual term to the effect that employees must abide by 'the currently operative works rules' affords management the maximum degree of flexibility.[46]

There may be rules that constitute employer guidance or policy and are therefore not appropriate as contractual terms. Such a situation might arise when the employer is setting out practice and procedures rather than conferring rights on individuals.

CASE STUDY

WANDSWORTH LONDON BOROUGH COUNCIL v D'SILVA

In *Wandsworth London Borough Council v D'Silva*[47] changes to a code of practice on staff sickness were made by the employer without consultation with employees or their representatives. The EAT held that these changes amounted to alterations to a code of good practice rather than an attempt to unilaterally alter the contract of employment.

Discussion point

How should employers make it clear to employees that changes to a code of practice will not amount to a variation of contractual rights?

However, the dismissal of an employee for failing to comply with revised works rules or policy guidance will not necessarily be fair because it will depend on what an employment tribunal regards as being 'reasonable in all the circumstances' (see Chapter 13).

REFLECTIVE QUESTION

What is the essential difference between works rules and collective agreements?

CUSTOM AND PRACTICE

In the days when written contracts of employment were less common and written statements of particulars were not required by statute, custom and practice played an important part in helping to identify the contractual terms. Today custom and practice is not such an important source of law, although it may still be invoked occasionally to fill gaps in the employment relationship. To do so, a custom or practice must be definite, reasonable and generally applied in the area or trade in question. If these criteria are met, the fact that the particular employee against whom the custom is applied is ignorant of its existence appears to be of no consequence.[48] In determining whether a policy drawn up unilaterally by management has become a term of the employee's contract on the grounds that it is an established custom and practice, all the circumstances have to be taken into account. Among the most important circumstances are whether the policy has been drawn to the attention of employees by management or has been followed without exception for a substantial period.[49]

The major drawback of custom and practice is its uncertain legal effect and therefore its unreliability. After what period of time can it be said that a non-union member who has always worked in accordance with current collective agreements is bound to accept future agreements? If a custom and practice is useful to management, it is logical that efforts should be made to convert it into an express term of the contract. This may not always be possible, either because of the imprecise nature of the custom or because unions might oppose such a move as being contrary to the interests of their members. It almost goes without saying that a union will be in a better position to modify a custom or practice if it has not become embodied in a contract of employment. Finally, it should be noted that there may still be a place for custom and practice as an aid to interpreting a contractual term that is ambiguous.[50]

TERMS IMPLIED BY STATUTE AND REGULATIONS

There are a number of examples of statutes and regulations implying terms into contracts of employment:

1 *Terms and conditions awarded by the CAC*
Under section 185 TULRCA 1992 (on disclosure of information) these terms operate as part of the contract of employment of each worker affected. However, the terms and conditions imposed may be superseded or varied by a collective agreement between the employer and the union 'for the time being representing the employee' or an express or implied agreement between the employer and the employee so far as that agreement effects an improvement in the terms and conditions awarded by the CAC.

2 *The sex equality clause*
This is inserted by virtue of section 66 of the Equality Act 2010 (EA 2010).

3 *The National Minimum Wage Act 1998*
This allows the Secretary of State to make provision for determining the hourly rate to be paid. Section 2(3) allows provision to be made with respect to when a person is to be treated as working and when he or she is not.

4 *The Working Time Regulations*
These provide for maximum hours to be worked in various situations and occupations (see Chapter 10).

TERMS IMPLIED BY THE COMMON LAW

There are two distinct types of common-law implied terms. First, where there is a gap in the contract of employment it is possible to imply a term if a court can be persuaded that it is necessary to do so in the circumstances of the particular case (**implied terms of fact**). Second, there are terms which are regarded by the courts as being inherent in all contracts of employment (**implied terms of law**). The next chapter examines the major obligations which are automatically imposed on the parties to a contract of employment.

It is a basic principle that a contractual term can be implied only if it is consistent with the express terms of the contract. However, despite the increased use of written contracts and statements, it is not unusual for the parties to discover that they have failed to provide for a particular contingency. If there is a dispute over something which is not expressly dealt with in the contract of employment, a court or tribunal may be asked to insert a term to cover the point at issue. The party wishing to rely on an implied term must satisfy a court either that such a term was so obvious that the parties did not think it necessary to state it expressly (the 'officious bystander' test) or that such a term was necessary to give 'business efficacy' to the relationship.[51]

KEY LEARNING POINTS

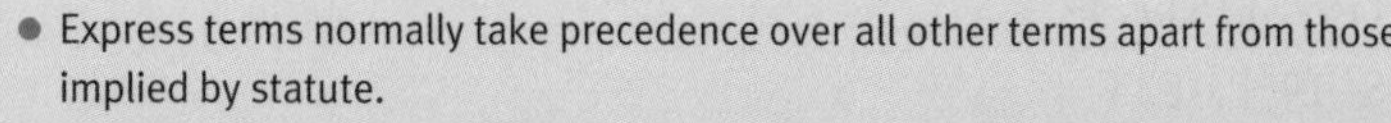

- Express terms normally take precedence over all other terms apart from those implied by statute.
- Not later than two months after the start of employment the employer must supply written particulars of employment, as provided in sections 1–3 ERA 1996.
- The statement does not constitute a contract of employment. It is merely the employer's version of what has been agreed.
- Terms of a contract may be derived from collective agreements as well as being individually negotiated.
- Substantive terms from a collective agreement may be incorporated into an employee's contract of employment expressly or impliedly or as a result of custom and practice.
- Workforce agreements can provide for a variation in the Working Time Regulations and other specified rights where there is no collective agreement.
- Works rules are normally determined by the employer and can be expressly or impliedly incorporated into a contract of employment.
- Custom and practice, if it is definite, reasonable and generally applied, can be used to fill gaps in the employment relationship.

- Terms, such as the sex equality clause in section 66 Equality Act 2010, can be implied in the contract of employment by statute.
- Terms can also be implied by the common law if they are consistent with the express terms.

REFERENCES

1 On apprenticeship contracts see *Flett v Matheson* (2006) IRLR 277

2 On the relevance of the Unfair Contract Terms Act 1977 see *Commerzbank AG v Keen* (2007) IRLR 132

3 Although tribunal jurisdiction in anti-discrimination cases may not depend on the existence of an enforceable contract of employment; see *Vakante v Governors of Addey and Stanhope School (No.2)* (2005) ICR 231

4 See *Annandale Engineering v Samson* (1994) IRLR 59

5 See (2004) IRLR 210

6 (1991) IRLR 473

7 *Enfield Technical Services Ltd v Payne* (2008) IRLR 500

8 See *Deeley v British Rail Engineering Ltd* (1980) IRLR 147

9 Sections 1–2 ERA 1996

10 (2001) IRLR 244

11 See sections 2(2) and (3) ERA 1996

12 For a discussion of this see *Secretary of State v Bearman* (1998) IRLR 431

13 See *Affleck v Newcastle Mind* (1999) IRLR 405

14 Sections 215 and 216 ERA 1996

15 SI 2006/246

16 (1997) IRLR 17

17 SI 1998/1833

18 See section 88(1)(d) ERA 1996

19 See *Leisure Leagues Ltd v Maconnachie* (2002) IRLR 600

20 See *Mihlenstedt v Barclays Bank* (1989) IRLR 522

21 See *Glitz v Watford Electrical* (1978) IRLR 89

22 See *Rutten v Cross Medical Ltd* (1997) IRLR 249

23 See *Werhof v Freeway Traffic Systems GmbH & Co.* (2006) IRLR 400

24 Directive 96/71

25 Section 3(1) ERA 1996

26 Section 7A ERA 1996

27 See section 4 ERA 1996

28 See *Systems Floors (UK) Ltd v Daniel* (1981) IRLR 475
29 (1983) IRLR 302
30 (1981) IRLR 477; see also *Aparau v Iceland Frozen Foods* (1996) IRLR 119
31 See *Gascol Conversions v Mercer* (1974) IRLR 155
32 See *Southern Cross Ltd v Perkins* (2011) IRLR 247
33 Section 11 ERA 1996
34 *Eagland v British Telecom plc* (1992) IRLR 323
35 Section 12(2) ERA 1996
36 Section 38(5) EA 2002 deals with exceptional circumstances
37 See *Adams v British Airways* (1996) IRLR 574
38 See *Gibbons v Associated British Ports* (1985) IRLR 376
39 See *Airlie v City of Edinburgh District Council* (1996) IRLR 516
40 See *Hamilton v Futura Floors* (1990) IRLR 478 and *Henry v LGTS Ltd* (2002) IRLR 472
41 See *Singh v British Steel* (1974) IRLR 478
42 See *Lakshmi v Mid Cheshire Hospitals NHS Trust* (2008) IRLR 956
43 Keeley v Fosroc *Ltd* (2006) IRLR 961. On the enforceability of a recognition agreement *see NCB v NUM* (1986) IRLR 439
44 *Malone v British Airways* (2011) IRLR 32
45 There are provisions which allow employers with fewer than 20 employees to have the majority of those employees sign in order for a workforce agreement to come into being
46 See *Cadoux v Central Regional Council* (1986) IRLR 131
47 (1998) IRLR 193
48 See *Sagar v Ridehalgh* (1931) Ch 310
49 See *Quinn v Calder* (1996) IRLR 126
50 See *Dunlop Tyres Ltd v Blows* (2001) IRLR 629 on the interpretation of an ambiguous collective agreement
51 See *United Bank v Akhtar* (1989) IRLR 507

EXPLORE FURTHER

Reading

- Deakin, S. and Morris, G. (2012) *Labour Law*. Hart, Chapter 4
- Smith, I. and Thomas, G. (2010) *Smith & Wood's Employment Law*. Butterworths, Chapters 2 and 3

Websites

- Advisory, Conciliation and Arbitration Service www.acas.org.uk
- Chartered Institute of Personnel and Development www.cipd.co.uk
- Department for Business Innovation and Skills www.bis.gov.uk
- Trades Union Congress www.tuc.org.uk

CHAPTER 3

Formation of the Contract of Employment (2): Implied terms of law

CHAPTER OVERVIEW

In the previous chapter we looked at the different ways in which contractual terms may come into existence and observed that certain terms could be implied into all contracts of employment. Here we examine the major obligations imposed on both employers and employees by law. Some of these are based on long-established common law principles, while others (such as those connected with unfair dismissal) are of relatively recent origin, having emerged as a result of legislative intervention.

LEARNING OUTCOMES

After studying this chapter you will be able to:

- understand and explain the implied duties of both parties to the employment relationship
- advise colleagues about how to operate the employment relationship without breaching legal obligations – for example, in respect of health and safety and disclosures of information.

DUTIES OF THE EMPLOYER

TO PAY WAGES

This is the most basic obligation of employers and is normally dealt with by an express term. Where the contractual pay is not specified, the law implies a reasonable sum.[1] In certain circumstances, however, the law does not leave the parties entirely free to determine the amount of remuneration payable – eg in the application of the national minimum wage or if a sex equality clause operates. Pay issues are considered in Chapter 5.

TO PROVIDE WORK

Employers are generally not obliged to provide work, and most employees who receive their full contractual remuneration cannot complain if they are left idle. Nevertheless, in certain circumstances the failure to provide work may amount to a breach of contract.

If a person's earnings depend upon work being provided

Employees who are paid by results or commission or who receive shift premiums must be given the opportunity to work because the payment of basic wages alone would deprive them of a substantial part of what they had bargained for – the opportunity to earn more.

Where the lack of work could lead to a loss of publicity or affect the reputation of an employee

Indeed, in one tribunal case it was held that the higher a person is in the management structure, the more important it is for work to be given when it is available.[2]

Where an employee needs to practise in order to preserve his or her skills

The Court of Appeal has suggested that such employees should be given the opportunity of performing work.[3] This is linked to the issue of 'garden leave' (see below), which is the practice of continuing to pay an employee for a period but not allowing him or her to work during that time. It has sometimes been used to prevent a valuable employee from leaving and immediately taking up employment with a competitor. A problem arises when such a period without work has a detrimental affect on an employee's skills.

CASE STUDY

WILLIAM HILL ORGANISATION v TUCKER

In *William Hill Organisation Ltd v Tucker*[4] the Court of Appeal held that the employer had an obligation to provide work when the work was available. This was partly because of the need to practise and partly because there was a contractual obligation on the employee to 'work those hours necessary to carry out his duties in a full and professional manner'.

Discussion point

Is it true to say that most employees now have the right to be provided with work when it is available?

The High Court has subsequently held that the right to work is subject to the qualification that the employee has not, as a result of some prior breach of duty, demonstrated in a serious way that he or she is not ready or willing to work. Thus in *SG&R Valuation Service v Boudrais*[5] the employer was granted an interim injunction which had the effect that the defendants had to remain on 'garden leave' for the rest of their notice periods.

TO CO-OPERATE WITH THE EMPLOYEE

Originally this duty amounted to little more than an obligation not to impede employees in the performance of their contracts and there is no general requirement to advise employees of their rights.[6] However, one of the effects of the unfair dismissal provisions has been that the courts have displayed a greater willingness to accept that employers have a positive duty to ensure that the purposes of the contract are achieved. Thus it has frequently been stated that employers must not destroy the mutual trust and confidence upon which co-operation is built without reasonable and proper cause.[7] However, the Supreme Court has ruled that such a term is concerned with preserving the continuing employment relationship and does not apply to the way that the relationship is terminated.[8] There are also limits as to how positive this obligation should be.

CASE STUDY

UNIVERSITY OF NOTTINGHAM v EYETT

In *University of Nottingham v Eyett*,[9] for example, a failure by an employer to warn an employee who was proposing to exercise important rights in connection with pension benefits, that the way the employee was proposing to exercise those rights was not the most financially advantageous was not seen as breaching a duty of mutual trust and confidence.

Discussion point

In what circumstance will the duty of trust and confidence require employers to advise employees about their rights?

Each case depends on its particular set of facts, but some examples of situations in which employers have been held to be in breach of this implied term are:

- changing the terms of employment without prior notice, consultation or discussion[10]
- the operation by an employer of a business in a dishonest and corrupt manner which damaged an innocent employee's reputation.[11] However, the employee may only be able to claim damages if he or she can show that the damage to reputation actually caused financial loss[12]
- an employer's discretion under a mobility clause being exercised in a way that made it impossible for the employee to comply with a contractual obligation to move[13]
- a failure to investigate a genuine safety grievance[14]
- employees not being afforded a reasonable opportunity to obtain redress of a grievance[15]
- a false accusation of theft on the basis of flimsy evidence[16]
- suspension as a knee-jerk reaction to allegations without considering the alternatives[17]
- reprimanding an employee in public[18]
- the persistent attempt by an employer to vary an employee's conditions of service[19]

- without reasonable cause, denying the employee the opportunity given to everyone else of signing a revised contract with enhanced redundancy payments[20]
- a serious failure over a period of time to make reasonable adjustments to accommodate a disabled person[21]
- failing to notify an employee on maternity leave of a vacancy for which she would have applied had she been aware of it.[22]

This duty should also inhibit employers from issuing unjustified warnings which are designed not to improve performance but to dishearten employees and drive them out.[23]

The Supreme Court has also accepted that in certain circumstances it will be necessary to imply an obligation on the employer to take reasonable steps to bring a contractual term to the employee's attention. Such a duty will arise when:

- the contractual terms have not been negotiated with individuals but result from collective bargaining or are otherwise incorporated by reference, and
- a particular term makes available to employees a valuable right contingent upon action being taken by them to avail themselves of its benefit, and
- employees cannot in all the circumstances reasonably be expected to be aware of the term unless it is drawn to their attention.[24]

Although employers should provide sufficient information to enable employees to understand the choices available to them, the Court of Appeal has ruled that they do not have to ensure that the information was actually communicated. All the employer has to do is to take reasonable steps to inform the employees about their rights.[25]

Finally, it should be noted that the relationship of trust and confidence is a mutual one. However, this does not mean that because the employer's confidence in the employee has been undermined, the employer is entitled to damage the employee's trust and confidence.[26]

TO TAKE REASONABLE CARE OF THE EMPLOYEE

In addition to this duty implied by law, there are a number of key statutes in the area of health and safety. We shall be looking at the legislation in Chapter 9, although it is important to note at this stage that a person who is injured in the course of employment may be able to bring an action for damages based either on the common law duty or breach of statute or other regulations. 'In the course of employment' means the claimant was doing something that he or she was employed to do, or something reasonably incidental to it.

CASE STUDY

CHIEF ADJUDICATION OFFICER v RHODES

In *Chief Adjudication Officer v Rhodes*,[27] an employee of the Benefits Agency was assaulted at her home, when off sick from work, by a neighbour whom she had reported for suspected fraud. The Court of Appeal decided that although the incident arose out of her employment it did not take place in the course of that employment.

Recognising that employers cannot guarantee that no employees will be injured at work, the standard of care which the law demands is that which 'an ordinary prudent employer would take in all the circumstances'.[28] Generally speaking, if a job has risks to health and safety which are not common knowledge but about which an employer knows or ought to know, and against which she or he cannot guard by taking precautions, then the employer should tell anyone to whom employment is offered what those risks are if, on the information then available, knowledge of those risks would be likely to affect the decision of a sensible prospective employee about accepting the offer.[29] Thus the common law accepts that employers should be held liable only if they fail to safeguard against something which was reasonably foreseeable.[30] In terms of damages, the Supreme Court held in *Corr v IBC Ltd*[31] that it is the foreseeability of the risk of physical injury that is important. In this case depression was a direct and foreseeable consequence of the accident and suicide was the direct result of the depression.

It should also be observed that the general duty of care does not extend to taking all reasonable steps to protect the economic welfare of employees, whether by insuring them against special risks known to the employer or by advising them of those risks so that they can obtain appropriate cover.

Employers' single personal duty of care to each employee

Employers are entitled to follow recognised practices in their industry, unless the practices are obviously unsafe, but must make arrangements to ensure that they keep abreast of current developments.

REFLECTIVE QUESTION

What steps can employers take to ensure that they are aware of safe working practices within their industry?

Once an employer knows of a source of danger, or could have been expected to know of it, it is necessary to take all reasonable steps to protect employees from risks which have hitherto been unforeseeable.[32] The duty is to assess the likelihood of injury and to weigh the risk against the cost and inconvenience of taking effective precautions to eliminate it. Employers owe a single personal duty of care to each of their employees, having proper regard to the employee's skill and experience, etc. Thus even if the employer delegates this duty to another person who is reasonably believed to be competent to perform it, the employer will remain personally liable for injuries to an employee caused by that other person's negligence.[33] Similarly, where an employee's labour is subcontracted, the employer's duty of care is still owed.[34]

Having considered some general issues, it may be useful to subdivide this duty into the following headings:

Safe premises

CASE STUDY

LATIMER v AEC LTD

Latimer v AEC Ltd[35] provides a suitable illustration of what is required of employers in this connection. Owing to exceptionally heavy rainfall, a factory was flooded. A layer of oil and grease was left on the floor which the employers attempted to cover with sawdust. However, this was not spread across all of the factory floor and an employee slipped in an area that was uncovered. It was held by the Supreme Court that the employers had taken reasonable precautions and they could not be expected to close down their factory in order to avoid what was a fairly small risk of injury.[36]

It has also been acknowledged that in certain circumstances UK-based employers may have to satisfy themselves as to the safety of overseas sites. According to the Court of Appeal, the employer's duty to take all reasonable steps to ensure the safety of employees applies whether the premises where the employee is required to work are occupied by the employer or by a third party.[37]

Safe plant, equipment and tools

If employers know that a tool or a piece of machinery could be a source of danger, it is incumbent upon them to take reasonable precautions to safeguard employees. Where tools or equipment are purchased from a reputable supplier and employers have no reason to suspect that they are defective, they cannot be held liable at common law. If in these circumstances an employee were to sustain an injury as a result of a defect, in order to recover damages he or she would be obliged to sue the person responsible, such as the supplier or manufacturer, under the general law of negligence.

Safe system of work

Under this heading are included all the matters which relate to the manner in which the work is performed: job design, working methods, the provision of protective clothing, training and supervision. Indeed, it is now accepted that employers have a duty not to cause their employees psychological damage by the volume or character of the work that they are required to perform.[38] However, the Court of Appeal has ruled that unless an employer knows of some particular problem or vulnerability, it is usually entitled to assume that the employee can withstand normal pressures of the job. According to the Appeal Court, there are no occupations which should be regarded as intrinsically dangerous to mental health.[39] Equally contentious is the view that if the only reasonable way of safeguarding the employee would be to demote or dismiss, an employer will not be in breach of the duty of care in allowing a willing employee to continue in the job. Thus in *Coxall v Goodyear Ltd* [40] it was held that the employer was under a duty either to take the claimant off the job or, as a matter of last resort, to dismiss. If safety rules and procedures exist, employees must be informed of their content, and if safety clothing or equipment is required, it must be readily available.[41] Clearly, the more dangerous the task or workplace situation, the greater is the need for precautions to be taken.

REFLECTIVE QUESTION

What efforts should an employer make to ensure that safety devices are properly used?

In *Crouch v British Rail Engineering* [42] the Court of Appeal decided that where an employee is regularly performing tasks which involve a reasonably foreseeable risk to the eyes, the employer has the duty actually to put goggles into the employee's hands. Similarly, employees who are likely to do a great deal of typing should be told that they must take breaks and rest pauses.[43] In *Pape v Cumbria County Council* [44] the High Court ruled that an employer has a duty to warn cleaners of the dangers of handling chemicals with unprotected hands and to instruct them on the need to wear gloves at all times. The circumstances that have to be considered in ascertaining the extent of the duty of care include: the risk of injury; the gravity of any injury which might result; the difficulty of providing protective equipment or clothing; the availability of that equipment or clothing and the distance the worker might have to go to fetch it; the frequency of occasions on which the employee is likely to need the protective equipment or clothing; and the experience and degree of skill to be expected of the employee. Bearing in mind both this common law duty and the obligations imposed by legislation (see Chapter 9), managers would be advised to ensure that an unreasonable refusal to follow safety rules or procedures is classed as a breach of discipline which could ultimately lead to dismissal for misconduct.

HONE v SIX CONTINENTS RETAIL LTD

CASE STUDY

Mark Hone was a licensed house manager for five years before he collapsed and never returned to work. He had complained that he did not have adequate support and that he was regularly working 90 hours a week. As a result of a meeting, the operations manager accepted that an assistant manager should be appointed, but apart from some occasional relief no help was provided.

Mr Hone sought damages on the basis that he had suffered psychological injury caused by the stress of being required to work excessive hours without proper support. In upholding an award of £21,840, the Court of Appeal confirmed that the correct test for deciding whether psychological injury was reasonably foreseeable was that: 'The indications of impending harm to health arising from stress at work must be plain enough for any reasonable employer to realise that he should do something about it.'[45]

Discussion point

In this case could a breach of trust and confidence also have been the basis for Mr Hone's legal action?

Competent and safe colleagues

Employers are required to take reasonable steps to ensure that employees do not behave in such a fashion that they are a source of danger to others. This means that employers must engage competent staff, or train recruits to a safe-worker level, must instruct their employees in safe working methods, and must then provide adequate supervision to check that these methods are being adhered to.

REFLECTIVE QUESTION

Does it follow from the law on health and safety that those who play practical jokes with tools or equipment should be removed from the workplace?

TO PROVIDE REFERENCES

SPRING v GUARDIAN ASSURANCE PLC

CASE STUDY

In *Spring v Guardian Assurance plc*[46] the complainant argued that a reference provided by a former employer was a malicious falsehood and/or a negligent misstatement and/or a breach of an implied term in the contract of employment that any reference would be compiled with all reasonable care. The Supreme Court concluded that an employer has a duty to take reasonable care in compiling a reference by ensuring the accuracy of the information upon which it was based.

Discussion point

Would it be helpful to have statutory guidance about the contents of employee references?

The duty is to provide a reference which is in substance true, accurate and fair, and this will usually involve making a reasonable enquiry into the factual basis of any statements made.[47] The provider of a reference must not give an impression that is unfair or misleading overall, even if the component parts of the reference are accurate.[48] Similarly, in *McKie v Swindon College* [49] an employer was held liable for a negligently prepared email where economic damage through job loss was eminently foreseeable.

REFLECTIVE QUESTION

Does the law relating to employment references require the inclusion of matters not in the employee's favour as well as those that are?

DUTIES OF THE EMPLOYEE

TO CO-OPERATE WITH THE EMPLOYER

We are concerned here with the duty to obey lawful and reasonable orders and the duty not to impede the employer's business. In this context the obligation to carry out lawful orders has two distinct aspects. First, it means that employees are not required to comply with an order if to do so would break the law – for example, by producing false accounts. Second, it also means that employees are not obliged to accept orders which fall outside the scope of the contract. This is consistent with the view that (at least in theory) the terms of a contract cannot be varied unilaterally[50] (see Chapter 11). However, the EAT has suggested that there can be an implied term that an employee may be obliged to perform duties that are different from those expressly required by the contract or to perform them at a different place. Nevertheless, it is likely to be legitimate to find an implied obligation to undertake a duty which is outside the express terms only where: the circumstances are exceptional; the requirement is plainly justified; the work is suitable; the employee suffers no detriment in terms of contractual benefits and status; and the change is temporary.[51] Additionally, as we shall discover later (Chapter 13), the law of unfair dismissal does not prevent employees from being fairly dismissed for refusing to follow instructions which may be outside their contractual obligations.[52]

As regards the duty not to impede the employer's business, it is clear that going on strike breaches a fundamental term of the contract because the essence of the employment relationship is that the employee is ready and willing to work in exchange for remuneration. However, is there a duty on employees not to engage in industrial action which falls short of a strike?

CASE STUDY

SECRETARY OF STATE v ASLEF

In the leading case of the *Secretary of State v ASLEF*,[53] which involved a work to rule on the railways, the Court of Appeal gave different reasons for reaching the conclusion that such a duty exists. Lord Justice Roskill thought that there is an implied term that employees ought not to obey lawful instructions in such a way as to disrupt the employer's business. Lord Justice Buckley extended the notion of fidelity (see below) and proclaimed that 'the employee must serve the employer faithfully with a view to promoting those commercial interests for which he is employed'. Lord Denning chose to focus attention on motive – ie the wilfulness of the disruption caused – and his formulation leads to the conclusion that all forms of industrial action are likely to be unlawful.

The High Court has also ruled that it is a professional obligation on teachers to co-operate in running schools and that the failure to cover for absent colleagues amounts to a breach of contract.[54] (On the options open to an employer where an employee only partly performs the contract, see Chapter 11.)

FIDELITY

Employees must avoid putting themselves in a position whereby their own interests conflict with the duty they owe their employer or an employer to whom they have been seconded.[55] Thus employees must not accept any reward for their work other than from their employer – for example, a gift or secret commission. There is no implied obligation on employees to disclose their own misconduct, and whether there is a duty to report the misconduct of fellow employees depends on the individual contract of employment and the circumstances.[56] However, the Court of Appeal has suggested that senior employees have a duty to disclose both their own wrongdoing and that of others.[57] There are two particular aspects of the duty of fidelity which we must now consider: the obligation not to compete with the employer, and the obligation not to disclose confidential information.

The obligation not to compete with the employer

Generally the spare-time activities of employees are no business of the employer, although an injunction may be granted to prevent employees from working for competitors during their own time if it can be shown that the employer's business would be seriously damaged. However, in *Nova Plastics Ltd v Froggatt* [58] the EAT rejected the argument that there is a general implication that any work for a competitor should be regarded as being a breach of trust or a failure to give loyal service. It should be noted that the intention to set up in competition with the employer is not in itself a breach of the implied duty of loyalty, although there is a line over which the employee must not go.[59] The renting and equipping of premises in an employee's spare time and the arranging of financial backing to set up in competition may be construed as a breach of an implied duty of fidelity.[60] If the employer has reasonable grounds for believing that the employee has committed or is about to commit some wrongful act, dismissal may be justified (see Chapter 13).[61]

Restraint clauses

Normally, ex-employees are entitled to make use of the skills and knowledge which they have acquired and are allowed to compete with a former employer provided they do not rely on confidential information (see below). However, this is not the position if there is an express clause in the contract of employment which restrains competition by employees when they leave.[62] Such restraint clauses (**restrictive covenants**) will be enforced by the courts only if they provide protection against something more than competition alone, if they are shown to be reasonable in the circumstances, and if they are not contrary to the public interest.[63] A clause stopping an ex-employee ever dealing with any of the plaintiff's customers with whom he or she dealt might be unreasonable, but one restricting contact with customers dealt with during the previous six months might be acceptable.[64] The reasonableness of the restraint is to be assessed as at the date the contract was made.[65] According to the Court of Appeal, the employer must establish that the nature of the employment was such as to expose the employee to the kind of information capable of protection beyond the duration of the contract.[66] Non-competition clauses in a contract may be reasonable to protect the employer's proprietary interests in the customer connections that have been built up by the departing employees, although non-solicitation clauses should not be too broad.[67] It would be an unreasonable restraint of trade to stop employees or ex-employees soliciting even the most junior of employees.[68]

'Garden leave'

What about the enforcement of 'garden leave' clauses – ie clauses which provide that during the period of notice an employee is not obliged to work but will receive full pay and meanwhile must not work for anyone else? Such clauses will not be enforced if it appears that the organisation for which the employee wishes to work before the notice expires has nothing to do with the employer's business. On the other hand, where the period during which the employee is not required to work is not excessive and there is a risk of damage to the employer's business, it may be appropriate to restrain the employee from taking other employment during the notice period, either under a specific clause or as a breach of duty of fidelity.[69] However, the wrongful dismissal of an employee will prevent the employer from relying on a restrictive covenant.[70] Finally, one effect of Regulation 4 of the Transfer Regulations (see Chapter 16) is that the transferee may benefit from a restrictive covenant in contracts of employment made with the transferor. Thus an employee may be restrained from doing or seeking to do business with anyone who had dealt with the transferor during the period stipulated in the original contract.[71]

The obligation not to disclose confidential information

CASE STUDY

FACCENDA CHICKEN LTD v FOWLER

In *Faccenda Chicken Ltd v Fowler*[72] the following principles were enunciated by the Court of Appeal. First, an individual's obligations are to be determined by the contract of employment and, in the absence of any express term, the employee's obligations in respect of the use and disclosure of information are the subject of implied terms. Second, while the individual remains in employment the obligations are included in the implied term which imposes a duty of fidelity on the employee. The extent of this duty varies according to the nature of the contract and would be broken if an employee copied a list of the employer's customers for use after the employment ended, or deliberately memorised such a list.[73] Third, the implied term which imposes an obligation on the employee as to his or her conduct after the employment has terminated is more restricted than that imposed by the duty of fidelity. The obligation not to use or disclose information might cover secret processes of manufacture or designs, or any other information of a sufficiently high degree of confidentiality as to amount to a trade secret.[74] However, this obligation does not extend to information which is only 'confidential' in the sense that any unauthorised disclosure to a third party while the employment subsisted would be a breach of the duty of fidelity.

Fourth, in order to determine whether any particular item of information falls within the implied term thus preventing its use or disclosure after the employment has ceased, it is necessary to consider all the circumstances of the case. Among the matters to which attention must be paid are:

- the nature of the employment – a high obligation of confidentiality might be imposed if the employment was such that confidential material was habitually handled
- the nature of the information – in deciding whether there is a legitimate trade secret to be protected, a distinction needs to be made between information which can be legitimately regarded as the property of the employer and the skill, know-how and general knowledge which can be regarded as the property of the employee. According to the courts, 'objective knowledge' is the employer's property and 'subjective knowledge' belongs to the employee[75]
- whether the employer impressed on the employee the confidentiality of the information – however, an employer cannot prevent the use or disclosure of information merely by telling the employee that it is confidential.

In practice it can be very difficult to differentiate between use and abuse of the knowledge which an ex-employee possesses – for example, of the former employer's customers. Thus employers should be advised to draft express restraint clauses which set precise limits on the future employment of key workers. Such clauses must be carefully worded, for it is a court's duty to give effect to covenants as they are expressed rather than to correct errors or remedy omissions.[76] Because breaches are relatively easy to identify, enforcing such clauses should be a fairly simple process. Indeed, the mere presence of a restraint clause can be valuable as a reminder to the employee that disclosure of confidential information will not be condoned. The employer who relies solely on the implied term is at a serious disadvantage, because an employee can be stopped from disclosing confidential information only when the employer has proved that such information has already been divulged. Only then will an aggrieved employer have a remedy against a third party to whom the employee has passed trade secrets or confidential information.[77]

Two further points must be considered. First, in an appropriate case a court has power to grant injunctions against ex-employees to restrain them from fulfilling contracts already concluded with third parties.[78] Second, although the Data Protection Act 1998 imposes additional constraints on an employee's ability to disclose information, the Public Interest Disclosure Act 1998 protects workers who make certain disclosures in the public interest (see below).

TO TAKE REASONABLE CARE

Employees must exercise reasonable skill and care in the performance of their contracts.[79] If they do not do so, apart from any disciplinary action that may be taken against them, there is an implied duty to indemnify the employer in respect of the consequences of their negligence.[80] Thus, if by virtue of the doctrine of **vicarious liability** (see Chapter 4) an employer is required to pay damages to an injured third party, in theory the amount paid out could be recovered by suing the negligent employee. In practice, such embarrassing litigation is avoided because it is the employer's insurance company that actually pays the damages.

PUBLIC INTEREST DISCLOSURES

The purpose of the Public Interest Disclosure Act 1998, which primarily amended the ERA 1996, is to protect individuals who make certain disclosures of information in the public interest. There is no statutory definition of 'information' for these purposes, but the EAT has drawn a distinction between 'information' and the making of an allegation.[81] Section 43A ERA 1996 defines a 'protected disclosure' as a qualifying disclosure which is made to the persons mentioned in sections 43C–43H ERA 1996 (below). Section 43B(1) defines a 'qualifying disclosure' as one which a worker *reasonably believes* [82] tends to show one or more of the following: (a) a criminal offence; (b) a failure to comply with any legal obligation;[83] (c) a miscarriage of justice; (d) danger to the health and safety of any individual (ie not necessarily a worker); (e) damage to the environment; or (f) the deliberate concealment of information tending to expose any of the matters listed above. Four general points about these categories should be noted. Firstly, they are not restricted to confidential information. Secondly, there is no requirement for any link between the matter disclosed and the worker's employment. Thirdly, the matter disclosed may have occurred in the past, be currently occurring, or be likely to occur. Fourthly, the statute does not protect actions which are directed at establishing or confirming the reasonableness of a belief.[84]

Section 43C(1) ERA 1996 protects workers who make qualifying disclosures *in good faith* to their employer or to another person who is responsible for the matter disclosed. It would seem that the burden is on the employer to show that the claimant lacked good faith and, if an ulterior motive was the dominant purpose for making the disclosure, protection will not be afforded.[85]

REFLECTIVE QUESTION

If information amounts to a qualifying disclosure, why is good faith a relevant consideration in determining whether protection should be afforded to a worker?

According to section 43C(2) ERA 1996, workers are to be treated as having made disclosures to their employer if they follow a procedure which the employer has authorised, even if the disclosure has been made to someone else such as an independent person or organisation. Section 43D ERA 1996 enables workers to seek legal advice about their concerns and to reveal to their adviser the issues about which a disclosure may be made. Under these circumstances, section 43B(4) ERA 1996 provides that the legal adviser is bound by professional privilege and cannot make a protected disclosure.

Section 43E ERA 1996 protects workers in government-appointed organisations if they make a disclosure in good faith to a Minister of the Crown rather than to their legal employer. Section 43F(1) ERA 1996 protects workers who make disclosures in good faith to a person prescribed for the purpose by the Secretary of State.[86] However, the worker must reasonably believe (a) that the matter falls within the remit of the prescribed person, and (b) that the information and any allegation contained in it are substantially true.

Section 43G ERA 1996 enables workers to make a protected disclosure in other limited circumstances. In order to be protected, workers must:

- act in good faith
- reasonably believe that the information and any allegation contained in it are substantially true[87]
- not act for personal gain (according to section 43L(2) ERA 1996, in determining whether a person has acted for personal gain, a reward payable under any enactment will be disregarded)
- have already disclosed substantially the same information to the employer or to a person prescribed under section 43F ERA 1996, unless they reasonably believe that they would be subject to a detriment for doing so, or that the employer would conceal or destroy the evidence if alerted
- act reasonably. For these purposes regard shall be had, in particular, to:

- the identity of the person to whom the disclosure is made (for example, disclosure to an MP may be reasonable whereas disclosure to the media may not be)
- the seriousness of the matter
- whether there is a continuing failure or one likely to recur
- whether the disclosure is made in breach of a duty of confidentiality owed by the employer to another person
- any action the employer (or prescribed person) has taken or might have been expected to take in relation to a previous disclosure
- whether the worker has complied with any procedure authorised by the employer for making a disclosure.

Section 43H ERA 1996 deals with disclosures about exceptionally serious wrongdoing. Again, in order to be protected:

- workers must act in good faith
- they must reasonably believe that the information and any allegation contained in it are substantially true
- they must not act for personal gain
- the relevant failure must be of an exceptionally serious nature
- in all the circumstances it must be reasonable to make the disclosure. In this respect particular regard will be had to the identity of the person to whom the disclosure is made.

Section 43J ERA 1996 prevents employers from generally contracting out of the provisions in Part IVA. In particular, it deals with 'gagging clauses' by invalidating a worker's agreement (whether contained in a contract or settlement of legal proceedings) not to make a protected disclosure.

Section 43K(1) ERA 1996 is designed to enable everyone who works to benefit from Part IVA, irrespective of whether they fall within the section 230 ERA 1996 definition of 'employee' or 'worker'. Thus for these purposes the definition of 'worker' is extended to include certain agency workers; certain workers who would not otherwise be covered because they are not obliged to carry out all of their duties personally; NHS practitioners such as GPs, certain dentists, pharmacists and opticians; and certain trainees.[88] Section 43K(2) ERA 1996 extends the definition of 'employer' accordingly.

Section 47B(1) ERA 1996 gives workers the right not to be subjected to any detriment by the employer on the ground that he or she has made a protected disclosure.[89] According to the Court of Appeal, this section will be infringed if such a disclosure materially influences the employer's treatment of the whistleblower.[90] For these purposes, the extended meaning of 'worker' in section 43K applies and it is made clear that 'detriment' covers both actions and a deliberate failure to act. Thus the following would be covered: discipline or dismissal, or being denied a pay rise or facilities that would otherwise be provided. However, it should be noted that the ERA 1996 does not make an employer vicariously liable for detriments inflicted by a worker's colleagues.

In addition, workers who have been dismissed for making a protected disclosure and are not qualified to claim unfair dismissal under Part X of the ERA 1996 (the general unfair dismissal provisions) can bring a claim under section 47B ERA 1996. The obvious example here is a worker who does not have a contract of employment. Section 48(1A) ERA 1996 enables a worker to complain to an employment tribunal that section 47B has been infringed, and compensation for injury to feelings is available.[91]

DISCLOSURE AND DISMISSAL

Section 103A ERA 1996 makes it automatically unfair to dismiss employees if the reason (or, if more than one, the principal reason) is that they have (at any time)[92] made a protected disclosure. No qualifying period of service is required.[93] Similarly, section 105(6A) ERA 1996 makes it unfair to select employees for redundancy if the reason for doing so is that they have made a protected disclosure. Finally, it should be noted that there is no limit on the compensation that can be awarded by an employment tribunal if section 103A ERA 1996 applies and damages are available for injury to feelings.[94]

THE LAW GOVERNING INVENTIONS AND COPYRIGHT

According to section 39(1) of the Patents Act 1977, an invention belongs to an employer if:

- it was made in the course of the employee's normal duties or those specifically assigned to him or her, and the circumstances in either case were such that an invention might reasonably be expected to result from the carrying out of those duties, or
- it was made in the course of the employee's duties and at the time of making the invention, because of the nature of the duties and the particular responsibilities arising from them, there was a special obligation to further the interests of the employer's undertaking.

In all other circumstances the invention belongs to the employee notwithstanding any contractual term to the contrary.

CASE STUDY

REISS ENGINEERING v HARRIS

This section was considered in *Reiss Engineering v Harris*[95] where the Patents Court held that, for these purposes, employees' 'normal duties' are those which they are actually employed to do. Section 39(1)(a) was interpreted as referring to an invention which achieves or contributes to achieving whatever was the aim or object to which the employee's efforts in carrying out his or her duties were directed – ie an invention similar to that made but not necessarily the precise invention as that actually made. The extent and nature of the 'special obligation' in section 39(1)(b) will depend on the status of the employee and the attendant responsibilities and duties of that status.

Even if the invention belongs to the employer, an employee can apply to the Patents Court or Controller of Patents for an award of compensation. This may be granted if the patent is of outstanding benefit (in money or money's worth) to the employer and it is just to make an award. The burden of proof lies on the employee to show that the employer has derived benefit from the patented invention. Where inventions belong to employees and their interests have been assigned to the employer, they are still entitled to seek compensation if they can show that the financial benefit they have derived is inadequate in relation to the benefit derived by the employer from the patent and it is just that additional compensation should be paid. However, no compensation can be paid if, at the time the invention is made, there is in force a 'relevant collective agreement' (an agreement between a trade union to which the employee belongs and the employer or an association to which the employer belongs) which provides for the payment of compensation for inventions made by the employee. It is expected that collective agreements will improve upon the statutory rights, yet there appears to be nothing to prevent employers and unions from negotiating less favourable compensation schemes.

According to section 11 of the Copyright, Designs and Patents Act 1988, where a literary, dramatic, musical or artistic work is made by an employee in the course of employment, the employer is the first owner of any copyright, subject to any agreement to the contrary.

KEY LEARNING POINTS

The law regards employers and employees as having certain obligations to each other. These obligations arise out of long-established common law principles and more recent statutory intervention in the employment relationship.

The duties of the employer include:

- paying wages if an employee is available for work and not making unlawful deductions
- providing work in circumstances where a lack of work will affect an employee's earnings, reputation or skills
- co-operating with the employee and preserving the mutual trust and confidence upon which this co-operation depends
- taking reasonable care of the employee by providing a safe working environment and safe working practices
- taking reasonable care with regard to references.

The duties of the employee include:

- co-operating with the employer and obeying lawful and reasonable instructions
- not damaging the employer's business by competing with the employer in breach of a duty of fidelity
- not disclosing certain confidential information to competitors
- taking reasonable care and exercising reasonable skills in the performance of his or her contract.

REFERENCES

1 See *Driver v Air India* (2011) IRLR 992, where the Court of Appeal upheld a claim for ad hoc overtime to be paid

2 *Bosworth v A Jowett* (1977) IRLR 341

3 *Langston v AUEW* (1974) ICR 180

4 (1998) IRLR 313

5 (2008) IRLR 770

6 See *Fraser v South West London St Georges Mental Health Trust* (2012) IRLR 100

7 See *Hilton v Shiner Ltd* (2001) IRLR 727

8 See *Johnson v Unisys Ltd* (2002) IRLR 271 and *Eastwood v Magnox plc* (2004) IRLR 733

9 (1999) IRLR 87. See also *Crossley v Faithful & Gould Ltd* (2004) IRLR 377

10 *McBride v Falkirk FC* (2012) IRLR 22

11 *Malik v BCCI* (1997) IRLR 462

12 See *Bank of Credit and Commerce International SA v Ali (No.3)* (1999) IRLR 508

13 *United Bank v Akhtar* (1989) IRLR 507

14 *BAC v Austin* (1978) IRLR 332

15 *Goold Ltd v McConnell* (1995) IRLR 516
16 *Robinson v Crompton Parkinson* (1978) IRLR 61
17 See *Crawford v Suffolk Mental Health Partnership NHS Trust* (2012) IRLR 402
18 *Morrow v Safeway Stores* (2002) IRLR 9
19 *Woods v WM Car Services* (1982) IRLR 413
20 See *Transco plc v O'Brien* (2002) IRLR 444
21 See *Greenhof v Barnsley M.B.C.* (2006) IRLR 98
22 See *Visa v Paul* (2004) IRLR 42
23 *Walker v J Wedgewood Ltd* (1978) IRLR 105
24 See *Scally v Southern Health Board* (1991) IRLR 522
25 See *Ibekwe v LGTS Ltd* (2003) IRLR 697
26 See *Tullett Prebon PLC v BG Brokers LP* (2010) IRLR 648
27 (1999) IRLR 103
28 *Paris v Stepney B.C.* (1951) AC 376
29 See *White v Holbrook Ltd* (1985) IRLR 215
30 See *Hewett v Brown Ltd* (1992) ICR 530 on the duty owed to the employee's family
31 (2008) ICR 372
32 See *Baxter v Harland & Wolff* (1990) IRLR 516
33 See *McDermid v Nash Dredging* (1987) IRLR 334
34 On dual vicarious liability for borrowed employees see *Viasystems v Thermal Transfer Ltd* (2005) IRLR 953
35 (1953) AC 643
36 See also *Smith v Scot Bowyers Ltd* (1986) IRLR 315
37 See *Cook v Square D Ltd* (1992) IRLR 34
38 See *Walker v Northumberland County Council* (1995) IRLR 35 and *Cross v Highlands and Islands Enterprise* (2001) IRLR 336
39 *Sutherland v Hatton* (2002) IRLR 263. See also *Hartmann v South Essex NHS Trust* (2005) IRLR 293
40 *Coxall v Goodyear Great Britain Ltd* (2002) IRLR 742
41 See *Pentney v Anglian Water Authority* (1983) ICR 463
42 (1988) IRLR 404
43 See *Pickford v Imperial Chemical Industries* (1996) IRLR 622
44 (1991) IRLR 404
45 *Hone v Six Continents Retail Ltd* (2006) IRLR 49. See also *Intel Corporation Ltd v Daw* (2007) IRLR 355

46 (1994) IRLR 460

47 See *Cox v Sun Alliance Ltd* (2001) IRLR 448

48 See *Jackson v Liverpool City Council* (2011) IRLR 1019

49 (2011) IRLR 575

50 See *Smith v London Metropolitan University* (2011) IRLR 884

51 *Luke v Stoke on Trent City Council* (2007) IRLR 305

52 See *Farrant v The Woodroffe School* (1998) IRLR 176

53 (1972) QB 443

54 See *Sim v Rotherham M.B.C.* (1986) IRLR 391

55 *Macmillan Inc v Bishopsgate Investment Trust plc* (1993) IRLR 393

56 See *Ranson v Customer Systems plc* (2012) IRLR 769

57 See *Item Software UK Ltd v Fassihi* (2004) IRLR 928

58 (1982) IRLR 146

59 See *Ranson v Customer Systems plc* (2012) IRLR 769

60 See *Lancashire Fires Ltd v SA Lyons & Co. Ltd* (1997) IRLR 113

61 See *Laughton v Bapp Industrial Ltd* (1986) IRLR 245 and *Adamson v B&L Cleaning Ltd* (1995) IRLR 193

62 See *Caterpillar Logistics Services (UK) Ltd v Huesca de Crean* (2012) IRLR 410. On injunctions to prevent economic losses see *UBS Ltd v Vestra LLP* (2008) IRLR 965

63 See *TFS Derivatives Ltd v Morgan* (2005) IRLR 246

64 See *Dentmaster (UK) Ltd v Kent* (1997) IRLR 636

65 See *Patsystems v Neilly* (2012) IRLR 979

66 See *Thomas v Farr Plc* (2007) IRLR 419

67 See *Landmark Brickwork Ltd v Sutcliffe* (2011) IRLR 976

68 See *Dawnay, Day & Co. v de Bracconier d'Alphen* (1997) IRLR 285

69 See *Eurobrokers Ltd v Rabey* (1995) IRLR 206 and *Credit Suisse Ltd v Armstrong* (1996) IRLR 450

70 See *Cantor Fitzgerald International v Callaghan* (1999) IRLR 234 and *Rock Refrigeration Ltd v Jones* (1996) IRLR 675

71 See *Morris Angel v Hollande* (1993) IRLR 169

72 (1986) IRLR 69

73 See *Crowson Fabrics Ltd v Rider* (2008) IRLR 288 and *PennWell Publishing (UK) Ltd v Ornstein* (2007) IRLR 700

74 See *Lancashire Fires Ltd v SA Lyons & Co. Ltd* (note 60)

75 See *SBJ Stephenson Ltd v Mandy* (2000) IRLR 233

76 See *WAC Ltd v Whillock* (1990) IRLR 23; on the possibility of severing unlawful clauses and enforcing the remainder see *Marshall v NM Financial Management* (1996) IRLR 20

77 See *Sun Printers Ltd v Westminster Press Ltd* (1982) IRLR 92

78 See *PSM International v McKechnie* (1992) IRLR 279

79 See also section 7 HASAWA 1974 (Chapter 9)

80 See *Janata Bank v Ahmed* (1981) IRLR 457

81 See *Cavendish Munro Professional Risks Management Ltd v Geduld* (2010) IRLR 38

82 See *Babula v Waltham Forest College* (2007) IRLR 346

83 See *Hibbins v Hester Way Neighbourhood Project* (2008) UKEAT/0275/08

84 See *Bolton School v Evans* (2006) IRLR 500

85 See *Street v Derbyshire Unemployed Worker Centre* (2004) IRLR 687

86 See The Public Interest Disclosure (Prescribed Persons) Order 1999 SI 1549

87 See *Korashi v Abertawe Bro Morgannwg University Local Health Board* (2012) IRLR 4

88 See *Croke v Hydro Aluminium Worcester Ltd* (2007) ICR 1303

89 See *Woodward v Abbey National plc* (2006) IRLR 677 on post-dismissal detriment

90 See *Fecitt v NHS Manchester* (2012) IRLR 64

91 See *Virgo Fidelis School v Boyle* (2004) IRLR 268

92 See *Miklaszewicz v Stolt Offshore Ltd* (2002) IRLR 344

93 On the burden of proof see *Kuzel v Roche Products Ltd* (2008) IRLR 530

94 See *Commissioner of Police of the Metropolis v Shaw* (2012) IRLR 291

95 (1985) IRLR 232

EXPLORE FURTHER

Reading

- Deakin, S. and Morris, G. (2012) *Labour Law.* Hart, Chapters 1 and 2
- Smith, I. and Thomas, G. (2010) *Smith & Wood's Employment Law.* Butterworths, Chapters 2 and 3

Websites

- Advisory, Conciliation and Arbitration Service www.acas.org.uk
- Chartered Institute of Personnel and Development www.cipd.co.uk
- Department for Business Innovation and Skills www.bis.gov.uk
- Trades Union Congress www.tuc.org.uk

CHAPTER 4

Recruitment and Selection

CHAPTER OVERVIEW

In this chapter we raise some of the issues that will have to be considered by the human resources department. Firstly, is it preferable to hire employed or self-employed persons? Secondly, what are the possible implications of outsourcing the work to be done? Thirdly, if employees are engaged, should they have indefinite, fixed-term, part-time or some other form of contract of employment? Fourthly, what are the issues concerned with employing workers on a temporary basis? Lastly, is it necessary to impose a probationary period on new recruits? At the end of the chapter we deal with some of the regulatory constraints which impinge upon the process of recruitment and selection, including rules about vetting and barring, rehabilitated offenders and migrant workers. (The law relating to the employment of disabled persons and to sex, race and age discrimination is dealt with in Chapters 6 and 7.)

LEARNING OUTCOMES

After studying this chapter you will be able to:

- understand and explain the legal constraints that affect the process of recruitment and selection and participate in policy-making
- advise colleagues about the practical implications of engaging particular types of worker – for example, self-employed, fixed-term, part-time and agency staff.

EMPLOYMENT STATUS

Before recruiting or selecting an individual, one of the first important decisions to be reached is what sort of contract he or she is to be hired under:

- Is it to be a contract of service (ie an employee) or a contract for services (ie a self- employed person or independent contractor)?
- Is it to be a fixed-term or an open-ended contract?
- Is it to be a full-time or a part-time contract?
- Would it be better to use the services of an employment agency and take on a temporary agency worker?

Although some statutes apply to all of these categories of worker – for example, the Equality Act 2010 – some do not, and some categories of workers are provided with special protection. Examples include:

- Employees gain the benefit of a number of statutory rights, such as protection against unfair dismissal, the right to maternity and parental leave.
- Employees are subject to the unwritten general obligations implied into all contracts of employment (see Chapter 3).
- When employees are engaged, employers are required by statute to deduct tax as well as social security contributions. In addition, employers are obliged to pay employers' National Insurance contributions and to insure against personal injury claims brought by employees.

Perhaps the most significant difference at common law is that the doctrine of vicarious liability applies to employees but not to the self-employed. However, in exceptional circumstances employers will be liable for the tortious acts of their independent contractors – for example, if they authorise the commission of the wrongful act or have a responsibility which cannot, by law, be delegated to someone else.

The essence of the doctrine of vicarious liability is that employers are held liable to third parties for the civil wrongs committed by employees in the course of their employment. Determining what is 'in the course of employment' has caused immense difficulties over the years but the position today appears to be as follows. Employees act 'in the course of employment' where they carry out acts which are authorised by the employer. Similarly, where their actions are so closely connected with the employment as to be incidental to it, although prohibited and unauthorised by the employer, employees act 'in the course of employment'.[1] Thus in *Lister v Hedley Hall Ltd*[2] the employers were held vicariously liable for a warden who sexually abused the claimants while they were in his care. However, if an employee's action is so outside the scope of employment as to be not something the employee was employed to do, then the employer is not liable.

Before an employer can be held vicariously liable, some nexus has to be established between the employee's wrongful act and the circumstances of employment. Thus a contractor engaged to clean offices (including telephones) was not vicariously liable when one of the contractor's employees dishonestly used the phones for his own purposes.[3] Employees remain personally liable for their own acts and theoretically may be required to reimburse the employer for any damages paid out as a result of their failure to take care (see Chapter 3). It should also be noted that in some cases the criminal law regards an employee's act as being that of the employer, in which case the latter will be responsible for the wrongs committed by the former.

Additionally, a company might be liable as a substitute employer for the negligence of employees not directly employed by it if it can be shown that the substitute employer had sufficient power of control and supervision properly to be regarded as the effective employer at the critical time.[4]

DISTINGUISHING EMPLOYEES FROM OTHER TYPES OF WORKER

Given all the consequences of having an employee on the books, is it always possible to discern whether a contract is a contract of service or a contract for services? Unfortunately, the answer is no. The courts have ruled that the intention of the parties cannot be the sole determinant of contractual status; otherwise, it would be too easy to contract out of employment protection legislation. It is the operation of the contract in practice that is crucial, rather than its appearance, so tribunals must consider whether the written words of a contract represent the true intentions or expectations of the parties both at its commencement and subsequently.[5] To discover the parties' true legal obligations a tribunal must examine all the relevant evidence. This will include the written terms which are to be read in the context of the whole agreement. It will also include evidence of how the parties behaved in practice and what expectations they had of each other. In *Autoclenz Ltd v Belcher*[6] the Supreme Court upheld the tribunal's decision that a 'right to refuse work' clause was not genuine. It also stated that the conclusion that a contract is in part a sham does not require a finding that both parties intended to paint a false picture of their obligations. Thus the practice of the parties may be so persuasive that an inference can be drawn that it reflects the true obligations of the parties. However, the fact that the parties behave in a particular way does not of itself mean that their conduct accurately reflects their legal rights and obligations. Significantly, the court accepted that the relative bargaining power of the parties must be taken into account in determining whether the written terms represent what was agreed.

REFLECTIVE QUESTION

Should the declared intention of the parties be a factor taken into account by tribunals or courts in determining employment status?

CARMICHAEL v NATIONAL POWER PLC

CASE STUDY

In *Carmichael*,[7] the Supreme Court held that the applicant's case 'founders on the rock of the absence of mutuality'. The case was about whether two tour guides had contracts of employment and were therefore entitled to a written statement giving particulars of their terms of employment (see Chapter 2). An important factor was that there was no requirement for the employer to provide work or for the individual to carry out that work. The Court heard that there were a number of occasions when the applicants had declined offers of work and ruled that there was an 'irreducible minimum of mutual obligation' that was necessary to create a contract of service. There had to be an obligation to provide work and an obligation to perform that work in return for a wage or some form of remuneration.

Discussion point

If a document states that the employer has no obligation to provide work, does that mean that no contract of employment exists?

However, a lack of any mutual obligations when no work is being performed is of little significance when determining the status of the individual when work is performed.[8]

Of crucial importance is whether one person working for another is required to perform his or her service in person or not.

CASE STUDY

EXPRESS AND ECHO PUBLICATIONS v TANTON

In *Express and Echo Publications v Tanton*,[9] a contract allowed a worker to provide a substitute if he was not available. This prevented the worker from being treated as an employee because the obligation to do the work in person was, according to the Court of Appeal, an 'irreducible minimum'.

Discussion point

Will a worker's option to provide a substitute always prevent a contract from being one of employment?

However, this was held not to apply to gymnasts working for a local authority who were able to provide substitutes for any shift that they were unable to work.[10] The difference in approach resulted from the fact that the local authority paid the substitutes directly and the gymnasts could only be replaced by others on the Council's approved list.

Unless the relationship is dependent solely upon the true construction of a written contract, whether a person is engaged under a contract of employment is a question of fact for a court or tribunal to determine.[11]

REFLECTIVE QUESTIONS

To what extent is it true to say that personal service and the payment of wages are the only mandatory requirements for a contract of employment to exist?

How important is it that employment tribunals deal strictly with sham employment relationships?

OUTSOURCING

Increasingly, employers have been choosing to outsource parts or all of their non-core activities. Outsourcing can mean an arrangement whereby a contractor supplies staff who will be under the supervision of the hirer, or it can mean the outsourcing of the complete activity, so that the hirer is concerned only with the outcomes rather than with the means of achieving them. Activities that are commonly outsourced include catering and the cleaning of premises.

When an organisation decides on outsourcing an activity it must also decide what is to happen to its current employees who work in the part to be contracted out. It also has an obligation to inform and consult those employees at the earliest opportunity. There may be no need for redundancies because the employees currently working in the part to be transferred may be protected by the Transfer of Undertakings (Protection of Employment) Regulations 2006[12] (these Regulations are further considered in Chapter 16). Their contracts of employment are likely to transfer with the outsourcing contract. The contractor will become their employer and be liable for any debts arising out of the employment relationship. It will be as if they signed their original contract of employment with the new contractor and any outstanding claims from employees, whether they concern contractual or other obligations arising from the contract of employment, will transfer. For example, where two employees had claims for sex discrimination outstanding at the time of the transfer, these were transferred to the contractor who was faced with the need to settle a dispute in which it had not taken part.[13]

Examples of outsourcing situations where the Transfer Regulations have been held to apply include the contracting out of a local authority refuse collection and cleansing work,[14] a contract to deliver Audi and Volkswagen cars around the country,[15] and the transfer of a security contract.[16] It has not always been clear when the Transfer Regulations apply (see Chapter 16) and there has been considerable litigation over the meaning of a transfer of an undertaking or business.

FIXED-TERM OR INDEFINITE CONTRACT?

Assuming that a decision has been taken that the organisation will engage employees itself, another matter for consideration is whether to hire for a fixed term or for an indefinite period. Concern that employers might abuse the use of fixed-term contracts was one of the motivations behind the EU Directive on Fixed-Term Work.[17] The aims of the Directive were twofold. Firstly, it aimed to improve the quality of fixed-term work by ensuring the application of the principle of non-discrimination. Secondly, it aimed to establish a framework to prevent abuse arising from the use of successive fixed-term contracts. The Directive was implemented in the United Kingdom by the Fixed-term Employees (Prevention of Less Favourable Treatment) Regulations 2002.[18]

The main features of the Regulations are:

- Fixed-term employees should not be treated less favourably than comparable permanent employees with respect to their terms and conditions of employment, unless there is an objective reason to justify the treatment.[19]
- Fixed-term employees should be able to compare their terms and conditions with permanent employees who do the same or similar work for the same employer if they think that they are being treated less favourably.[20]
- The use of successive fixed-term contracts should be limited. This was effected by setting a maximum period of four years for such successive contracts unless there are objectively justifiable reasons for their renewal.[21] This four-year period is calculated on the basis of continuous service.

According to the CJEU,[22] objective reasons must mean precise and concrete circumstances which justify the use of successive fixed-term contracts. The Court held that a rule which allowed gaps of more than 20 days to break continuity so that a new fixed-term contract need not be justified was contrary to the Directive. This is a problem for the United Kingdom because the rules normally only require a week's break to end continuity (see Chapter 16). In relation to pay, the CJEU has ruled that unequal treatment must be justified by precise and concrete factors in the specific context in which it occurs and on the basis of objective and transparent criteria. This is to ensure that there is a genuine need and that the unequal treatment is appropriate for achieving the objective pursued and is necessary for that purpose.[23] Where a fixed-term contract is converted into an indefinite one, the CJEU has stated that if the tasks remain unchanged, there must not be material amendments that are unfavourable overall.[24]

If an employee considers that he or she has been treated less favourably than a comparable permanent employee, then he or she may request a written statement from the employer giving the reasons for the treatment. The employee is entitled to the statement within 21 days of the request and the statement is admissible as evidence in any subsequent tribunal proceedings.

CASE STUDY

DEPARTMENT FOR WORK AND PENSIONS v WEBLEY[25]

Atasha Webley worked as an administrative officer at Leyton Job Centre from 4 February 2002 to 17 January 2003. She was employed on a series of short, fixed-term contracts. Her letter of engagement had specified that she was employed on a short-term temporary and non-permanent basis. This was because the employer had a policy of terminating temporary employees after 51 weeks' service.

Mrs Webley brought a complaint under the Fixed-term Employees Regulations that the termination of her contract amounted to less favourable treatment compared to comparable permanent employees. Thus the question was whether the non-renewal of a fixed-term contract, amounting to dismissal, was capable of being less favourable treatment.

The Court of Appeal held that the ending of a fixed-term contract by the effluxion of time could not constitute less favourable treatment when compared to a permanent employee. If fixed-term contracts of employment were lawful, then the ending of those contracts must also be lawful.

Discussion point

Is it fair to say that this decision will encourage employers to use fixed-term contracts?

An employee may present a complaint to an employment tribunal that he or she has received less favourable treatment. It will be for the employer to identify the reason for the less favourable treatment. If the employment tribunal finds that such treatment has taken place, it may make a recommendation for action by the employer and award compensation to the employee.[26] Employers will have to be aware of these legal requirements when deciding whether to employ individuals on a permanent or a fixed-term contract. It should also be noted that the expiry of a fixed-term contract without its renewal on the same terms amounts to a dismissal in law (see Chapter 12).

PART-TIME OR FULL-TIME?

In deciding whether to employ full-time or part-time staff, account will have to be taken of the Part-time Workers (Prevention of Less Favourable Treatment) Regulations[27] (PTW Regulations) which give effect to a European Council Directive.[28] The purpose of the Regulations is to give part-time workers the right not to be treated less favourably than comparable full-time workers as regards the terms of the contract, or be subjected to some detriment by any act or failure to act.[29] This right applies only if there is an actual as opposed to a hypothetical **comparator**, and the treatment is on the grounds that a worker is a part-timer and cannot be justified on objective grounds.[30] However, the EAT has indicated that the part-time nature of the worker's status does not have to be the sole reason for discrimination. Indeed, the fact that not all part-timers are adversely treated does not mean that those who are cannot bring proceedings if being part-time is a reason for their less favourable treatment.[31]

PART-TIME WORKERS AND COMPARABLE FULL-TIME WORKERS

The principle of non-discrimination applies to 'workers'. This has a wider meaning than 'employees', and the definition given in the PTW Regulations[32] is identical to that in section 230(3) ERA 1996.

Regulation 2 PTW Regulations has a similar definition of both full-time and part-time workers. They are individuals who are paid wholly or in part by reference to the amount of time worked and who are, in relation to other workers employed under the same type of contract, defined as full-time or part-time.

Comparable full-timers, in relation to part-timers, are individuals who are:

- employed by the same employer under the same sort of contract[33]

- engaged in the same or broadly similar work, having regard, where relevant, to whether they have similar levels of qualifications, skills and experience[34]
- based at the same establishment or, if there is no full-time comparator at the same establishment, at a different one.[35]

According to Regulation 2(4) PTW Regulations, the moment for deciding whether an individual is a full-time comparator is the time when the alleged less favourable treatment takes place. This is a very demanding test for establishing whether an individual's job can be used as a comparator on which to base a claim of discrimination. If there is not a full-timer who meets the criteria, it will not be possible to make a claim for discrimination based upon the PTW Regulations.

REFLECTIVE QUESTION

In a business where all the management staff are full-time and all the operatives are low-paid part-timers, is it likely that the PTW Regulations would be of any help to the part-time workers?

CASE STUDY

MATTHEWS v KENT AND MEDWAY FIRE AUTHORITY

In *Matthews v Kent and Medway Fire Authority*,[36] some 12,000 'retained' firefighters brought claims under the PTW Regulations that they were being less favourably treated than full-time firefighters. They complained that they did not receive a number of benefits which their full-time colleagues had. These included not being in the Firemen's Pension Scheme, a lack of pay for additional responsibilities and a less favourable sick pay scheme. The Supreme Court held that the retained firemen worked under the same sort of contract within the meaning of Regulation 2. Even though the full-time firefighters had a fuller and wider job, it was important to look at the work they were both engaged in to decide whether it was the same work or, importantly, whether it was broadly similar work.

There are a limited number of exceptions to these strict rules on comparators. These are:

- workers who become part-time. If a full-time worker varies or terminates his or her contract in order to work fewer hours each week and thus become a part-timer, it is permissible to assume that there is a full-time comparator employed on the same terms as applied before the variation or termination.[37]
- full-time workers who return to work for the same employer after an absence of less than 12 months but are then required to work fewer hours per week. This is conditional upon the returning individual working in the same job, or at the same level, as that in which he or she worked before the break. In such a situation it is possible to assume that there is a full-time comparator employed

on the same terms and conditions as applied to the individual before the break in employment.[38]

LESS FAVOURABLE TREATMENT

In determining whether a part-timer has been discriminated against, the pro rata principle applies, unless it is inappropriate.[39] This means that a part-time worker is entitled to receive pay or any other benefit in proportion to the number of weekly hours that he or she works in comparison with a comparable full-time worker.[40] The one exception to this concerns overtime. Not paying overtime rates to a part-time worker until he or she has completed at least the basic working hours of the comparable full-time worker will not be regarded as less favourable treatment.

In the government's guidance accompanying the PTW Regulations the following are examples given as arising from the application of the principle of non-discrimination:

- Previous or current part-time status should not of itself constitute a barrier to promotion.
- Part-time workers should receive the same hourly rate as full-time workers.
- Part-time workers should receive the same hourly rate of overtime pay as full-time workers, once they have worked more than normal full-time hours.
- Part-time workers should be able to participate in profit-sharing or share option schemes available to full-time workers.
- Employers should not discriminate between part-time workers and full-time workers over access to pension schemes.
- Employers should not exclude part-timers from training simply because they work part-time.
- In selection for redundancy, part-time workers must not be treated less favourably than full-time workers.

DETRIMENT AND DISMISSAL

There is a distinction in the protection offered by the Regulations between employees and workers. Dismissal of employees, for any of the reasons listed below, will be regarded as an unfair dismissal in accordance with Part X of the ERA 1996 (see Chapter 13).[41] Regulation 6(1) PTW Regulations entitles a worker who considers that he or she has been treated less favourably to request in writing a statement giving particulars of the reasons for the treatment.[42] The worker is entitled to receive this statement within 21 days of the request. The written statement is admissible as evidence in any future proceedings and a tribunal may draw its own inferences if the statement is not provided or if it is 'evasive or equivocal'.[43]

Workers (which includes employees) have the right not to be subjected to a detriment by any act, or any deliberate failure to act, by the employer on the grounds that the employer believes that the worker has (or intends in due course to have):

- brought proceedings against the employer under the PTW Regulations

- requested from the employer a written statement of reasons under Regulation 6
- given evidence or information in connection with any proceedings brought by any worker
- done anything else under the PTW Regulations in relation to the employer or any other person
- alleged that the employer has infringed the Regulations
- refused, or proposes to refuse, to give up any rights held under the PTW Regulations.

COMPLAINTS TO EMPLOYMENT TRIBUNALS

A worker who believes that he or she has suffered less favourable treatment or other detriment in accordance with the Regulations may complain to an employment tribunal.[44] The complaint must be made within a period of three months from the date of treatment or detriment, although a longer period will be allowed if the tribunal finds it just and equitable to do so.[45] The options open to the employment tribunal are to:[46]

- make a declaration of the rights of the complainant in respect of the complaint
- order the employer to pay compensation to the complainant. Compensation does not include injury to the complainant's feelings and the complainant has a duty to mitigate his or her losses[47]
- recommend that the employer takes action to obviate or reduce the adverse effect on the complainant of any matter to which the complaint relates. The tribunal may specify a reasonable period during which this action should be taken. If the employer fails to follow the recommendation, without justification, the tribunal may increase the amount of compensation to be paid to the complainant.[48]

SHOULD TEMPORARY EMPLOYEES OR AGENCY STAFF BE HIRED?

In deciding whether to employ on a temporary or 'permanent' basis (see Chapter 11 on notice provisions), it should be noted that temporary staff have exactly the same statutory rights as other employees so long as they possess any necessary qualifying period of service. The only two exceptions to this proposition arise where an individual is employed on a temporary basis as a replacement for a woman on maternity leave or to replace someone absent from work under the statutory provisions relating to medical suspension (see Chapters 8 and 5 respectively).

Occasionally an organisation may ask an agency to provide staff, and if the worker engaged by the client organisation is under a personal obligation to perform the work, a contract of employment may exist. The exact relationship between the client and the individual supplied by the agency is a question of fact for an employment tribunal to decide. We will look firstly at issues relating to the relationship between the individual and the agency, and secondly at the relationship, if any, between the individual and the client.

CASE STUDY

McMEECHAN v SECRETARY OF STATE FOR EMPLOYMENT

McMeechan v Secretary of State for Employment[49] involved a temporary worker who completed a series of individual assignments through an employment agency. He was given a job sheet and a standard written statement of terms and conditions for each assignment. The statement specified that he was providing services as a self-employed worker and was not operating under a contract of service, although the agency did deduct tax and National Insurance contributions. When the agency became insolvent, the individual made a claim to the Secretary of State for wages owed. The claim was refused because, it was argued, the individual was not an employee of the insolvent company. The question for the Court of Appeal was whether the individual assignment could amount to a contract of service or not. The arguments for there being a contract for services were that there was an express statement that the individual was self-employed and that the worker had freedom to work for a particular client on a self-employed basis. On the side of there being a contract of service were the power of the agency to dismiss for misconduct, the power to bring any assignment to an end, the establishment of a grievance procedure and the stipulation of an hourly rate of pay, which in turn was subject to deductions for unsatisfactory timekeeping, work, attitude or misconduct. The Court concluded that despite the label put on it by the parties, there was a contract of service between the temporary worker and the agency.

Discussion point

Would it be fairer if courts and tribunals looked only at the realities of the employment relationship and disregarded any label used by the parties?

The courts will consider all aspects of the relationship in deciding whether the agency worker has a contract of employment or not.[50]

MUTUALITY OF OBLIGATION AND CONTROL

The second question is whether there can be an employment relationship between the individual, supplied on a temporary basis by an employment agency, and the client employer.

CASE STUDY

MONTGOMERY v JOHNSON UNDERWOOD LTD

In *Montgomery v Johnson Underwood Ltd*[51] a woman was placed by an agency with a client company and remained there for two years. Eventually the company asked the agency to terminate the assignment. As a result the individual made a complaint of unfair dismissal naming both the client company and the agency as her employer. The Employment Appeal Tribunal found that the agency had exercised little or no 'control, direction or supervision' over the individual during the assignment, and this proved crucial. There had to be the essential elements of mutuality of obligation and control. The Court of Appeal relied upon *Carmichael*[52] to decide that 'mutuality of obligation' and 'control' are the minimum legal requirements for the existence of a contract of employment. The following three conditions have to be fulfilled:

- the individual agrees, in return for wages or other remuneration, that he or she will provide his or her own work and skill in performance of some duty for the employer (mutuality of obligation)
- he or she agrees, expressly or impliedly, to be subject to the other's control in the performance of the duties (control)
- the other provisions of the contract are consistent with those of a contract of service.

Whether there exists a mutuality of obligation and the necessary level of control is a matter for the employment tribunal to decide. In this case the lack of control by the agency meant that the individual could not be regarded as an employee of that agency.

CASE STUDY

MOTOROLA LTD v DAVIDSON

An employer–employee relationship was established with the client in *Motorola Ltd v Davidson*.[53] This case concerned a long-term agency worker who, eventually, was suspended by the client company after a disciplinary hearing. This led to the client terminating the individual's assignment. The EAT held that once the individual was at the client's site, he was largely subject to the same control as if he had been an ordinary full-time employee. It was the client who decided 'the thing to be done, the way in which it shall be done, the means to be employed in doing it, the time when and the place where it shall be done'.[54]

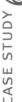

CASE STUDY

DACAS v BROOK STREET BUREAU (UK) LTD[55]

Patricia Dacas worked as a cleaner for Brook Street Bureau. She had a contract with Brook Street which stated that her 'temporary worker agreement' would not give rise to a contract of employment between her and the agency.

For a number of years she was assigned to the same client of Brook Street, namely Wandsworth Borough Council. She was assigned exclusively to work at a Council-run hostel for the long-term care of people with mental health problems. The agency paid her wages and deducted tax and National Insurance. Eventually, after some trouble, the Council asked the agency to withdraw Ms Dacas from the contract. She then made a complaint of unfair dismissal on the basis that she was either an employee of the agency or of the Council.

The first question to be decided was who, if anyone, was the employer of Ms Dacas. The Court of Appeal concluded that it could not be Brook Street Bureau because the agency was under no obligation to provide her with work and she was under no obligation to accept any work offered. There was thus no mutuality of obligation. On the other hand, the degree of control exercised by the Council, as well as a mutuality of obligation between the parties, suggested that she was actually an employee of the client.

Discussion point

Should there be a presumption that those who work for an agency are employed by it?

Thus in cases involving a triangular relationship consisting of a worker, an employment agency and an end user, tribunals should consider the possibility of an implied contract between the worker and the end user.[56] According to the Court of Appeal, the relevant question is whether it is necessary to imply mutual contractual obligations between the end user to provide work and the worker to perform it. Thus the implication of a contract of employment is not inevitable in a long-term agency situation.[57] It should also be remembered that it is impossible to imply into a contract a term that contradicts an express one.[58]

The Agency Worker Regulations 2010[59]

These came into force in 2011 and were designed to implement Directive 2008/104/EC. The Regulations introduced the principle of equal treatment for agency workers after they have been in 'the same role' with the same hirer for a qualifying period of 12 continuous calendar weeks.[60] Regulation 5 gives agency workers the right to the same 'basic working and employment conditions' as they would have been entitled to if they had been engaged directly by the hirer. The Regulation uses the expressions 'ordinarily included' and 'comparable employee' with the effect that individually negotiated terms are not covered. Regulation 6 makes it clear that it is terms and conditions relating to pay, the duration of working time, night work, rest periods, rest breaks and annual leave that are relevant. In relation to pay, Regulation 5 does not apply where there is a permanent contract between the agency worker and a temporary work agency. There are a number of conditions that must be met in relation to the form and terms of this contract, and there must be a minimum amount of pay between assignments.[61] Regulations 7 and 8 deal with the completion of the qualifying period and the effect of breaks during or between assignments. In essence, the individual must work 'in the same role with the same hirer', and a test of 'substantively different' will be applied. According to Regulation 9, the qualifying period will be treated as satisfied if a worker is prevented from fulfilling it by the structuring of assignments.

Regulations 12 and 13 both apply from the commencement of work. Regulation 12 provides a right to be treated no less favourably than a comparable worker in relation to 'collective facilities and amenities' provided by the hirer unless such treatment can be justified on objective grounds. Regulation 13 gives agency workers the right to be informed by the hirer of any vacant relevant posts and may be achieved by 'a general announcement in a suitable place in the hirer's establishment'. Regulation 14 states that a temporary work agency and hirer can both be liable to the extent that they are responsible for breaching Regulation 5. The hirer is liable for breaches of Regulations 12 and 3. Agency workers also have the right to receive information from the temporary work agency or hirer, as applicable, about the rights and duties in Regulations 5, 12 and 13. Regulation 16 refers to written requests for a written statement to be supplied within 28 days. Regulation 17 introduces the right not to be unfairly dismissed or subjected to a detriment for a reason relating to the Regulations, and Regulation 18 offers remedies for breach. This includes a minimum award of two weeks' pay and an additional award of up to £5,000 where Regulation 9 applies. There is no cap on compensation, but no award can be made for injury to feelings. Finally, Regulation 20 deals with the liability of employers and principals, and Regulation 15 restricts contracting out generally.

Employment agencies

The Conduct of Employment Agencies and Employment Businesses Regulations 2003[62] came into effect in April 2004. The government's stated objective was to help promote a flexible labour market, and this is underpinned by a set of regulations that ensure fairness and minimum standards in the industry.

In seeking the 'proper conduct' of agencies and employment businesses, the government aimed to protect the interests of work-seekers and those of hirers. There is an attempt to ensure clarity of agreement between the work-seeker and the employment agency or business. Generally the Employment Agencies Act 1973 and the Regulations regulate the relationship between the hirer and the agency or business and the relationship between the job-seeker and the agency or business. They set down the requirements for the communication of information between all the parties involved and the terms of the agreements between each of the parties. Anyone who contravenes the prohibition on charging fees to work-seekers, fails to comply with regulations to secure the proper conduct of the agency or business, falsifies records, or fails without reasonable excuse to comply with a prohibition order, will be guilty of an offence and subject to a fine.[63]

An employment tribunal may make an order prohibiting a person from operating an employment agency or business for up to 10 years on the grounds that the person is unsuitable because of misconduct or any other sufficient reason. In addition, terms of contracts with hirers or work-seekers that are invalid as a result of the Act or Regulations will be unenforceable.

SHOULD A PROBATIONARY PERIOD BE IMPOSED?

We shall see in Chapter 12 that (save in exceptional circumstances) only those who have been continuously employed for one year or more can claim that they have been unfairly dismissed. In a sense this requirement serves to impose a probationary period. However, some employers may regard one year as excessive for the purpose of establishing whether a person's appointment should be confirmed, and frequently a shorter period will be deemed appropriate. Some employers prefer to make an assessment within four weeks in order to avoid having to give statutory notice to terminate the contract (see Chapter 11). The great advantage of operating a probationary period is that new recruits are made aware that they are on trial and must therefore establish their suitability.

REFLECTIVE QUESTION

What are the advantages and disadvantages of operating a lengthy probationary period at the start of employment?

REGULATORY CONSTRAINTS

At common law, employers have the right to decide what policies to adopt in relation to recruitment but this position has been altered by a series of statutory and non-statutory interventions designed to protect certain categories of job applicant. Such interventions mostly concern provisions designed to prevent discrimination in recruitment and employment on the grounds of gender, race, disability, sexual orientation, religion or belief, age and membership or non-membership of a trade union. Many of these issues are considered in later chapters.

VETTING AND BARRING SCHEME

This scheme has operated since October 2009 and – although it is being reviewed at the time of writing – the Safeguarding Vulnerable Groups Act 2006 is still in force. People who are prohibited from working with children or vulnerable adults will accordingly be acting illegally if they try to work or volunteer with those groups. It is also unlawful to knowingly employ someone who is barred to work with those groups, so it is vital that employers carry out appropriate pre-recruitment checks. Finally, if a worker or volunteer leaves because they have harmed a child or vulnerable adult, employers must notify the Independent Safeguarding Authority. This agency maintains lists of barred people and offers guidance about the implementation of the legislation.

REHABILITATION OF OFFENDERS ACT 1974

The law does not require applicants to disclose facts about themselves which could hinder them in getting jobs (unless their silence amounts to fraud). Thus if employers believe that certain information is important, they should seek it specifically before the job is offered.

Section 4 of this Act relieves certain rehabilitated persons from the obligation to disclose 'spent' convictions to a prospective employer and makes it unlawful for an employer to deny employment on the grounds that the applicant had a conviction which was 'spent'. It is the policy of the Act that applicants should not be questioned about spent convictions, although if this situation does arise, applicants are entitled to deny that they have ever been convicted. There are a number of exceptions to these rules. Protection under the Act is not given to certain occupations such as doctors, nurses, teachers, social workers and those working with children, including those applying to become registered day-care providers.

Sentences of over two-and-a-half years' imprisonment never become 'spent'; otherwise, convictions become 'spent' after periods which are related to the gravity of the sentence imposed. Thus for a sentence of imprisonment of between six months and two-and-a-half years the rehabilitation period is 10 years. Imprisonment for less than six months requires a seven-year rehabilitation period, and fines or community service orders take five years to become 'spent'. A probation order, conditional discharge or binding over need not be disclosed after a year or until the order expires (whichever is the longer), and absolute discharges can be concealed if six months have elapsed since sentence. Despite the existence of the Act, the courts cannot compel an employer to engage a rehabilitated offender: they can only declare the exclusion of the applicant to be unlawful.

MIGRANT WORKERS

A new method for migrant workers to enter the UK came into force in November 2008. Employers wanting to engage skilled persons from outside Europe and sponsor their entry to the UK must apply for a licence. Migrants have to pass a points-based assessment before they are given permission to enter or remain. The system consists of five tiers, each with different requirements.The number of points the migrant needs and the way the points are awarded depend on the tier they are applying under. Points are awarded to reflect the migrant's ability, experience, age and, when appropriate, the level of need within the sector the migrant will be working. Except for tier 1, migrants will have to be sponsored in order for their application to be successful. If an employer wishes to recruit a migrant under tiers 2, 4 or 5, they will have to apply for a licence. The tiers are: (1) highly skilled workers – for example, scientists and entrepreneurs; (2) skilled workers with a job offer – for example, teachers and nurses; (3) low-skilled workers filling specific temporary labour shortages – for example, construction workers for a particular project; (4) students; (5) youth mobility and temporary workers – for example, musicians coming to play in a concert.[64]

KEY LEARNING POINTS

- Organisations have to decide whether to use employees or independent contractors; there are differences in taxation and employment costs as well as in vicarious liability.
- It is not always clear whether a worker is employed under a contract of employment or is working under a contract for services; the intention of the parties is important but may not be the deciding factor.
- The factors leading to a decision on whether a contract of employment exists or not are likely to include a 'sufficient' level of control by the employer and an 'irreducible minimum' of mutuality of obligation between employer and worker.
- Outsourcing is an option for many employers, but it is important to be aware of the effect of the Transfer of Undertakings (Protection of Employment) Regulations 2006.
- Employers may be faced with decisions regarding whether to employ individuals on part-time, fixed-term or temporary contracts. Care will have to be taken with the regulatory constraints on the way an employer treats such employees/workers.
- There are Regulations dealing with employment agencies which aim to clarify the rights of both hirers and work-seekers.
- Probationary periods may be useful in deciding whether to confirm an appointment; the law normally places a requirement for one year's continuous employment before there is a right to claim unfair dismissal.
- Rehabilitated offenders have the right, in certain circumstances, not to reveal information about spent convictions.
- Employers may have to apply for a licence in order to recruit certain types of migrant labour.

REFERENCES

1 See *Weddall v Barchester Health Care* (2012) IRLR 307
2 (2001) IRLR 472
3 See *Heasmans v Clarity Cleaning* (1987) IRLR 286
4 See *Sime v Sutcliffe Catering* (1990) IRLR 228
5 See *Protectacoat Ltd v Szilagi* (2009) IRLR 365
6 (2011) IRLR 820
7 *Carmichael v National Power plc* (2000) IRLR 43 HL
8 See *Quashie v Stringfellows Restaurants Ltd* (2012) IRLR 536
9 (1999) IRLR 367
10 *MacFarlane v Glasgow City Council* (2001) IRLR 7
11 See *Clark v Oxfordshire Health Authority* (1998) IRLR 125
12 SI 2006/246
13 See *DJM International Ltd v Nicholas* (1996) IRLR 76
14 *Wren v Eastbourne Borough Council* (1993) IRLR 425

15 *ECM (Vehicle Delivery Services) Ltd v Cox* (1999) IRLR 559

16 *Securicor Guarding Ltd v Fraser Security Services* (1996) IRLR 552

17 Council Directive 99/70/EC

18 SI 2002/2034

19 Regulations 3 and 4. In *Gaviero v Galicia* (2011) IRLR 504 the CJEU accepted that a length of service increment is an employment condition

20 Regulation 2

21 See *Duncombe and others v Secretary of State for Children, Schools and Families* (2011) IRLR 498

22 Case C-212/04 *Adeneler v Ellinikos Organismos Galaktos* (2006) IRLR 716

23 *Alonso v Osakidetza-Servicio* (2007) IRLR 911

24 *Huet v Université de Bretagne Occidentale* (2012) IRLR 703

25 (2005) IRLR 288

26 Regulation 7

27 SI 2000/1551; subsequently amended by the Part-time Workers (Prevention of Less Favourable Treatment) Regulations 2001 SI 2001/1107

28 Council Directive 97/81/EC OJ L14/9 20.1.98

29 Regulation 5(1) PTW Regulations

30 See *Carl v University of Sheffield* (2009) IRLR 616

31 See *Sharma v Manchester City Council* (2008) IRLR 336

32 Regulation 1(3) PTW Regulations

33 Regulation 2(4)(i) PTW Regulations; amended in 2002 (SI 2002/2035) so that there was no distinction between permanent and fixed-term contracts

34 Regulation 2(4)(ii) PTW Regulations

35 Regulation 2(5) PTW Regulations

36 (2006) ICR 365

37 Regulation 3 PTW Regulations

38 Regulation 4 PTW Regulations

39 Regulation 5(3) PTW Regulations

40 Regulation 2(2) PTW Regulations

41 Regulation 7(1) PTW Regulations

42 If the less favourable treatment is dismissal, the employee would be able to exercise his or her right to request written reasons for the dismissal under section 92 ERA 1996.

43 Regulation 6(3) PTW Regulations

44 There are special rules for members of the armed forces; see Regulation 13 PTW Regulations

45 Regulation 8(1)–(3) PTW Regulations

46 Regulation 8(7) PTW Regulations

47 Regulation 8(11)–(12) PTW Regulations

48 Regulation 8(14) PTW Regulations

49 (1997) IRLR 353

50 See *O'Kelly v Trust House Forte* (1983) IRLR 286

51 (2001) IRLR 269

52 *Carmichael v National Power plc* (2000) IRLR 43

53 *Motorola Ltd v (1) Davidson and (2) Melville Craig Group Ltd* (2001) IRLR 4

54 This was a quotation from MacKenna, J. in *Ready Mixed Concrete (South East) Ltd v Minister of Pensions and National Insurance* (1968) 1 All ER 433

55 (2004) IRLR 358

56 See *Cable & Wireless v Muscat* (2006) IRLR 355

57 See *James v London Borough of Greenwich* (2008) IRLR 302

58 See *Consistent Group Ltd v Kalwak* (2008) IRLR 505, where it was alleged that some of the contractual obligations were a sham

59 SI No.93

60 Regulation 3 provides a definition of 'agency worker', and Regulation 4 defines 'temporary work agency'

61 See Regulations 10 and 11

62 SI 2003/3319

63 See sections 15 and 16 of EA 2008

64 See http://www.ukba.homeoffice.gov.uk/

EXPLORE FURTHER

Reading

- Davies, A. (2009) *Perspectives on Labour Law.* Oxford University Press, Chapter 5
- Deakin, S. and Morris, G. (2012) *Labour Law.* Hart, Chapters 1 and 2
- Smith, I. and Thomas, G. (2010) *Smith & Wood's Employment Law.* Butterworths, Chapters 2 and 3

Websites

- Advisory, Conciliation and Arbitration Service www.acas.org.uk
- Chartered Institute of Personnel and Development www.cipd.co.uk
- Department for Business Innovation and Skills www.bis.gov.uk
- Trades Union Congress www.tuc.org.uk
- WorkSmart www.worksmart.org.uk

CHAPTER 5

Pay Issues

CHAPTER OVERVIEW

This chapter is concerned with a number of issues related to pay, beginning with the duty to pay wages or salaries. There is then some detailed consideration of the National Minimum Wage Act 1998 and the complexities associated with trying to establish the actual rates paid in a variety of work circumstances. We also consider the employer's duty to provide pay statements and make guarantee payments when employees are not provided with work. Finally, we examine issues related to pay and sickness, including statutory sick pay and the right of employers to suspend employees on medical grounds.

LEARNING OUTCOMES

After studying this chapter you will be able to:

- understand and explain the content of the employer's duty to pay wages and advise colleagues about how to avoid making unlawful deductions
- advise colleagues about the impact of the national minimum wage and the circumstances in which sick and guarantee payments must be provided.

THE DUTY TO PAY WAGES

This is a basic obligation of employers and is normally dealt with by an express term. There are a number of issues to be considered.

1 *An employer may be required to pay wages even if there is no work for the employee to do*
The general rule is that wages must be paid if an employee is available for work,[1] but everything will depend on whether there is an express or implied term of fact in the contract which deals with the matter. Thus an express term to the effect that 'no payment shall be made during a period of lay-off' will eliminate the possibility of a contractual claim being brought in such a situation.

2 *Deductions from wages or payment by the employee are unlawful unless required or authorised by statute – for example, PAYE or social security contributions – or the worker has agreed to it* [2]

Section 27(1) ERA 1996 defines 'wages' as 'any sum payable to the worker in connection with his employment'. This includes holiday pay and commission earnings which are payable after an employee has left. It also includes discretionary bonus payments where the employee has been told that he or she will receive the payments.[3] Before payment of such 'wages' the employer would be entitled to deduct an amount to repay any advances that had been given to the employee.[4]
The worker must give oral or written consent to the deduction before it is made,[5] and where the agreement constitutes a term of the contract of employment, it must be in writing and drawn to the employee's attention (or its effect must have been notified to the worker in writing).[6] To satisfy the requirements of ERA 1996 there must be a document which clearly states that a deduction is to be made from the employee's wages and that the employee agrees to it.[7] Even if an employee has entered into a compromise agreement to settle an unfair dismissal complaint over non-payment of wages, he or she may still be able to make a claim for that underpayment.[8] If a tribunal is not persuaded on the evidence that a deduction was authorised by a provision of the employee's contract, the individual is entitled to be paid the money deducted. Thus, in *IPC Ltd v Balfour*,[9] the EAT held that a reduction in pay following the unilateral introduction of short-time working amounted to an unauthorised deduction. However, if the contract of employment allowed the employer to change the hours or shift-patterns of an employee, the employer would be entitled to adjust the pay levels to reflect those changes.[10]

For these purposes there is no valid distinction between a deduction and a reduction of wages. The issue is whether, for whatever reason, apart from an error of computation, the worker is paid less than the amount of wages properly payable.[11] Nevertheless, employers who take a conscious decision not to make a payment because they believe that they are contractually entitled to take that course are not making an error of computation.[12] Although section 13(4) refers to an 'error of any description', it does not include an error of law.[13] Where there is a dispute over the justification for a deduction, it is the employment tribunal's task to resolve it.[14] However, tribunals do not have jurisdiction to determine whether a deduction by reason of industrial action was contractually authorised.[15]

Written agreements under which employers pay a proportion of wages to third parties are not affected by ERA 1996, and in retail employment, deductions or payments made to an employer in relation to stock or cash shortages are subject to a limit of one-tenth of gross pay, except for the final payment of wages.[16]

3 *Payments in lieu are not wages within the meaning of ERA 1996 if they relate to a period after the termination of employment*

CASE STUDY

DELANEY v STAPLES

According to the Supreme Court in *Delaney v Staples*,[17] ERA 1996 requires wages to be construed as payments in respect of the rendering of services during employment. Thus the only payments in lieu covered by the legislation are those in respect of 'garden leave' (see below), since these can be viewed as wages owed under a subsisting contract of employment. In the same case the Court of Appeal accepted that non-payment of wages constitutes a deduction for these purposes, as does the withholding of commission and holiday pay.[18]

Discussion point

After this decision, is it now clear what will amount to wages for the purposes of ERA 1996?

Indeed, the withholding of commission may amount to an unlawful deduction even where it is discretionary so long as commission was normally expected by the employee.[19]

4 *A complaint that there has been an unauthorised deduction must normally be lodged with an employment tribunal within three months of the deduction being made* [20]

If the complaint is well-founded, the tribunal must make a declaration to that effect and must order the reimbursement of the amount of the deduction or payment to the extent that it exceeded what should lawfully have been deducted or received by the employee. Employment tribunals can also provide compensation for workers who suffer financial losses as a result of unlawful deductions from wages.[21] The only method of contracting out of the requirements of ERA 1996 is if an agreement is reached following action taken by ACAS or there is a valid compromise agreement (see Chapter 15).

5 *A worker who is ready and willing to perform his or her contract but is unable to do so because of an avoidable impediment is not entitled to claim his or her wages*

CASE STUDY

BURNS v SANTANDER UK PLC

In this case a branch manager was arrested and remanded in custody for six months as a result of being charged with a number of criminal offences. He was subsequently convicted of two offences and was given a non-custodial sentence. He brought proceedings, asserting that he was entitled to be paid during the period that he was in custody. He claimed that he was ready and willing to work but could not do so because of an unavoidable impediment. The EAT found that the impediment was avoidable; it was the result of his own actions and was different from unavoidable impediments such as sickness or injury.

Discussion point

Can you imagine any situation in which an employer would be obliged to pay wages to an employee if the employee was imprisoned?

6 *Overpayments*
Employers may be entitled to restitution of overpayments made to an employee owing to a mistake of fact but *not* a mistake of law. For example, an overpayment that arose as the result of a misunderstanding of the National Minimum Wage Act would be irrecoverable.[22] However, employees may commit theft if they fail to notify the employer of an accidental overpayment.[23] Section 16(1) ERA 1996 makes specific provision for the recovery of overpayments, and tribunals cannot inquire into the lawfulness of a deduction for this purpose.[24]

THE NATIONAL MINIMUM WAGE

The National Minimum Wage Act 1998 (NMWA 1998) provides a minimum hourly wage for workers. 'Worker' is defined in section 54(3) as someone working under a contract of employment or any other contract under which an individual undertakes to do or perform in person any work or service for another. From October 2012, the standard rate was £6.19 per hour. There are also two development rates for younger workers: for those aged 18 years to 20 years inclusive it is set at £4.98 per hour, and for 16- and 17-year-olds it was set at £3.68 per hour. In addition, a minimum wage was introduced in 2010 for apprentices who are either under 19 years or over this age but in the first year of their apprenticeship. From October 2012 this rate was set at £2.65 per hour. Any other allowances paid by the employer to workers in relation to their work cannot be used to offset the fact that an individual's basic hourly rate is less than the NMW. It is possible to reduce those other rates in order to increase the basic rate without contravening the requirements of the National Minimum Wage Regulations 1999 (NMW Regulations),[25] although doing this might result in the employer making an unlawful deduction from wages in contravention of section 13(1) ERA 1996.[26]

Regulation 12 of the NMW Regulations describes those who do not qualify for the national minimum wage at all. These include:

- a worker who is participating in a scheme designed to provide him or her with training, work, or temporary work, or which is designed to assist him or her to obtain work
- a worker who is attending higher education up to first degree level or a teacher-training course, and who, before the course ends, is required as part of the course to attend a period of work experience not exceeding one year

- a homeless person who is provided with shelter and other benefits in return for performing work.

WHEN IS A WORKER 'WORKING'?

Workers who work and live in the employer's household and who are treated as members of the family are also excluded.[27] This includes live-in domestic workers such as those in the case of *Julio v Jose* [28] in which a number of live-in domestic workers in different situations unsuccessfully claimed an entitlement to the national minimum wage. However, workers who, by arrangement, sleep on the employer's premises may be entitled to payment for all the hours that are required to be spent at those premises.

CASE STUDY

SCOTTBRIDGE LTD v WRIGHT

In *Scottbridge Ltd v Wright* [29] a night-watchman was required to be on the premises between 5 pm and 7 am each night. Apart from some minor duties he was mainly required to be present in case of intruders. He was provided with sleeping facilities and allowed to sleep during the course of the night. The Court of Session upheld the EAT decision that he was entitled to be paid at least the national minimum wage rate for the specific hours that he was required to be at work. It was up to the employer to provide him with work and the fact that he was not required to do any did not nullify his entitlement to be paid.

CASE STUDY

BRITISH NURSING ASSOCIATION v INLAND REVENUE[30]

The employers were a national organisation providing emergency 'bank' nurses for nursing in homes and other institutions. Part of the work involved a 24-hours-a-day telephone booking service. This service was carried on at night by employees working from home. The 'duty' nurse would take the diverted call and contact the appropriate person to do the work requested. The duty nurse was paid an amount per shift.

The issue was whether this person was 'working' within the meaning of the NMW Regulations when they were not actually receiving or making phone calls – even when watching television while waiting for contacts. The Court of Appeal endorsed the EAT's view that in deciding when a worker is working for the purposes of the NMW Regulations, an employment tribunal should look at the type of work involved and its different elements to see if altogether it could be properly described as work. Aspects to be examined include:

- the nature of the work
- the extent to which the worker's activities are restricted when not performing the particular task
- the mutual obligations of employer and worker, although the way in which remuneration is calculated is not conclusive

- the extent to which the period during which work is being performed is readily ascertainable.

Thus the duty nurses were held to be working throughout their shift and entitled to payment for it.

Discussion point

What are the implications of these decisions for employers who need staff to be available for long hours but are likely to require them to work only during a small proportion of them?

CALCULATING REMUNERATION

The hourly rate is calculated by adding up the total remuneration, less reductions, and dividing by the total number of hours worked[31] during a pay reference period.[32] Total remuneration[33] in a pay reference period is calculated by adding together:

- all money paid by the employer to the worker during the reference period
- any money paid by the employer to the worker in the following reference period which is in respect of work done in the current reference period
- any money paid by the employer to the worker later than the end of the following pay reference period in respect of work done in the current reference period and for which the worker is under an obligation to complete a record and has not done so
- the cost of accommodation, calculated by an approved formula.[34]

Deductions that can be made from this total remuneration figure are set out in Regulation 31 and include:[35]

- any payments made by the employer to the worker in respect of a previous pay reference period
- in the case of non-salaried work, any money paid to the worker in respect of periods when the worker was absent from work or engaged in taking industrial action
- in the case of time-work, the difference between the lowest rate of pay and any higher rates of pay paid during the reference period
- any amounts paid by the employer to the worker that represent amounts paid by customers in the form of service charge, tips, gratuities or cover charge – that is, not paid through the payroll[36]
- the payment of expenses.

CALCULATING HOURS

The calculation of the hours worked can be complex and for these purposes work has been classified into the following different types:

1 *salaried hours work* [37]

This is where the worker is paid for a number of ascertainable hours in a year (the basic hours) and where the payment, which normally consists of an annual salary and perhaps an annual bonus, is paid in equal instalments, weekly or monthly.

2 *time-work* [38]
This is work that is paid for under a worker's contract by reference to the time worked, and is not salaried hours work.

3 *output work* [39]
This is work that is paid for by reference to the number of pieces made or processed, or by some other measure of output such as the value of sales made or transactions completed. The rated output hours, in a reference period, will be the total number of hours spent by the worker in doing output work. The employer has to arrive at a 'fair' piece rate by reference to the time taken by the average employee doing the same job.

4 *unmeasured work* [40]
This is any work that is not salaried hours work, time-work or output work, especially work where there are no specified hours and the worker is required to work when needed or whenever work is available. The unmeasured work hours will be the total hours, in a pay reference period, spent by the worker in carrying out his or her contractual duties.[41] Regulation 28 allows for a 'daily average' agreement to be reached between the employer and the worker.[42]

UNDERPAYMENT OF THE NMW

Section 9 NMWA 1998[43] allows the Secretary of State to require employers to keep and preserve records for at least three years. Workers have the right to inspect these records if they believe, on reasonable grounds, that they are being paid at a rate less than the national minimum wage.[44] When inspecting these records a worker may be accompanied by another person of his or her choice,[45] and that individual must be identified in the 'production notice' that the worker gives to the employer requesting the production of the records.[46] The employer must provide these records within 14 days following receipt of the notice and must make them available at the worker's place of work or some other reasonable place.[47] Failure to produce the records or to allow the workers to exercise their rights can lead to a complaint at an employment tribunal.[48] In these circumstances the tribunal can make an award of up to 80 times the national minimum wage. If a worker has been remunerated during the reference period at a rate less than the national minimum wage, there is a contractual entitlement to be paid the amount underpaid. There is a reversal of the normal burden of proof and a presumption that the worker both qualifies for the national minimum wage and is underpaid.[49]

Sections 5–8 of the NMWA 1998 established the Low Pay Commission and gave the Secretary of State discretion to refer matters to it. HM Customs and Revenue has the task of ensuring that workers are remunerated at a rate that is at least equivalent to the NMW. It has wide powers to inspect records and enforce the Act.[50] If it is discovered that workers are not being paid the national minimum wage, the Revenue can issue enforcement notices requiring payment of the national minimum wage together with arrears and a financial penalty.[51] Section 14 allows HMRC officers to take information away from the employer's premises in order to copy it and Section 31 enables serious offences to be tried in the Crown Court.

Workers have a right not to suffer detriment[52] if they assert in good faith their right to the national minimum wage, to inspect records or to recover underpayment.

REFLECTIVE QUESTION

To what extent does the National Minimum Wage Act 1998 ensure that no worker receives less than the prescribed rate?

PAY STATEMENTS

Under section 8 ERA 1996 employers must give their employees an itemised pay statement containing the following particulars:

- the gross amount of wages or salary
- the amount of any variable or fixed deductions and the purposes for which they are made (on the legality of such deductions see above)
- the net wages or salary payable and, where the net amount is paid in different ways, the amount and method of payment of each part.

Such a statement need not contain separate particulars of a fixed deduction – for example, of union dues – if it specifies the total amount of fixed deductions and each year the employer provides a standing statement of fixed deductions which describes the amount of each deduction, its purpose and the intervals at which it is made. If no pay statement is issued, an employee may refer the matter to an employment tribunal to determine what particulars ought to have been included. Where a tribunal finds that an employer failed to provide such a statement or the statement does not contain the required particulars, the tribunal must make a declaration to that effect. Additionally, where it finds that any unnotified deductions have been made during the 13 weeks preceding the application, it may order the employer to pay compensation to the employee. This refund cannot exceed the total amount of unnotified deductions.[53] Thus there is here a penal aspect to the discretion that tribunals have to exercise.

GUARANTEE PAYMENTS

Employees with one month's continuous service qualify for a guarantee payment if they are not provided with work throughout a day in which they would normally be required to work in accordance with their contract of employment because of:

- a diminution in the requirements of the employer's business for work of the kind which the employee is employed to do, or
- any other occurrence that affects the normal working of the employer's business in relation to work of that kind.[54]

The words 'normally required to work' are significant for two reasons. First, an employee who is not obliged to work when requested may be regarded as not being subject to a contract of employment.[55] Second, if contracts of employment are varied to provide for a reduced number of working days – for example, four instead of five – employees will be unable to claim a payment for the fifth day because they are no longer 'required to work' on that day. 'Any other occurrence ...' would seem to comprehend something like a power failure or natural disaster rather than works holidays.

No guarantee payment is available if the workless day is a consequence of a strike, lock-out or other industrial action involving any employee of the employer or any associated employer.[56] The entitlement to a guarantee payment may be lost in two other circumstances:

- where the employer has offered to provide alternative work which is suitable in the circumstances (irrespective of whether it falls inside or outside the scope of the employee's contract) but this has been unreasonably refused;[57] and
- where the employee does not comply with reasonable requirements imposed by the employer with a view to ensuring that his or her services are available.[58] This is to enable the employer to keep the workforce together, perhaps in the hope that the supplies which have been lacking will be delivered.

CALCULATING GUARANTEE PAYMENTS

A guarantee payment is calculated by multiplying the number of normal working hours on the day of lay-off by the guaranteed hourly rate. Accordingly, where there are no normal working hours on the day in question, no guarantee payment can be claimed.[59] The guaranteed hourly rate is one week's pay divided by the number of normal hours in a week and, where the number of normal hours varies, the average number of such hours over a 12-week period will be used.[60] Payment cannot be claimed for more than five days in any period of three months.[61] There is a maximum daily sum payable of £23.50 in 2011 but this increases or decreases each year in line with the retail price index.[62] It should be noted that contractual payments in respect of workless days not only discharge an employer's liability to make guarantee payments for those days[63] but are also to be taken into account when calculating the maximum number of days for which employees are entitled to statutory payments.[64] Where guaranteed weekly remuneration has been agreed, this sum is to be 'apportioned rateably between the workless days'.[65] If an employer fails to pay the whole or part of a guarantee payment, an employee can complain to an employment tribunal within three months of the last workless day. Where a tribunal finds a complaint to be well-founded, it must order the employer to pay the amount which it finds owing to the employee.[66]

If guaranteed remuneration is the subject of a collective agreement currently in force, all the parties may choose to apply for an exemption order. So long as the Secretary of State is satisfied that the statutory provisions should not apply, the relevant employees will be excluded from the operation of section 28 ERA 1996. However, the Secretary of State cannot make an order unless a collective agreement permits employees to take a dispute about guaranteed remuneration to arbitration, an independent adjudicating body or an employment tribunal.[67]

PAY AND SICKNESS

THE RIGHT TO SICK PAY AT COMMON LAW

In the absence of an express term in the contract of employment, the correct approach to determining whether there is an obligation upon the employer to pay wages to an employee absent through sickness is to look at all the facts and circumstances to see whether such a term can be implied. Such a term may derive from the custom or practice in the industry or from the knowledge of the parties at the time the contract was made. The nature of the contract will have to be taken into account and, on occasions, it will be permissible to look at what the parties did during the period of the contract. Only if all the factors and circumstances do not indicate what the contractual term is will it be assumed that wages should be paid during sickness. If such a term is implied, it is likely to provide for the deduction of sums received under social security legislation.[68]

CASE STUDY

HOWMAN & SONS v BLYTH

In *Howman & Sons v Blyth*[69] it was held that the reasonable term to be implied in respect of duration in an industry where the normal practice is to give sick pay for a limited period only is the term normally applicable in the industry. The EAT did not accept that where there is an obligation to make payments during sickness, in the absence of an express term to the contrary, sick pay is owed so long as the employment continues.

ENTITLEMENT TO BENEFITS AND THE INDIVIDUAL'S CONTRACT OF EMPLOYMENT

The courts have intervened to ensure that employees' entitlements to disability benefits under health insurance schemes have not been frustrated by a strict interpretation of the contract of employment.

ADIN v SEDCO FOREX INTERNATIONAL

CASE STUDY

In *Adin v Sedco Forex International*[70] an employee's contract of employment included provisions for short-term and long-term disability benefits. It also contained a clause which allowed the employers, at their sole discretion, to terminate the contract for any reason whatsoever. The Court of Session concluded that because the right to these benefits was established in the contract of employment, the employer could not take them away by dismissing the employee.

The courts have also been willing to imply terms into contracts which will give effect to agreed health insurance schemes.

ASPDEN v WEBBS POULTRY GROUP

CASE STUDY

In *Aspden v Webbs Poultry Group*,[71] a manager had a contract of employment which did not mention the generous health insurance scheme which, the High Court held, had been mutually agreed by the employers and the senior management. The employee was dismissed while on sick leave as a result of angina. It was claimed that there was an implied term that the employee would not be dismissed while incapacitated because this would frustrate the permanent health insurance scheme. The court accepted this argument, even though there was an express term in the contract that allowed the employer to dismiss employees for reasons of prolonged incapacity.

It should also be noted that an employee can rely on contractual terms to pay long-term benefits, even if the employer has stopped paying the premiums on his or her health insurance policy.[72]

HILL v GENERAL ACCIDENT[73]

CASE STUDY

Mr Hill started employment with the company in 1988. In March 1994 he became ill and remained absent from work for medical reasons until his employment was terminated on the grounds of redundancy in November 1995.

During his absence he had received sick pay in accordance with the contractual scheme. Under that scheme employees could receive full pay for 104 weeks. After this period employment was to be terminated and the employee would receive either an ill-health retirement pension or sickness and accident benefit. When Mr

Hill was made redundant he was still four months away from qualifying for his long-term sickness provision. He claimed that there was an implied term in his contract of employment that he would not be made redundant where this would frustrate his entitlement to long-term benefit.

The contract contained an express provision for the retention of sick employees for a period of two years' absence before they were able to qualify for the ill-health retirement scheme. The Court held that this did not exclude the possibility of the employee's being dismissed for redundancy, despite the unfortunate consequence. To allow this exclusion would put sick employees at an advantage compared to those who were well and attending work when it came to selecting those who would be dismissed.

Discussion point

How would this case be decided today if Mr Hill was recognised as disabled in accordance with section 6 of the Equality Act 2010? (See Chapter 7.)

STATUTORY SICK PAY

The Social Security Contributions and Benefits Act 1992 (SSCBA 1992) and the Statutory Sick Pay Act 1994 make employers responsible for paying statutory sick pay (SSP) to employees working within the EU. SSP is paid for up to 28 weeks of absence due to sickness or injury in any single 'period of entitlement'.[74] As well as those who pay full Class 1 National Insurance contributions, married women and widows paying reduced contributions are eligible for SSP. Part-timers who earn more than the lower earnings limit (£107 per week for 2012/13) are to be treated in the same way as full-time employees, and there is no minimum service qualification. Indeed, an employee may be entitled to SSP under more than one contract or with more than one employer if the relevant conditions are satisfied.

The rate of SSP for 2012/13 is £85.85 per week, and the daily rate is the appropriate weekly rate divided by the number of 'qualifying days' in the week (starting with Sunday).[75] Employers must pay the stipulated amount of SSP for each day that an employee is eligible, but any other sums paid in respect of the same day can count towards the SSP entitlement – eg normal wages.[76] Any agreement which purports to exclude, limit or modify an employee's right to SSP or which requires an employee to contribute (directly or indirectly) towards any cost incurred by the employer is void.[77] For many employees SSP will be worth less than state incapacity benefit because the former is subject to tax and National Insurance contributions and will be paid at a flat rate without additions for dependants. It is therefore hardly surprising that trade unions endeavour to negotiate sick pay schemes which ensure that their members do not suffer any detriment as a result of this legislation.

Normally, employers cannot recover the sums they pay out by way of SSP. However, if in any tax month the amount of SSP exceeds 13% of National

Insurance contributions' liability for that month, the employer can recoup the excess from the contributions due.[78]

Section 14(3) of the Social Security Administration Act 1992 gives employees the right to ask their employer for a written statement, in relation to a period before the request is made, of one or more of the following matters:

- the days for which the employer regards himself or herself as liable to pay SSP
- the reasons the employer considers himself or herself not liable to pay for other days
- the amount of SSP to which the employer believes the employee to be entitled.

And, to the extent to which the request is reasonable, the employer must comply with it within a reasonable time.

THE DUTY TO KEEP RECORDS

Employers are obliged to keep records showing:

- the amount of SSP paid to each employee on each pay day
- the amount of SSP paid to each employee during each tax year
- the total amount of SSP paid to all employees during the tax year.

Additionally, Regulation 13 of the SSP Regulations 1982 (as amended) stipulates that for three years after the end of each tax year employers must in relation to each employee keep a record of the following matters:

a) any day in that tax year which was one of four or more consecutive days of incapacity for work, whether or not the employee would normally have been expected to work on that day

b) any day recorded under (a) for which the employer paid SSP.

PENALTIES

An employer who knowingly produces false information in order to recover a sum allegedly paid out as SSP commits an offence.

SUSPENSION ON MEDICAL GROUNDS

Employees with at least one month's continuous service who are suspended from work in consequence of a requirement imposed by specified health and safety provisions or a recommendation contained in a code of practice issued or approved under section 16 HASAWA 1974 are entitled to a week's pay (see Chapter 16) for each week of suspension up to a maximum of 26 weeks.[79] The relevant health and safety provisions are listed in section 64(3) ERA 1996 and cover hazardous substances and processes – for example, lead and ionising radiation. It should be observed that this statutory right can be invoked only where the specified safety legislation has affected the employer's undertaking and not the employee's health. Employees are therefore not entitled to remuneration under this provision for any period during which they are incapable of work by reason of illness or injury. Additionally, if employees unreasonably refuse to perform suitable alternative work (whether or not it is within the scope of their contract), or they do not comply with reasonable requirements imposed by their employer with a view to ensuring that their services are available, no payment is owed.[80]

It is important to note that these sections do not grant employers the right to suspend: they merely give rights to employees who are lawfully suspended. If there is no contractual right to suspend, employees will be entitled to sue for their full wages anyway, although any amounts already paid in respect of this period can be set off.[81] Where the employer fails to pay remuneration which is owed to the employee by virtue of the statute, the employee can apply to an employment tribunal normally within three months. Section 70(3) ERA 1996 provides that if the tribunal finds a complaint to be well-founded, the employer must be ordered to pay the amount due to the employee. As long as any replacement for a suspended employee is informed in writing by the employer that the employment will be terminated at the end of the suspension, dismissal of the replacement in order to allow the original employee to resume work will be deemed to have been for a 'substantial reason of a kind such as to justify the dismissal of an employee holding the position which that employee held'.[82] However, an employment tribunal must still be satisfied that it was reasonable in all the circumstances to dismiss (see Chapter 13).

- Subject to express or implied contractual terms, an employer is normally obliged to pay wages if there is no work.
- Deductions from wages are unlawful unless approved by statute or by agreement with the employee.
- The standard rate for the national minimum wage is set at £6.19 per hour from October 2012.
- The types of hours worked, for the purposes of the NMWA 1998, are salaried hours work, time-work, output work and unmeasured work.
- Employers are obliged to give their employees itemised pay statements.
- Statutory sick pay is payable for up to 28 weeks of absence due to sickness or injury in any single period of entitlement.
- Employees suspended from work as a result of a requirement imposed by any provisions or code of practice under the HASAWA 1974 are entitled to a week's pay for each week of suspension up to a maximum of 26 weeks.

REFERENCES

1 See *R v Liverpool City Corporation* (1985) IRLR 501

2 See sections 13(1) and 15(1) ERA 1996; wages are defined in section 27, and a worker is defined in section 230(3) ERA 1996

3 *Farrell, Matthews & Weir v Hansen* (2005) IRLR 160

4 See *Robertson v Blackstone Franks Investment Management Ltd* (1998) IRLR 376

5 See *Discount Tobacco v Williams* (1993) IRLR 327

6 Section 13(2) ERA 1996; see *Kerr v The Sweater Shop* (1996) IRLR 424

7 See *Peninsula Business Services Ltd v Sweeney* (2004) IRLR 49

8 See *Dattani v Trio Supermarkets Ltd* (1998) IRLR 240

9 (2003) IRLR 11

10 *Hussman Manufacturing Ltd v Weir* (1998) IRLR 288

11 See sections 13(3) ERA 1996 and *New Century Cleaning v Church* (2000) IRLR 27. On the distinction between a deduction in respect of wages and a deduction in respect of expenses, see *London Borough of Southwark v O'Brien* (1996) IRLR 240

12 See *Yemm v British Steel* (1994) IRLR 117

13 See *Morgan v West Glamorgan County Council* (1995) IRLR 68

14 See *Fairfield Ltd v Skinner* (1993) IRLR 3

15 See section 14(5) ERA 1996 and *Sunderland Polytechnic v Evans* (1993) ICR 196

16 See section 13 ERA 1996

17 (1992) IRLR 191

18 *Delaney v Staples t/a De Montfort Recruitment* (1991) IRLR 112

19 See *Kent Management Services v Butterfield* (1992) IRLR 394 and compare *Coors Ltd v Adcock* (2007) IRLR 440

20 'Or, within such further period as the tribunal considers reasonable in a case where it is satisfied that it was not reasonably practicable for the complainant to be presented within three months': sections 23(2)–(4) ERA 1996. This 'escape clause' applies to other statutory provisions and throughout the rest of the book will be referred to as the 'time-limit escape clause'; see *List Design Ltd v Douglas and Catley* (2003) IRLR 14

21 See section 24 ERA 1996

22 See *Avon County Council v Howlett* (1993) 1 All ER 1073

23 See Attorney General's reference (No.1 of 1983) 1 All ER 369

24 See *SIP Ltd v Swinn* (1994) IRLR 323

25 SI 1999/584 (as amended)

26 This was the case in *Laird v A K Stoddart Ltd* (2001) IRLR 591

27 Regulation 2 NMW Regulations 1999

28 *Julio v Jose* (2012) IRLR 180

29 (2003) IRLR 21

30 (2002) IRLR 480

31 Regulation 14 NMW Regulations 1999

32 Regulation 10 NMW Regulations 1999; a pay reference period is one month or a shorter period if a worker is usually paid at more frequent intervals.

33 Regulation 30 NMW Regulations 1999

34 Regulation 36 NMW Regulations 1999

35 On deductions for gas and electricity in tied accommodation see *HM Revenue and Customs v Leisure Management Ltd* (2007) IRLR 450

36 See *Revenue and Customs Commissioners v Annabel's Ltd* (2008) ICR 1076

37 Regulation 16 NMW Regulations 1999

38 Regulation 15 NMW Regulations 1999

39 Regulation 17 NMW Regulations 1999

40 Regulation 18 NMW Regulations 1999

41 Regulation 27 NMW Regulations 1999

42 See *Walton v Independent Living Organisation* (2003) IRLR 469

43 See also regulation 38 NMW Regulations 1999

44 Sections 10(1) and 10(2) NMWA 1998

45 Section 10(4)(b) NMWA 1998

46 Sections 10(5) and 10(6) NMWA 1998

47 Sections 10(8) and 10(9) NMWA 1998

48 Section 11 NMWA 1998; section 11(3) requires that the complaint should normally be made within three months of the end of the 14-day notice period.

49 Section 28 NMWA 1998

50 Sections 13–17 NMWA 1998

51 See the National Minimum Wage (Enforcement Notices) Act 2003 and sections 19–9H NMWA 1998

52 Section 23 NMWA 1998

53 Section 12(4) ERA 1996

54 Section 28(1) ERA 1996

55 See *Mailway (Southern) Ltd v Willsher* (1978) IRLR 322

56 Section 29(3) ERA 1996; 'associated employer' is defined by section 231 ERA 1996

57 Section 29(4) ERA 1996

58 Section 29(5) ERA 1996

59 Section 30(1) ERA 1996

60 Section 30(2)–(4) ERA 1996

61 Section 31(1)–(3) ERA 1996

62 Section 34 ERel Act 1999

63 Section 32(2) ERA 1996

64 See *Cartwright v Clancey Ltd* (1983) IRLR 355

65 Section 32(3) ERA 1996

66 Section 34(3) ERA 1996
67 Section 35 ERA 1996
68 See *Mears v Safecar Security* (1982) IRLR 501
69 (1983) IRLR 139
70 (1997) IRLR 280
71 (1996) IRLR 521
72 See *Bainbridge v Circuit Foil UK Ltd* (1997) IRLR 305
73 (1998) IRLR 641
74 Section 155 SSCBA 1992 sets the entitlement limit at '28 times the appropriate weekly rate'.
75 See section 157 SSCBA 1992
76 See Schedule 12 paragraph 2 SSCBA 1992
77 Section 151(2) SSCBA 1992
78 SSP Percentage Threshold Order 1995 SI 1995/512
79 Section 64(1) ERA 1996
80 Section 65 ERA 1996
81 See section 69(3) ERA 1996
82 See section 106(3) ERA 1996

EXPLORE FURTHER

Reading

- Davies, A. (2009) *Perspectives on Labour Law.* Oxford University Press, Chapter 8
- Deakin, S. and Morris, G. (2012) *Labour Law.* Hart, Chapter 4
- Simpson, R. (2004) 'The national minimum wage five years on: reflections on some general issues', *Industrial Law Journal*, Vol.33, No.1: 22–41
- Smith, I. and Thomas, G. (2010) *Smith & Wood's Employment Law.* Butterworths, Chapter 3

Websites

- Advisory, Conciliation and Arbitration Service www.acas.org.uk
- Chartered Institute of Personnel and Development www.cipd.co.uk
- Department for Business Innovation and Skills www.bis.gov.uk
- Directgov – Employment www.direct.gov.uk
- HM Revenue and Customs www.hmrc.gov.uk/nmw/
- Trades Union Congress www.tuc.org.uk

CHAPTER 6

Discrimination Against Employees (1)

CHAPTER OVERVIEW

In this chapter we consider the Equality Act 2010, which sets out nine *protected characteristics* – namely: age, disability, gender reassignment, marriage and civil partnership, pregnancy and maternity, race, religion or belief, sex and sexual orientation – in respect of which the Act gives protection against discrimination. We go on to consider the types of *prohibited conduct* – namely: direct discrimination, discrimination arising from disability, gender reassignment discrimination, pregnancy and maternity discrimination, indirect discrimination, failure to make reasonable adjustments, harassment and victimisation. We conclude the chapter by noting that as a general rule discrimination is unlawful at all stages of employment.

LEARNING OUTCOMES

After studying this chapter you will be able to:

- understand and explain the legal principles that apply to the different types of discrimination, such as that on grounds of sex, race, religion or belief, etc
- advise colleagues on the employer's role in, for example, ensuring that company rules and practices do not result in indirect discrimination, that reasonable adjustments are made for disabled employees and applicants, and on avoiding any discrimination in respect of pregnant employees or applicants – even in relation to a fixed-term contract.

EQUALITY LAW

Equality law[1] aims to protect certain groups of people who experience disadvantage and unequal treatment due to prejudice and stereotyping related to their characteristics. In relation to the workplace, UK equality law attempts to ensure that these people have the same opportunity as everyone else to obtain and retain work and to progress in their careers.

The sources for equality law in the UK are the Equality Act 2010 as well as EU law in the form of treaty articles and secondary legislation (see Chapter 1). Prior to 2010 the UK law on equality was fragmented into a number of different statutes and sets of regulations dealing with different areas of discrimination:

- Race discrimination was dealt with by the Race Relations Act 1976.
- Discrimination between men and women was covered by the Sex Discrimination Act 1975 and the Equal Pay Act 1970.
- Disability discrimination law was contained in the Disability Discrimination Act 1995.
- Sexual orientation, religion or belief and age discrimination each had a separate set of regulations.

For several years the Government had given consideration to having a single statute which would cover all the different strands of discrimination law. A Bill was presented to Parliament in 2009, and the Equality Act 2010 (EA 2010) received the Royal Assent on 8 April 2010, much of it coming into force on 1 October 2010. EA 2010 replaced almost all the previous UK equality law. There are very helpful *Explanatory Notes* to EA 2010 issued by the Government which are referred to throughout this chapter and Chapter 7.[2] Another very readable source of information which explains EA 2010 in straightforward language comprises the Codes of Practice issued by the Equality and Human Rights Commission (EHRC) and available online on the EHRC website.[3] A Code of Practice is not law in itself but is admissible in evidence, and where relevant must be taken into account by a tribunal or court.

Apart from putting all equality law into one statute, EA 2010 also made some important changes to the law. However, the essential principles and rules of equality law have not changed a great deal and consequently much of the previous case law would be likely to be decided in the same way under EA 2010. The old case law is therefore referred to below and in the following chapter.

EA 2010 deals not only with equality in employment but also in other areas of life such as education and the provision of services or premises. Our concern is only with equality and discrimination in employment but we may observe that much of the law in relation to those other areas of life is very similar. However, there are important differences too – for instance, there are particular exceptions which apply only to discrimination in employment.

The discrimination which is made unlawful under EA 2010 is set out by listing the 'protected characteristics' and 'prohibited conduct'.

PROTECTED CHARACTERISTICS

The protected characteristics are, in total, nine attributes in respect of which EA 2010 gives protection against discrimination. It is unlawful, unless an exception applies, to discriminate against a person because of such a characteristic. The characteristics are:

- age
- disability
- gender reassignment
- marriage and civil partnership
- pregnancy and maternity
- race

- religion or belief
- sex
- sexual orientation.

PROHIBITED CONDUCT

Prohibited conduct covers the different acts of discrimination which are unlawful under the Act, unless one of the exceptions applies.

These are:

- direct discrimination
- combined discrimination (but this has not been implemented)
- discrimination arising from disability
- gender reassignment discrimination
- pregnancy and maternity discrimination
- indirect discrimination
- failure to comply with a duty to make reasonable adjustments.

There are two other types of 'prohibited conduct':

- harassment
- victimisation.

THE PROTECTED CHARACTERISTICS

Section numbers throughout this chapter refer to EA 2010 unless otherwise stated.

AGE (SECTION 5)

This protected characteristic is defined as belonging to a particular age group, and 'age group' is defined to cover people either of the same particular age or of a range of ages within that group. Thus examples of age groups, given in the *Explanatory Notes*, would include 'over fifties' (range of ages) and people of twenty-one years old (same age).[4]

DISABILITY (SECTION 6 AND SCHEDULE 1)

This is defined in section 6 as

> a physical or mental impairment which has a substantial and long-term adverse effect on a person's ability to carry out normal day-to-day activities.

This is similar to the former definition of a disability under the Disability Discrimination Act 1995. For those new to this area of law it is necessary to discard any preconceived notions that 'disability' simply means something that keeps someone in a wheelchair! The definition covers a large number and variety of conditions, both physical and mental, if they have the stated substantial and long-term effect. Examples of a *physical or mental impairment* might include, among many other conditions,[5]

- a sight or hearing impairment
- rheumatoid arthritis

- asthma
- stroke and heart disease
- cancer
- HIV
- learning difficulties
- depression
- schizophrenia
- dementia.

'A substantial and long-term adverse effect'

Examining other parts of the definition, the impairment must have a *long-term* adverse effect. This is defined in Schedule 1 paragraph 2, which states that a disability is long-term if it has lasted or is likely to last at least 12 months or is likely to last the rest of a person's life – for example, a terminal illness. The effect must also be *substantial* – this simply means 'more than minor or trivial' (section 212(1)), so the effect need not be a very great one.

'Normal day-to-day activities'

The effect of the impairment must be on the person's ability to carry out *normal day-to-day activities*. This would cover, again, a large number and variety of matters but would be likely to include the following examples given in the Guidance on the definition of disability produced under the Disability Discrimination Act 1995:[6]

> Shopping, reading and writing, having a conversation or using the telephone, watching television, getting washed and dressed, preparing and eating food, carrying out household tasks, walking and travelling by various forms of transport, and taking part in social activities.

Two examples of a disability are given in the *Explanatory Notes*: [7,8]

> A young woman has developed colitis, an inflammatory bowel disease. The condition is a chronic one which is subject to periods of remissions and flare-ups. During a flare-up she experiences severe abdominal pain and bouts of diarrhoea. This makes it very difficult for her to travel or go to work. This has a substantial adverse effect on her ability to carry out normal day-to-day activities. She is likely to be considered a disabled person for the purposes of the Act.
>
> A man with depression finds even the simplest of tasks or decisions difficult – for example, getting up in the morning and getting washed and dressed. He is also forgetful and can't plan ahead. Together, these amount to a 'substantial adverse effect' on his ability to carry out normal day-to-day activities. The man has experienced a number of separate periods of this depression over a period of two years, which have been diagnosed as part of an underlying mental health condition. The impairment is therefore considered to be 'long-term' and he is a disabled person for the purposes of the Act.

Other conditions treated as a disability

There are a number of situations, where the condition may be treated as a disability even though it does not fulfil the requirements of the main definition in section 6.

1 *In deciding whether the impairment has a substantial effect one does not take into account any measures which are being taken to treat or correct it, such as medical treatment* [9]
Example:

A person has a heart condition which is being controlled by medication as result of which he or she can live a normal life. In deciding whether this is a person with a disability, the test is what would be the effects of the condition if the medication was not being taken

2 *If the impairment has ceased to have a substantial adverse effect but the effect is likely to recur, it is still treated as continuing to have that effect* [10, 11]

3 *Progressive conditions*
Three specific conditions – cancer, HIV and multiple sclerosis – are treated as a disability without the need for there to be any adverse effect on the person's life.[12]

Other progressive conditions are treated as disabilities from the time the condition begins to have some adverse effect, even though it is not *substantial*, if the prognosis is that the effect is likely to become substantial.[13]

4 *A person who has had a disability in the past is protected even if he or she has made a full recovery* [14]

5 *A severe disfigurement is treated as a disability* [15]

Further explanation has been provided by the Equality Act 2010 (Disability) Regulations 2010 (SI 2010/2128), which state, among other things, that certain conditions do *not* constitute a disability. These conditions include:

- an addiction, including a dependency on alcohol, nicotine or other substance
- certain conditions including a tendency to set fires, steal or abuse other persons, exhibitionism and voyeurism
- hay fever.

Additional clarification of what comes within the definition is contained in the Equality Act 2010 Guidance published by the government Office for Disability Issues. This is guidance on matters to be taken into account in determining questions in relation to the definition of disability. (The web address for this guidance can be found at the end of this chapter.)

GENDER REASSIGNMENT (SECTION 7)

A person who has proposed, started or completed a process to change his or her sex has the protected characteristic of **gender reassignment** under the Act. This would cover both a male making a transition to female and a female making a transition to male. There is no longer a requirement, as there was under the Sex Discrimination Act, for the person to be under medical supervision.[16]

The *Explanatory Notes* give an example of a person born as a female who decides to live the rest of her life as a man. He starts and continues to live as a man and seeks no medical advice as he can successfully pass as a man without medical intervention. He would have the protected characteristic of gender reassignment under the Act.[17]

MARRIAGE AND CIVIL PARTNERSHIP (SECTION 8)

A person who is married or is in a civil partnership has the protected characteristic of 'marriage and civil partnership'. The single characteristic covers both these relationships, so a married man and a woman in a civil partnership share the protected characteristic of 'marriage and civil partnership'.[18] The *Explanatory Notes* point out that someone who is engaged to be married is not married and so does not have this protected characteristic. Similarly, someone who is divorced or whose civil partnership has been dissolved does not have the protection within this section.[19]

PREGNANCY AND MATERNITY

The period from conception to birth and maternity leave has long been a specially protected period for women. Traditionally, action against a woman in relation to pregnancy or maternity has been treated as sex discrimination. Only women can be pregnant, so discrimination in relation to pregnancy is discrimination against women.

CASE STUDY

MAYR v BÄCKEREI UND KONDITOREI GERHARD FLÖCKNER

Ms Mayr was undergoing *in vitro* fertilisation treatment. During her treatment she was dismissed from her job as a waitress. At the time of dismissal two ova had been taken from her and fertilised but had not yet been transferred to her uterus. That procedure was carried out three days later. The question was whether Ms Mayr was a pregnant worker at the time of her dismissal. The CJEU held that, for reasons of legal certainty, the fact that the process had not been completed meant that she was not protected. The problem is that sometimes the transfer back to the woman can be delayed for a considerable period of time – for example, when the eggs are frozen and preserved. It would not desirable to give the worker protection for possibly years ahead.

Discussion point

Do you think that this was a fair decision? Ms Mayr was in the process of having her treatment and if she had received the eggs a few days earlier might have been protected.

RACE (SECTION 9)

Race is defined to include colour, nationality and ethnic or national origins. This is a similar definition to that under the Race Relations Act 1976.

CASE STUDY

MANDLA v DOWELL LEE

In a famous case decided under the Race Relations Act, *Mandla v Dowell Lee*,[20] it was held that Sikhs were a racial group by reference to 'ethnic origin'. 'Ethnic' was a wider term and included groups who might not be a separate 'race' in the biological sense. In this case a Sikh boy was refused entrance to a private school unless he gave up wearing a turban and had his hair cut. This conflicted with his religion but there was no law against religious discrimination in mainland UK at that time. It was held by the Supreme Court that this was race discrimination. As well as being a religious group, Sikhs were a racial group by reference to 'ethnic origin', even though they were not biologically any different from other Indian people coming from the Punjab.

Discussion point

This case does show the link between discrimination on the grounds of race and discrimination on the grounds of religion or religious belief. These are two separate characteristics now and this case would have been dealt with differently now – consider why this is so.

CASE STUDY

R v GOVERNING BODY OF Jewish Free School

In an interesting recent case, *R v Governing Body of JFS*,[21] an Orthodox Jewish school in London, the JFS, was held by the Supreme Court to be discriminating on racial grounds when it refused entry to the school to a boy who was not Jewish as laid down by the religious law of Orthodox Judaism, because his mother was not Jewish according to that law. Jewish religious status in the Orthodox Jewish community is passed down to a person by descent on his or her mother's side, and may also be acquired by conversion. Unusually, nine judges sat to hear this case and the case was decided by a majority of only 5–4 against the school. It was held that it was direct discrimination to treat someone less favourably because he or she *lacked* necessary ethnic origins just as much as it is direct discrimination to treat someone less favourably because he or she *does* possess certain ethnic origins. The fact that this decision by the school was not based on racism but on sincerely held religious convictions made no difference – the motive was irrelevant. (On this last point, see further below.)

Discussion point

Do you think that the court in this case is interfering with a religious group's own religious law to decide who is an adherent and who is not?

Note that Sikhs and Jewish people would also have the possibility of a claim in appropriate cases for discrimination because of religion or belief (see below).

Romany gypsies have also been held to be an ethnic group.[22] Muslims[23] and Rastafarians,[24] however, have been held not to be racial groups and so have been unable to bring a claim for race discrimination, but may bring a claim for discrimination because of religion or belief.

A racial group may be based on more than one element. An example given by the *Explanatory Notes* is 'black Britons', which would encompass people who are both black and of British nationality.[25]

A new point under EA 2010 is that the Government is given the power to add 'caste' to the definition of race. The caste system is generally associated with countries in South Asia, particularly India and its diaspora. It involves different classes which are ranked on a perceived scale of ritual purity.[26]

RELIGION OR BELIEF (SECTION 10)

Religion is defined as meaning any religion, and belief as any religious or philosophical belief. Religion also includes lack of religion, and belief includes lack of belief. This is a similar broad definition to that in the Employment Equality (Religion or Belief) Regulations 2003 which formerly covered this area of equality law, and it is likely to be interpreted in the same way. It is probable that to be covered by the definition the religion would require a clear structure and belief system.

Examples are given in the *Explanatory Notes*:

> The Baha'i faith, Buddhism, Christianity, Hinduism, Islam, Jainism, Judaism, Rastafarianism, Sikhism and Zoroastrianism are all religions for the purposes of this provision. Beliefs such as humanism and atheism would be beliefs for the purposes of this provision, but adherence to a particular football team would not be.[27]

Equally, it will apply to groups within religions, such as Roman Catholics and Protestants.

The coverage of the words 'any … philosophical belief' was examined in relation to a belief about climate change in a recent case brought under the 2003 Regulations.

CASE STUDY

GRAINGER v NICHOLSON

In *Grainger v Nicholson* [28] Mr Nicholson claimed he was dismissed because of his belief in the importance of climate change. He no longer travelled by aeroplane; he had eco-renovated his home; he tried to buy local produce; he had reduced his consumption of meat; and he composted his food waste. The EAT held in this case that a genuine belief in man-made climate change was capable of being a philosophical belief for the purposes of the Regulations. The EAT said that in order to decide whether a belief came within the definition it was directly relevant to consider the case law relating to Article 9 of the European Convention on Human Rights, which guarantees freedom of religion and belief. Accordingly:

(i) the belief must be genuinely held;

(ii) it must be a belief and not an opinion or viewpoint based on the present state of information available;

(iii) it must be a belief as to a weighty and substantial aspect of human life and behaviour;

(iv) it must attain a certain level of cogency, seriousness, cohesion and importance; and

(v) it must be worthy of respect in a democratic society, be not incompatible with human dignity and not conflict with the fundamental rights of others.

Principle (ii) above was the issue in *McClintock v Department of Constitutional Affairs*.[29]

CASE STUDY

McCLINTOCK v DEPARTMENT OF CONSTITUTIONAL AFFAIRS

Mr McClintock was a magistrate and member of the Family Panel (magistrates who hear cases involving children). He was a practising Christian. He did not wish to place children with same-sex couples for adoption. His request to be relieved of the duty to officiate in such cases was refused and he resigned from the Family Panel. The reason he gave was that he thought there was no evidence that such adoptions would work and that this was an experiment in social sciences. He did not say that the reason was because of his religious convictions. The EAT held that the dismissal was not unlawful under the Regulations. The reason he gave was not a religious or philosophical belief – it was an opinion.

Discussion point

Note that even if Mr McClintock had given a reason of religious belief, it would appear that he would still have had no claim. See the case of *Ladele v London Borough of Islington*.[30]

As regards political beliefs: in the *Grainger* case it was stated that although the support of a particular political party might not be a 'philosophical belief', a belief based on a political philosophy, such as socialism or free-market capitalism, might qualify. However, a belief based on a political philosophy which was objectionable such as a racist or homophobic political philosophy would not be covered because it would not be worthy of respect in a democratic society and would be incompatible with human dignity – principle (v) above.

SEX (SECTION 11)

Sex discrimination was formerly covered by the Sex Discrimination Act 1975. The protected characteristic of sex under section 10 is being a man or a woman.

CASE STUDIES

SCHMIDT v AUSTICKS BOOKSHOPS

In *Schmidt v Austicks Bookshops*[31] women could not wear trousers and had to wear overalls, men were not allowed to wear tee-shirts. Ms Schmidt claimed that not being allowed to wear trousers was direct sex discrimination. The EAT held that there was no discrimination – there was a common standard of smartness or conventionality being applied and it was not necessary that the code should require men and women to wear identical items and clothing.

SMITH v SAFEWAY

This approach was approved by the Court of Appeal in *Smith v Safeway*[32] in regard to hair length rules. Female employees of Safeway could have long hair if it was clipped back, men could not. Both men and women had to have conventional hairstyle and colouring. Mr Smith was dismissed for refusing to cut off his ponytail. The court held there was no discrimination – the code had a common standard of smartness and conventionality, both men and women were being required to have a conventional appearance.

DEPARTMENT FOR WORK AND PENSIONS v THOMPSON

In *Department for Work and Pensions v Thompson*[33] the EAT followed this approach again. Both male and female staff had to dress in a professional and businesslike way. Men had to wear a collar and tie, women just had to 'dress appropriately and to a similar standard'. Mr Thompson claimed this was sex discrimination. The EAT held (in sending the case back for a fresh tribunal hearing) that the test was whether the rules required an equivalent level of smartness for men and women. If, however, this could be achieved in the case of men by some way of dressing other than requiring a collar and tie, then the lack of flexibility and choice for them in the dress code would suggest there was discrimination.

Discussion point

Is it direct sex discrimination for an employer to have different rules of dress and appearance for its male and its female employees? The approach of the courts has been to say that it is not discrimination, as long as the dress code has a common standard of smartness or conventionality.

SEXUAL ORIENTATION (SECTION 12)

This was previously covered by the Employment Equality (Sexual Orientation) Regulations 2003. The definition is similar to the former one and defines the sexual orientation characteristic as orientation towards:

- persons of the same sex
- persons of the opposite sex, or
- persons of either sex.

Thus heterosexual, gay, lesbian and bisexual people are protected by the definition.

PROHIBITED CONDUCT

DIRECT DISCRIMINATION (SECTION 13)

Direct discrimination occurs if a person (A) treats another (B) less favourably than A treats or would treat someone else because of a protected characteristic. It is often based on prejudice or making unwarranted assumptions. So, for example, if a woman applies for a job but her application is rejected because the employer assumes that she would be a less satisfactory employee than a male applicant with comparable qualifications, this would be direct sex discrimination. It would of course also be the case if a male were rejected in the opposite situation – but see later in this chapter with regard to *positive discrimination.*

If the less favourable treatment is for some other reason, it is not direct discrimination.

CASE STUDY

B v A

In *B v A*[34] a jealous employer dismissed his PA who had been in a relationship with him because she was now going out with someone else.

She claimed direct sex discrimination on the basis that she had only been dismissed because she was a woman. The EAT held there was no sex discrimination. The PA hadn't been dismissed because she was a woman but because of the breakdown of the relationship. The comparison had to be with a man in a similar situation. If the employer had been a gay man in a relationship with a male PA, the male secretary would also have been dismissed.

In regard to eight out of the nine protected characteristics there is direct discrimination even if it is not the individual's own characteristic but the characteristic of someone else with whom the individual is associated. This is known as *discrimination by association.*[35, 36]

CASE STUDY

EBR ATTRIDGE LAW v COLEMAN (No. 2)

In *EBR Attridge Law v Coleman (No. 2)*[37] it was held by the EAT, after reference to the European Court of Justice, that a legal secretary who had a child with a disability and claimed she suffered direct discrimination at work as a result could claim disability discrimination. The Disability Discrimination Act 1995 could, and should, be interpreted to cover claims based on another person's characteristics with whom the employee was associated.

Discussion point

Do you think that it is right for discrimination law to cover discrimination by association?

However, under section 13(4), with regard to the protected characteristic of marriage and civil partnership there is only direct discrimination if the treatment is because of the individual's own marriage or civil partnership status, not someone else associated with the individual.

It is direct discrimination even if the treatment takes place on the basis of an employer's mistaken perceptions – so if, for example, an employer thinks that an employee is gay and discriminates against him or her, the employee has a claim even if the assumption was incorrect.[38]

In the interesting decision of *English v Thomas Sanderson Blinds Ltd* [39] (which was a claim for harassment rather than direct discrimination) the Court of Appeal held that there might be discrimination because of sexual orientation even where the harassers knew that the victim was not gay.

CASE STUDY

ENGLISH v THOMAS SANDERSON BLINDS LTD

Mr English was subjected to banter at work which referred to him as a gay man. His colleagues knew he was not gay, and Mr English knew this, but nevertheless found the banter very unpleasant. The Court of Appeal held that this conduct was capable of being unlawful harassment, because it was 'on grounds of sexual orientation'. In the same way as cases of mistaken perception were covered (see above), so were the facts of this case. There was little difference between harassment of a heterosexual employee wrongly thought to be gay and an employee, known to be heterosexual, being treated as if he were gay. In both cases it was the imagined sexual orientation which was the ground of the harassment.

Can direct discrimination be justified?

Except with regard to age (see below) there is no justification defence for direct discrimination. The motive for direct discrimination is irrelevant – a good motive is no defence.

CASE STUDY

MOYHING v BARTS AND LONDON NHS TRUST

In *Moyhing v Barts and London NHS Trust*[40] male nurses had to be chaperoned when performing intimate procedures on female patients whereas female nurses in the reverse situation did not have to be chaperoned. Mr Moyhing claimed this was sex discrimination. The EAT held in favour of Mr Moyhing – this was sex discrimination, even though there were good reasons for the policy, namely, the risk of assault on female patients or the risk of false accusations of assault by the female patients.

Discussion point

Do you think that there should be a justification defence for all forms of direct discrimination?

Similarly, in *Amnesty International v Ahmed*[41] it was held by the EAT to be unlawful race discrimination to refuse to appoint a woman of Sudanese origin to the post of 'researcher' for Sudan, even though this was with good motives: a) so as to avoid the possible appearance of bias, and b) for the researcher's own safety if he or she had to visit Sudan.

However, with regard to age, under section 13(2), the employer does have a defence of justification for direct discrimination. The definition of justification is 'a proportionate means of achieving a legitimate aim'.

CASE STUDY

HOMER v CHIEF CONSTABLE OF WEST YORKSHIRE POLICE

In this case the employer imposed a requirement for a law degree in order to be promoted to a certain grade. Mr Homer did not think that he could complete studies for a degree and enjoy the benefits of that study before he reached retirement age. He therefore claimed that the new rule amounted to indirect age discrimination, because older employees would not be able to obtain the necessary qualification to be promoted. The Court of Appeal held that this was not a case of discrimination. The reason Mr Homer could not achieve the qualification for promotion was because of his impending retirement. In objecting to the need for a degree to be promoted he was in fact asking for more favourable treatment on account of his age.

Discussion point

Do you agree with this decision? Was the effect of this policy to stop older people being promoted?

DISCRIMINATION ARISING FROM DISABILITY (SECTION 15)

We saw above that except with regard to age discrimination there is no defence of justification for *direct discrimination* which occurs because of one of the protected characteristics, including disability. However, in regard to disability there may be many situations where a person's disability means that they cannot perform satisfactorily in a particular job, and the law recognises this. Section 15 provides for another type of discrimination which applies only to a person with a disability. This is 'discrimination arising from disability', which is defined as where A treats B unfavourably for a reason arising in consequence of B's disability. In these cases, unlike with direct discrimination against a person with a disability, the employer will be able to justify the discrimination if it is a proportionate means of achieving a legitimate aim. An example is given in the *Explanatory Notes*:

> … a man who has severe back pain and cannot bend is rejected for a job as carpet fitter. He has been treated unfavourably in being rejected for the job, but it is likely that this would be justified.

An additional 'get-out' for the employer is that there is no liability 'if A did not know and could not reasonably have been expected to know that B had the disability'. The *Explanatory Notes* give another example from a non-employment context:

> The licensee of a pub refuses to serve a person who has cerebral palsy because she believes that he is drunk as he has slurred speech. However, the slurred speech is a consequence of his impairment. If the licensee is able to show that she did not know, and could not reasonably have been expected to know, that the customer was disabled, she has not subjected him to discrimination arising from his disability.[42]

GENDER REASSIGNMENT DISCRIMINATION: CASES OF ABSENCE FROM WORK (SECTION 16)

Section 16 provides for a specific type of discrimination against transsexual people. Transsexual people may have to be absent from work if they are undergoing gender reassignment – for example, to have hormone treatment. Under the section it is discrimination to treat them less favourably for being absent from work because they propose to undergo, are undergoing or have undergone gender reassignment than they would be treated if they were absent because they were ill or injured. It is also discrimination if they are less favourably treated than they would be if they were absent for some reason other than sickness or injury and it is not reasonable to treat them less favourably.

PREGNANCY AND MATERNITY DISCRIMINATION: WORK CASES (SECTION 18)

Under section 18 it is discrimination to treat a pregnant woman unfavourably because of her pregnancy, because of pregnancy-related illness or because of exercising or wishing to exercise her maternity leave rights, during what is called the *protected period*. This period, in the case of a woman entitled to *statutory maternity leave* (see Chapter 8), runs from the beginning of the pregnancy until the end of the statutory maternity leave period. If the woman is not entitled to statutory maternity leave (see Chapter 8), then the protected period ends two weeks after the baby is born.[43]

For this type of claim the woman is not required to compare herself to a man.

The protection applies even in relation to employment on a short fixed-term contract.

CASE STUDY

TELE DANMARK (2001)[44]

Marianne Brandt-Nielsen was recruited by the employer on a six-month fixed-term contract to work in its customer service department for mobile telephones. The job commenced on 1 July 1995, and she was to be trained for the first two months. She was pregnant but did not tell the employer of her condition before starting the job. She told the employer in August, and she was then given notice of dismissal terminating at the end of September. The European Court of Justice held that this was unlawful discrimination. The protection applied even where:

- it was a short fixed-term contract and the employee would be unavailable for a substantial proportion of the duration of the contract
- her presence at work was essential for the business, and
- she did not tell the employer before obtaining the job.

Refusing to employ a pregnant employee in the same situation would be equally unlawful.

Discussion point

Do you think that the high degree of legal protection given to pregnant women by this decision could cause some employers to avoid recruiting women of child-bearing age?

If, however, the claim relates to unfavourable treatment outside the protected period, the employee will have no claim under this section. She will have to make a claim for sex discrimination (see above), which will involve comparison with a comparable man.

CASE STUDY

BRITISH TELECOMMUNICATIONS v ROBERTS AND LONGSTAFFE[45]

Helen Roberts and Annette Longstaffe wanted to work on a job-share basis after they came back from maternity leave. The employers refused to permit this. The EAT held that this was not a case of discrimination within the *protected period*. The refusal of their request 'had nothing to do with them being pregnant but with having children to look after'. Because their maternity leave had ended, in order to claim sex discrimination a comparison with a male was necessary and the claimants hadn't brought any evidence to support a claim that they had been treated less favourably than a man. It should be noted, however, that if the facts of this case were to recur today, the women would have a right to request **flexible working** – see Chapter 8.

INDIRECT DISCRIMINATION (SECTION 19)

Indirect discrimination is more subtle discrimination than direct discrimination. Direct discrimination involves treating people in different ways, so that a person with one of the protected characteristics is treated less favourably than someone without that characteristic. With indirect discrimination the behaviour is, on the face of it, 'neutral' – the same for everyone – but it has a disproportionate adverse effect on people with a protected characteristic. A very simple example of indirect discrimination would be a height requirement. If an employer stipulates in a job advertisement that 'applicants must be six foot tall', this will not be *direct* sex discrimination because both men and women are required to meet the same criterion. However, it is likely to be *indirect* sex discrimination against women, who are generally shorter than men, and will therefore be put at a disadvantage by this criterion. Nonetheless, as may be seen below, the employer will have the possible defence of justification for indirect discrimination.

The essence of the definition of indirect discrimination in section 19[46] is that

- there is a rule – a 'provision, criterion or practice' (PCP) – which the employer applies to everyone but
- which has more of an impact on some groups than on others (such as the height criterion we have just referred to) and
- which causes a disadvantage to the claimant personally, as well as to his or her group.

If these three elements exist, the claimant will win an indirect discrimination claim unless the employer can justify the discrimination – can show it to be *a proportionate means of achieving a legitimate aim.*

We can further explain and illustrate this by looking at a well-publicised religion or belief discrimination case:

CASE STUDY

AZMI v KIRKLEES M.B.C.[47]

Mrs Azmi was employed as educational support worker. Due to her beliefs as a Muslim woman, she wanted to wear a veil covering all her head and face apart from her eyes when in the presence of the male teachers with whom she would be working. The school took advice from the education authority, which advised that the veil reduced non-verbal signals to the children and prevented full and effective communication between Mrs Azmi and the pupils. After her teaching was observed on two occasions she was instructed not to wear the veil while teaching and was suspended when she refused to obey the instruction. She claimed religion or belief direct and indirect discrimination (as well as harassment and victimisation). It was held by the EAT that:

1) There was no direct discrimination (less favourable treatment) against Mrs Azmi because of her religion. The comparison would be with a woman, whether Muslim or not, who wanted to cover her face for a reason not relating to religion. Such a person would have been treated in the same way.

2) There was no indirect discrimination.

- What was the provision, criterion or practice (PCP)?

  The PCP here was the requirement not to wear clothing which covered the whole or a considerable part of the face or mouth and/or the requirement not to wear clothing which interfered unduly with the ability to communicate with pupils.

- Did the PCP put persons of Mrs Azmi's belief at a particular disadvantage?

  Yes.

- Did the PCP put Mrs Azmi herself at a particular disadvantage?

  Yes – therefore an indirect discrimination claim would succeed unless the school could show it was *justified.*

- Was the potential indirect discrimination justified? Was the PCP a proportionate means of achieving a legitimate aim?

  Yes, because:

  – The requirement had not been imposed immediately.

  – The instruction to Mrs Azmi to remove her veil had only related to the occasions when she was teaching children.

  – The instruction had been given only after she had twice been observed teaching and assisting the children.

In *Ladele v London Borough of Islington* [48] the Court of Appeal held that the Council had the defence of justification for indirect discrimination against a registrar for marriages who because of her strong Christian beliefs refused to carry out civil partnership ceremonies. Promoting equal opportunities was a *legitimate aim* and it was a *proportionate means* for the Council to achieve this aim by requiring all registrars to carry out the civil partnership ceremonies.[49]

An essential element in the definition of indirect discrimination is that not only must the *claimant personally* be put at a particular disadvantage but also the *group* to which he or she belongs. Mrs Azmi's personal belief was that she was required to cover her face and this was a belief shared by a significant number of Muslim women, though not all, who would similarly have been put at a disadvantage. This may be contrasted with the equally well-publicised case of Mrs Eweida.

CASE STUDY

EWEIDA v BRITISH AIRWAYS[50]

Mrs Eweida was employed by British Airways (BA) as one of the check-in staff. She was a practising Christian and wished to wear a small, visible cross outside her uniform. The BA staff dress code forbade the wearing of a visible adornment outside the uniform, although items which were a mandatory religious requirement could be worn if other conditions were fulfilled. Mrs Eweida wished to wear the cross visibly as a personal choice – she did not claim that it was a requirement of the Christian religion to do so. She brought a claim of religion or belief discrimination at the tribunal. There was no evidence provided by Mrs Eweida that anyone else among 30,000 uniformed BA employees had ever made such a request or demand, or that because of the BA dress code rule any Christians had been deterred from applying for a job with BA. The Court of Appeal held that for a finding of indirect discrimination, some identifiable section of a workforce, quite possibly a small one, must be shown to suffer a particular disadvantage which the claimant shares. No disadvantage for Christians as a group had been shown to exist in this case and the claim therefore failed.

FAILURE TO COMPLY WITH A DUTY TO MAKE REASONABLE ADJUSTMENTS (SECTION 20)

An employer has a duty to make reasonable adjustments which would make a job suitable for a person with a disability. The duty comprises three requirements, relating to different aspects of the employment, if any of these place the disabled person at a substantial disadvantage in comparison with non-disabled people. The three requirements relate to:

- a provision, criterion or practice applied by the employer
- physical features of a building
- providing auxiliary aids or services.

An example of the first type of adjustment would be allowing a disabled employee to be absent during working hours for rehabilitation or treatment. The 'provision, criterion or practice' that is being adjusted in this example is the practice that employees should be present during working hours.

An example of the second type is given by the *Explanatory Notes*:[51]

> A bank is obliged to consider reasonable adjustments for a newly recruited financial adviser who is a wheelchair user and who would have difficulty

> negotiating her way around the customer area. In consultation with the new adviser, the bank rearranges the layout of furniture in the customer area and installs a new desk. These changes result in the new adviser being able to work alongside her colleagues.

An example of the third type, in a non-employment context, given in the *Explanatory Notes* is:[52]

> The organiser of a large public conference knows that hearing-impaired delegates are likely to attend. She must therefore consider how to make the conference accessible to them. Having asked delegates what adjustments they need, she decides to engage BSL/English interpreters, have a palantypist and an induction loop to make sure that the hearing-impaired delegates are not substantially disadvantaged.

A failure by an employer to comply with the duty to make reasonable adjustments amounts to discrimination (section 21).

HARASSMENT AND VICTIMISATION

HARASSMENT (SECTION 26)

There are three types. The first type (section 26(1)) involves unwanted conduct which is related to a relevant characteristic and has the *purpose or effect* of creating an intimidating, hostile, degrading, humiliating or offensive environment for the complainant or violating the complainant's dignity. This type applies to all the protected characteristics apart from

- pregnancy and maternity, and
- marriage and civil partnership.

It is interesting to note that anyone who is affected by the conduct may have a claim.

The *Explanatory Notes* give an example of a white person who sees a black colleague being subjected to racially abusive language. The white person could also have a claim if the language also causes an offensive environment for him or her.[53]

The definition may cover even a single remark, although there is a reasonableness test – see below.

CASE STUDY

RICHMOND PHARMACOLOGY v DHALIWAL[54]

A British woman of Indian origin was project manager in the clinical department of a company which conducts trials of new medicines. She had a good working relationship with her managers until she gave notice. She had a conversation with Dr Lorch, the medical director, who remarked 'We will probably bump into each other in future – unless you are married off in India.' Ms Dhaliwal found this offensive and claimed that it was racial harassment. The Employment Appeal Tribunal held that this remark might have been 'close to the borderline' but that it fell 'on the wrong side of the line' and was harassment. The EAT also examined the meaning of 'purpose or effect' and stated that under the definition there will be liability even if the purported harasser merely *intends* to create an intimidating, hostile, etc, environment but does not do or, conversely, does not intend to create that effect but does so.

The second type (section 26(2)) is sexual harassment, which is unwanted conduct *of a sexual nature* where this has the same purpose or effect as the first type of harassment. Again, even a single remark might amount to harassment of this type, if it has the said purpose or effect.

An example of less obvious conduct which might come under this type, given in the *Explanatory Notes*, is that of an employer who displays material of a sexual nature, such as pornography, where this has the effect of creating a hostile or degrading environment for any male or female employee.[55]

The third type (section 26(3)) is treating someone less favourably because they have either submitted to or rejected sexual harassment, or harassment related to sex or gender reassignment. Suppose, for instance, a manager makes unwelcome sexual advances to his secretary, who rejects him, and as a result she is demoted. The secretary would have two potential harassment claims: the second type of claim and the third type.

In deciding whether harassment has taken place it is necessary for the tribunal to take into account not only the perceptions of the claimant and other circumstances but also whether it was reasonable for the conduct to have that effect (section 26(4)). So an over-sensitive claimant who is unreasonably offended would not succeed in his or her claim. Thus Ms Dhaliwal's claim (above) was, according to the EAT, only just 'on the wrong side of the line'!

We will see below that an employer may be liable for repeated harassment committed against an employee by a third party such as a customer.

VICTIMISATION (SECTION 27)

In everyday speech 'victimisation' may be more or less synonymous with 'harassment'. But in equality law victimisation has a specific technical definition which is entirely different from harassment. Victimisation is defined in section 27 as where A subjects B to a 'detriment' because B has done one of the 'protected acts', or A believes that B has done or may do one of these acts. 'Protected acts' are defined as

- bringing discrimination proceedings themselves
- giving evidence or information in proceedings
- doing any other thing for the purposes of or in connection with EA 2010

- making an allegation that B (or anyone else) has done something in breach of EA 2010.

For example: Julie makes an allegation that Bob, her manager, has sexually harassed her and she brings a claim in an employment tribunal. Patricia gives evidence at the tribunal on Julie's behalf. Julie wins her harassment claim, but after the case, Bob dismisses her and also demotes Patricia. Julie will have a new claim for victimisation (and very possibly unfair dismissal, see Chapter 13), and so will Patricia.

It is sufficient if the protected act was an 'important cause' of the victimisation or a 'significant influence' on it – see *Nagarajan v London Regional Transport.*[56]

In an interesting case, *Rank Nemo (DMS) v Coutinho,*[57] it was held that when an employee had won a case for discrimination and been awarded compensation by the tribunal, the employer, in not paying the judgment debt to Mr Coutinho, might be held to be victimising him if the evidence showed that in not paying the judgment debt the employer was treating him less favourably than its other creditors. Note that although this case was decided on the wording of the definition of 'victimisation' under the previous law, the same might apply under EA 2010.

LIKE FOR LIKE COMPARISON

Under section 23, in cases of *direct* and *indirect discrimination*, the claimant must be compared with someone whose circumstances are not materially different, apart from the protected characteristic. This is known as a 'like for like' comparison.

For example: a female solicitor who has only one year's experience of family law is unsuccessful in her application to a law firm which has advertised for a family lawyer. The successful applicant is a male solicitor with five years' family law experience. The successful applicant is better qualified and the claimant is unlikely to be able to win a claim for direct sex discrimination.

If there is an actual person with whom to make the comparison (called the 'comparator'), all the better. Otherwise, the employee can compare himself or herself with a 'hypothetical comparator' – ie a theoretical person who the claimant shows, on the evidence, *would* have been treated less favourably.

CASE STUDY

CHIEF CONSTABLE OF WEST YORKSHIRE POLICE v VENTO

In *Chief Constable of West Yorkshire v Vento,*[58] a female probationary police officer was not given a permanent post after she gave a dishonest reply to a superior officer. In deciding that she had been treated less favourably the EAT held that it was legitimate for the tribunal to decide that a hypothetical male probationary officer who had done what she did would have been offered the permanent post, basing this on the situations of four male officers whose cases were somewhat similar, though not identical, to Ms Vento's case.

DISCRIMINATION AT WORK

Assuming that one or more of the prohibited acts have taken place because of one or more of the protected characteristics, we next need to consider at what stage of the employment this occurred, and whether there are any applicable *exceptions* available to the employer.

Section 39 makes clear that an employer must not discriminate at any stage of the employment relationship – from hiring through to termination, and even beyond termination in some cases –

- in relation to job offers, including an outright refusal to hire, or offering the job but on inferior terms
- during employment, in relation to access to promotion, transfer or training, or other benefits, or subjecting the employee to some other detriment
- dismissal.

So if, for example, an employer refuses to shortlist an applicant because he or she is of Afro-Caribbean origin, or if a pregnant woman is selected for redundancy because of her pregnancy, there will be potential discrimination claims.

It should be noted that under section 83 the definition of 'employment' includes employment under not only a contract of employment but also a contract personally to do work. This means that some self-employed people are able to bring discrimination claims as well as employees, in contrast to, for instance, unfair dismissal or redundancy claims which are limited to employees only.

Section 108 makes it unlawful to discriminate even once the employment has ended. This applies if the discrimination arises out of and is closely connected to the former employment relationship. So if an employer refuses to give a reference to an ex-employee because of his or her religion or belief, this would be unlawful.

Discriminatory job advertisements are unlawful, but proceedings in relation to the advertisement cannot be brought by an individual – the action must be brought by the Equality and Human Rights Commission: see Chapter 7.

Under section 60, unless one of the following situations is applicable it is unlawful for an employer to ask about the health of a job applicant until that person has received a job offer or has been included in a pool of candidates to be offered a job when a position arises. The situations when an employer may make enquiries *at an earlier stage* are for the purposes of:

- finding out whether a job applicant would be able to participate in an assessment to test his or her suitability for the work

- making reasonable adjustments to enable a disabled applicant to participate in the recruitment process
- finding out whether a job applicant would be able to undertake a function that is intrinsic to the job, with reasonable adjustments in place if required
- monitoring diversity in applications for jobs
- supporting positive action in employment for disabled people
- enabling an employer to identify suitable candidates for a job where there is an occupational requirement for the person to be disabled.[59]

As with discriminatory advertisements, it is only the Equality and Human Rights Commission who can take action against an employer who has made enquiries in breach of section 60. However, if the employer relies on the answer given by the applicant and rejects the application, the applicant may use this as evidence in support of a discrimination claim which the employer must then disprove – see burden of proof, Chapter 7.

- The Equality Act 2010 covers all areas of discrimination law.
- There are nine *protected characteristics* – namely: age, disability, gender reassignment, marriage and civil partnership, pregnancy and maternity, race, religion or belief, sex, sexual orientation.
- There are eight types of *prohibited conduct* – namely: direct discrimination, discrimination arising from disability, gender reassignment discrimination, pregnancy and maternity discrimination, indirect discrimination, failure to make reasonable adjustments, harassment and victimisation.
- Discrimination is generally unlawful at all stages of employment, from hiring through to termination and sometimes beyond. Advertisements which discriminate are also unlawful but proceedings may only be brought by the Equality and Human Rights Commission.
- Unless one of a number of situations pertains, it is unlawful to ask a job applicant about his or her health until a job offer has been made.
- Under section 23, in cases of direct and indirect discrimination, the claimant(s) must be compared with someone whose circumstances are not materially different, apart from the protected characteristic. This is known as a 'like for like' comparison.

REFERENCES

1 **This chapter contains extracts from or close paraphrasing of legislation, and explanatory notes to that legislation which is on the opsi.gov.uk website (and its successor) and is subject to crown copyright. Its reproduction here is licensed under the open government licence v1.0**

2 Equality Act 2010 *Explanatory Notes*, Revised edition August 2010

3 At the time of writing these Codes are in draft form

4 *Explanatory Notes* page 13 paragraph 37

5 See Guidance on matters to be taken into account in determining questions relating to the definition of disability, in force from May 2006, on the EHRC website

6 *Ibid* page 22 paragraph D4

7 *Explanatory Notes* page 14 paragraph 40

8 *Explanatory Notes* page 142 paragraph 675

9 EA 2010 Schedule 1 paragraph 5

10 EA 2010 Schedule 1 paragraph 2(2)

11 'Likely' means 'could well happen': *SCA Packaging Ltd v Boyle* (2009) IRLR 746

12 EA 2010 Schedule 1 paragraph 6

13 EA 2010 Schedule 1 paragraph 8

14 EA 2010 Section 6(4)

15 EA 2010 Schedule 1 paragraph 3

16 See *ibid* pages 14–15 paragraphs 41–43

17 See *ibid* page 15 paragraph 43

18 *Ibid* page 15 paragraph 45

19 See *ibid* pages 15–16 paragraph 46

20 (1983) IRLR 209

21 (2010) IRLR 136

22 *Commission for Racial Equality v Dutton* (1989) IRLR 8

23 See *Nyazi v Rymans Ltd* (1988) IRLIB 367 24 *Dawkins v Department of the Environment sub nom Crown Suppliers PSA* (1993) IRLR 284

24 *Explanatory Notes* page 16 paragraph 50

25 *Ibid* page 16 paragraph 49

26 *Ibid* page 16 paragraph 53

27 (2010) IRLR 4

28 (2008) IRLR 29

29 (2010) IRLR 211

30 (1977) IRLR 360

31 (1996) IRLR 456

32 (2004) IRLR 348

33 (2007) IRLR 576

34 *Explanatory Notes* page 18 paragraph 59

35 The claim of a BNP member for discrimination by association on grounds of race failed in *Redfearn v Serco Ltd* (2006) IRLR 623

36 (2010) IRLR 10

37 *Explanatory Notes* page 18 paragraph 59

38 (2009) IRLR 206

39 (2006) IRLR 860

40 (2009) IRLR 884

41 *Ibid* page 22 paragraph 70

42 EA 2010 section 18(6)

43 *Tele Danmark A/S v Handels- og Kontorfunktionærernes Forbund i Danmark* (2001) IRLR 853

44 (1996) IRLR 601

45 Section 19 reads as follows:
(1) A person (A) discriminates against another (B) if A applies to B a provision, criterion or practice which is discriminatory in relation to a relevant protected characteristic of B's.

(2) For the purposes of subsection (1), a provision, criterion or practice is discriminatory in relation to a relevant protected characteristic of B's if –

(a) A applies, or would apply, it to persons with whom B does not share the characteristic,

(b) it puts, or would put, persons with whom B shares the characteristic at a particular disadvantage when compared with persons with whom B does not share it,

(c) it puts, or would put, B at that disadvantage, and

(d) A cannot show it to be a proportionate means of achieving a legitimate aim.

46 (2007) IRLR 484

47 (2010) IRLR 211

48 See also *McFarlane v Relate Avon* (2010) IRLR 872

49 (2010) IRLR 322

50 *Explanatory Notes* page 26 paragraph 86

51 *Ibid* page 26 paragraph 86

52 *Ibid* page 29 paragraph 99

53 (2009) IRLR 336

54 *Explanatory Notes* page 30 paragraph 99

55 (1999) IRLR 572

56 (2009) IRLR 672

57 (2001) IRLR 124

58 *Explanatory Notes* page 51 paragraph 197

EXPLORE FURTHER

Reading

- Smith, I. and Thomas, G. (2010) *Smith & Wood's Employment Law.* Butterworths, Chapter 5.
- Wadham, J., Ruebain, D., Robinson, A. and Uppal, S. (eds) (2010) *Blackstone's Guide to the Equality Act 2010.* Oxford University Press

Websites

- ACAS www.acas.org.uk
- Chartered Institute of Personnel and Development www.cipd.co.uk
- Department for Business Innovation and Skills www.bis.gov.uk
- Directgov – Employment www.direct.gov.uk
- Equality Act 2010 Guidance http://odi.dwp.gov.uk/docs/wor/new/ea-guide.pdf
- Equality and Human Rights Commission http://www.equalityhuman rights.com

CHAPTER 7

Discrimination (2): Lawful Discrimination, Vicarious Liability, Burden of Proof, Enforcement and Equality of Terms

CHAPTER OVERVIEW

In this chapter we begin by examining the exceptional situations in which it is permissible to discriminate. We then consider when an employer may be vicariously liable for an act of discrimination that has been committed by one employee against another. We discuss who carries the 'burden of proof' in a discrimination claim, and the remedies awarded by an employment tribunal. We examine the role of the Equality and Human Rights Commission and the equality duty placed on public authorities. In the final part of our discussion of equality law we look at the right to equality of contract terms of male and female employees.

LEARNING OUTCOMES

After studying this chapter you will be able to:

- understand and explain the legal principles that apply to matters pertaining to the exceptional situations when discrimination is permissible, and the law on equality of terms of the contract in respect of men and women
- advise colleagues on such matters as the obligatory procedure to be followed in relation to compulsory retirement, the employer's possible liability for acts of discrimination committed by one employee against another and how to protect against it, and job evaluation studies in order to avoid inequality of contract terms.

LAWFUL DISCRIMINATION: THE EXCEPTIONS

There are some general exceptions when it is lawful to discriminate, which apply to discrimination in employment as well as other areas of life such as education, the provision of goods and services, etc. There are also specific exceptions which apply only to potential employment law discrimination.

Section numbers in this Chapter refer to sections of EA 2010 unless otherwise stated.

GENERAL EXCEPTIONS – PART 14 AND SCHEDULE 22 OF EA 2010 [1]

Statutory authority

Under section 191 and Schedule 22 an act of discrimination is lawful if done under *statutory authority*, meaning that there is another law which requires the discrimination to take place. This applies only in relation to age, disability, religion or belief, sex and sexual orientation discrimination.

An example is cited in the Equality Act 2010 *Explanatory Notes*:

> An employer can lawfully dismiss a disabled employee if health and safety regulations leave him with no other choice.[2]

CASE STUDY

AMNESTY INTERNATIONAL v AHMED

In *Amnesty International v Ahmed*[3] (see Chapter 6), which was a claim under the Race Relations Act, the employer argued that its action was necessary to comply with its duty to ensure Ms Ahmed's health and safety at work under the Health and Safety at Work Act 1974 section 2(1). This argument was rejected because Amnesty could have assigned that part of the job to someone else by sending someone else to Sudan. Under the EA 2010 there would in any case be no such exception – even if that part of the job could not have been given to anyone else – because there is no statutory authority exception for race discrimination.

National security

Under Section 192 an act of discrimination which is proportionate, for the purpose of safeguarding national security, is lawful. In the light of contemporary fears of a terrorist attack this is an exception which may perhaps arise more frequently than in the past – for example, in relation to race discrimination and religion or belief discrimination. We may note the requirement that the act must be proportionate, so that groundless fears or otherwise disproportionate actions would not be excepted from liability.

WORK EXCEPTIONS (SCHEDULE 9)

Occupational requirements: paragraph 1

This is an exception to what would otherwise be unlawful direct discrimination in relation to work. The exception applies where being of a particular sex, race, disability, religion or belief, sexual orientation or age – or not being a transsexual person, married or a civil partner – is a crucial requirement for the work, and the person who it is applied to does not meet it (or, except in the case of sex, does not meet it to the reasonable satisfaction of the person who applied it). It must also be a proportionate means of achieving a legitimate aim.[4]

The *Explanatory Notes* give a number of examples:

> The need for authenticity or realism might require someone of a particular race, sex or age for acting roles (for example, a black man to play the part of Othello) or modelling jobs.
>
> Considerations of privacy or decency might require a public changing room or lavatory attendant to be of the same sex as those using the facilities.
>
> An organisation for deaf people might legitimately employ a deaf person who uses British Sign Language to work as a counsellor to other deaf people whose first or preferred language is BSL.
>
> Unemployed Muslim women might not take advantage of the services of an outreach worker to help them find employment if they were provided by a man.
>
> A counsellor working with victims of rape might have to be a woman and not a transsexual person, even if she has a Gender Recognition Certificate, in order to avoid causing them further distress.[5]

Religious requirements relating to sex, marriage, etc, sexual orientation: paragraph 2

There is a specific exception which applies to *employment for the purposes of an organised religion*, which is intended to cover the employment of

- ministers of religion and
- a small number of lay posts which can also be said to be *for the purposes of an organised religion* – see examples below.

Where employment is for the purposes of an organised religion, this exception allows the employer to apply a requirement to be of a particular sex or not to be a transsexual person, or to make a requirement related to the employee's marriage or civil partnership status or sexual orientation, but only if –

- appointing a person who meets the requirement in question is a proportionate way of complying with the doctrines of the religion, or
- because of the nature or context of the employment, employing a person who meets the requirement is a proportionate way of avoiding conflict with a significant number of the religion's followers' strongly held religious convictions.[6]

You will note that there are two possible situations covered here. One is that the *doctrines* – that is, what we might call the core beliefs – of the religion contain such rules. The second situation is that although the religion in question may not have a doctrine on the point, a significant number of its followers nevertheless have strong beliefs about it.

The *Explanatory Notes* give several examples.

> This exception would apply to a requirement that a Catholic priest be a man and unmarried.
>
> This exception is unlikely to permit a requirement that a church youth worker who primarily organises sporting activities is celibate if he is gay – because this would not be employment *for the purposes of an organised religion* – but it may apply if the youth worker mainly teaches Bible classes.
>
> This exception would not apply to a requirement that a church accountant be celibate if he is gay because this would not be employment *for the purposes of an organised religion.*[7]

Exception for ethos relating to religion or belief: paragraph 3

This exception is broader than the previous one. It applies where an employer has an 'ethos' based on religion or belief. It allows that employer to discriminate in relation to work by applying a requirement to be of a particular religion or belief, but only if, having regard to that ethos,

- being of that religion or belief is a requirement for the work, and
- applying the requirement is proportionate so as to achieve a legitimate aim.

An example is given in the *Explanatory Notes*:

> A religious organisation may wish to restrict applicants for the post of head of its organisation to those people that adhere to that faith. This is because in order to represent the views of that organisation accurately it is felt that the person heading it must have an in-depth understanding of the religion's doctrines. Discrimination in relation to this post might be lawful. However, the exception would probably not apply to other posts within the organisation that do not require this kind of in-depth understanding, such as administrative posts.[8]

The armed forces: paragraph 4

The armed forces have an exemption, if the conditions are fulfilled, from discrimination against women, transsexuals, disability and age.

EXCEPTIONS TO AGE DISCRIMINATION (SCHEDULE 9 PARAGRAPHS 7–16)

As far as age discrimination is concerned there are a number of different exceptions set out in Schedule 9. The biggest exception is the possibility of *compulsory retirement.*[9]

Retirement

The default retirement age was abolished with effect from October 2011. This means that the provisions allowing an employer to automatically dismiss someone just because they had reached a certain age were removed. If an employer now wishes to compulsorily retire an individual or group, the employer will have to show that the policy of retirement is a proportionate means of achieving a legitimate aim. This is known as an employer-justified retirement age

(EJRA). It is likely to be something that applies only in exceptional circumstances.

CASE STUDY

SELDON v CLARKSON WRIGHT AND JAKES

Mr Seldon was a senior partner in a law firm where the partnership deed contained a mandatory retirement clause. There was a requirement for the partners to retire from the partnership at the end of the year when the age of 65 was reached. When his turn came, Mr Seldon put forward a number of proposals to the partners that would enable him to continue working for another three years. The partners rejected this and he eventually began proceedings alleging direct age discrimination.

The firm had put forward a number of 'legitimate aims' to the employment tribunal, which accepted that compulsory retirement was an appropriate means of achieving the aims of staff retention, workforce planning and allowing an older and less capable partner to leave without the need to justify the departure and damage dignity.

The outcome was that although the Supreme Court accepted the justification of the firm for having a retirement age, the matter was referred back to the employment tribunal to consider whether retirement at the age of 65 years was an appropriate age for these legitimate aims.

REFLECTIVE QUESTION

Should employers ever be allowed to make someone retire if the individual does not wish to do so?

Benefits based on length of service: paragraph 10

This exception is concerned with the issue of benefits related to length of service and seniority. It is not uncommon for employees to be given extra benefits related to length of service with an organisation. Pay scales and holiday entitlement are obvious examples of benefits that might be linked to length of service. Other examples include entry into health schemes and employee discount schemes. Without further provisions such benefits might constitute unlawful *indirect* (see Chapter 6) age discrimination, because it will tend to mean that older (and longer-serving) employees receive greater benefits than less experienced (and often younger) employees.

Paragraph 10 provides that it is not unlawful for A to award a benefit to employee B which is less than that awarded to employee C, when the reason for the difference is that B has a shorter period of service.[10] This exception is absolute and straightforward if B has served for five years or less. However, if B has served for more than five years, then the exception only applies if a further proviso is fulfilled. The proviso is that A must 'reasonably believe' that using the criterion of length of service 'fulfils a business need'.[11] Examples of 'fulfilling a business need' would include encouraging loyalty or motivation or rewarding experience. It is difficult to see why the government bothered with this proviso – its wording is so broad that an employer's reliance on it for justification of discrimination will be almost impossible to disprove!

The *Explanatory Notes* give further information:

> An employer's pay system includes an annual move up a pay spine, or a requirement that a certain amount of time must elapse before an employee is entitled to be a member of an employee benefits scheme. Provided that the pay spine or time it takes to get the benefit is no longer than five years or can be justified, the exception will apply.
>
> An employer's terms and conditions relating to annual leave entitlement provide that employees are entitled to an additional five days' leave after ten years of service. Such an entitlement needs to be justified as reasonably fulfilling a business need.[12]

It is for the employer to decide which formula to use to calculate length of service. It may be either the length of time a worker has been working at or above a particular level, or it can be the length of time the worker has been working for the employer in total.[13] This distinction is important because if the employer chooses the first option it will be possible to use the absolute exception applicable to service of five years or less on more than one occasion. Thus if a worker is employed as a shopfloor operative for four years and is then promoted to being supervisor, the five-year period can start all over again.

CASE STUDY

ROLLS-ROYCE PLC v UNITE THE UNION

The case of *Rolls-Royce v Unite*[14] concerned two collective agreements which had an agreed matrix to be used to choose who should be selected for redundancy. Those with the lowest number of points overall were selected for redundancy. There were five criteria (eg self-motivation and expertise/knowledge) against which an individual could score a maximum total of 130 points. In addition there was a length-of-service criterion which awarded 1 point for each year of continuous service. Thus older employees would have an important advantage over younger ones, which was potentially unlawful age discrimination. The Court of Appeal held that:

- The length-of-service criterion was *justified* – it was a proportionate means of achieving a legitimate aim. (On justification, see Chapter 6.) The legitimate aim was to reward loyalty and achieve a stable workforce through a fair selection for redundancy. The proportionality was shown by the fact that length of service was only one of a substantial number of criteria.
- It could also come under the exception in Schedule 9 paragraph 10.[15] The criterion gave employees with longer service an advantage in making it less likely that they would be chosen for redundancy. This

advantage came within the meaning of a 'benefit' in paragraph 10.

Exception for the national minimum wage: paragraphs 11 and 12

This exception allows employers to base their pay structures on the National Minimum Wage Act 1998 and the National Minimum Wage Regulations 1999 – see Chapter 5. The exception for workers is dealt with in paragraph 11 and apprentices in paragraph 12. As we saw in Chapter 5, there are two lower bands for **young workers**: one for those aged 16 and 17 years; the other for those aged between 18 and 20 inclusive. This exception only applies to the age bands and pay levels established by the statutory measures on the national minimum wage.

The *Explanatory Notes* again give further information:

> It is lawful for an employer to pay 16- to 21-year-olds a lower rate of minimum wage than that given to adults, when based on the development bands set out in 1999 Regulations [see Chapter 5].
>
> Rather than pay the amounts stated by the 1999 Regulations, this paragraph also permits an employer to base its pay scales on the development bands and so, for example, it may pay 16–17-year-olds £4 per hour, 18–21-year-olds £5 per hour and those over 22 £6 per hour.[16]

However, if an employer wished to pay a 16-year-old at a different rate from a 17-year-old, this exception would not apply because it applies only where an employer bases its pay structure on the national minimum wage law. In this case the employer would need to show *justification* for the discrimination.

The objective in having a lower rate for young people is, according to the government, to make the employment of young people more attractive to employers but, at the same time, not set the rates at a level that would act as an incentive for young people to give up education and go into work. If the government was ever challenged on these lower rates (which do discriminate against younger workers), it would have to show that these were legitimate aims and that the means for achieving these aims – namely, the national minimum wage – are proportionate.

Exception for the provision of enhanced redundancy payments: paragraph 13

As we will see in Chapter 14, *statutory* redundancy payments are calculated using a combination of length of service and age. The greater the age and length of service, the higher the payment. This is using an age-related criterion but is in any case lawful because of the exception for *statutory authority* in Schedule 22 – see above. The exception in paragraph 13 is for an employer who wishes to pay *enhanced* redundancy payments – ie to pay more than the statutory amounts. This is allowed as long as the employer follows the same formula as under the statutory scheme – eg one week's pay for each year of employment in which the employee was aged 21–40 years old.

The *Explanatory Notes* give more detailed information:[17]

> An employer may pay qualifying employees an enhanced redundancy payment based on their actual week's pay rather than the maximum amount as specified in section 227 ERA 1996 (currently £380).
>
> So an employee (P) aged 45 with 18 years' continuous employment earning £600 a week would receive one and a half weeks' pay for each year of employment in which he was not below the age of 41 and one week's pay for each year of employment in which he was not below the age of 22. P would therefore receive the following:
>
> 3 × (1.5 × £600) + (15 × £600) = £11,700.

Life assurance cover for retired workers: paragraph 14

As the *Explanatory Notes* explain, an employer who provides life assurance cover will usually wish to provide it only in respect of people below the age of 65 (or the employer's normal retirement age, if different). Such cover is not provided in respect of older people because it becomes more and more expensive to provide. If employers were no longer able to impose a 'cut-off' for the provision of such cover to those who have retired early, there is a real risk they would simply cease to offer it to anyone. This exception is intended to avoid that happening.[18]

The *Explanatory Notes* furnish examples:

> An employer who has no normal retirement age provides life assurance cover for an employee who has retired early due to ill health. If the employer then ceases to provide such cover when the employee reaches the age of 65, this is lawful.
>
> An employer who operates a normal retirement age of 70 provides life assurance cover for an employee who has retired early due to ill health. If the employer then ceases to provide such cover when the employee reaches the age of 70, this is lawful.[19]

Child care: paragraph 15

This exception allows an employer to discriminate in the provision of a child care benefit which relates to the provision of child care and to which access is restricted to children of a particular age group. This would otherwise be discrimination against those with parental responsibility for children of other ages.

More examples from the *Explanatory Notes*:

> An employer may provide a crèche for employees' children aged two and under; or a holiday club open only to employees' children aged between five and nine. In each of these examples, the exception allows an employer

to discriminate against employees because of their association with a child who does not fall within the specified age groups.[20]

Personal pensions: paragraph 16

A further exception is provided in relation to age discrimination for employer contributions to personal pension schemes in paragraph 16.

OTHER WORK EXCEPTIONS NOT RELATED TO AGE

- In relation to pregnancy and maternity discrimination, an employer is not required to make a *non-contractual* payment, such as a discretionary bonus, to a woman on maternity leave if the only condition for eligibility is for the employee to be in active employment (paragraph 17).
- There is a specific exception relating to sexual orientation discrimination relating to benefits dependent on marital status (paragraph 18) in respect of service before the coming into force of the Civil Partnership Act 2004.
- An employer providing services to the public who discriminates in relation to those services against an employee will not be liable for *discrimination at work*. Instead, the employee will have to bring a claim for discrimination in the provision of services (Part 3 of EA 2010).
- Insurance contracts which provide for the payment of different benefits or premiums for men and women, persons who are or are not married or in a civil partnership, pregnancy or maternity or gender reassignment, are lawful if done by reliance on actuarial or other data.

POSITIVE ACTION

Positive *discrimination* may be defined as giving preferential treatment to one or more groups in order, for example, to redress a historical inequality. An example in relation to recruitment would be giving automatic preference to black candidates who have the same qualifications as white applicants for a position. With very limited exceptions, this type of discrimination is not generally permitted under EA 2010, except in relation to disability discrimination where positive discrimination is allowed. However, as will be seen below, section 159 comes close to permitting a measure of positive discrimination in recruitment and promotion if the conditions are met.

Positive *action*, however, is permitted. By positive action is meant measures to increase equality of opportunity by, for example, targeting advertising at a particular group to encourage applicants from that group to come forward. The rules on positive action are found in sections 158 and 159 of the Act.

Section 158 states that positive action measures are not prohibited to alleviate disadvantage experienced by people who

- suffer a disadvantage connected to a protected characteristic
- have particular needs because of that characteristic
- are under-represented in relation to particular activities.

The action taken must be proportionate.

The *Explanatory Notes* provide an example:

> Having identified that its white male pupils are under-performing at maths, a school could run supplementary maths classes exclusively for them.[21]

Section 159 goes somewhat further. Under this section an employer is permitted to take a protected characteristic into consideration when deciding who to recruit or promote, where people having the protected characteristic are at a disadvantage or are under-represented. Two points should be noted. Firstly, this can be done only where the candidates are as qualified as each other. Secondly, the employer is only permitted to take the characteristic *into consideration* on a case-by-case basis – a policy giving automatic preference to the under-represented group would be unlawful.

REFLECTIVE QUESTION

Do you think that section 159 is good policy, or do you think it goes too far – or not far enough?

More examples from the *Explanatory Notes*:

> A police service which employs disproportionately low numbers of people from an ethnic minority background identifies a number of candidates who are equally qualified for recruitment to a post, including a candidate from an under-represented ethnic minority background. It would not be unlawful to give preferential treatment to that candidate, provided the comparative merits of other candidates were also taken into consideration.
>
> An employer offers a job to a woman on the basis that women are under-represented in the company's workforce when there was a male candidate who was more qualified. This would be unlawful direct discrimination.[22]

However, in regard to disability discrimination it *is* permitted to treat a disabled person more favourably than a person who is not disabled.

CASE STUDY

ARCHIBALD v FIFE COUNCIL

In *Archibald v Fife Council* Mrs Archibald, a road sweeper, became unable to do her job and was confined to a wheelchair. She was interviewed at competitive interviews for over 100 alternative jobs but did not succeed in any of the applications. The Supreme Court held that the duty to make reasonable adjustments could extend to placing a disabled person in a post of the same or higher grade without competitive interview, as long, of course, as it was a job for which he or she was suitable. Thus the employer was required in this case to treat a disabled job applicant *more* favourably than a non-disabled one, who would have to go through the competitive interview process.[23]

AN EMPLOYER'S VICARIOUS LIABILITY FOR DISCRIMINATION BY EMPLOYEES

Under section 109, when an act of discrimination is committed by an employee 'in the course of [the employee's] employment', the employer is vicariously liable for the act, even if the employer doesn't know about or approve of the act. The employee himself or herself will also be personally liable under section 110.

The crucial words here are 'in the course of [the employee's] employment'. Until the landmark decision of *Jones v Tower Boot* [24] the courts and tribunals interpreted these words in the narrow sense in which they had been interpreted in the law of torts (civil wrongs which are not a breach of contract – eg the law of trespass). In tort law these words were understood to mean that an employer was liable for an act of an employee which caused injury or damage only if the act was either fully or partly authorised by the employer – ie an act which at least to some extent came under the employee's job duties. This had the unfortunate effect that the employer was not liable for acts of discrimination which had nothing to do with the job. The issue is well illustrated by the facts of *Jones v Tower Boot*, in which the Court of Appeal took a different approach. The court held in this case that the words 'course of the employee's employment' should be understood in the sense that they are used in everyday speech.

CASE STUDY

JONES v TOWER BOOT

Raymondo Jones was of mixed race origin, aged 16, and was starting his first job as a lathe operative in a shoe factory. He was subjected to very unpleasant acts of racial harassment from work colleagues. He was branded with a hot screwdriver, whipped across the legs and metal bolts were thrown at his head. He was also subjected to unpleasant verbal racial abuse. He resigned after a month in the job and claimed race discrimination. The EAT (reversing the employment tribunal's decision) followed the established law and said that the employer could not be liable, as the harassment could not have been said to be in any way part of the employees' job duties. But the Court of Appeal held that the employers *were* liable. The court held that the words 'in the course of [the employee's] employment' should be given the broad meaning they are given in everyday speech, and so could cover acts which were nothing to do with the discriminator's job duties. 'In the course of employment' might cover acts done even while on rest breaks or outside the workplace. Deciding whether an act was in the course of employment in particular cases was a question of fact for each tribunal to resolve.

Discussion point

Why is it the policy under EA 2010 to make the employer liable for discrimination carried out by an employee (as well as the employee)?

This approach was taken up and developed further in two more cases.

CASE STUDIES

CHIEF CONSTABLE OF LINCOLNSHIRE POLICE v STUBBS

In *Chief Constable of Lincolnshire Police v Stubbs* [25] the police force was held liable for acts of sexual harassment of a female officer by a male colleague which took place off-duty at a pub with work colleagues and while at a work-related leaving party. On the facts of the case these situations were held to be an extension of the workplace and the harassment was therefore held to have taken place in the course of employment.

SIDHU v AEROSPACE COMPOSITE TECHNOLOGY

However, in *Sidhu v Aerospace Composite Technology* [26] racial harassment of an employee took place during a weekend day out at a theme park arranged by the employer annually for employees and their families. The Court of Appeal affirmed the employment tribunal decision that this harassment was not 'in the course of employment'. It took place outside the work premises, outside working hours and because families of employees were also present, most of the people at the scene were not employed by the employer.

Discussion point

Are the facts of *Stubbs* and *Sidhu* really so significantly different from each other? The reality is that different employment tribunals may take a different view of similar facts!

Even if the acts were done 'in the course of employment', the employer has a defence under section 109 if it has taken *all reasonable steps* to prevent the employees from doing those acts. Such steps would include:

- having a good equal opportunities policy which has been properly publicised to the workforce: see *Balgobin and Francis v London Borough of Tower Hamlets* [27]

- giving training in the policy
- proper supervision of staff.

Even if the employer has taken some steps, the tribunal must ask whether there were any other reasonable steps it could have taken: see *Canniffe v East Riding Council.* [28]

If the employer is able to avoid liability because it has taken all reasonable steps, the individual employee will still remain personally liable.[29]

A related but separate section (section 111) makes it unlawful to instruct, induce or cause discrimination in relation to any of the protected characteristics. Both the person given the instruction and the intended victim have a claim if they have suffered a 'detriment'. Interestingly, the claims may be made even if the instruction was not carried out. Proceedings may also be taken against the person giving the instruction by the Equality and Human Rights Commission.

For example: a car rental firm instructs a receptionist not to rent cars to anyone of Afro-Caribbean or Asian origin. The receptionist would have a claim against the firm if subjected to a detriment for not doing so. A potential customer would also have a claim against the firm if he or she discovered the instruction had been given and was put off applying to hire a car. (The receptionist's claim against the firm would be brought before the employment tribunal as it relates to employment, while the potential customer's claim would be brought in the county court because it relates to services.[30])

THE LIABILITY OF THE EMPLOYER FOR HARASSMENT BY A THIRD PARTY

Employees will sometimes face problems of harassment in the workplace not at the hands of their employer or fellow employees but by third parties, such as customers or guests. Third parties are, by definition, not employed by the employer and so the rules of vicarious liability under Section 109 are not applicable. Instead, section 40 provides that if, with the employer's knowledge, there has been harassment of an employee by a third party on at least two previous occasions, the employer will be liable if it has not taken reasonably practicable steps to prevent it. It need not be the same third party who has carried out the harassment. The section applies to harassment related to all the protected characteristics (see Chapter 6) apart from marriage and civil partnership and pregnancy and maternity.[31]

CASE STUDY

SHEFFIELD CITY COUNCIL v NOROUZI

Mr Norouzi was a residential social worker of Iranian origin in a small home for troubled children. One of the children was often abusive and offensive to him on racial grounds, including mocking his accent. He raised his concerns with several people over a period of time, but, before any action was taken, he became so upset by the child's behaviour that he went off sick. The EAT concluded that the employer had not taken sufficient steps to deal with the problem and that mocking a person's accent could amount to racial abuse.

Discussion point

How far should employers go in protecting their employees from abuse or harassment from clients or customers?

THE BURDEN OF PROOF IN DISCRIMINATION CLAIMS

Discrimination is often hard to prove. Occasionally there might be a give-away remark by the employer (as, for example, in *Owen & Briggs v James* [32] – 'I cannot understand why any English employer would want to take on a coloured girl when English girls are available'). But it is not usually made explicit why a person was unsuccessful in, for example, a job application. So in order to make it less difficult to prove that discrimination has occurred, the rule is that the employee merely has to produce sufficient evidence from which a court or tribunal *could* conclude that there has been discrimination. In legal parlance this is known as a *prima facie* case. Once the employee has produced such evidence it is for the employer to *disprove* that discrimination has occurred, and if the employer cannot do so, the tribunal must find in favour of the employee. This is usually, therefore, a two-stage process – namely:

- Stage 1
  The employee has to prove facts from which the tribunal *could* conclude, in the absence of an adequate explanation from the employer, that the employer has committed discrimination. This is a *prima facie* case, a case for the employer to answer.
- Stage 2
  If the employee has proved a *prima facie* case, the tribunal will uphold the complaint unless the employer proves it did not commit discrimination – ie proves that there was an innocent explanation for these facts.

A good illustration of how the section operates is the case of *King v Great Britain-China Centre*. Note that this case is being used *as an illustration only* – the law on the burden of proof at that time was slightly different from the position today.

CASE STUDY

KING v GREAT BRITAIN-CHINA CENTRE[33]

Karen Lily King was of Chinese origin, born in China but educated in Britain. She applied for the job of deputy director of the *Great Britain-China Centre*, which aims to promote closer ties between Britain and China. The criteria were that applicants should have first-hand knowledge of China and speak fluent modern Chinese. Ms King did speak fluent modern Chinese and had travelled in China for three months. Eight applicants were short-listed but she was not one of them. None of the five ethnically Chinese applicants for the job was short-listed. In fact, it turned out that no ethnic Chinese person had ever been employed in the Centre! All the short-listed applicants were white, and the successful candidate was a young English graduate in Chinese. The facts strongly suggested that the reason Ms King failed to get the job was race discrimination, and the employer was unable to produce an innocent explanation to disprove her claim.

If these facts were to occur in a case today, the tribunal would be bound to find in favour of Ms King if the employer was unable to provide an innocent explanation.

But in order to succeed, an employee must show a *prima facie* case:

CASE STUDY

LAING v MANCHESTER CITY COUNCIL

In *Laing v Manchester City Council*[34] Mr Laing, a difficult and confrontational employee, came into conflict with Ms Taylor, an inexperienced manager with poor management skills. Mr Laing claimed that the way he had been treated was race discrimination. At the tribunal the employer brought evidence to show that Ms Taylor had poor management skills and treated *all* subordinates in an abrupt fashion. The EAT held that Mr Laing had failed to establish a *prima facie* case and the claim therefore failed at the first stage.

REFLECTIVE QUESTION

One reason why proving a claim is problematic is the difficulty for an employee in getting colleagues to give evidence at the tribunal. Can you remember what legal protection is given to a colleague who gives evidence in a discrimination claim for the claimant, and is badly treated by the employer because of it? See Chapter 6.

THE OBTAINING INFORMATION PROCEDURE (SECTION 138 [35])

Further help for the employee in proving his or her case may be obtained by use of the 'obtaining information' procedure. The employee may send questions to the employer asking about the way he or she was treated, and both the questions and the replies are admissible in evidence. The questions may be sent either before putting in a tribunal claim or once the claim has been presented.[36] If the employer fails to answer a question within eight weeks, or gives an evasive or equivocal reply, the tribunal may draw inferences from this.

So, for example, in the case of *King v Great Britain-China Centre* (above), Ms King – who did send a questionnaire to the Centre – might have asked such questions as:

- 'Why was I not short-listed?'
- 'How many people of ethnic Chinese origin applied for this job, and how many were short-listed?'
- 'How many people of ethnic Chinese origin have been employed in the Centre over the past three years?'

The Centre's replies, or lack of them, would have helped Ms King in proving her case.

The section provides for certain circumstances when the tribunal may not draw inferences, such as where the employer claims that to have answered the questionnaire differently, or at all, might have prejudiced a criminal matter. This assertion by the employer must be 'reasonable'.[37]

ENFORCEMENT

TIME-LIMITS IN MAKING A DISCRIMINATION CLAIM

Claims of discrimination in employment begin in the employment tribunal. No period of continuous employment is needed. The time-limit, under section 123(1), is three months from the act of discrimination, with an extension of time for late applications where the tribunal considers it 'just and equitable'. This gives the tribunal more flexibility in allowing late claims than in relation to late unfair dismissal claims where the statute is differently worded (see Chapter 15).

In *Department of Constitutional Affairs v Jones* a claimant with severe depression and anxiety who missed the deadline in a disability discrimination claim because he had not wanted to admit to himself that he had a disability was allowed to bring a claim out of time.[38]

REMEDIES (SECTION 124)

If the employee's claim is successful, a tribunal may make three orders.

- *A declaration that the employee's rights have been infringed.*
- *An order for compensation.* This has no limit on it, in contrast to the compensation awarded in other claims such as unfair dismissal.
  It will often include compensation for *injury to feelings* (again in contrast to unfair dismissal awards, which may not include such compensation – see Chapter 15). The compensation involved is occasionally for a very large sum, such as £100,000 or more.
  But the Court of Appeal has said that only in 'the most exceptional case' should injury to feelings awards be for more than £30,000 (*Vento v Chief Constable of West Yorkshire Police (No.2)*,[39] updated in *Da'Bell v NSPCC*[40]). In exceptional cases a tribunal may award aggravated or exemplary damages.
- *A recommendation.* Under the law existing before EA 2010, the only recommendation a tribunal could make was for the employer to take action which was likely to reduce the effect of the discrimination *on the claimant.* But since in the majority of discrimination claims the employee has already left the organisation, this remedy was not generally appropriate. Under EA 2010 section 124 a tribunal is now able to give a recommendation for action that will

benefit not only the employee but also any other person. So even though the successful claimant may have left the organisation, the tribunal could still make a recommendation – for example, that the employer adopt an equal opportunities policy which will benefit other employees
If a recommendation is not complied with by the employer without reasonable justification, the tribunal may order compensation instead or increase the amount of compensation if already ordered.

THE EQUALITY AND HUMAN RIGHTS COMMISSION

The Equality and Human Rights Commission (EHRC) was set up under the Equality Act 2006. Its activities include:

- monitoring the effectiveness of discrimination law
- undertaking research and education,
- producing publications, including Codes of Practice
- conducting inquiries and investigations
- assisting in bringing litigation.[41]

An investigation by the EHRC may be undertaken if it suspects that a person or organisation has committed an 'unlawful act' of discrimination. After the investigation, the EHRC will draw up a report which will only be finalised once the party investigated has been sent a draft and has had at least 28 days to make representations.[42] If the EHRC is satisfied that the party investigated has committed an unlawful act, it may issue an 'Unlawful Act Notice' and require the party involved to prepare an action plan.[43] The person may appeal to a court or tribunal within six weeks claiming that he or she has not committed the act or that the action plan is unreasonable.[44] The EHRC may apply to a court at any time within five years for an order requiring the person to act in accordance with the action plan.[45]

It will often be more effective for the EHRC to seek progress by agreement. The EHRC is therefore given the power to enter into a legally binding agreement with a person who undertakes not to commit an unlawful act, and in return EHRC undertakes not to proceed with an investigation or issue an Unlawful Act Notice.[46]

In the late 1990s the Commission for Racial Equality (a predecessor of the EHRC) carried out a lengthy investigation into racism in the British Army, particularly in the Household Division (the Guards). In the light of major improvements made by the army, the Commission decided not to issue a Non-Discrimination Notice (the equivalent of the Unlawful Act Notice).

Discriminatory advertisements, as we have seen, are unlawful, but it is the EHRC who may bring a court action, under section 25 of the Equality Act 2006 – not an individual.

PUBLIC SECTOR EQUALITY DUTY

Under section 149 of EA 2010, all public authorities listed in Schedule 19 are subject to an *equality duty* which requires them in carrying out their functions to have due regard to:

- the need to eliminate prohibited conduct
- advancing equality of opportunity
- fostering good relations.

To take examples from the *Explanatory Notes*, the duty might lead a local authority to:

- target training and mentoring schemes at disabled people to enable them to stand as local councillors
- review its policy of Internet-only access to council services, which might not meet the needs of older people
- introduce measures to try to foster links between people from different religious groups in the area.[47]

The duty is also imposed on some other public bodies in respect of their public functions.

As for the private and voluntary sector, large employers employing 250 or more employees in the UK will be expected to publish information on a voluntary basis about the differences in pay between their male and female employees. If sufficient progress on voluntary publication has not taken place by April 2013, the Government may introduce regulations under section 78.

EQUALITY OF TERMS FOR EQUAL WORK

That female employees receive lower pay than comparable male employees is a major and long-standing problem, and although there has been legislation in force for around 35 years to deal with the issue, there is still significant inequality. Average weekly earnings for a full-time male employee are currently around 17% higher than for a comparable female employee. The issue of equal pay for women was the subject of the British film *Made in Dagenham*, released in 2010: a dramatisation of the female workers' strike at Ford's Dagenham assembly plant in 1968.

The right to equality of pay and other terms between men and women under their contracts – if they are employed to do equal work – is dealt with in Part 5 Chapter 3 of EA 2010. It was formerly dealt with in the Equal Pay Act 1970. Typically, the claimant is a woman, and so we refer below to a female claimant throughout, but of course if a man is receiving lower pay than a comparable female employee, he too will be able to claim equality. The inequality does not just refer to basic pay but all aspects of the pay and benefits package such as overtime rates, non-discretionary bonuses and fringe benefits, and also non-monetary terms such as leave entitlement. As with other discrimination claims discussed above, much of the case law under the previous statute is thought to be still relevant and so is referred to below.

Equality in relation to an employer's occupational pension scheme has its own parallel regime under the Act. Under section 67 there must be equal treatment of men and women in relation both to the terms on which they are permitted to join the pension scheme, and to the terms on which they are treated once they have become members. As with the equal work provisions there is a 'material factor' defence (see below) available to the employer under section 69.

Under section 70 the equal terms part of the Act does not operate where the sex discrimination provisions apply, and vice versa. The equal terms provisions cover sex discrimination in relation to *the terms of the contract* whereas the sex discrimination provisions deal with sex discrimination in matters *outside the contract*, such as

- non-contractual pay and benefits
- promotion, transfer and training
- job offers of employment or appointment.

However, there is an exception to this where there is no comparator doing equal work – see below, on section 71.

WHO IS THE COMPARATOR?

Under this part of the Act, the woman must compare herself to *an actual named male comparator or comparators*, in contrast to the sex discrimination provisions we saw in Chapter 6, where she can compare herself to either an actual comparator or a hypothetical one. This can be a major problem for the claimant, especially if she works for an organisation in which the jobs are in practice segregated along gender lines – for example, all the canteen chefs are female. The problem is lessened in two ways. Firstly, as we will see, it is possible for the claimant to compare herself to a man doing a totally different job, if it is comparable work. So although the canteen chef in our example might not have a male chef with whom to compare her pay, there might be a painter working for the same company, whose job may be claimed to be comparable in terms of the effort and skill required, to whom she can compare herself.

Secondly, where there is no comparator doing equal work, section 71 enables a person who is treated less favourably than others by being paid less either

- because of the person's sex, or
- because of a combination of two protected characteristics including sex,

to pursue a claim for direct or dual (combined) discrimination in these circumstances, if there is evidence of such discrimination.

An example is given in the *Explanatory Notes*:

> An employer tells a female employee 'I would pay you more if you were a man,' or tells a black female employee 'I would pay you more if you were a white man.' In the absence of any actual male comparator the woman cannot bring a claim for equality of terms but she can bring a claim of direct sex discrimination or dual discrimination (combining sex and race) against the employer.[48]

Leaving aside the possibility of a claim for direct sex discrimination or dual (combined) discrimination, how may an equality of terms claim be made?

Under section 65 of EA 2010, a claim may be made if

- ss(1)(a) – the woman is employed on work like the comparator's work
- ss(1)(b) – the woman is employed on work rated as equivalent to the comparator's
- ss(1)(c) – the woman is employed on work of equal value to the comparator's.

As we will see below, the first category covers a situation where the male comparator is doing broadly the same job as the claimant. 'Work rated as equivalent' and 'work of equal value' cover situations where the job of the comparator is quite different but comparable.

The right to equality in any of these three situations is given by a *term implied by statute*, which we saw in Chapter 2. Section 66 of the Act says that the woman's contract is to be treated as including a *sex equality clause*. This implied term has the effect of giving the woman the legal right to have her contract modified to bring it in line with the contract of her comparator.

The comparison must be made on a term-by-term basis.

CASE STUDY

HAYWARD v CAMMELL LAIRD

In the leading case of *Hayward v Cammell Laird*, the Supreme Court held that an employer cannot claim that less favourable terms in the woman's contract are offset by other terms which are more favourable. In the case itself the court therefore held that a canteen chef was entitled to the same basic rate of pay as her male comparators (a painter, engineer and joiner) even though she had other terms of employment (sickness benefits, holidays, meal breaks) which were better than her comparators'.[49]

Under section 79 the comparator must work for the same employer, or an associate employer, either at the same establishment or at a different establishment in Great Britain which observes common terms and conditions of employment. For these purposes 'common terms and conditions' means terms and conditions which are substantially comparable on a broad basis rather than the same terms and conditions.

It should be noted that the class of comparators defined in section 79 is more restricted than applies under Article 157 of the Treaty on the Functioning of the European Union (TFEU) (formerly Article 141 EC). Article 157, which is EU law, takes precedence over EA 2010 which is domestic UK law, and under Article 157 the crucial question is whether the applicant and the comparators are employed 'in the same establishment or service'. Thus the EAT has allowed a teacher employed by a Scottish local education authority to bring an equal pay claim comparing herself with a teacher employed by a different education authority in Scotland.[50] However, according to the European Court of Justice, a situation where the differences in pay of employees performing work of equal value cannot be attributed to a single source does not come within Article 157. This is because there is no body which is responsible for the inequality and which could restore equal treatment.[51]

The effect of the sex equality clause is that any term in a person's contract (whether concerned with pay or not) which is less favourable than in the contract of a person of the opposite sex is modified so as to be not less favourable.

CASE STUDY

BROWNBILL v ST HELENS & KNOWSLEY HOSPITAL NHS TRUST

The complainants in this case chose comparators who earned higher premium rates than themselves for working unsocial hours. The Court of Appeal held that there might be non-discriminatory reasons for this, but the evidence relating to this contractual difference had to be considered by the tribunal. This was despite the fact that the female complainants earned more overall than their male comparators.

Discussion point

Even if a female earns more than a male comparator, the court will still look at individual terms to make sure that any differences are examined. Do you think that this is fair? Should it be possible to compare the value of the contract as a whole rather than each term?

In *Evesham v North Hertfordshire Health Authority* [52] the EAT held that this meant being placed at the same point on an incremental scale as the comparator, not being placed on that scale at a level that was commensurate with her experience. It should also be noted that paragraph 2 of Article 157 states that 'pay' means 'the ordinary basic minimum wage or salary and any other consideration, whether in cash or in kind, which the worker receives directly or indirectly, in respect of his employment, from his employer'. According to the European Court of Justice, a benefit is pay if the worker is entitled to receive it from his or her employer by reason of the existence of the employment relationship. Thus Article 157 covers not only occupational retirement and survivors' pensions,[53] travel concessions on retirement, end-of-year bonuses and statutory and contractual severance payments, but also paid leave or overtime for participation in training courses given by an employer under a statutory scheme.[54] Attention focuses on each aspect of remuneration rather than on any general overall assessment of all the consideration paid to the workers.[55] However, for the purposes of comparison, the Court of Appeal has accepted that attention should focus on all the monetary payments that an employee receives for performing the contract during normal working hours.[56]

WHAT IS 'WORK LIKE THE COMPARATOR'S WORK'?

This is the simplest route to claiming equality of terms – the claimant is claiming that the work she is doing is like that of her comparator. Once the woman has shown that her work is of the same or broadly similar nature as that of her comparator, unless the employer can prove that any differences are of no practical importance in relation to terms and conditions of employment, that person is to be regarded as employed on 'like work'.[57] In comparing work, a broad approach should be taken and attention must be paid to the frequency with which any differences occur in practice as well as their nature and extent. Trivial differences or 'differences not likely in the real world to be reflected in terms and conditions of employment' are not to be taken into account.[58] Similarly, tribunals are required to investigate the actual work done rather than rely on theoretical contractual obligations. The performance of supervisory duties may constitute 'things done' of practical importance[59] but the time at which the work is done would seem to be irrelevant.

In *Dugdale v Kraft Foods*,[60] the men and women were employed on broadly similar work but only men worked the night shift. It was held that the hours at which the work was performed did not prevent the same *basic rate* of pay being required because the men could be compensated for the night shift by an additional payment.

The work is not like work if persons of one sex are remunerated for something which persons of the other sex do not do.[61] It is not permissible, however, to ignore part of the work which a person actually performs on the grounds that his or her pay includes an additional element in respect of that work,[62] although there might be an exception where part of the work is, in effect, a separate and distinct job. Finally, in determining whether differences are of practical importance, a useful guide is whether the differences are such as to put the two employments in different categories or grades in an evaluation study.[63]

WHAT IS 'WORK RATED AS EQUIVALENT'?

If the only situation in which a woman could claim equality of terms was where she was doing work which is broadly the same as that of her comparator, it would certainly be a valuable legal right – but only up to a point. It would not deal with the inequality of terms experienced by those working in low-paid occupations which are carried out predominantly by women (often, in the case law, for local authorities), such as cleaners, caterers and carers. The pay for these 'women's jobs' has historically often been lower than comparable but different male jobs, such as work for men as street cleaners, refuse collectors and gardeners. So EA 2010 provides for another route to equality of terms in which the woman compares herself with a man doing a totally different job but one that is comparable in the demands of the job and the skills required. This second way in which a woman can claim equality of terms is if her job and that of the male comparator have been rated as equivalent under a job evaluation study which the employer has voluntarily carried out.

Job evaluation studies decide the relative importance of different jobs within an organisation. There are a number of different reasons why an employer might carry out such a study. These might include, for example:

- employee dissatisfaction with the way jobs are graded
- too many job grades
- problems with recruitment and retention
- equality of terms issues.[64]

According to section 65(4) of EA 2010, a person's ('A') work will only be regarded as rated as equivalent to that of a person of the opposite sex ('B') if either

- it has been given equal value under a job evaluation study which gives an equal value to A's job and B's job in terms of the demands made on a worker, or
- it would have given an equal value to A's job and B's job in those terms if the job evaluation study had not been carried out in a discriminatory way, because it set values for men which were different from those it set for women.

An example is given in the *Explanatory Notes*:

> A job evaluation study rated the jobs of women and their better-paid male comparators as not equivalent. If the study had not given undue weight to the skills involved in the men's jobs, it would have rated the jobs as equivalent. An equality clause would operate in this situation.[65]

Section 80(5) states that the study must be undertaken with reference to factors such as effort, skill and decision-making. In other words, a job evaluation study will only enable a woman to claim equal terms if it has been properly carried out by the employer with reference to objective criteria, and not on a subjective (ie biased) basis.

In *Springboard Trust v Robson* [66] it was accepted that the applicant was employed on work rated as equivalent, notwithstanding that the comparator's job scored different points, where the result of converting the points to grades provided for under the evaluation scheme was that the jobs were to be treated as in the same grade.

A valid job evaluation exercise will evaluate the job and not the person performing it, and if evaluation studies are to be relied on, they must be analytical in the sense of dividing a physical or abstract whole into its constituent parts. It is clearly insufficient if benchmark jobs – ie jobs the employer considers to have been correctly graded – have been evaluated using a system of job evaluation whereas the jobs of the applicant and comparators have not.[67] Employers are not prevented from using physical effort as a criterion if the tasks involved objectively require a certain level of physical strength, so long as the evaluation system as a whole precludes all sex discrimination by taking into account other criteria.[68] If the work has been rated as equivalent, a claimant does not have to show that the employees concerned have actually been paid in accordance with the evaluation scheme.[69]

WHAT IS 'WORK OF EQUAL VALUE'?

The previous category is of great assistance to the claimant where the employer has carried out a job evaluation study. But employers have no legal requirement to carry out such studies. If an employer has not done so, an employee wishing to compare her terms to a man carrying out a different but comparable job would have no means of comparison. For this reason there is a third way of presenting an equal terms claim – namely, the woman claiming that her job is *of equal value* to that of her male comparator. As with work rated as equivalent, this category of case is used to compare quite different sorts of jobs – for example, the job of a cook may be compared to a painter (*Hayward v Cammell Laird*) or a speech therapist to a psychologist (*Enderby v Frenchay Health Authority*). Again, the comparison means looking at the demands of the two jobs such as effort, skill and decision-making. A tribunal deciding an equal value claim will generally (though not always) decide the issue by commissioning an independent expert to carry out a report which compares the jobs in question (section 131). Because the case cannot not be decided until the report is completed (unless the tribunal withdraws its commission), this used to lead to delays of considerable length in processing equal value claims. In recent years, however, reforms to the procedure have meant that cases are heard more quickly.

The Supreme Court has ruled that an equal value claim can be brought so long as the applicant's comparator is not engaged on like work or work rated as equivalent.[70]

THE MATERIAL FACTOR DEFENCE

Where a woman can show that she is employed on work like her comparator's, or work rated as equivalent or of equal value, section 69 says that an employer can still defend the claim for equal terms by showing that the inequality is due to a *material factor.* There are two types of material factor provided by the section. Put simply, these amount to saying that the reason for the inequality is either not based on sex at all, or even if it does involve a particular disadvantage for one sex, it is justified because it is a proportionate means of achieving a legitimate aim.

A material factor which does not involve treating the claimant less favourably because of her sex – ie there is no *direct discrimination*

If the woman's terms are less good than those of her comparator but the reason is a 'material factor' which is nothing to do with the difference of sex, then the employer has a defence to the claim. The following are examples under the previous law of reasons which may come under the material factor defence: the method of entering employment,[71] working in a different part of the country,[72] responsibility allowances,[73] financial constraints,[74] longer service,[75] physical effort and unpleasantness,[76] better academic qualifications, and higher productivity.

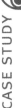

CASE STUDY

RAINEY v GREATER GLASGOW HEALTH BOARD

In *Rainey v Greater Glasgow Health Board*, a new service for fitting artificial limbs (prosthetics) within the NHS was set up in Scotland. Mrs Rainey joined the service straight after qualifying and received an annual salary of £7,295. In order to attract enough experienced prosthetists the Board offered 20 staff from the private sector, who all happened to be men, their existing higher salaries. Mr Crumlin, who was Mrs Rainey's chosen comparator, received an annual salary of £10,085. Mrs Rainey brought an equal terms claim. The Supreme Court held that the Board had a defence to the claim. It was not just personal qualities such as skill, experience and training which a person brings to a job which would justify inequality of terms between the man and woman. 'Material' meant 'significant and relevant' and all the circumstances of the case had to be considered.

There was objective justification given the need to expand the service within a reasonable time.[77] However, even if there is no direct discrimination involved, there may be indirect discrimination – in which case the second type of material factor defence may be available.

A material factor which involves a particular disadvantage for one sex but is justified

In this category of cases, one sex has been put at a disadvantage (ie suffered indirect discrimination – see Chapter 6) but it is justified because the inequality is a proportionate means of achieving a legitimate aim.

CASE STUDY

BLACKBURN v CHIEF CONSTABLE OF WEST MIDLANDS POLICE

In *Blackburn v Chief Constable of West Midlands Police*,[78] Ms Blackburn was a front-line police officer in the West Midlands police force. Front-line officers generally had to work a 24/7 rotating shift pattern which involved some **night-time working**. As a reward for this, a bonus was paid to those who worked the shift pattern. Ms Blackburn was excused from working the 24/7 shift because of childcare responsibility and therefore did not receive the bonus. She claimed that this was an unequal term in her contract which put female front-line officers at a particular disadvantage because of their childcare responsibilities. She claimed that she should receive the bonus too even though she did not work the 24/7 shift. The Court of Appeal held that the claim failed. The wish to reward night-time working was a legitimate aim, and paying the bonus to those who worked it was a proportionate way of achieving that aim. It was difficult to see how that objective could be achieved if those who did *not* work the shift were also paid the same amount.

The fact that inequality is caused by different collective bargaining arrangements is not a justification.[79]

RED-CIRCLING

The practice of drawing a circle around the names of those within a protected group – for example, employees demoted through no fault of their own as the result of reorganisation – is one device that has to be scrutinised because it may be in breach of the law on equal terms. Such action may be perfectly lawful – eg where employees accept lower-paid work in a redundancy situation – but if the underlying reason for different treatment is sex-based, it cannot be accepted as a defence.[80] Employers have to justify the inclusion of every employee in a red-circled group and must prove that at the time of admission to the circle the more favourable terms were related to a consideration other than sex.[81] Again, if a person's wages are protected on a transfer, perhaps because of age or illness, tribunals must be satisfied that this was not merely because of sex or that the new job was not one which was open only to one sex. The prolonged maintenance of a red circle may not only be contrary to good industrial relations practice but may in all the circumstances give rise to a doubt whether the employers have discharged the statutory burden of proof imposed on them. Thus in *Home Office v Bailey*,[82] the EAT ruled that arrangements that were objectively justified in 1987 provided an unsatisfactory explanation 12 years later.

ENFORCEMENT

Where there is a dispute as to the effect of an equality clause, both the employee and the employer can apply to an employment tribunal. Equality of terms claims must be lodged on or before a qualifying date. Normally, this will be six months after the last day on which the claimant was employed.[83] Similarly, where the proceedings relate to a period during which a 'stable employment relationship' (a series of fixed- or short-term contracts) subsists, the qualifying date is six months after the day on which that stable employment relationship ended.[84] Arrears can be awarded back to the 'arrears date' in respect of any time when there was unequal pay. Normally, the arrears date will be six years before the date on which the claim is made.[85] Complainants must identify a comparable person of the opposite sex and cannot launch an application without some sort of *prima facie* case.[86] Although, as said above, a comparison cannot be made with a hypothetical person, the ECJ has decided that Article 157 EC allows a complainant to compare himself or herself with a previous job incumbent.[87] The EAT has now held, however, that a comparison may not be made with a successor in the post.[88]

THE MATERNITY EQUALITY CLAUSE

The *sex equality clause*, as we have seen, is implied into the employment contract to remove inequality between men and women in the terms of the contract.

Under section 74 a *maternity equality clause* is another statutory implied term which has the effect that a woman's pay is protected while she is on maternity leave. The protection is threefold:

- Any pay increase a woman receives (or would have received if she had not been on maternity leave) must be taken into account in the calculation of her maternity-related pay.
- Pay, including any bonus, must be paid to the woman at the time she would have received it if she had not been on maternity leave.
- On a woman's return to work following maternity leave, her pay must take account of any pay increase which she would have received if she had not been on statutory maternity leave.[89]

There are some examples in the *Explanatory Notes*:

> Early in her maternity leave, a woman receiving maternity-related pay becomes entitled to an increase of pay. If her terms of employment do not already provide for the increase to be reflected in her maternity-related pay, the employer must recalculate her maternity pay to take account of the increment.
>
> A woman becomes entitled to a contractual bonus for work she undertook before she went on maternity leave. The employer cannot delay payment of the bonus and must pay it to her when it would have been paid had she not been on maternity leave.[90]

A clause with similar effect is implied into an occupational pension scheme under section 75.

Under section 76 the pregnancy and maternity discrimination sections of the Act (see Chapter 6) do not apply where a maternity equality clause or rule operates. This section parallels the mutual exclusion of the equal work and sex discrimination claims under section 70. The maternity equality clause applies in relation to discrimination in relation to the terms of the contract, whereas the maternity discrimination provisions prohibit discrimination in relation to non-contractual pay and benefits such as promotion, transfer and training and in relation to offers of employment or appointment.

The *Explanatory Notes* give a further example:

> A woman who is in line for promotion tells her employer that she is pregnant. The employer tells the woman he will not promote her because she is likely to be absent on maternity leave during a very busy period. This will be direct pregnancy discrimination and is not a situation where the *maternity equality clause* will operate, because it is not discrimination regarding a term of the woman's contract.[91]

DISCUSSIONS WITH COLLEAGUES

Section 77 aims to protect a person who tries to find out from discussions with colleagues if her contract has unequal terms. The section makes unenforceable terms in the contract – known colloquially as 'gagging clauses' – that prevent or restrict people from disclosing their pay, or asking colleagues about their pay if this is done with a view to finding out if differences exist that are related to a protected characteristic. Any action taken against them by the employer as a result of their doing so is treated as victimisation, as defined in section 27 (see Chapter 6). But this is only if the purpose of the disclosure or the enquiry is to find out if there is discrimination occurring. If the disclosure is for some other reason, the contract term will be enforceable.

Examples are provided in the *Explanatory Notes*:

> A female employee thinks she is underpaid compared with a male colleague. She asks him what he is paid, and he tells her. The employer takes disciplinary action against the man as a result. The man can bring a claim for victimisation against the employer for disciplining him.
>
> A female employee who discloses her pay to one of her employer's competitors with a view to getting a better offer could be in breach of a confidentiality clause in her contract. The employer could take action against her in relation to that breach because her disclosure did not relate to lower pay resulting from discrimination.[92]

- There are exceptional situations where it is permissible to discriminate. These include where there is an occupational requirement., Positive discrimination, which means giving preferential treatment to the person with a protected characteristic, is not generally permitted – but positive *action* measures which increase equality of opportunity are permitted if they are proportionate.
- Under section 108, when an act of discrimination is committed by an employee 'in the course of [the employee's] employment', the employer is vicariously liable for the act, even if the employer does not know about or approve of the act. The employee himself or herself will also be personally liable under section 110.
- Once the employee has produced *prima facie* evidence of discrimination, it is for the employer to *disprove* that discrimination has occurred, and if the employer cannot do so, the tribunal must find in favour of the employee.
- The choice of remedies awarded by an employment tribunal are a declaration, compensation, and/or a recommendation.
- The body which oversees and helps to enforce discrimination law is the Equality and Human Rights Commission.
- All public authorities listed in Schedule 19 are subject to an equality duty in carrying out their functions.
- Men and women have the right to equality of contract terms due to the implied *sex equality clause* if they are employed on work like their comparator, or work which has been rated as equivalent or is work of equal value.
- An employer can defend the claim for equal terms by showing that the inequality is due to a *material factor.*
- A maternity equality clause is a statutory implied term which has the effect that a woman's pay is protected while she is on maternity leave.

REFERENCES

1 **This chapter contains extracts from or close paraphrasing of legislation, and explanatory notes to that legislation which is on the opsi.gov.uk**

website (and its successor) and is subject to crown copyright. It also contains other public sector information. The reproduction of this material here is licensed under the open government licence v1.0

2 Equality Act 2010 *Explanatory Notes* (August 2010) revised edition, page 205 paragraph 977

3 (2009) IRLR 884

4 See *Explanatory Notes* page 66 paragraph 787

5 *Ibid* page 167 paragraph 789

6 See *ibid* page 167 paragraph 790

7 *Ibid* page 168 paragraph 793

8 *Ibid* page 169 paragraph 796

9 Unsuccessfully challenged in *R (on the application of Age UK) v Secretary of State for Business, Innovation and Skills* (2009) IRLR 1017

10 Equality Act 2010 Schedule 9 paragraph 10(1)

11 *Ibid* Paragraph 10(2)

12 *Explanatory Notes* page 173 paragraph 824

13 Equality Act 2010 Schedule 9 paragraph 10(3)

14 (2009) IRLR 576

15 The case was actually decided under the equivalent provisions in the Employment Equality (Age) Regulations

16 *Explanatory Notes* page 174 paragraph 826

17 *Ibid* page 175 paragraph 834

18 *Ibid* page 176 paragraph 837

19 *Ibid*

20 *Ibid* page 177 paragraph 841

21 *Ibid* page 113 paragraph 517

22 *Ibid* page 114 paragraph 521

23 (2004) IRLR 651

24 (1997) IRLR 168

25 (1999) IRLR 81

26 (2000) IRLR 602

27 (1987) IRLR 401

28 (2000) IRLR 555

29 EA 2010 section 110(2)

30 See similar example in *Explanatory Notes* page 84 paragraph 367

31 *Ibid* page 39 paragraph 146

32 (1982) IRLR 502

33 (1991) IRLR 513

34 (2006) IRLR 748

35 And see the Equality Act 2010 (Obtaining Information) Order 2010 SI 2010/2194

36 *Ibid* Regulation 4. If the questions are to be sent after presenting a tribunal claim, this must be within 28 days of submitting the claim

37 EA 2010 section 138(5)

38 (2008) IRLR 128

39 (2003) IRLR 102

40 (2010) IRLR 19

41 See Part 1 of the Equality Act 2006

42 *Ibid* section 20

43 *Ibid* sections 21 and 22

44 *Ibid* section 21(5)

45 *Ibid* section 22(6)(c)

46 *Ibid* section 23

47 See *Explanatory Notes* page 107 paragraph 484

48 *Ibid* page 60 paragraph 246

49 (1988) IRLR 257

50 *South Ayrshire Council v Morton* (2002) IRLR 256

51 *Allonby v Accrington and Rossendale College* (2004) IRLR 224 and *Armstrong v Newcastle NHS Trust* (2006) IRLR 124

52 (1999) IRLR 155

53 See *Ten Oever's* case [*ten Oever v Stichting Bedrijfspensioenfonds voor het Glazenwassers- en Schoonmaakbedrijf*] (1993) IRLR 601

54 See *Botel's* case [*Arbeiterwolfahrt der Stadt Berlin v Botel*] (1992) IRLR 423

55 See *Brunnhofer v Bank der Österreichischen Postsparkasse AG* (2001) IRLR 571. See also *Hayward v Cammell Laird* above, footnote 49

56 *Degnan v Redcar B.C.* (2005) IRLR 615

57 EA 2010 section 65(2)(b)

58 See *Capper Pass Ltd v Lowton* (1976) IRLR 366

59 See *Eaton v Nuttall* (1977) IRLR 71

60 (1976) IRLR 368

61 See *Thomas v* NCB (1987) IRLR 451 and *Calder v Rowntree Mackintosh* (1993) IRLR 212

62 See *Maidment v Cooper & Co.* (1978) IRLR 462

63 See *British Leyland v Powell* (1978) IRLR 57

64 Taken from the ACAS booklet *Job Evaluation: Considerations and risks*, which can be downloaded from the website http://www.acas.org.uk/CHttpHandler.ashx?id= 922&p=0 [accessed 18 October 2010]. **THIS INFORMATION IS SUBJECT TO CROWN COPYRIGHT**

65 *Explanatory Notes* page 56 paragraph 221

66 (1992) IRLR 261

67 See *Bromley v Quick Ltd* (1988) IRLR 249

68 See *Rummler v Dato-Druck GmbH* (1987) IRLR 32

69 See *O'Brien v Sim-Chem Ltd* (1980) IRLR 373

70 See *Pickstone v Freemans plc* (1988) IRLR 357

71 See *Rainey v Greater Glasgow Health Board* (1987) IRLR 26

72 *NAAFI v Varley* (1976) IRLR 408

73 *Avon and Somerset Police Authority v Emery* (1981) ICR 229

74 *Beneviste v University of Southampton* (1989) IRLR 122

75 On the relationship between experience and the better performance of duties see *Cadman v Health and Safety Executive* (2006) IRLR 969

76 *Christie v Haith Ltd* (2003) IRLR 670

77 *Rainey v Greater Glasgow Health Board* (1987) IRLR 26

78 (2009) IRLR 135

79 *Enderby v Frenchay Health Authority* (1993) IRLR 591

80 See *Snoxell v Vauxhall Motors* (1997) IRLR 123

81 See *Methuen v Cow Industrial Polymers* (1980) IRLR 289

82 (2005) IRLR 757

83 Equality Act 2010 section 129

84 *Ibid*

85 *Ibid* section 132

86 See *Clwyd C.C. v Leverton* (1985) IRLR 197

87 See *Kells v Pilkington plc* (2002) IRLR 693 and *Alabaster v Barclays Bank (No. 2)* (2005) IRLR 576

88 *Walton Centre for Neurology v Bewley* (2008) IRLR 588

89 *Explanatory Notes* page 61 paragraphs 253–5

90 *Ibid* page 62 paragraph 256

91 See *ibid* page 63 paragraph 268

92 *Ibid* page 64 paragraph 271

EXPLORE FURTHER

Reading

- Smith, I. and Thomas, G. (2010) *Smith & Wood's Employment Law*. Butterworths, Chapter 5.
- Wadham, J., Ruebain, D., Robinson, A. and Uppal, S. (eds) (2010) *Blackstone's Guide to the Equality Act 2010*. Oxford University Press.

Websites

- ACAS www.acas.org.uk
- Chartered Institute of Personnel and Development www.cipd.co.uk
- Department for Business Innovation and Skills www.bis.gov.uk
- Directgov – Employment www.direct.gov.uk
- Equality and Human Rights Commission http://www.equalityhuman rights.com

CHAPTER 8

Parental Rights

CHAPTER OVERVIEW

This chapter discusses the rights of parents in certain circumstances – in particular, the rights of pregnant women and those who have recently given birth together with the right to ordinary, compulsory and additional maternity leave. Other rights examined here are the rules associated with parental leave, adoption leave and paternity leave. We then consider the right to time off to deal with emergencies and the right to ask for more flexible working arrangements for the care of children and adults.

LEARNING OUTCOMES

After studying this chapter[1] you will be able to:

- understand and explain the legal principles that apply in relation to 'family-friendly' rights for primary carers, including maternity, paternity, parental and adoption leave
- advise colleagues on the employer's role in periods of leave, such as ensuring the right of employees to return to their jobs after leave, the position of replacement employees, and the possible duty to carry out a risk assessment in relation to a pregnant employee.

TIME OFF FOR ANTENATAL CARE

Irrespective of the length of service or the number of hours she works, a pregnant woman who, on the advice of a registered medical practitioner, midwife or health visitor, has made an appointment to receive antenatal care has the right not to be unreasonably refused time off during working hours to enable her to keep the appointment. Apart from the first appointment, the woman may be required to produce a certificate and some documentary evidence of the appointment for the employer's inspection. A woman who is permitted such time off is entitled to be paid for her absence at the appropriate hourly rate.[2]

If time off is refused or the employer has failed to pay the whole or part of any amount to which she feels she is entitled, a woman can complain to an employment tribunal. Unless the tribunal allows a late claim to be made, her claim must be presented within three months of the date of the appointment concerned.[3] Where a tribunal finds that the complaint is well-founded, it must make a declaration to that effect, and if time off has been unreasonably refused, the employer will be ordered to pay a sum equal to that which she would have been entitled to had the time off not been refused. If the complaint is that the employer failed to pay the amount to which she was entitled, the employer must pay the amount that the tribunal finds due to her. Any payment made to the woman under her contract in respect of a period of time off under this section, however, goes towards discharging the liability under the statute. Conversely, any payment made as a result of this section goes towards discharging any contractual liability to pay for the period of time off.[4]

REFLECTIVE QUESTION

Is the issue of what is an unreasonable refusal likely to cause problems of uncertainty?

MATERNITY LEAVE

European Community law, in particular the Pregnant Workers Directive,[5] and the European Court of Justice, have played an important part in developing rules that protect women during their pregnancy and maternity leave period. The CJEU has regarded discrimination against pregnant women as acts of sex discrimination which are in breach of Article 157 of the Treaty on the Functioning of the European Union (ex-Article 141 TEC) and the Equal Opportunities and Equal Treatment (EOET) Directive.[6] We dealt with pregnancy and maternity discrimination in Chapter 7, but here we consider the related topic of maternity leave.

Part VIII of the ERA 1996 contains provisions for maternity rights, and further detail is provided in the Maternity and Parental Leave Regulations 1999 (MPL Regulations),[7] as amended.

ORDINARY MATERNITY LEAVE AND ADDITIONAL MATERNITY LEAVE

In the past all pregnant employees were entitled to a period of 26 weeks' **ordinary maternity leave** no matter how short a period of time they had been employed by their current employer, but only employees with a minimum of six months' service were entitled to a further 26 weeks' **additional maternity leave**. This changed from April 2007, when the right to additional maternity leave became available to all those who are entitled to ordinary maternity leave. All pregnant employees are therefore now entitled to a maximum of 52 weeks' maternity leave, made up of 26 weeks' ordinary maternity leave and 26 weeks' additional maternity leave. The additional maternity leave period begins on the day after the last day of the ordinary maternity leave period.

Although the ordinary maternity leave will almost always be a maximum period of 26 weeks, it can be a longer period. Firstly, it will always include the two-week **compulsory maternity leave** period (four weeks for those who work in a factory), beginning with the day of the birth (see below), even if (which is unlikely) this makes the ordinary maternity leave longer than 26 weeks in total. Secondly, the ordinary maternity leave may be extended beyond 26 weeks if there is another law which prohibits her from working after the end of the leave because she has recently given birth. But these exceptions will rarely be applicable.

Previously, there were important differences between the rights of the employee during the two leave periods, but there is now little to distinguish them. One difference that remains is in respect of the right to return to work – see below.

Maternity leave is taken before and/or after the '**expected week of childbirth**'. This is defined as the week (beginning with midnight between Saturday and Sunday) in which it is expected that childbirth will occur.[8] The employee may decide when to start her leave, but this cannot be earlier than the beginning of the 11th week before the beginning of the expected week of childbirth.[9]

Regulation 2 of the MPL Regulations defines childbirth as 'the birth of a living child or the birth of a child whether living or dead after 24 weeks of pregnancy'. This means that a woman who gives birth to a stillborn child after 24 weeks of pregnancy will be entitled to the same leave as a person who gave birth to a live child.

THE EMPLOYEE'S DUTY TO NOTIFY THE EMPLOYER

In order to enable the employer to make plans to deal with her absence on maternity leave, the employee is ordinarily required to give advance notification to the employer. Regulation 4 states that an employee's entitlement to maternity leave is conditional on the following:[10]

- that no later than the 15th week before her expected week of childbirth she notifies her employer of her pregnancy and the date on which she intends to start her ordinary maternity leave. If it is not reasonably practicable to inform the employer by this time, the requirement is that notice must be provided as soon as is reasonably practicable. The employee may subsequently vary the date, provided that she does so at least 28 days before the date to be varied or the new date, whichever is earlier
- that the employee must give these notices in writing if the employer so requests
- that the employer is able to request, for inspection, a certificate from a registered medical practitioner or a registered midwife stating the expected week of childbirth.

However, Regulation 6 provides exceptions to the need for advance notification. This regulation deals with a situation where an employee delays taking the leave and tries to continue working for as long as possible before the birth. Before she has commenced her leave she is then either absent from work due to the pregnancy or actually gives birth. Under Regulation 6, if the ordinary maternity leave has not commenced

- by the first day after the beginning of the fourth week before the expected week of childbirth on which the employee is absent from work wholly or partly because of pregnancy, or
- by the day on which childbirth occurs,

then the ordinary maternity leave automatically commences on the day following that day. But this is provided that the employee notifies her employer, in writing if requested, as soon as reasonably practicable about the reason for the absence or the birth.

For example: Gillian wants to delay taking her maternity leave as long as possible so that the family will not suffer a drop in income. She does not notify her employer of her pregnancy or of a date for starting her maternity leave. Three weeks before the baby is born Gillian's legs swell up due to the pregnancy and she is unable to go into work. She informs her employer as soon as she can that she is absent because of a pregnancy-related illness. Gillian's ordinary maternity leave period begins automatically on the day after her first day of this period of absence.

The additional maternity leave period commences on the day after the last day of the ordinary maternity leave period.

REFLECTIVE QUESTION

Do you think that employees should be employed for a qualifying period before they become entitled to 52 weeks' maternity leave?

THE COMPULSORY MATERNITY LEAVE PERIOD

Within the ordinary maternity leave, and forming part of it, is the *compulsory maternity leave* period. This is normally a two-week period (four weeks for factory workers), beginning with the day of the birth, during which the employer must not permit the employee to work.[11] An employer who allows an employee to work during this period will be subject to a fine.[12]

CASE STUDY

EVERSHEDS LEGAL SERVICES LTD v DE BELIN

The employer decided that one of two employees had to be made redundant. One of the two employees was absent on maternity leave, which resulted in her being given extra marks in the scoring for deciding who to make redundant. Subsequently, the male employee was terminated for redundancy and brought a claim for sex discrimination – which he won. The EAT held that it was not permitted to favour a woman on maternity leave beyond what was reasonably necessary (ie proportionate).

Discussion point

Do you agree with the EAT and its decision, or should women on maternity leave be protected no matter what?

THE DATE OF THE RETURN TO WORK

In order to avoid any confusion, an employer who has been notified by its employee under Regulation 4 (see above) about the *start* of her maternity leave must, in turn, notify the employee of the date on which the leave will *end*. This must be done within 28 days of the date on which the employer received the notification.[13]

If the employee wishes to return early and not take her full entitlement of additional maternity leave, she must give eight weeks' notice, in writing, of her intended return date (no such notice is required by her unless an early return is planned). If she does not give this notice, the employer may delay her return for up to eight weeks.[14]

'KEEPING IN TOUCH' DAYS

Employers and employees are encouraged to stay in contact with each other during the maternity leave. Regulation 12A provides that the employer is entitled to maintain 'reasonable' contact with the employee during maternity leave; the same Regulation enables the employee to do up to 10 days' work for her employer without this having the effect of bringing her maternity leave to an end. These days are known as 'keeping in touch' days. Any amount of work done on any day constitutes a day's work. This is all a matter of agreement between the employer and employee – the employer cannot demand that this work be done, nor can the employee demand work.

REFLECTIVE QUESTION

Do you think that the employer should be legally required to offer work on 'keeping in touch' days if the employee wishes to work?

TERMS AND CONDITIONS DURING PERIODS OF MATERNITY LEAVE

Regulation 9 of the MPL Regulations state that an employee on ordinary or additional maternity leave is entitled to the benefit of all the terms and conditions of employment under her employment contract which would have applied had she not been absent. This does not include terms and conditions relating to wages or salary – as we will see below, the employee instead receives statutory maternity pay – but she is entitled to other benefits.[15]

So, for example:

- The maternity leave is part of the employee's period of continuous employment and will count towards the calculation of her seniority and pension rights.
- The employee's holiday entitlement under her contract will continue to accrue.
- She will continue to be entitled during the leave to the use of a company car, mobile phone and private health insurance.

In return, during her maternity leave an employee will also continue to be bound by all obligations arising under her terms and conditions – except the obligation to provide work!

THE RIGHT TO RETURN TO WORK AFTER MATERNITY LEAVE

The Regulations distinguish between those employees who take shorter periods of leave – who have the right to return to their old job – and those who take longer periods – who in some circumstances may instead be offered another suitable job. In all cases, though, the right to return to work is a right to return with seniority, pension rights and similar rights preserved as they would have been if she had not been absent.[16] The right to return might also be affected by the employee's position becoming *redundant* before or during the leave – see below.

The detailed rules are as follows.

Returning after ordinary maternity leave

An employee who is returning to work after a period of ordinary maternity leave will be entitled to return to the job in which she was employed before the absence. This is provided that this was either an isolated period of leave or that it was the last of two or more consecutive periods of statutory leave which did not include any periods of additional maternity or adoptive leave, or parental leave of more than four weeks.[17] If these conditions are not fulfilled, the employee still has the right in the first place to return to her old job – but if this is not reasonably practicable, the right is to return to another job which is both suitable and appropriate in the circumstances.[18]

For example: Julia, who was expecting her second child, took four weeks' parental leave to spend time with her three-year-old child, and then took her full 26 weeks' ordinary maternity leave. She decided not to take additional maternity leave. She would be entitled to return to her previous job. But if she had taken five weeks' parental leave followed by her ordinary maternity leave, and if it was then not reasonably practicable to keep her old job open, her employer could offer her another suitable job instead.

Returning after additional maternity leave

An employee who returns from additional maternity leave is entitled to return from that leave to the job in which she was employed prior to the absence. But if this is not reasonably practicable, the right is to return to another job which is both suitable and appropriate in the circumstances.[19]

PROTECTION FROM DETRIMENT AND DISMISSAL

Whereas some employers will be helpful and supportive to a pregnant employee wishing to take maternity leave, others will not be! An employee wishing to take maternity leave might find that she is penalised in some way by her employer for it, or even dismissed. It is therefore an essential component of the right to maternity leave that the employee is given protection both against dismissal and also against action short of dismissal – the latter referred to in the Regulations as being *subjected to a detriment.* As we will see later, the same dual legal protection is given in respect of the other parental rights covered in this chapter. As far as pregnancy and maternity leave is concerned, the employee is protected from being subjected to a detriment for one of the following reasons:

- that she is pregnant or has given birth to a child
- that she took ordinary or additional maternity leave or availed herself of the benefits of her terms and conditions of employment during such leave
- that she undertook, considered undertaking or refused to undertake work on 'keeping in touch' days.[20]

Similarly, it is an *automatically unfair* dismissal (see Chapter 13) to dismiss an employee, irrespective of her length of service, for any of the above reasons as well as several others relating to maternity leave.[21]

It is possible that before or during the maternity leave the employee's position will become *redundant.* Redundancy, as we will see in Chapter 14, is a fair reason for dismissal, but the dismissal may nevertheless become automatically unfair in the following circumstances:

- if the principal reason that this employee was selected for redundancy dismissal, rather than a colleague, was because of her maternity leave[22]
- if her employer, or an associated employer, does not offer her other suitable and appropriate employment if it is available.[23, 24]

Where an employee is dismissed while she is pregnant or during her maternity leave period, she is entitled to written reasons for her dismissal. This right does not depend on any qualifying period of service and the woman does not need formally to request the reasons.[25]

Section 106 of the Employment Rights Act 1996 deals with the issue of the dismissal of a replacement who is taken on to cover for an employee absent because of pregnancy (among other reasons). The section provides that if the replacement has been informed in writing, on being engaged, that his or her employment will be terminated on the woman's return to work, the dismissal of the replacement is treated as being for a 'substantial reason', which is one of the *potentially fair reasons* for dismissal – see Chapter 13.

TRANSFERRING MATERNITY LEAVE TO THE FATHER

An important change was introduced by the Additional Paternity Leave Regulations 2010, which applies to parents of babies whose expected week of birth or whose notification of matching for adoption was on or after 3 April 2011. A woman who qualifies for maternity leave but wishes to return to work rather than taking up her full 52-week entitlement may transfer up to 26 weeks of the leave to the father of the child. This will be taken as additional paternity leave – see further below under Paternity leave.

STATUTORY MATERNITY PAY

Employees who meet the qualifying conditions are entitled to receive statutory maternity pay (SMP) for the first 39 weeks of maternity leave. Under the Work and Families Act 2006 regulations may be made to extend this entitlement to 52 weeks but this has not yet taken place.

Those who do not qualify for SMP may be entitled to Maternity Allowance.

In order to qualify for SMP an employee must:

- have been continuously employed by the same employer for at least 26 weeks preceding the 14th week before the week in which the baby is due, and
- have been earning a gross wage (ie before tax) which is at least at or above the lower earnings limit for the payment of National Insurance contributions (£107 per week for 2012/13) for at least eight weeks preceding the 14th week before the week in which the baby is due.

For example: Rukhsana started working for her employer on 1 January 2012. Her baby is due in the week beginning 1 November 2012. She earns £110 per week before tax. She has been employed by her employer for (more than) 26 weeks by the week beginning 26 July, which is the 14th week before her baby is due. She is also earning just above the minimum required gross wage. She is therefore entitled to SMP.

SMP may start as early as the 11th week before the week in which the baby is due, but no later than the day following the baby's birth. If the pregnant woman is off sick from work for a pregnancy-related reason at the start of, or during, the four weeks before the week in which the baby is due, SMP will start on the day following the first day of absence.

HOW MUCH IS SMP?

During the first six weeks the employee will receive a sum equivalent to 90% of her average gross weekly earnings (usually calculated by reference to the eight-week period prior to the 14th week before childbirth), with no upper limit. During the remaining weeks she will receive a flat rate sum (£135.45 in 2012) or 90% of gross average earnings if this is less than the flat rate figure. The employer must deduct tax and National Insurance contributions from these sums.

The Maternity Allowance (MA) is managed by Jobcentre Plus. In order to qualify for MA, a pregnant woman must

- not qualify for SMP
- have been employed and/or self-employed for at least 26 weeks in the 66-week period before the week in which the baby is due
- have earned at least £30 per week in any 13-week period during this time.

The earliest time at which MA can start is the 11th week before the week in which the baby is due. The amount paid (in 2012) is a flat rate of £128.73 per week or 90% of the employee's average earnings if this is less than the flat rate figure. MA is paid for a maximum of 39 weeks.

REFLECTIVE QUESTION

Do you think that maternity pay is set at a fair level?

PARENTAL LEAVE

An employee who has been continuously employed for a period of not less than one year and who has, or expects to have, responsibility for a child[26] is entitled to be absent from work on parental leave for the purposes of caring for that child.[27]

The Directgov website[28] gives examples of when parental leave might be taken:

> Caring for a child does not necessarily mean being with the child 24 hours a day. Parental leave might be taken simply to enable you to spend more time with your young child. Examples of the way parental leave might be used include:

- straight after your maternity, paternity or adoption leave
- spending more time with your child in their early years
- time with your child during a stay in hospital
- looking at new schools
- settling your child into new childcare arrangements
- allowing your family to spend more time together – for example, taking your child to stay with grandparents.

The entitlement to parental leave is in respect of a child who is less than five years old. When the child reaches his or her fifth birthday, the entitlement ends. There are three exceptions to this:

- when a child is adopted or placed for adoption with an employee. In such cases the entitlement ends on the fifth anniversary of the date on which the placement began, and the usual upper age limit, therefore, does not apply. The Regulations place an absolute upper age limit of the date of the child's eighteenth birthday
- when a child is in receipt of, or entitled to, a disability living allowance. In this case the upper age limit of 18 years applies
- when the employer exercises its right to delay parental leave (see below) and this results in the child reaching its fifth birthday. The entitlement can still be taken at the end of the period for which leave has been postponed, even though the child will now be over five years old.

An employee is entitled to 13 weeks' leave in respect of any individual child.[29] The leave is *unpaid*. The leave entitlement is for 'any individual child', so that an employee/parent of multiple-birth children will be entitled to 13 weeks' leave in respect of each child. This figure is increased to 18 weeks for those with responsibility for a child who is entitled to a disability living allowance.[30]

REFLECTIVE QUESTION

Do you think that the leave should be with pay?

THE DEFAULT PROVISIONS

Under the MPL Regulations, the following additional conditions – called the default provisions – apply to parental leave unless otherwise stipulated by collective or workforce agreements (see Chapter 2).[31]

The employee must:

- not take the leave in periods other than a week or multiples of a week (see *Rodway v South Central Trains*, below) except where the child is entitled to disability living allowance
- not take more than four weeks' leave in respect of any individual child in any particular year
- comply with any request from the employer to produce for inspection evidence of the employee's responsibility for the child as well as evidence of the child's age
- give the employer notice of the period of leave. This notice must specify the dates on which the leave is to begin and end and be given at least 21 days before the date upon which the leave is to start. Where the leave is in respect of a child to be adopted and the leave is to begin on the date of the placement, the notice must specify the week of the placement and the period of leave. The notice must be given at least 21 days before the beginning of that week, or if that is not reasonably practicable, as soon as it is so.

The employer has the right to postpone the leave – see below.

CASE STUDY

RODWAY v SOUTH CENTRAL TRAINS

Mr Rodway was employed as a train conductor and had a son aged 2 years, who lived with his former partner. She informed him that he would have to look after his son on Saturday 26 July. He applied for annual leave for that day but was told that this could not be guaranteed. Because of this uncertainty he applied for parental leave for that day but this was refused on the grounds that his job could not be covered. He took the day off and was subsequently disciplined for it. He brought a claim in the employment tribunal that he had been subjected to a detriment (see below) because he had sought to take parental leave.

The Court of Appeal held that Mr Rodway's claim failed. The default provisions (see above) which apply to parental leave require the leave to be taken in blocks of at least one week. Such an approach, according to the court, made practical sense as employers might well prefer to make arrangements for temporary cover for a week rather than a single day or two odd days.[32]

Discussion point

Should the default provisions be made more flexible?

THE EMPLOYER'S RIGHT TO POSTPONE PARENTAL LEAVE

Under the default provisions, the employer is given the right to postpone a period of parental leave, except where the employee wants to take it immediately after the birth or placement of the child, where:

- the employee has applied and given the necessary notice, and
- the operation of *the employer's business would be unduly disrupted* if the employee took leave during the period identified in the notice, and
- the employer permits the employee to take a period of leave of the same length that had been requested within six months of the date on which it was due to begin, and
- the employer gives notice in writing of the postponement stating the reasons for it and specifying the dates on which the employee may take parental leave. This notice must be given to the employee not later than seven days after the employee's notice was given to the employer.

An employee may complain to an employment tribunal if the employer has unreasonably postponed a period of parental leave or attempted to prevent the employee from taking it.[33] The tribunal may award such compensation that it considers 'just and equitable'.

We should note that the right to postpone the leave, like the other conditions in the default provisions, may be removed or modified by a collective or workforce agreement.

REFLECTIVE QUESTION

Do the default provisions allow too much freedom to the employer to postpone a short period of unpaid leave?

TERMS AND CONDITIONS DURING PERIODS OF PARENTAL LEAVE

While an employee is on parental leave, only some of the terms and conditions of the contract of employment continue to apply. This is in contrast to an employee on maternity leave – see above. Regulation 17 MPL Regulations 1999 provides that as regards an employee on parental leave, he or she is entitled to, or bound by, the following terms only:

- the benefit of the employer's implied obligation of trust and confidence (see Chapter 3) and any terms of employment relating to:
  - notice of the termination of the employment contract by the employer
  - compensation in the event of redundancy
  - disciplinary and grievance procedures
- the implied obligation of good faith to the employer and any terms and conditions of employment relating to:
  - notice of the termination of the employment contract by the employee
  - the disclosure of confidential information
  - the acceptance of gifts or other benefits, or
  - the employee's participation in any other business.[34]

THE RIGHT TO RETURN TO WORK AFTER PARENTAL LEAVE

We saw above in relation to maternity leave that the Regulations distinguish between those employees who take shorter periods of leave and those who take longer leave. The same distinction applies to parental leave. Again, in all cases, however, the right to return to work is a right to return with seniority, pension rights and similar rights preserved as they would have been if he or she had not been absent.[35]

Returning after shorter periods of leave

An employee who is returning to work after a period of parental leave of not more than four weeks' duration, will be entitled to return to the job in which he or she was employed before the absence. This is provided that the period of leave was either an isolated one or that it was the last of two or more shorter periods of statutory leave, as for maternity leave, above. If these conditions are not fulfilled, the employee still has the right in the first place to return to his or her old job, but if this is not reasonably practicable, the right is to return to another job which is both suitable and appropriate in the circumstances.[36]

Returning after longer periods of leave

An employee who takes parental leave of more than four weeks is entitled to return from that leave to the job in which he or she was employed prior to the absence. But if this is not reasonably practicable, the right is to return to another job which is both suitable and appropriate in the circumstances.[37]

PROTECTION FROM DETRIMENT AND DISMISSAL

An employee is entitled not to be subjected to any detriment for taking or seeking to take parental leave,[38] and it is an automatically unfair dismissal to dismiss him or her for this.[39]

ORDINARY PATERNITY LEAVE

Paternity leave was first provided for by the Employment Act 2002[40] and the Paternity and Adoption Leave Regulations 2002 (the PAL Regulations).[41] The PAL Regulations were amended in 2006 by a further set of regulations[42] but a more significant change came about in 2010 with the Additional Paternity Leave Regulations 2010,[43] which provided for additional paternity leave under certain circumstances – see further below.

Entitlement to paternity leave is, according to Regulation 4(1), for the purpose of caring for a child or supporting the child's mother. It is a very short period of leave: a maximum of two weeks – see below. In order to qualify for paternity leave an individual must meet certain conditions and comply with the notice requirements.[44] The conditions are:

- that the employee has been continuously employed for a period of at least 26 weeks ending with the week immediately preceding the 14th week before the expected week of childbirth
- that the employee is the father of the child or, if not the father, then married to, or partner or civil partner of, the child's mother
- that if he is the father, he has, or expects to have, responsibility for bringing up the child; if he is not the father but the partner or civil partner of the mother, that he has, or expects to have, the main responsibility (apart from any responsibility of the mother) for bringing up the child.

There are a number of complications to this simple formula, which are dealt with by the Regulations. These are, firstly, that if the child is born earlier than expected, the original date is still used in order to calculate whether the employee has 26 weeks' service before the 14th week preceding the expected week of childbirth. Secondly, if the child's mother dies, her husband or partner or civil partner would still be assumed to be married to or the partner or civil partner of the mother. Thirdly, an employee will be assumed to have responsibility for bringing up the child even if the child is stillborn after 24 weeks of pregnancy or dies. All these measures are aimed at ensuring that the employee is still entitled to paternity leave if these issues arise.

The notice and evidence requirements are:[45]

- An employee must give his employer notice of his intention to take paternity leave, specifying the expected week of childbirth, the length of the period of leave (see below) and the date on which the employee has chosen that his period of leave will begin.
- This notice must be given to the employer in or before the 15th week before the expected week of childbirth, or if it was not reasonably practicable to do so, then as soon as it is so.
- If the employer requests it, the employee must give a signed declaration stating that the purpose of the leave is either for caring for the child or supporting the child's mother and that he satisfies the conditions of entitlement listed above.

Unlike parental leave, multiple births from the same pregnancy do not have any effect on the amount of paternity leave the father is entitled to.[46] An employee may take either one week's leave or two consecutive weeks' leave in respect of the child (or children). This leave must be taken between the date of the birth and a date 56 days after that. It is for the employee to choose whether he takes the leave commencing with the date of the birth or at some time after that, within the 56-day period.[47] Partly because dates of birth are not entirely predictable, there are opportunities for the employee to vary the start date for the leave, provided that the employee gives the employer 28 days' notice or, if this is not reasonably practicable, then gives such notice as soon as it is reasonably practicable.

Employees who are married to, or the partner of, an adopter have the same entitlement to paternity leave. They must meet similar conditions and abide by similar notice rules. The important date is that on which the child is placed with the adopter, because this is the date from which the critical 56-day period commences.[48]

Other rules relating to paternity leave are identical to those which apply to maternity leave. The leave is paid, the employee receives the same flat rate figure paid for maternity pay – see above (£135.45 in 2012) – or 90% of average earnings, if lower. There is the same right to return to the job in which the employee was employed before the absence, in a case where the paternity leave is an isolated period of leave or the last of two or more consecutive periods of short statutory leave. Where it is a return after longer periods of leave, there is the right to return to the same job or, if that is not reasonably practicable, to one that is similar and appropriate in the circumstances. In all cases the employee will return with his seniority, pension and other rights as if he had not been absent.[49]

There is, once again, protection against being subjected to a detriment and against dismissal.

REFLECTIVE QUESTION

Is the current paternity leave policy of any value?

ADDITIONAL PATERNITY LEAVE

As seen above, under the Additional Paternity Leave Regulations 2010 additional paternity leave will be available in relation to fathers (both natural and adoptive) of babies whose expected week of birth, or whose notification of matching for adoption, was on or after 3 April 2011. As with paternity leave, it will also be available to husbands or partners of the mother but who are not the father of the child. For ease of reference we will refer to all those who may be entitled as 'the father'. Under these regulations it will be possible for the mother to transfer up to 26 weeks of her maternity leave to the father. The father will take this leave as additional paternity leave. There are various eligibility criteria which apply, both to the mother and to the father.[50] These include:

- The mother must have been entitled to maternity leave.
- She must have returned to work.
- The father must have been employed continuously by his employer for a minimum of 26 weeks on 'the relevant date', which is the 14th week before the expected week of birth.

- He must also have remained in continuous employment with that employer until the week before the leave begins.
- There are notice and evidence requirements similar to those we saw above for paternity leave. He must also give his employer a declaration signed by the mother of the child stating information about her identity and about his eligibility to take the leave.[51]

A minimum of two weeks and a maximum of 26 weeks will be transferable.[52] The earliest point at which the leave may begin is at 20 weeks after the child's birth and the leave must end within 12 months of the birth or placement for adoption.[53] The leave will be paid if the qualifying conditions are met,[54] with the father receiving additional statutory paternity pay at the same flat rate figure as above (£135.45 in 2012). The other rules relating to matters such as the right of the father to return to the job in which he was employed are once again identical to those applicable to maternity leave.

> For example: Brian and Fiona's baby was born on 1 January 2012. Brian has been employed by his employer continuously since 1 January 2011. Fiona took a total of 30 weeks' maternity leave and returned to work on 28 May 2012. Brian has the necessary period of continuous employment and would be able to take the unused 22 weeks of Fiona's leave as additional paternity leave (as well as two weeks' 'ordinary' paternity leave), provided the other eligibility criteria are met.

There are provisions for variation of the dates of the leave or cancellation of the leave before it has begun,[55] and for a longer period of leave when the mother or primary adopter has died during the 12 months after the birth or placement.

REFLECTIVE QUESTION

To what extent do you think that fathers will take up the new right?

PROTECTION FROM DETRIMENT AND DISMISSAL

An employee is entitled not to be subjected to any detriment for taking or seeking to take paternity leave or additional paternity leave, and it is an automatically unfair dismissal to dismiss him for this.

If, prior to or during the paternity leave or additional paternity leave, the employee's position becomes redundant, the dismissal may nevertheless become automatically unfair in the following circumstances:

- in relation to both paternity leave and additional paternity leave – if the principal reason that this employee was selected for redundancy dismissal, rather than a colleague, was because of his paternity leave or additional paternity leave.

- in relation to additional paternity leave only – if the employer, or an associated employer, does not offer him other suitable and appropriate employment if it is available.

ADOPTION LEAVE

The right to adoption leave was introduced by the Employment Act 2002 and the PAL Regulations (2002),[56] with some amendments being made by the 2006 Regulations. An employee who meets the necessary conditions and complies with the notice and evidential requirements is entitled to adoption leave. As with maternity leave, this is divided into ordinary and additional adoption leave, each period comprising 26 weeks, although there is no equivalent of compulsory maternity leave. Another important difference from maternity leave is that adoption leave is only available if the employee has been employed by the employer for a minimum period – see below. Statutory adoption pay (SAP) is payable for a total of 39 weeks, at 135.45 per week (in 2012) or 90% of average gross earnings, if lower. Only one partner may take adoption leave: it is the partners' choice which of them shall take it.

An employee is entitled to adoption leave if the employee:[57]

- is the child's adopter
- has been continuously employed for a period of not less than 26 weeks ending with the week in which the employee was notified of being matched with the child, and
- has notified the agency that he agrees that the child should be placed with him on the date of placement.

An employee's entitlement to adoption leave is not affected by the placement for adoption of more than one child as part of the same arrangement.

ORDINARY ADOPTION LEAVE

An obvious difference from maternity leave is that the employee will not have a need to start the leave until shortly before the child is placed with him or her. An employee may choose between two options when deciding when ordinary adoption leave starts. The choices are between the date on which the child is placed for adoption, and some other predetermined date which is *no more than 14 days before* the date on which the child is expected to be placed, and no later than this date. This may be contrasted with maternity leave which, as we saw above, may commence 11 weeks before the expected birth.

The notice and evidential requirements are:[58]

- An employee must give the employer notice of intention to take ordinary adoption leave, specifying the date on which the child is expected to be placed for adoption and the date on which the employee has chosen when the period of leave should begin.
- *The notice must be given to the employer no more than seven days after the date on which the employee has been notified of having been matched with a child* or, if this was not reasonably practicable, then as soon as it is so.

- Where the employer requests it, the employee must provide evidence, in the form of documents issued by the adoption agency, of the name and address of the agency, the date on which the employee was notified of the match and the date on which the agency expects to place the child with the employee.

  For example: Barbara, who is intending to take adoption leave, is informed by the adoption agency on 1 March 2012 that she and her partner have been matched with a child. She forgets to inform her employer until 15 March. She will very probably lose her right to take adoption leave. (Forgetting to do something does not mean that it was 'not reasonably practicable'!)

Within 28 days of the receipt of the employee's notification, the employer must give the employee notice of when the period of additional adoption leave, if there is an entitlement, will end. There are also provisions for the employee to vary the start date, subject to notice being given to the employer.

ADDITIONAL ADOPTION LEAVE

An employee is entitled to additional adoption leave if:

- the child was placed with the employee for adoption
- the employee took ordinary adoption leave
- the ordinary adoption leave did not end prematurely (see below).

The leave begins on the day after the last day of ordinary adoption leave.[59]

PREMATURE ENDING

As stated, ordinary adoption leave and additional adoption leave will normally last for 26 weeks each. It may be less, of course, if the employee is dismissed before the end of this period.[60] It may also end early if the placement is disrupted.[61] The circumstances where this applies are:

- where the adoption leave starts before the placement (see above) and the employee is subsequently notified that the placement will not take place
- if the child dies
- if the child is returned to the adoption agency under section 30(3) of the Adoption Act 1976.

Unless the employee has less than eight weeks to go before his or her leave comes to an end, the adoption leave, in these circumstances, will end after a period of eight weeks after the week in which the employee was informed that the placement is not to be made, or the child dies, or the child is returned. If the employee has less than eight weeks' *ordinary* maternity leave to go, he or she will be entitled to some *additional* maternity leave as well to give a total of eight weeks' leave.

> For example: Marian adopted a child and has taken 20 weeks of her ordinary adoption leave when the child dies. Marian will be entitled to take the final six weeks of her ordinary adoption leave plus two weeks' additional maternity leave.

OTHER ISSUES

Other matters arising out of adoption leave are identical to those concerning maternity leave, as outlined earlier in this chapter. These matters concern the right to return to work,[62] notice periods for early return,[63] matters concerning terms and conditions during adoption leave, and contact between the employer and employee during adoption leave, including the right to carry out up to 10 days' work with the employer without bringing the statutory adoption leave period to an end.[64] An employee is entitled not to be subjected to any detriment for taking or seeking to take adoption leave, and it is an automatically unfair dismissal to dismiss him or her for it. If the employee's job becomes redundant during adoption leave, the position is also as noted in relation to maternity leave.

TIME OFF FOR DEPENDANTS

Section 57A ERA 1996 states that an employee is entitled to be permitted by the employer to take a reasonable amount of *unpaid* time off during the employee's working hours in order to take action necessary:

- to provide assistance on an occasion when a dependant falls ill, gives birth or is injured or assaulted
- to make arrangements for the provision of care for a dependant who is ill or injured
- in consequence of the death of a dependant
- because of the unexpected disruption or termination of arrangements for the care of a dependant, or
- to deal with an incident which involves a child of the employee and which occurs unexpectedly in a period during which an educational establishment which the child attends is responsible for him or her.

On the meaning of 'dependant', see below.

CASE STUDY

ROYAL BANK OF SCOTLAND v HARRISON

Royal Bank of Scotland v Harrison concerned a situation coming under the fourth of the above bullet points, and the meaning of 'unexpected disruption ... of arrangements'. Mrs Harrison worked part-time as a home insurance claims adviser. She had two young children aged 5 and 15 months respectively, who were looked after by a childminder when she was at work. On 8 December 2006 she learned that her childminder would not be available in two weeks' time (the 22nd) to look after the children, and Mrs Harrison was unable to find any replacement. On 13 December she told her line manager about the problem and asked if she could take the day off on the 22nd. On the 20th she was told that she could not take the day off and it would be treated as an unauthorised absence if she did so. She took the day off nonetheless and was given a verbal warning. She claimed in the employment tribunal that in giving her the warning, her employer was subjecting her to a detriment (see below) because she had sought to take time off under section 57A. The tribunal found in her favour and this was affirmed by the EAT. The EAT held that in deciding whether the employee's action was 'necessary', a tribunal could take into account all relevant circumstances, including urgency and time. The longer the time the employee had to make alternative arrangements, the less likely that it would be necessary for her to take the time off. However, the words 'unexpected disruption' in the statute did not mean that the situation had to be an emergency. On the facts of this case Mrs Harrison had been entitled to the time off under section 57A and the warning she had been given was unlawfully subjecting her to a detriment.[65]

There is an obligation on the employee to inform the employer of the reason for absence and of its duration as soon as reasonably practicable. The time off is limited to incidents involving a dependant, who is defined as:[66]

- a spouse or civil partner
- a child
- a parent
- a person who lives in the same household as the employee but who is not an employee, tenant, lodger or boarder
- any person who reasonably relies on the employee for assistance if he or she is ill or assaulted[67]
- any person who reasonably relies on the employee to make arrangements for the provision of care in the event of illness or injury.[68] The references to illness or injury include mental illness or injury.[69]

Section 57B ERA 1996 asserts that an employee may apply to an employment tribunal to complain about a failure to be allowed time off. A tribunal may make a declaration and award compensation which the tribunal considers 'just and equitable in the circumstances'. There is the usual protection which we have seen throughout this chapter against being subjected to a detriment or being dismissed for taking or seeking to take the time off.

CASE STUDY

QUA v JOHN FORD MORRISON SOLICITORS

Ms Qua was a single mother with a small child who had medical problems. She was dismissed from her job as a legal secretary after taking time off for a total of 17 days during her ten months of employment to deal with the child's illnesses. She claimed that her dismissal was automatically unfair because the reason for it was that she had taken time off to which she was entitled under section 57A. The employment tribunal decided against Ms Qua on the grounds that she had not properly notified her employer in regard to the absences. The EAT held that the tribunal had not clarified the facts properly and ordered the case to be reheard. But more importantly, the EAT in this case also gave general guidance about the right to time off under section 57A. The EAT stated that the right to time off did not enable employees to take time off in order to look after a sick child *except* to deal with an immediate crisis. Longer-term care would be covered by the employee's parental leave entitlement. The right to time off was the right to a 'reasonable' amount of time in order to take action that is 'necessary'. The decision whether it was necessary depended upon a number of factors, including, for example:

- the nature of the incident that has occurred
- the closeness of the relationship between the employee and the dependant, and
- the extent to which anyone else was available to help out.

As far as what was a 'reasonable' amount of time off was concerned, this would depend upon the circumstances in each case. An employee was not, however, entitled to unlimited amounts of time off and the employer may take into account the number and length of previous absences, as well as the dates on which they occurred, when deciding whether the time off sought for a subsequent occasion is reasonable.

Furthermore, the time off is to deal with unforeseen circumstances. Thus if a child were known to be suffering from an underlying medical condition causing regular relapses, then time off for dealing with these illnesses would not come within the terms of section 57A.

A final important point made by the EAT was that in determining the reasonableness of the amount of time taken off, the disruption to an employer's business by the employee's absence cannot be taken into account.[70]

Discussion point

Should the effect on an employer's business be a relevant factor here, as it is in relation to the right to apply for flexible working (see below)?

FLEXIBLE WORKING

Section 47 of the Employment Act 2002 created the right to apply for flexible working, inserting new sections 80F to 80I into the ERA 1996 to provide for this. Two points should be noted. Firstly, it should be stressed that there is no right to work flexibly but only a right for an employee who qualifies (see below) to *apply* to the employer to agree to it! Secondly, the right to apply for flexible working is a right to apply to vary terms of the employment contract which relate, currently, to three specific matters only. These matters are:

- hours of work,
- times when required to work
- place of work.[71]

The purpose of the application must be to enable the employee to care for a child or an adult within the categories mentioned below.

CASE STUDY

SHAW v CCL LTD

Mrs Shaw became pregnant and took maternity leave. While on leave she submitted an application to return to work on a part-time basis. She was flexible about which days and what hours to work but wanted the total to be no more than 14 hours per week. Her application was refused by her employer. The employment tribunal decided that she had suffered direct sex discrimination as a result of not being allowed to return to work on a part-time basis and indirect discrimination as a result of the rule requiring her to work full-time on her return from maternity leave. The EAT also held that this discrimination amounted to a fundamental breach of contract, specifically the duty of mutual trust and confidence, and thus also allowed her claim for constructive dismissal.

Discussion point

Do you think that these rules are a real burden for employers?

REFLECTIVE QUESTION

Should there be a right to flexible working rather than just a right to apply for it?

The details of the employee's rights are spelled out in several sets of regulations.[72] The effect of these regulations, combined with section 12(10) of the Work and Families Act 2006, is that the definition of a child now includes anyone under the age of 17, or 18 if disabled. In addition, section 12(2)(b) of the Work and Families Act 2006 introduced a significant extension to the right so as to include carers for people aged 18 and over who need care.

A qualifying employee, as regards *caring for a child*, is an individual who:

- has been continuously employed for a period of not less than 26 weeks, and
- is the mother, father, adopter, guardian or foster parent of the child, or is married to, or partner of, the child's mother, father, adopter, guardian or foster parent, and
- has, or expects to have, responsibility for the upbringing of the child.

As regards *caring for an adult*, the qualifying requirements are that the employee:

- has been continuously employed for a period of not less than 26 weeks, and
- is caring or expects to be caring for a person in need of care who is either:
  - married to the partner or civil partner of the employee
  - a relative of the employee, or
  - living at the same address as the employee.

THE PROCEDURE

The application must be made at least 14 days before the child reaches the age of 17, or, if disabled, 18 years. The application must be in writing.

The employer must hold a meeting with the employee within 28 days from the date when the application is made, unless the employer simply agrees to the application and notifies the employee accordingly.

In cases where a meeting is held, the employer must give notice, in writing, of the decision within 14 days of the meeting. The notice must consist of

- *either* the employer's agreement, specifying the variation to the contract and the date on which the change becomes effective
- *or* a refusal of the application, stating the grounds for refusing it (see below), an explanation as to why the grounds apply, and details of an appeals procedure.

An employee is entitled to appeal, in writing, against the employer's decision within a further 14 days. The appeal meeting itself must take place within 14 days of the date of the appeal notice and the employer then has a further 14 days in which to give written notice of the appeal decision. The decision will again be either to agree to the variation or to refuse it, giving the grounds and an explanation. All these periods of time can be extended by agreement between the employer and the employee.

The times and dates of the meetings must be convenient for both parties, and the employee has the right to be accompanied by a fellow worker who may address the meeting. If the employer fails to allow this, the employee may complain to an employment tribunal and obtain an award of up to two weeks' pay

GROUNDS ON WHICH THE EMPLOYER MAY REFUSE

The employer may only refuse the application on one or more of the following grounds:[73]

- the burden of additional costs
- a detrimental effect on the ability to meet customer demand
- an inability to reorganise work among existing staff
- an inability to recruit additional staff
- a detrimental impact on quality
- a detrimental impact on performance
- insufficiency of work during the periods the employee proposes to work
- planned structural changes
- such other grounds as the Secretary of State may specify.

An employee may complain to an employment tribunal that his or her employer has failed to comply with the duty under section 80G, or that a decision to reject the application was based upon incorrect facts. Failure to comply with the duty includes a failure to hold the required meeting, or a failure to notify a decision. The maximum amount of compensation that can be awarded is eight weeks' pay. The tribunal may also order the employer to reconsider the application. There is, once again, protection against being subjected to a detriment or being dismissed for exercising or seeking to exercise rights in relation to flexible working.

CASE STUDY

COMMOTION LTD v RUTTY[74]

Mrs Rutty was an employee of a mail order company when she became legally responsible for the care of her grandchild. She had problems coping with her full-time job as a warehouse assistant and informally asked her employer if she could change to a three-day week. After this request was turned down, she put in a formal application under section 80F ERA 1996. Her employer refused the application, giving as the grounds that it would have a detrimental effect on the company's ability to meet customer demand and a detrimental effect on performance.

Mrs Rutty resigned and claimed, amongst other matters, a breach of her right to request flexible working.

The EAT held that the employer had failed to establish that it had refused her request on one or more of the grounds set out in section 80G. In order to establish whether or not the employer's decision to reject the request was based on incorrect facts, the tribunal is entitled to enquire what would be the effect of granting the application – for example, could it have been granted without disruption? What did other staff feel about it? Could they have made up the time? In this case the tribunal was entitled to find that the evidence did not support the employer's statements about the effects of agreeing to the request.

REFLECTIVE QUESTION

Are the rules in relation to various parental rights too complex and confusing for both employees and employers?

RISK ASSESSMENT

Where an employee is pregnant, has given birth within the past six months or is breast-feeding, the employer must assess the special risks which the woman faces in the workplace and take measures to avoid them.[75] However, the EAT recently made clear[76] that there is no general obligation to carry out a risk assessment on pregnant employees but it should certainly take place when certain preconditions are met – namely:

- the employee has notified the employer in writing that she is pregnant
- the work is of a kind which could involve a risk of harm or danger to the health and safety of the expectant mother or baby
- the risk arises either from either processes or working conditions or physical or biological or chemical agents in the workplace at the time.

If an assessment has found risk to be present and preventative action is impossible or would be inadequate to avoid the risk, the employee's working conditions or hours of work must be altered. If that would be unreasonable or still would not avoid the risk, the employer must offer suitable alternative work, or where none is available, suspend her from work on full pay.[77] Alternative work will be suitable if it is both suitable in relation to the employee and appropriate for her to do in the circumstances. The terms and conditions applicable must not be substantially less favourable than those which apply to her normal work. An employment tribunal may award compensation to a woman if her employer fails to offer suitable alternative employment.[78]

CASE STUDY

BRITISH AIRWAYS v MOORE AND BOTTERILL

In *British Airways v Moore and Botterill*,[79] the case concerned two cabin crew employees who became grounded, by agreement, after their 16th week of pregnancy. They were given alternative duties and continued to receive their normal basic salary but not the allowances that they had previously received while flying. Despite the fact that these arrangements were in accord with a collective agreement, the EAT held that the employees concerned had not been offered suitable alternative employment, because the terms and conditions were substantially less favourable.

Under section 68 of the Employment Rights Act 1996, a woman who is suspended on maternity grounds is entitled to be paid by her employer during the suspension. However, this right is lost if she unreasonably refuses an offer of suitable alternative work. The remuneration is a week's wage for each week of suspension and pro rata for any part of a week of entitlement. Any remuneration paid under the employee's contract goes towards discharging the employer's liability under section 68. Conversely, any payment under section 68 goes towards discharging any contractual obligation the employer may have. Where an employer fails to pay all or any of the amount due, an employment tribunal will order the employer to pay the remuneration owed.[80]

Rights comparable to the above have now been given to agency workers by the Agency Workers Regulations 2010.[81]

REFLECTIVE QUESTIONS

Should small employers be exempt from providing some of the parental rights for their employees?

Should any or all of these rights be available to other members of staff who are not employees?

KEY LEARNING POINTS

- A pregnant woman is entitled to paid time off for antenatal care.
- The maternity leave period is divided into ordinary, compulsory and additional leave periods; adoptive leave is divided into ordinary and additional leave periods.
- An employee has the right to return to his or her job under the original contract of employment and on terms and conditions not less favourable than those which would have applied if the employee had not taken maternity, adoption, parental or paternity leave; if this is not practicable, the right is to be offered a suitable and appropriate alternative position.
- Where an employee is pregnant, has given birth within the last six months, or is breast-feeding, the employer must assess the special risks faced by the woman in the workplace and take measures to avoid those risks.
- It is automatically unfair, regardless of length of service, to dismiss an employee for reasons connected with pregnancy or the taking of maternity, adoption, parental or paternity leave.
- Parents with child responsibilities are entitled to time off for parental leave for a maximum of 13 weeks or 18 weeks for a child in receipt of invalidity benefit.
- Employees are entitled to time off to provide assistance for dependants in certain circumstances.
- A qualifying employee may make an application to the employer to vary his or her contractual terms in relation to hours of work, times when required to work or place of work. The purpose of the application is to enable the employee to care for a child or for an adult requiring care.

REFERENCES

1 **This chapter contains extracts from or close paraphrasing of legislation which is on the opsi.gov.uk website (and its successor) and is subject to crown copyright. It also contains other public sector information. The reproduction of this material here is licensed under the open government licence v1.0**

2 See section 56(1) ERA 1996

3 Section 57 ERA 1996

4 Section 56(6) ERA 1996

5 Directive 92/85/EEC of 19 October 1992

6 2006/54/EC (consolidating seven Directives, including the Equal Pay and Equal Treatment Directives)

7 SI 1999/3312

8 Regulation 2(1) MPL Regulations 1999

9 Regulation 4(2)(b) MPL Regulations 1999

10 Regulation 4 MPL Regulations 1999

11 Section 72(3) ERA 1996 and Regulation 8 MPL Regulations 1999

12 Section 72(5) ERA 1996

13 Regulation 7(6) MPL Regulations 1999
14 Regulation 11 MPL Regulations 1999
15 Section 73(5) ERA 1996
16 Regulation 18A(1) MPL Regulations 1999
17 Regulation 18(1) MPL Regulations 1999
18 Regulation 18(2) MPL Regulations 1999
19 Regulation 18(2) MPL Regulations 1999
20 Regulation 19 MPL Regulations 1999
21 Regulation 20(1) MPL Regulations 1999
22 Regulation 20(2) MPL Regulations 1999
23 Regulation 20(1) MPL Regulations 1999
24 If for some reason other than redundancy it is not practicable for the employee to return to either her old job or another suitable job, but an associated employer offers her such a job and she unreasonably refuses it, the dismissal will not be automatically unfair. If she *accepts* the job, she will also have no claim.
25 Section 92(4) ERA 1996
26 Responsibility for a child means having parental responsibility or being registered as the child's father in accordance with the provisions of the Births and Deaths Registration Act 1953 or the Registration of Births, Deaths and Marriages (Scotland) Act 1965 – Regulation 13(2) MPL Regulations 1999.
27 Regulation 13(1) MPL 1999
28 From the DirectGov website www.direct.gov.uk/en/parents/moneyandwork entitlementsparentalleaveandpay/dg_10029416 [accessed 17 October 2010] **subject to Crown Copyright**
29 Regulation 14 MPL Regulations 1999
30 Regulation 14(1)(A) MPL Regulations 1999
31 Schedule 2 MPL Regulations 1999
32 (2005) IRLR 583
33 Section 80 ERA 1996
34 Regulation 17 MPL Regulations 1999
35 Regulation 18A(1) MPL 1999
36 Regulation 18(1) MPL Regulations 1999
37 Regulation 18(2) MPL 1999
38 Regulation 19(2) MPL 1999
39 Regulation 20(1) MPL 1999
40 Now contained in sections 80A–80D ERA 1996 and sections 171ZA–171ZK Social Security Contributions and Benefits Act 1992

41 SI 2002/2788

42 Maternity and Parental Leave etc and the Paternity and Adoption Leave (Amendment) Regulations SI 2006/2014

43 With accompanying sets of regulations

44 Regulation 4(1) PAL Regulations 2002

45 Regulation 6 PAL Regulations 2002

46 Regulation 4(6) PAL Regulations 2002

47 Regulation 5 PAL Regulations 2002

48 See Regulations 8–11 PAL Regulations 2002

49 See Regulations 12–14 PAL Regulations 2002

50 Regulation 4 of Additional Paternity Leave Regulations SI/1055

51 *Ibid* Regulation 6

52 *Ibid* Regulation 5(2)

53 *Ibid* Regulation 5(1)

54 Additional Statutory Paternity Pay (General) Regulations SI 2010/1056

55 *Ibid* Regulation 7

56 Now contained in sections 75A–75D ERA 1996 and sections 171ZL–171ZT Social Security Contributions and Benefits Act 1992

57 Regulation 15 PAL Regulations 2002

58 Regulation 17 PAL Regulations 2002

59 Regulation 20 PAL Regulations 2002

60 Regulation 24 PAL Regulations 2002

61 Regulation 22 PAL Regulations 2002

62 Regulation 26 PAL Regulations 2002

63 Regulation 25 PAL Regulations 2002; changed to eight weeks from 28 days for those whose adoption placements start after 1 April 2007

64 Regulation 21 PAL Regulations 2002 and Regulation 21A for those whose adoption placements start after 1 April 2007

65 *Royal Bank of Scotland v Harrison* (2009) IRLR 28

66 Section 57A(3) ERA 1996

67 Section 57A(4)(a) ERA 1996

68 Section 57A(4)(b) ERA 1996

69 Section 57B ERA 1996

70 (2003) IRLR 184

71 ERA 1996 section 80F(1)(a)

72 Namely the Flexible Working (Eligibility, Complaints and Remedies) Regulations 2002, the Flexible Working (Procedural Requirements)

Regulations 2002 and the Flexible Working (Eligibility, Complaints and Remedies) (Amendment) Regulations 2009

73 ERA 1996 section 80G(1)(b)

74 (2006) IRLR 171

75 See the revised ACOP issued with the 1999 Health and Safety (Miscellaneous Modifications) Regulations; the revised ACOP refers employers to HSE guidance entitled *New and Expectant Mothers at Work: A guide for employers*

76 *O'Neill v Buckinghamshire County Council* (2010) IRLR 384

77 Regulation 16 of the Management of Health and Safety at Work Regulations 1999, SI 1999/3242

78 Sections 66–67 ERA 1996

79 (2000) IRLR 296

80 Sections 68–70 ERA 1996

81 See now *ibid* sections 68A–68D, 69A and 70A

EXPLORE FURTHER

Reading

- Deakin, S. and Morris, G. (2012) *Labour Law.* Hart, Chapter 6
- Smith, I. and Thomas, G. (2010) *Smith & Wood's Employment Law.* Butterworths, Chapter 4

Websites

- ACAS www.acas.org.uk
- Chartered Institute of Personnel and Development www.cipd.co.uk
- Department for Business Innovation and Skills www.bis.gov.uk
- Directgov – Employment www.direct.gov.uk
- Equality and Human Rights Commission http://www.equalityhuman rights.com
- Walsh, I. (May 2009) 'A review of how to extend the right of flexible working to parents of older children': available online at http://www.berr.gov.uk/files/file46092.pdf . Although the right has since been extended, this review is still worth looking at

CHAPTER 9

Health and Safety at Work

CHAPTER OVERVIEW

This chapter is a slightly amended version of one originally written by Professor Brenda Barrett of Middlesex University

In this chapter we examine occupational health and safety law. Having distinguished between injury prevention and injury compensation law, including the respective roles of civil and criminal law, common law and statute, the Health and Safety at Work Act 1974 is explained, noting the role of the Health and Safety Executive, and the duties of employers not to endanger the health, safety and welfare of their employees while at work and not to put others at risk by their activities. There is then an examination of the Management of Health and Safety at Work Regulations 1999 and a brief description of other Regulations, including the COSHH Regulations 2002.

LEARNING OUTCOMES

After studying this chapter[1] you will be able to:

- understand and explain the legal principles that apply in relation to the law pertaining to health and safety – in particular, duties under the Health and Safety at Work Act (HASAWA) and the principal health and safety regulations[2]
- advise colleagues about the strict level of liability which employers have under HASAWA and regulations such that in some cases they have to adopt a proactive approach and seek out risks
- advise about matters such as the duty to undertake risk assessments, working with safety representatives, and the powers of the Health and Safety inspectors.

INJURY PREVENTION AND INJURY COMPENSATION

The primary purpose of the law should be to make work safe so that it does not cause personal injury – but provision also has to be made for the compensation of people who nevertheless suffer injury. 'Injury' covers both physical and mental impairment caused by accident or illness. Compensation law has been developed largely through judges deciding the claims of accident victims. The victims of work-related injury may sue in the civil courts for damages, claiming that the defendant has caused the injury either by negligent conduct or by breaking a statutory duty. On the other hand, in the UK, legislation with criminal sanctions imposes duties on employers and others for the purpose of injury prevention. This chapter focuses on the principal preventative legislation but makes some reference to compensation case law.

SCOPE OF THE CURRENT INJURY PREVENTION LEGISLATION

The principal Act is the Health and Safety at Work Act 1974 (HASAWA 1974). It is a framework Act enabling the making of regulations, and it is the vehicle through which EEC Directives have normally been implemented. An important feature of the Act and of the Management of Health and Safety at Work Regulations 1999 (MHSW Regulations)[3] – the most important and comprehensive set of regulations made under the 1974 Act – is that they apply to the behaviour of people as well as to the condition of premises and equipment. The Act sets out general duties which employers have towards their employees, other workers and members of the public. It also imposes duties on employees to protect themselves and others.

The MHSW Regulations make more explicit what employers are required to do to manage health and safety under the Act. Like the Act, these Regulations apply to every work activity. They also seek to protect persons other than those at work against risks to their health and safety arising out of, or in connection with, work activities. While a breach of HASAWA 1974 or Regulations amounts to a criminal offence, civil liability does not arise from breach of the general duties contained in the Act; it arises only if there is a failure to comply with Regulations.[4]

The Act is administered and enforced by the Health and Safety Executive (HSE).[5] Now that the Health and Safety Commission has been abolished the HSE is responsible both for keeping the law under review and for initiating research, as well as making arrangements for enforcing the law, either through its own or local authority inspectors. Where the HSE considers there is a need to strengthen the law or assist duty-holders to comply with the law, it has three main options. It can issue:

1. *Guidance*, which has three purposes: firstly, to help people understand the law by interpreting it; secondly, to help people comply with the law; and thirdly, to provide technical advice. Guidance has no standing in a prosecution. Since 2002 the EU has made less use of Directives and the European social partners have issued autonomous agreements to Member States. In Britain these agreements have been published by the CBI and TUC as guidance, but two of them – namely, work-related stress[6] and harassment and violence at work[7] – have been endorsed by the HSE.
2. *Approved codes of practice* (ACOPs), which offer practical guidance about how to comply with the law. A failure to observe any provision of an approved code of practice does not of itself render a person liable to any civil or criminal proceedings. However, such a code is admissible in evidence in a criminal court, and proof of a failure to meet its requirements will be

sufficient to establish a contravention of a statutory provision, unless a court is satisfied that the provision was complied with in some other way.[8] A duty-holder who has complied with an ACOP is considered to have done enough to satisfy the law on the specific issues addressed by the code.

3 *Regulations*, which are made under HASAWA 1974. Regulations are proposed by the HSE and approved by Parliament. They identify specific risks and set out particular actions that must be taken.[9] In practice most Regulations are made to comply with European Union Directives.[10]

THE HEALTH AND SAFETY AT WORK ACT 1974

Section 2(1) provides that 'It shall be the duty of every employer to ensure, so far as is reasonably practicable, the health, safety and welfare at work of all his employees.' The inclusion of the words 'so far as reasonably practicable' was unsuccessfully challenged[11] by the European Commission as an incorrect implementation of Directive 89/391/EEC, which introduced measures to encourage improvements in health and safety. The European Court of Justice held that the Commission were arguing that the legislation should impose criminal liability on employers for all accidents in the work place – a proposition which the Court did not accept.

The matters to which this duty extends include:[12]

- the provision and maintenance of plant[13] and systems of work that are, so far as is reasonably practicable, safe and without risks to health
- arrangements for ensuring, so far as is reasonably practicable, safety and absence of risks to health in connection with the use, handling, storage and transport of articles and substances[14]
- the provision of such information, instruction, training and supervision as is necessary to ensure, so far as is reasonably practicable, the health and safety at work of employees
- so far as is reasonably practicable as regards any place of work under the employer's control, the maintenance of it in a condition which is safe and without risks to health and the provision and maintenance of means of access to and egress from it that are safe and without such risks
- the provision and maintenance of a working environment for his employees that is, so far as is reasonably practicable, safe, without risks to health, and adequate as regards facilities and arrangements for their welfare at work.[15] (On working time, see Chapter 10.)

HASAWA 1974 requires the duty-holder (usually an employer) to ensure that systems set down on paper are actually observed. In *R* v *Gateway Foodmarkets Ltd*,[16] the employer set down procedures for the maintenance of lifts in all its stores. However, when failings at store management level led to the death of an employee, the company was held to be in breach of its duties under section 2(1) HASAWA 1974.

It could be argued that these statutory duties merely enact the employer's common-law obligations developed in compensation cases. Although this is largely true, compensation law requires the defendant merely to take reasonable care whereas the statutory duties are usually either actually or virtually absolute, for even where the standard is qualified, the burden lies on the accused to escape liability by proving that it was not 'reasonably practicable' to do more than was in fact done to achieve a safe situation.[17] This defence is rarely invoked. It does not mean that the defendant must do everything that is physically possible to achieve safety – only that the risks be weighed against the trouble and expense of eliminating or reducing them.[18] Defendants are to be judged according to the knowledge they had or ought to have had at the time. In compensation cases it has been held that the existence of a universal practice is evidence which goes to the question whether any other method was reasonably practicable but it does not necessarily discharge the onus on the employer.[19]

EMPLOYEE INVOLVEMENT

From the outset it was intended that employees should be well informed and consulted about developing and maintaining measures to ensure the health and safety of employees. HASAWA 1974 section 2(4–7) enabled regulations to be made for safety representatives. The Safety Representatives and Safety Committees Regulations 1977[20] enabled recognised trade unions to appoint representatives and required employers to set up a safety committee if the appointed representative(s) so required. The Health and Safety (Consultation with Employees) Regulations 1996[21] gave similar rights to be consulted to employees lacking union representation. For further consideration of employee consultation see Chapter 17.

SAFETY POLICIES

Except where fewer than five employees are employed at any one time in an undertaking,[22] every employer must:

> prepare and, as often as may be appropriate, revise a written statement of his general policy with respect to the health and safety at work of his employees, and the organisation and arrangements for the time being in force for carrying out that policy, and bring the statement and any revision of it to the notice of all of his employees.[23]

The Act does not give any further indication about what the statement should contain, but advice and guidance notes, which are not legally enforceable, are available from the HSE. Clearly, it is intended that employers will seek solutions to their own particular safety problems and it will not be sufficient simply to adopt a model scheme drawn up by some other body. As an absolute minimum the safety policy should deal with the various responsibilities of all employees, from the board of directors down to the shop floor. Indeed, the statement may be used as evidence if a prosecution is launched under section 37 HASAWA 1974 (see below). It should also deal with general safety precautions, mechanisms for dealing with special hazards, routine inspections, emergency procedures, training and arrangements for consulting the workforce.

In industrial relations terms, it is obviously desirable to reach agreement with employee representatives on the contents of the written statement. However, this is not a legal requirement. No guidance is given as to how the statement should be brought to the notice of employees, although ideally a copy should be supplied to each person.[24] Special precautions may have to be taken in relation to those who have language difficulties.

REFLECTIVE QUESTION

Should there be a legal requirement that the safety policy be agreed with the employee representatives?

PERSONS OTHER THAN EMPLOYEES

Section 3 HASAWA 1974 imposes a duty on employers and self-employed persons to 'conduct their undertakings in such a way as to ensure, so far as is reasonably practicable, that persons not in their employment who may be affected thereby are not exposed to risks to their health and safety'. More specifically, Regulation 12 of the MHSW Regulations 1999 obliges employers and self-employed people to supply any person working in their undertaking who is not their employee with comprehensible information and instruction on any risks which arise out of the conduct of the undertaking.[25] It is clear that the word 'risk' should be given its ordinary meaning of denoting the possibility of danger rather than actual danger.[26] This may apply to subcontractors working on the employer's premises. The duty of the employer towards visiting workers is not very different from that owed to its own employees under section 2 of HASAWA 1974, since it may need to instruct the visitors (see *R v Swan Hunter Shipbuilders Ltd and Telemeter Installations Ltd* [27]).

The question of employer control

An employer cannot delegate its duty under section 3 HASAWA 1974, and criminal liability is not limited to the acts of the 'directing mind' or senior management of a company.[28] In *R v Associated Octel* [29] the House of Lords held that cleaning, repair and maintenance was necessary for the carrying out of the employer's business and part of the conduct of the undertaking and fell within the scope of section 3 when carried out by contractors.[30] It is unnecessary to show that the employer has some actual control over how the work is done. Nevertheless, as far as operations carried out by independent contractors are concerned, the question of control may be relevant. In most cases, the employer has no control over how a competent contractor does the work and it may not be reasonably practicable to do other than rely on the contractor. Thus it is important to clarify when making the contract the way the work should be done and, if it is clear that the contractor is not honouring the agreed system, the employer should order it off site.

SAFE PREMISES

Section 4 HASAWA 1974 provides that a person who has

> control of non-domestic premises used as a place of work must take such measures as it is reasonable for a person in his position to take to ensure that the means of access and egress and any plant or substance in the premises is safe and without risks to health.

According to the House of Lords, once it is proved that:

- the premises made available for use by others are unsafe and constitute a risk to health,
- the accused (who is usually an employer) had a degree of control over those premises, and
- having regard to the accused's degree of control and knowledge of the likely use, it would have been reasonable to take measures to ensure that the premises were safe,

the accused must demonstrate that, weighing the risk to health against the means (including cost) of eliminating it, it was not reasonably practicable to take those measures. However, if the premises are not a reasonably foreseeable cause of danger to people using them in the circumstances that might reasonably be expected to occur, it is not reasonable to require further measures to be taken. Unlike section 3 this section provides for shared responsibility where there is more than one occupier of the premises. This possibly explains why the employer was not liable under section 4 in a case[31] where the facts were very similar to those in the *Octel* case.

EMPLOYEE DUTIES

Section 7 of HASAWA 1974 imposes two general duties on employees while they are at work:[32]

- to take reasonable care of the health and safety of themselves and of others who may be affected by their acts or omissions
- as regards any duty imposed on their employers or any other person by any of the relevant statutory provisions, to co-operate with them so far as is necessary to enable that duty to be performed.

REGULATIONS

It is not possible to review all the sets of Regulations made under HASAWA 1974. The following paragraphs outline the Regulations made to implement the EEC Framework Directive, the five sets of Regulations immediately subsidiary to this, and the Control of Substances Hazardous to Health (COSHH) Regulations.

THE MHSW REGULATIONS

These Regulations are intended to implement the EEC Framework Directive[33] (but also cover all or part of certain other EEC Directives[34]), and Regulation 4 requires an employer to implement preventative and protective measures on the basis of certain general principles of prevention set out in this Directive. These general principles are:

- avoiding risks
- evaluating the risks which cannot be avoided
- combating the risks at source
- adapting the work to the individual, especially as regards the design of workplaces and the choice of work equipment and the choice of working and production methods with a view in particular to alleviating monotonous work and work at a predetermined work rate and to reducing their effect on health
- adapting to technical progress
- replacing the dangerous by the non-dangerous or less dangerous
- developing a coherent overall prevention policy which covers technology, organisation of work, working conditions, social relationships and the influence of factors related to the work environment
- giving collective protective measures priority over individual protective measures
- giving appropriate instructions to employees.

Risk assessment

The MHSW Regulations impose a duty on all employers and the self-employed to conduct a risk assessment. This assessment must be both suitable and sufficient and must consider the risk to the health and safety of all employees and other persons arising from the conduct of the undertaking.[35] The purpose of the assessment is to identify the measures that have to be taken to ensure compliance with the relevant statutory provisions. These provisions are specified in the Approved Code of Practice and include both the duties under HASAWA 1974 and regulations made under that Act. The risk assessment must be reviewed if there is reason to suspect that it is no longer valid or there has been a significant change in the matters to which it relates. An employer is specifically forbidden from employing a young person (someone under the age of 18 years[36]) unless a review has occurred which takes particular account of certain special characteristics such as the inexperience, lack of awareness of risks and the immaturity of young persons.[37] Regulation 19 provides employers with a particular duty to ensure that young employees are protected from risks to their health and safety arising out of their inexperience. If there are any women of child-bearing age working in an undertaking, there is a special obligation, in Regulation 16, to assess any potential risk that might affect the health and safety of a new or expectant mother – see Chapter 8.

REFLECTIVE QUESTION

Have you ever conducted or participated in conducting a risk assessment at work? Do you think the requirement to conduct one is a wise precaution or unnecessary regulation?

Regulation 5 requires employers to give effect to appropriate arrangements for the effective planning, organisation, control, monitoring and review of the measures they need to take as a result of the risk assessment. Again, such arrangements must be recorded if the employer has five or more employees. Regulation 6 obliges employers to provide appropriate health surveillance for their employees. Where prosecution has established that a person has been injured in the course of employment, the employer (and, indeed, senior managers) are unlikely to escape liability if no risk assessment of the work had been undertaken.[38]

Relating risk assessment to compensation cases

While the risk assessment requirements are clearly part of the preventative legislation, compensation cases can give insights into factors that the employer may have to consider when carrying out a risk assessment. For example, the employer may need to have regard to any particular issues relating to individual employees. Thus in *Tasci v Pekalp of London Ltd*,[39] a Kurdish refugee, who spoke little English, was employed as a wood machinist. The Court of Appeal (Civil Division) held that, given the claimant's background, the system of work operated by the employer fell short of that which was required by the relevant safety regulations and the employer's common-law duty of care.

It may be possible to identify a wide range of compensation cases which, like the one above, are indicative of the requirements of a comprehensive risk assessment, but of general importance is the developing awareness of the incidence of stress at the workplace. The HSE website cites estimates from the Labour Force Survey which claimed that:

- The total number of cases of stress in 2010/11 was 400 000 out of a total of 1,152,000 for all work-related illnesses. This is significantly lower than the number in 2001/02.
- The number of new cases of work-related stress has been reduced to 211,000 from 233,000 in 2009/10.
- The industries that reported the highest rates of work-related stress in the previous three years were health, social work, education and public administration.
- The occupations that reported the highest rates of work-related stress in the previous three years were health and social service managers, teachers and social welfare associate professionals.[40]

Recent compensation litigation has established that the employer must compensate an employee who suffers stress-related injury as a result of the employer's negligence, whether the injury is physical or psychological.[41] Yet health and safety legislation makes no express reference to the employer's having any duty to protect employees from stress-related ill health. However, the HSE considers that section 2 of the Act implicitly requires employers to take steps to make sure employees do not suffer stress-related illness as a result of their work. It similarly believes that employers must take account of the risk of stress-related ill health when carrying out risk assessments as required by Regulation 3.[42] The implication is therefore that employers can be criminally liable for operating stressful workplaces that put their employees at risk of ill health. For criminal liability to occur it is not necessary that any employee becomes ill; it is sufficient that employees are at risk of becoming ill.

Defining and appointing 'competent persons'

Under Regulation 7 employers must appoint one or more 'competent persons' to assist them in implementing the measures they need in order to comply with the relevant statutory provisions. The number of people appointed, the time available for them to fulfil their functions, and the means at their disposal must be adequate, having regard to the size of the undertaking and the risks to which employees are exposed. A 'competent person' is defined as someone who has sufficient training and experience or knowledge to enable him or her to assist properly in the undertaking.[43] However, there is a requirement for the employer to give preference to the appointment of a 'competent person' in his employment over one from outside.[44]

Regulation 8 obliges an employer to establish appropriate procedures to be followed in the event of 'serious and imminent danger to persons at work in his undertaking'. Employers must nominate a sufficient number of competent persons to implement these procedures and to be sure that employees are unable to enter dangerous areas without having received adequate health and safety instruction. It is made clear that this Regulation requires both the provision of information and procedures which enable employees to leave their work immediately in the event of 'serious and imminent danger'.[45]

THE SUBSIDIARY DIRECTIVES

At about the time of the adoption of the Framework Directive, the EEC adopted five subsidiary Directives. The following sets of Regulations were made in Britain to implement these Directives and many of them have been more tested in the civil than in the criminal courts. Some of them have also been subject to minor amendments.[46]

THE MANUAL HANDLING OPERATIONS REGULATIONS

These Regulations[47] require an employer to:

- avoid hazardous manual handling where reasonably practicable
- assess unavoidable hazardous manual handling operations
- reduce the risk of injury as far as reasonably practicable
- provide employees who are undertaking manual handling with as much information as reasonably practicable about the weight of the load(s) and the heaviest side of loads which have a centre of gravity that is not located centrally.

Manual handling is a major cause of workplace injuries and there have been many compensation claims. The HSE has published guidance.[48] The guidance lays emphasis on how to manage loads safely, and although the regulations do not place a duty on the employer to train employees who have to manually handle goods, it is clearly good practice for employers to do so.

THE WORKPLACE (HEALTH, SAFETY AND WELFARE) REGULATIONS 1992

These Regulations[49] provide standards for matters such as temperature, lighting, space, passageways, floors, doors, toilets, washing, eating and changing facilities, drinking water, and for maintenance of the workplace, equipment and facilities.

THE PERSONAL PROTECTIVE EQUIPMENT AT WORK REGULATIONS 1992

These Regulations[50] set out principles for selecting, providing, maintaining and using personal protective equipment (PPE). They do not apply where there are specific regulations relating to PPE.

THE HEALTH AND SAFETY (DISPLAY SCREEN EQUIPMENT) REGULATIONS 1992

These Regulations[51] apply where there is a 'user'.[52] Employers must:

- assess display screen equipment (DSE) workstations and reduce risks discovered by the assessment
- make sure that workstations satisfy minimum regulatory standards
- plan DSE work so that there are breaks or changes of activity
- provide information and training for users
- in some cases meet the cost of special reading glasses.

THE PROVISION AND USE OF WORK EQUIPMENT REGULATIONS 1998

These revised Regulations[53] were originally made in 1992. Work equipment is broadly defined to include everything from a hand tool to a complete plant. 'Use' includes starting, stopping, repairing, modifying, installing, dismantling, programming, setting, transporting, maintaining, servicing and cleaning. Minimum requirements are set down for work equipment to deal with selected hazards. The HSE has published an Approved Code of Practice and several sets of guidance.

THE CONTROL OF SUBSTANCES HAZARDOUS TO HEALTH (COSHH) REGULATIONS 2002

Each year, approximately 16,000 to 25,000 people become ill as a result of exposure to substances hazardous to health at work – eg respiratory disease, dermatitis, etc. This includes an estimated 3,000 to 12,000 cancer deaths mostly related to chemicals and asbestos.[54] The Control of Substances Hazardous to Health Regulations (COSHH) originally came into force in October 1989 but have been amended and replaced several times. The most recent version came into effect in November 2002 but has since been amended.[55]

According to the Health and Safety Executive, hazardous substances are anything that can harm your health when you work with them if they are not properly controlled – eg by using adequate ventilation. They can include:

- substances used directly in work activities – eg glues, paints, cleaning agents
- substances generated during work activities – eg fumes from soldering and welding

- naturally occurring substances – eg grain dust, blood, bacteria.

For the vast majority of commercial chemicals, the presence (or not) of a warning label will indicate whether COSHH is relevant. For example, household washing-up liquid doesn't require a warning label but bleach does – so COSHH applies to bleach but not washing-up liquid when used at work.[56]

COSHH provides employers with a general duty to prevent or adequately control the exposure of their employees and others who may be affected to hazardous substances. In addition there are a number of specific duties:

1 *Risk assessment*
An employer must not carry out work which is liable to expose any employees to any substance hazardous to health unless the employer has carried out an assessment of the risk to the health of employees and the steps that need to be taken to meet the requirements of the Regulations.[57] The risk assessment is to be reviewed regularly and appropriate changes made as a result of these reviews. All but the smallest of employers (those employing fewer than five employees) must record the 'significant' findings of the risk assessment and the steps that have been taken as a result.

2 *Prevention or control of exposure*
Every employer must ensure that the exposure of his employees to substances hazardous to health is either prevented or, where this is not reasonably practicable, adequately controlled.[58] Substitution by a substance that is not hazardous is preferred. However, if this is not reasonably practicable, the employer must comply with this duty by applying protection measures such as adequate ventilation, using appropriate work processes, and the provision of suitable protective equipment.

3 *Maintenance, examination and testing*
All employers who provide control measures must ensure, where relevant, that they are maintained in an efficient state, in efficient working order, in good repair and in a clean condition.[59] A suitable record of the examinations and tests plus any subsequent repairs carried out must be kept and made available for at least five years after it was done.

Where employees are, or are liable to be, exposed to a hazardous substance, they must be kept under suitable health surveillance. The employer should ensure that a health record is kept in respect of each of these employees and must make sure that it is kept and available for 40 years from the date it was made. Employees, and the Health and Safety Executive, have a right of access to their own records.[60] The employer also has a duty to ensure that all employees who may be exposed to hazardous substances are provided with suitable information, instruction and training. This will include details about the substances, maximum exposure limits, findings of the risk assessment and the precautions and actions that must be taken by the employee to safeguard himself or herself and others at the workplace.[61] The Regulations are supported by an Approved Code of Practice which gives detailed practical advice on compliance. The ACOP includes appendices dealing with carcinogens, biological agents and substances that cause occupational asthma.

CASE STUDY

DUGMORE v SWANSEA NHS TRUST

Dugmore v Swansea NHS Trust[62] concerned a nurse who, in 1994, developed an allergy to latex protein as a result of using powdered latex gloves in the course of her work. She was given vinyl gloves to use instead but still came into contact with an empty box that had contained the latex ones and suffered an illness which stopped her returning to work as a nurse. There was evidence that in the 1990s there was increasing scientific recognition of the problem of latex allergy. She claimed damages from her employers, alleging, amongst other matters, a breach of Regulation 7(1) of the COSHH Regulations (see point **2** above). The Court of Appeal held that the Regulations imposed an absolute duty on the employer to prevent exposure to health hazards and there was enough scientific knowledge of the allergy at that time for an employer with that duty to have been able to discover what needed to be done. The purpose of the COSHH Regulations was protective and preventative. Lady Justice Hale stated that the Regulations did not simply rely on criminal sanctions or civil liability to induce good practice. They involved positive obligations to seek out the risks and take precautions. In this case the employer had a duty to ensure that exposure was adequately controlled. The Court suggested that it would have been a simple matter to change the latex gloves to vinyl ones and the onus was on the employer to show that they were unable to do this. They failed to do so and the Court allowed Ms Dugmore's claim.

Discussion point

Do you think that this strict approach – putting the onus on employers to seek out the risks and take preventative measures – is the approach to be preferred in relation to health and safety law? Or is the old 'common law' approach fairer – by which the employer only has to take 'reasonable care' (see above)?

REGULATIONS ON REPORTING INJURIES

The Reporting of Injuries, Diseases and Dangerous Occurrences Regulations 1995 (RIDDOR 1995)[63] apply to events which arise 'out of or in connection with work'[64] activities covered by HASAWA 1974. Whenever any of the following arises it must be reported to the enforcing authority in writing and a record kept.[65] If any of **(a)**–**(d)** happens, the enforcing authority must first be notified by the quickest practicable means:

a) the death of any person as a result of an accident, whether or not he or she is at work
b) someone at work suffers a major injury as the result of an accident[66]
c) someone who is not at work suffers an injury as the result of an accident and is taken to a hospital for treatment
d) one of a list of specified dangerous occurrences takes place[67]

e) someone is unable to do his or her normal work for more than seven days (not counting the day on which the accident occurred)[68] as the result of an injury caused by an accident at work

f) the death of an employee, if it occurs after a reportable injury which led to the employee's death, but not more than one year afterwards

g) a person at work suffers a specified disease, provided that a doctor diagnoses the disease and the person's job involves a specified work activity.[69]

The duty to report the events listed above is imposed on the 'responsible person'.[70] Regulation 13 gives the HSE a limited power to grant exemptions from the requirements imposed by RIDDOR 1995.

INSPECTION AND ENFORCEMENT

Except where enforcement responsibilities have been assigned to local authorities,[71] HASAWA 1974 is enforced by inspectors appointed by the HSE. Inspectors appointed under HASAWA 1974 have the following powers:[72]

a) at any reasonable time (or, if there is a dangerous situation, at any time) to enter premises

b) to take with them a police officer, if they have reasonable cause to be apprehensive of any serious obstruction in the execution of their duty

c) to take with them any other authorised person and any equipment or materials required

d) to make such examination and investigation as may be necessary

e) to direct that the premises be left undisturbed for so long as is reasonably necessary for the purpose of examination or investigation

f) to take such measurements, photographs and readings as they consider necessary

g) to take samples of any articles or substances found in any premises and of the atmosphere in, or in the vicinity of, any such premises[73]

h) in the case of an article or substance which appears to have caused or to be likely to cause danger, to dismantle it or subject it to any process or test. The article or substance may be damaged or destroyed if it is thought necessary in the circumstances. However, if they are so requested by a person who is present and has responsibilities in relation to those premises, this power must be exercised in that person's presence unless the inspector considers that to do so would be prejudicial to the safety of the state

i) in the case of an article or substance which appears to have caused or to be likely to cause danger, to take possession of it and detain it for so long as is necessary in order to examine it, to ensure that it is not tampered with before the examination is completed, and to ensure that it is available for use as evidence in any proceedings for an offence or any proceedings relating to a notice under section 21 or 22 HASAWA 1974 (see below). An inspector must leave a notice giving particulars of the article or substance stating that he or she has taken possession of it and, if it is practicable, he or she should give a sample of it to a responsible person at the premises[74]

j) if carrying out examinations or investigations under **(d)**, to require persons whom they have reasonable cause to believe to be able to give any information to answer such questions as the inspector thinks fit to ask and to sign a declaration of the truth of their answers

k) to require the production of, inspect and take copies of an entry in, any books or documents which are required to be kept and any other books or documents which it is necessary for them to see for the purpose of any examination or investigation under **(d)** above

l) to require any persons to afford them such facilities and assistance with respect to any matters within that person's control or responsibilities as are necessary for the inspectors to exercise their powers

m) any other power which is necessary for the purpose of carrying into effect the statutory provisions.

However, inspectors appointed under HASAWA are empowered only to enforce the general duties in HASAWA 1974 and 'relevant statutory provisions' (that is, in effect, regulations made under the Act unless they have been given special authority – for instance, under the Working Time Regulations). Unusually, these inspectors are empowered to conduct prosecutions in their own right rather than through the Crown Prosecution Service.

If a person has been killed and homicide proceedings appear appropriate, these can only be taken by the police, with the Crown Prosecution Service. In practice the HSE and the police carry out a joint investigation. Very high financial penalties may be imposed under HASAWA – indeed, in August 2006 Transco plc was fined £15 million under HASAWA 1974 at the High Court of Justiciary in Edinburgh following a massive pipeline explosion that destroyed a house and killed the occupants. Nevertheless, there was public disquiet that there was insufficient stigma attached to conviction under HASAWA for causing fatalities.

At common law it was very difficult to convict a company of manslaughter and there was considerable public demand for reform. Eventually, after a long gestation period, the Corporate Manslaughter and Corporate Homicide Act 2007 was enacted. The Act created a new statutory offence of manslaughter which an organisation commits if the way in which its activities are managed or organised by its senior management a) causes a person's death, and b) amounts to a gross breach of a relevant duty of care owed by the organisation to the deceased. It is no longer possible to prosecute an organisation for common law manslaughter. Prosecutions cannot be brought under this Act against individuals, but a conviction for this new offence does not preclude a prosecution under HASAWA 1974, and the practice established under HASAWA 1974 of the HSE and the police conducting joint investigations is likely to be followed where prosecution is for manslaughter under the 2007 Act. At the time of going to press there has been only one conviction under the Act, but its existence may enable prosecutions of individuals for common law manslaughter in situations where previously there was a reluctance to charge individual managers or employees for manslaughter when such a charge would not lie against the corporate employer.[75]

THE SERVING OF NOTICES

HASAWA 1974 gave inspectors what were at that time novel powers – namely, the power to serve notices on persons requiring them to take actions which in the view of the inspectors are necessary in the interests of health and safety. Service of a notice does not of itself amount to being charged with a criminal offence. In practice inspectors more frequently serve notices than institute criminal proceedings, although it is possible for criminal proceedings to be instituted at the time of serving a notice. There are two forms of notice:

- *Improvement notices*
  Where an inspector is of the opinion that a person is contravening or has contravened a relevant statutory provision in circumstances that make it likely that the contravention will continue or be repeated, he or she may serve an 'improvement notice' stating that opinion. The notice must specify the provision, give particulars of the reasons why he or she is of that opinion, and will require that person to remedy the contravention within such period as may be specified in the notice.[76] This period must not be less than the time allowed for appealing against the notice – ie 21 days.[77]
- *Prohibition notices*
  In respect of an activity covered by a relevant statutory provision, if any inspector believes that activities are being carried on or are about to be carried on which will involve a risk of serious personal injury, the inspector may serve a 'prohibition notice'. Such a notice will state the inspector's opinion, specify the matters which give rise to the risk, and direct that the activities to which the notice relates must not be carried on by or under the control of the person on whom the notice is served (unless the matters specified in the notice have been remedied). A prohibition notice will normally take effect immediately.

Both types of notice may (but need not) include directions as to the measures to be taken to remedy the contravention or the matter to which the notice relates. Where a notice has been served but is not to take immediate effect, it may be withdrawn by the inspector within 21 days of service. Similarly, the period specified for rectification may be extended by an inspector at any time when an appeal against the notice is not pending.

A person on whom a notice is served may appeal to an employment tribunal, which has the power to cancel or affirm the notice or affirm it in a modified form.[78] For the purpose of hearing such appeals the tribunal may include specially appointed assessors. Bringing an appeal against an improvement notice has the effect of suspending the operation of that notice until the appeal is disposed of. Lodging an appeal against a prohibition notice suspends it only if the tribunal so directs and then only from the time when the direction is given.[79] Failure to comply with a notice is an offence.[80]

Because it is not possible to bring a prosecution against the Crown,[81] it is equally impossible to enforce improvement and prohibition notices against Crown bodies. However, the HSE has been prepared to issue 'Crown notices' where, in its opinion, an improvement or prohibition notice would have been appropriate. Such notices have no legal effect but may be of some value in so far as they put moral pressure on the employing body. Of course, trade union representatives who receive copies of these notices may be in a position to apply industrial pressure.

OFFENCES

Other than the Crown, any person or body corporate can be prosecuted for an offence under HASAWA 1974. However, if an offence is proved to have been committed with the consent or connivance of, or to have been attributable to neglect on the part of, any director, manager, secretary or other similar officer, then that person as well as the body corporate may be found guilty of an offence.[82] Thus in *Armour v Skeen*,[83] a local authority director of roads was prosecuted for failing to prepare and carry out a sound safety policy. His neglect led to breaches of safety provisions that resulted in the death of a Council employee.[84]

Where the commission of an offence by any person is due to the act or default of some other person, that other person may be charged whether or not proceedings are taken against the first-mentioned person.[85] Crown servants may be prosecuted despite the immunity of the Crown itself. Proceedings under this Act can be brought only by an inspector or with the consent of the Director of Public Prosecutions.

The Health and Safety (Offences) Act 2008 amended HASAWA in order to increase the penalties for the offences created by section 33 of HASAWA. In brief, most of the offences under section 33 are now triable either summarily or on indictment. On summary conviction the maximum penalty is imprisonment for a term not exceeding 12 months, or a fine not exceeding £20,000, or both. The penalty on conviction on indictment is now imprisonment for a term not exceeding two years, or a fine, or both. Where conviction follows trial upon indictment, there is no limit to the amount of fine that the court can impose.

In deciding on the level of the fine to be imposed, the court will take into account the ability of the defendant to pay. Generally, fines will not be so large as to endanger the earnings of employees or create a risk of bankruptcy, unless the offence is so serious that the firm should not be in business.[86] The questions to be asked, according to the Court of Appeal, which should guide courts in assessing fines were:

- What financial penalty does the offence merit?
- What financial penalty can a defendant reasonably be ordered to pay, and over what period? A longer period might be acceptable in the case of a company as opposed to an individual.[87]

In reaching a decision on the fine, the aggravating features to be taken into account will include:

- whether the defendant had failed to heed warnings

- whether the defendant deliberately profited financially from the failure to take the necessary health and safety measures.

Conversely, the features which might be taken in mitigation include:

- prompt admission of responsibility and a timely plea of guilty
- steps to remedy the deficiencies once they have been drawn to the defendant's attention
- a good safety record.

Where people are convicted of offences in respect of any matters that appear to the court to be within their power to remedy, the court may, in addition to or instead of imposing any punishment, order them to take such steps as may be specified to remedy those matters.[88]

CASE STUDY

DAVIES v HSE

Following a fatal accident at his plant hire business, Mr Davies was charged with an offence under section 3 HASAWA 1974. The judge ruled that section 40 HASAWA 1974, which states that 'it shall be for the accused to prove ... that it was not reasonably practicable to do more than was in fact done' was compatible with Article 6(2) of the European Convention on Human Rights. This provides that 'Everyone charged with a criminal offence shall be presumed innocent until proved guilty according to law.'

In dismissing an appeal against conviction, the Court of Appeal held that the imposition of a reverse legal burden of proof was justified, necessary and proportionate in the circumstances. Before any question of reverse onus arises, the prosecution must prove that the defendant owed the duty and that the safety standard was breached. Additionally, the facts relied on by the defendant should not be difficult to establish because they will be within the defendant's knowledge. Finally, whether the defendant could have done more will be judged objectively.[89]

Discussion point

'Innocent until proved guilty' is one of the most fundamental legal principles (and one which almost everyone is aware of!). Do you think that even with regard to health and safety law it is right for this principle to be reversed as it is in section 40 HASAWA 1974?

REFLECTIVE QUESTION

Do you think that the laws on health and safety at work are adequate? Are there any ways in which you think they could be strengthened, or do you think on the contrary that they are an excessive burden on business?

KEY LEARNING POINTS

- Occupational health and safety legislation is enforced through the criminal law. Accident victims may sue alleging common-law negligence or breach of statutory duty.
- HASAWA 1974 sets out the general duties which employers have towards employees, other workers and members of the public, and which employees have towards themselves and each other.
- The HSE has the option to propose and issue guidance, ACOPs or regulations.
- Every employer with five employees or more must prepare and revise a written statement of its general policy on health and safety at work, and the organisation and arrangements for carrying out that policy.
- HASAWA 1974 also places an obligation on employers to have regard for the health and safety of persons not in their employment.
- All employers have an obligation to conduct a risk assessment. The purpose of this assessment is to identify the measures that must be taken to ensure compliance with the statutory provisions contained in HASAWA 1974, and relevant regulations, taking into account any ACOP or guidance issued by the HSE.
- Employers are required not only to carry out but also respond to risk assessments; such assessments should include consideration of stress-related injury.
- COSHH requires employers to prevent or adequately control the exposure of their employees to, and others who may be affected by, hazardous substances.
- There is a duty on employers to provide information to and consult with employees and their representatives who are either trade-union-appointed or directly elected.

REFERENCES

1 **This chapter contains extracts from or close paraphrasing of legislation which is on the opsi.gov.uk website and is subject to crown copyright. The reproduction of this material here is licensed under the open government licence v1.0**

2 Most occupational health and safety regulations are made under section 5 of HASAWA and known as 'relevant statutory instruments', although some which represent the implementation of European Directives were made under other legislation and the HSE has been empowered to enforce them too – for example, the Supply of Machinery (Safety) Regulations 2008 (SI 2008/1597) and the Working Time Regulations 1998 (SI/1833) were made under section 2(2) of the European Communities Act 1972. The Working Time Regulations are covered in Chapter 10.

3 SI 1999/3242; see also the Management of Health and Safety at Work Regulations 1999 Approved Code of Practice and Guidance, HSE 2000

4 The Act says except in so far as the regulations provide otherwise – see section 47(2) HASAWA 1974 – however, following subsequent EEC requirements there is a presumption that breach of any of the regulations can lead to civil liability. The Regulatory Enforcement and Sanctions Act

2008 provides for new civil sanctions as an alternative to some prosecutions, but the HSE has expressed its opposition to making use of these.

5 HASAWA 1974 originally provided for both a Health and Safety Commission and a Health and Safety Executive but the Commission was abolished (Legislative Reform, (Health and Safety Executive) Order 2008 SI 2008/960)

6 www.hse.gov.uk/stress/pdfs/eurostress.pdf

7 www.hse.gov.uk/violence/preventing-workplace-harassment.pdf

8 Section 17 HASAWA 1974

9 The website of the Health and Safety Executive contains a large amount of free information about various regulatory requirements

10 Formerly, these were EEC Directives

11 *Commission v UK* (2007) IRLR 721. The difficulty was that the Commission failed to take into account the difference between the UK legal system and that of other Member States: the Court was satisfied that the UK social security system ensures that all victims of workplace injury and disease are given financial support

12 Section 2(2) HASAWA 1974. Note that the illustrations provided by section 2(2) are not intended to be exhaustive

13 Defined in section 53 HASAWA 1974 as including any machinery, equipment or appliance

14 Defined in section 54 HASAWA 1974 as 'any natural or artificial substance whether in solid or liquid form of a gas or vapour'

15 The legislation makes little explicit reference to welfare, but it may prove to be relevant to physical and psychological stress injury. See also the guide *Tackling Work-Related Stress* (HSG218) (2001). For more up to date information go to *http://www.hse.gov.uk/stress/standards/index.htm*

16 (1997) IRLR 189

17 Section 40 HASAWA 1974. There is some confusion as to whether section 40 provides a defence or whether the defendant's task is to show that the prosecution has failed to establish an offence was committed. See *R v Davies* (2002) EWCA Crim. 2949 and compare *R v HTM Ltd* (2006) EWCA Crim. 1156.

18 See, *West Bromwich Building Society v Townsend* (1983) IRLR 147

19 *Cavanagh v Ulster Weaving Co Ltd* (1959) 2 All ER 745

20 SI 1977/500

21 SI 1996/1513

22 An 'undertaking' is not statutorily defined for these purposes, but is likely to cover all enterprises or businesses

23 Section 2(3) HASAWA 1974

24 In recent times employers have tended to put this policy, and other policies, on their intranet. Arguably, this is less satisfactory than providing a hard copy

25 There are special requirements in relation to visiting workers where there is asbestos on the premises. See the Control of Asbestos Regulations 2012 (SI 2012/632) replacing earlier regulations in order to implement Council Directive 2009/148 EC

26 See *R v Trustees of the Science Museum* (1993) 3 All ER 853

27 (1981) IRLR 403

28 See *R v British Steel* (1995) IRLR 310. Regulation 21 of MHWR 1999 now provides that an employer cannot raise as a defence that a breach of the employer's duty was due to the fault of an employee; so it was thought the controversial case of *R v Nelson Group Services Ltd (Maintenance) Ltd* (1998) 4 All ER 331 was not likely to be followed but in *R v HTM* (2006) EWCA Crim. 1156 it was argued that an employer should not be liable if the employee's unsafe conduct could not be foreseen

29 (1997) IRLR 123

30 The site was classified as a hazardous installation and the employer did not ensure that the visitors followed the work permit system

31 See *Inspector of Factories v Austin Rover* (1989) IRLR 404

32 On the meaning of 'at work' see section 52(1) HASAWA 1974

33 Directive 89/391/EEC

34 Eg the Directives concerning employment of pregnant women (92/85/EC) and young persons (94/33/EC)

35 See HSE leaflet *A Guide to Risk Assessment Requirements*, HSE (2001)

36 Regulation 1(2) MHSW Regulations 1999

37 Regulation 3(5) MHSW Regulations 1999

38 See *R v Chargot* (2008) UKHL 73 per Lord Brown at para 42. Both employers and a senior manager were convicted; the manager under section 37

39 (2001) ICR 633

40 Taken from the HSE website http://www.hse.gov.uk/statistics/causdis/stress/ index.htm [accessed April 2012]

41 See *Pickford v ICI* (1998) IRLR 435 on repetitive strain injury, and *Sutherland v Hatton* (2002) IRLR 263 on psychological injury

42 *Tackling Work-Related Stress: A manager's guide to improving and maintaining employee health and well-being* (2001) HSG218 at paras 12 and 13; see also *Management Standards for Work Related Stress* http://www.hse.gov.uk/stress/ standards/, or the fuller explanation *Managing the Causes of Work-related Stress* HSG218, which may be downloaded from this website

43 See Regulation 6(5)

44 Regulation 6(8) 1999 Regulations

45 See Regulation7(2)

46 When seeking the full version of any regulations it is important to ensure that the copy contains all the amendments; this applies both to hard copies and Internet versions. The legislative practice is to 'cut and paste' amendments into the original rather than reissue the regulations as a whole

47 SI 1992/2793, implementing 90/269/EEC

48 *Simple Guide to Lifting Operations and Lifting Equipment Regulations 1998*

49 SI 1992/3004, implementing 89/6544/EEC

50 SI 1992/2966, implementing 89/656/EEC

51 SI 1992/2792, implementing 90/270/EEC

52 An employee who habitually uses DSE as a significant part of normal work

53 SI 1998/2306, revised to implement 95/63/EEC

54 Information from the Health and Safety Executive website

55 The Control of Substances Hazardous to Health Regulations 2002, SI 2002/2677

56 See HSE website. Section 6 of HASAWA places a general duty on the manufacturers and suppliers of articles and substances for use at work and this duty is underpinned by the Chemicals (Hazard Information and Packaging) Regulations 2009, SI 2009/716

57 Regulation 6 COSHH Regulations 2002

58 Regulation 7 COSHH Regulations 2002

59 Regulation 9 COSHH Regulations 2002

60 Regulation 11 COSHH Regulations 2002

61 Regulation 12 COSHH Regulations 2002

62 (2003) IRLR 164

63 SI 1995/3163

64 Defined by Regulation 2(2)c RIDDOR 1995

65 Regulation 7 RIDDOR 1995

66 Major injuries are listed in Schedule 1 RIDDOR 1995

67 Dangerous occurrences are listed in Schedule 2 RIDDOR 1995

68 The requirement to report an inability to work lasting three days (or more) was changed to one lasting seven days (or more) in April 2012

69 The specified diseases and corresponding work activities are listed in Schedule 3 RIDDOR 1995

70 Defined in Regulation 2

71 Health and Safety (Enforcing Authority) Regulations 1998 (SI 1998/494). These Regulations were made under Section 18(2) of HASAWA

72 Section 19

73 See *Laws v Keane* (1982) IRLR 500

74 See also section 25 HASAWA 1974 on the power to deal with an imminent cause of danger

75 Members of the crew of the ferry involved in the Zeebrugge disaster would have been more likely to have been prosecuted had it been possible to convict the ferry company of manslaughter

76 See *West Bromwich Building Society v Townsend* (note 18)

77 Rule 2 Schedule 4 Employment Tribunal (Constitution and Rules of Procedure) Regulations 1993, SI 1993/2687

78 Section 24(2) HASAWA 1974. Section 82(1)(c) defines 'modifications' as including additions, omissions and amendments. See *British Airways v Henderson* (1979) ICR 77

79 Section 24(3) HASAWA 1974

80 See section 33(1)(g) HASAWA 1974 and *Deary* v *Mansion Hide Upholstery Ltd* (1983) IRLR 195

81 Section 48 HASAWA 1974

82 Section 37 HASAWA 1974. Directors who are convicted of an offence can be disqualified from office under the Directors Disqualification Act 1986

83 (1977) IRLR 310. See also *R v Boal* (1992) IRLR 420

84 See also *R v Chargot* (2008) UKHL (note 38) 80 Section 36 HASAWA 1974

85 See *R v F Howe & Son* (1999) IRLR 434

86 See *R v Rollco Screw Co Ltd* (1999) IRLR 439

87 Section 42(1) HASAWA 1974

88 *Davies v HSE* (2003) IRLR 170

EXPLORE FURTHER

Reading

This topic now has very little coverage in the main student textbooks. Should you wish to find more detail, you might try:

- Ford, M. and Clarke, J. (2012) *Redgrave's Health and Safety at Work*, 8th edition. Butterworth's Law
- LexisNexis (2010) *Tolley's Health and Safety at Work Handbook.* Butterworth's Law

Website

- Health and Safety Executive http://www.hse.gov.uk/

CHAPTER 10

The Regulation of Working Time

CHAPTER OVERVIEW

This chapter is concerned with the Working Time Regulations 1998 and those occasions when there is a statutory right to time off work. (Issues relating to parental rights, including maternity leave, parental leave and time off for dependants, are dealt with in Chapter 8.) There is an examination of the contents of these Regulation and this is followed by a consideration of the rights of trade unionists for time off to take part in trade union duties and activities. Finally, we look at other rights to time off, including time off for carrying out public duties.

LEARNING OUTCOMES

After studying this chapter you will be able to:

- understand the principles behind the Working Time Regulations and the statutory rights to time off work, and advise colleagues about their practical implications
- participate in the formulation of a policy on working hours and time off.

THE WORKING TIME REGULATIONS 1998

The Working Time Regulations[1] (WT Regulations) implement the Working Time Directive[2] and provisions of the Young Workers Directive.[3] The preamble to the Working Time Directive states that 'in order to ensure the safety and health of Community workers, the latter must be granted minimum daily, weekly and annual periods of rest and adequate breaks' and that 'it is necessary in this context to place a maximum limit on working time'. Thus the legal basis for the Directive was Article 118a EC (now Article 153 TFEU) relating to health and safety. This was the subject of an unsuccessful challenge by the United Kingdom,[4] which claimed that this was wrong and that the regulation of working time was a matter for Member States and not a health and safety matter to be dealt with at Community level.

EXCLUSIONS FROM THE WT REGULATIONS

Certain activities and certain sectors were originally excluded from the scope of the WT Regulations, although these exclusions have been modified as a result of the Working Time (Amendment) Regulations 2003.[5] One of the problems with excluding whole sectors from the application of the Regulations is that all workers are affected. There may be special problems associated with limiting the number of hours of mobile workers, such as long-distance lorry drivers and those at sea, but a blanket exclusion includes non-mobile workers who perhaps should be included. This was the issue in *Bowden v Tuffnel Parcels Express Ltd*.[6] In this case three clerical workers employed in the road transport industry failed to receive paid holidays. The European Court of Justice held that the Directive's exclusions applied to all workers within an excluded sector. Thus the administrative workers were to be treated no differently from travelling workers in any such sector.

The effect of the 2003 Regulations was to distinguish between mobile workers and others.[7] A mobile worker is defined as 'any worker employed as a member of the travelling or flying personnel by an undertaking which operates transport services for passengers or goods by rail or air'.[8] Thus it is these mobile workers who are excluded from the WT Regulations and for whom arrangements are made to cope with the special nature of the work. Specifically excluded groups include seafarers and those that work on board both seagoing ships and on ships or hovercraft operating on inland waterways; mobile road transport workers; mobile workers in aviation; and those in the armed or civil forces, such as the army or police, whose duties would inevitably conflict with the requirements of the WT Regulations. Also excluded are jobs in domestic service,[9] and there were special transitional arrangements for doctors in training,[10] whose maximum working hours have been progressively reduced.

Defining 'workers'

Regulation 2 defines a 'worker' as an individual who has entered into, or works under, a contract of employment or 'any other contract, whether express or implied and (if it is express) whether oral or in writing, whereby the individual undertakes to do or perform personally any work or services for another party to the contract whose status is not by virtue of the contract that of a client or customer of any professional or business undertaking carried out by the individual'. Thus there may be a distinction between a worker and a self-employed person.

CASE STUDY

BACICA v MUIR

In *Bacica v Muir*,[11] a self-employed painter and decorator who had worked for one employer for seven years was held not to be a worker but a self-employed person running his own business. He had claimed that he was entitled to be paid for his holidays under the Working Time Regulations because he met the definition of worker under those Regulations. The court, however, stated that there were enough indications to show that he was running his own business, such as being able to work for others, not being paid when not working and receiving an overheads allowance.

A young worker is defined as an individual who is at least 15 years of age, over the compulsory school-leaving age, and who has not yet attained the age of 18 years. This does not include children who are covered by other legislation. Thus, in *Addison v Ashby*,[12] a 15-year-old paperboy could not be classified as a worker, within the definition of the WT Regulations, because he was not over the compulsory school-leaving age. Regulation 36 deals with agency workers, who are not otherwise workers, by deeming the agency or principal to be the employer depending upon who is responsible for paying the worker. Labour-only subcontractors have been held to be workers within the definition of worker in the WT Regulations.[13] This was despite the fact that their contracts allowed them to appoint substitutes in certain circumstances. The subcontractors spent most of their time working personally and they were to be distinguished, according to the EAT, from others who might be seen as running a business undertaking.

CASE STUDY

COMMISSIONERS OF INLAND REVENUE v POST OFFICE LTD

In *Commissioners of Inland Revenue v Post Office Ltd*,[14] a number of sub-postmasters and postmistresses claimed that they were workers for the purposes of the WT Regulations. Their claim failed because, the EAT held, they were carrying on a business undertaking such that the Post Office was a client of their business. This was despite the fact that they gave undertakings to work personally for at least 18 hours per week in their sub-post office.

Working time, in relation to the worker, is defined[15] as:

- any period during which the worker is working, at the employer's disposal and carrying out the worker's activity or duties
- any period during which the worker is receiving relevant training

- any additional period which is to be treated as working time for the purpose of these Regulations under a relevant agreement (see below).

One issue concerning the WT Regulations has been the position of people who are on call, but not necessarily working all the time that they are required to be available. An example of this is a hospital doctor who is required to be on call and, inevitably, also be available in the hospital. The European Court of Justice[16] considered one case where a doctor spent three quarters of his working hours on call, sometimes for periods up to 25 hours. He was provided with a room where he could sleep when his services were not required. The Court decided that all his hours on call should be counted as working time. The crucial point was that he was required to be present at the place decided by the employer.

THE MAXIMUM WORKING WEEK AND THE FACILITY TO OPT OUT

Regulation 4 provides that working time, including overtime, must not exceed 48 hours per week (ie seven days) averaged over a reference period of 17 weeks, unless the worker has first agreed in writing to perform such work. This must be agreed by the worker individually, 'expressly and freely', and it is not enough for the contract of employment just to refer to a collective agreement which allows more hours.[17]

The employer is unable to insist that the employee works longer hours. In *Barber v RJB Mining (UK) Ltd*,[18] the employees were granted a declaration by the High Court that having worked in excess of the permitted hours during the reference period, they need not work again until such time as their average working time fell within the limits specified in Regulation 4(1).

Calculating average hours

The Regulations supply a formula for calculating the average hours over the reference period.[19] The formula is:

$$\frac{A + B}{C}$$

where A is the total number of hours comprised in the worker's working time during the reference period; B is the total number of hours comprised in the working time during the course of the period immediately after the end of the reference period and ending when the number of days in that subsequent period on which he or she has worked equals the number of excluded days during the reference period; and C is the number of weeks in the reference period. The excluded days in B are periods including annual leave, sick and maternity leave and periods in which an individual opting-out agreement is in effect. For new employees the reference period is the number of weeks actually worked.

Regulations 4 and 5 allow a worker to effectively opt out of the maximum working week provided that the agreement:

- is in writing
- relates either to a specified period or applies indefinitely, and
- is terminable by the worker on seven days' notice, unless a different notice period is specified (subject to a maximum of three months).

REFLECTIVE QUESTION

Is the opt-out from the maximum working week a fundamental flaw in the protection provided for workers?

The Regulations set a maximum working time for young workers of eight hours per day or 40 hours per week.[20] There are some exceptions to this rule. These are where

- the young worker's employer requires him or her to undertake work necessary to maintain continuity of service or production, or to help cope with a surge in demand
- no adult worker is available to perform the work
- performing the work would not adversely affect the young worker's education or training.[21]

Night work

Regulation 2 defines 'night time' as a period which is not less than seven hours in length and includes the hours from 12 midnight to 5 am. A 'night-worker' is a worker who, as a normal course, works at least three hours of working time during 'night time'[22] or is a worker who is likely, during 'night time', to work a certain proportion of his or her annual working time as defined by a collective or workforce agreement (see below).

CASE STUDY

R v ATTORNEY-GENERAL FOR NORTHERN IRELAND

In *R v Attorney-General for Northern Ireland*,[23] the meaning of the term 'normal course' was considered. The employee in the case had been asked to change to a shift system, which meant working a night shift, between 9 pm and 7 am, one week in three. The court held that the definition which requires an individual to work at least three hours during night time as a 'normal course' meant no more than that this should be a regular feature of the individual's work. It would be wrong to confine the protection only to those who work night shifts exclusively or predominantly.

Discussion point

Was such an interpretation necessary in order to promote the purpose of the Regulations?

Regulation 6 states that a night-worker's normal hours of work must not exceed, in a reference period, an average of eight in any 24-hour period.

Night-worker's average hours

A night-worker's average normal hours of work for each 24 hours during a reference period are calculated by the formula:

$$\frac{A}{B-C}$$

where A is the number of hours during the reference period which are the normal working hours for that worker; B is the number of days during the reference period; and C is the total number of hours during the reference period spent in rest periods (see below) divided by 24.

There is an obligation upon the employer to ensure that no night-worker whose work involves special hazards or heavy physical or mental strain works for more than eight hours in any 24-hour period during which night work is performed.[24] Such hazards or strain can be identified in a collective or workforce agreement or as a result of a risk assessment carried out in accordance with Regulation 3 of the Management of Health and Safety at Work Regulations 1999 (see Chapter 9). Night-workers are also entitled to a free health assessment prior to taking up night work and at regular intervals thereafter.[25]

Regulation 7(6) also stipulates that where a medical practitioner informs the employer that a worker is suffering from health problems connected with working at night, the employer should, if it is possible, transfer the worker to more suitable work or work which is not night work. The employer also has an obligation to provide adequate rest breaks where the pattern of work is likely to cause health problems, such as where there is monotonous work or a predetermined work-rate.[26] Regulation 9 also ensures that employers keep adequate records for a period of at least two years.

A restricted period for working is also introduced. This period is between 10 pm and 6 am, or if a worker's contract provides for him or her to work after 10 pm, the restricted period is between 11 pm and 7 am. The significance of this restricted period is that employers must ensure that no young worker works during these hours.[27] This effective ban on night work for young workers is also qualified. The rule does not apply to work in hospitals or similar establishments and does not apply in connection with cultural, artistic, sporting or advertising activities. The restricted period is reduced to the hours between midnight and 4 am for young workers in a number of businesses such as agriculture, retail trading, postal or newspaper deliveries, catering, hotels and bakeries.[28]

Rest periods and rest breaks

According to Regulation 10, adult workers are entitled to a rest period of at least 11 consecutive hours in each 24-hour period. For young workers this period should be at least 12 consecutive hours. The rest period can be interrupted in the case of activities which involve periods of work that are split up over the day or are of short duration. In addition,[29] adult workers are entitled to an uninterrupted weekly rest period of at least 24 hours in each seven-day period. The employer may change this to two uninterrupted rest periods of 24 hours in each 14 days or one uninterrupted rest period of 48 hours every 14 days. Young workers are entitled to an uninterrupted 48-hour rest period every seven days, although this may be interrupted in cases of activities which involve periods of work that are split up over the day or are of short duration, or where there are technical or organisational reasons for reducing it.[30]

Regulation 12 provides that where an adult worker's daily working time is more than six hours, the worker is entitled to a rest break. The details of this rest break can be in accordance with a workforce or collective agreement, provided that it is for at least 20 minutes and the worker is entitled to spend it away from the workstation. It should be noted that individuals are only entitled to one break however long they work in excess of six hours,[31] and it is intrinsic in the rules that the break should be during the working day and not at the end of it.[32] Young workers are entitled to a break where their working time is more than four and a half hours. This is to be for at least 30 minutes and can be spent away from the workstation. There is an additional complication for employers in Regulation 12(5), which states that where a young worker is employed by more than one employer, the daily working time is the total number of hours that the young worker has worked.

CASE STUDIES

MACCARTNEY v OVERSLEY HOUSE MANAGEMENT

Elizabeth MacCartney was employed as the resident manager of a development of privately owned homes for the over-sixties. She had a variety of duties, including being on call for emergencies. She was required to work for four days per week 'of 24 hours on site cover'. This meant that she had to stay on site, in her employer-provided accommodation, during the whole of this period. She could not go out, but could receive visitors, during the on-call period. On average she would have to deal with three to four emergency calls and ten or eleven non-emergency calls per month.

She made a claim that she was being denied the daily rest periods and rest breaks to which she was entitled under the WT Regulations 1999.

The EAT held that the whole period when she was on call could be classified as working time. It did not matter how many times she was actually called out or whether she was sleeping or resting during some of the period. Nor was it relevant that she was in accommodation intended to be her home. Workers who are on call at a place where they are required by their employer to remain can be said to be 'working' during the whole period. Ms MacCartney was therefore entitled to the daily rest periods in accordance with Regulation 10(1). Following the decision in *Gallagher v Alpha Catering Services Ltd*[33] the EAT held that she was also entitled to her 20-minute rest breaks in accordance with Regulation 12.

HUGHES v CORPS OF COMMISSIONAIRES MANAGEMENT LTD

Mr Hughes was employed as a security guard. He was one of three guards assigned to a company's premises. The three guards rotated their hours so that two guards worked a twelve-hour shift while the third had a day off. This meant that there was only one guard on duty at any particular time, so when the guard took his rest break he was obliged to leave a notice with a telephone number of where he could be contacted. Regulation 12(3) of the WT Regulations provides that the 'rest break' should be an uninterrupted period of not less than 20 minutes. This was confirmed by the Court of Appeal in *Gallagher v Alpha Catering Services Ltd* (note 33). In Mr Hughes' case it was not possible to have a 'Gallagher' break because of the possibility of interruptions. In such a case the obligation was on the employer to provide compensatory rest breaks, which would have the characteristics of a Gallagher rest break and, as far as possible, be free of interruptions. In Mr Hughes' case, if he was interrupted he was able to start his period of rest over again, and the Court held that this policy met the employer's obligations.

Discussion point

How important is it that the approach taken to 'on call' hours is the same for the purposes of both limiting hours and providing a minimum wage?

ANNUAL LEAVE

In any leave year a worker is entitled to 5.6 weeks' paid leave.[34] Unless there is a relevant agreement for another date, the worker's leave year begins on the date employment commenced and every anniversary thereafter. If the worker commences employment on a date that is different from the date agreed for the commencement of a leave year, he or she is entitled to a proportion for that first year. The leave may be taken during the year, but there is only an entitlement to the amount that has accrued so far. This is calculated on the basis of one-twelfth of the annual entitlement for each month of service.[35] It does include all the elements that make up the normal remuneration linked to the performance of the tasks that the contract requires. Thus, for an airline pilot, for example, the holiday pay might include regular flying allowances even though, obviously, the pilot is not flying during his break.[36]

A worker is deemed to have been continuously employed if his or her relations with the employer have been governed by a contract during the whole or part of each of those weeks. The leave may only be taken in the leave year in respect of which it was due and cannot be replaced by a payment in lieu, unless the employment is terminated.[37] If leave is carried over to the next holiday year, it must not be replaced with a payment in lieu. The CJEU has stated[38] that the Directive includes the rule that a worker must be entitled to the actual rest. To pay money in lieu would create an incentive not to take leave, and this would be incompatible with the health and safety objectives of the Working Time Directive. Nor is it necessary for the employee to have actually been at work during the period when the right to take leave arose. If an employee was absent through sickness for the entire year, as happened in *Dominguez*,[39] he or she would still be entitled to paid leave.

CASE STUDY

ASOCIACIÓN NACIONAL DE GRANDES EMPRESAS DE DISTRIBUCIÓN v FEDERACIÓN DE ASOCIACIONES SINDICALES

A number of Spanish trade unions asked for a declaration that department store workers were entitled to paid annual leave even where the leave coincided with temporary absences though sickness. The CJEU held that a worker is entitled to such paid annual leave irrespective of the point at which someone became incapacitated for work. The actual leave could be scheduled for a later date if necessary.

The correct approach to calculating the appropriate daily rate when working out what is owed to an employee is to divide the annual salary by the number of working days in the year, rather than the number of calendar days.[40] If an employee's employment is terminated and he or she has taken in excess of the entitlement calculated on a pro rata basis, there is no opportunity for the employer to claw back any of the overpayment unless there is in existence a relevant agreement, such as a collective or workforce agreement, allowing it to be done.[41]

A worker must give the employer notice of when he or she wishes to take the leave.[42] This notice must be given by a date which is equivalent to twice the amount of leave the worker is proposing to take. However, an employer can require the worker not to take the particular period requested by giving notice equivalent to the amount of leave the worker wants to take.

CASE STUDY

RUSSELL v TRANSOCEAN INTERNATIONAL RESOURCES LTD

The claimants were offshore workers located on the UK's continental shelf. They worked two weeks offshore on 12-hour shifts, then they had two weeks onshore during which they could undertake whatever activities they wished. They claimed that the WT Regulations allowed them to take four weeks annual paid leave when they would otherwise be working offshore. The Supreme Court, however, stated that the employer was able to insist that that they took their paid annual leave during periods when they were onshore. All the WT Regulations and the WT Directive required were rest periods, which are simply periods when the worker is not working.

Discussion point

What are the arguments for and against the fairness of this decision?

Regulation 16 provides that in respect of annual leave workers are entitled to be paid a sum equivalent to a week's pay for each week of leave.[43]

CASE STUDY

STRINGER v HM REVENUE & CUSTOMS

In *Stringer v HM Revenue & Customs*,[44] the CJEU established that the right to paid annual leave cannot be made subject to a condition that the worker has actually worked during the leave year. Thus the right continues to accrue during sick leave and, on termination of employment, a worker who has been on sick leave and unable to take paid annual leave is entitled to payment in lieu. More generally, the CJEU stated that the Directive does not preclude national legislation prohibiting workers on sickness absence from taking paid annual leave during that absence, provided they can exercise their right during another period. Equally, national legislation could allow workers on sickness absence to take paid annual leave during this absence. Subsequently, the CJEU has ruled that workers who are off sick must be allowed to carry over their holiday even if that is to a different leave year although there may be a limit to how far this can go.[45, 46]

Discussion point

To what extent does the CJEU's approach cause practical difficulties for employers?

For a time there were contradictory approaches in the courts as to whether holiday pay could be 'rolled up' over the year, so workers did not receive extra pay when they took their holidays. In effect the employer claimed that part of the worker's remuneration was holiday pay and that this was paid throughout the year, so that there was no obligation to pay the worker when he or she took the holiday, because it had already been included in the pay rate.

CASE STUDY

ROBINSON-STEELE v RD RETAIL SERVICES LTD

In *Robinson-Steele v R.D. Retail Services Ltd*,[47] the CJEU held that the Working Time Directive precluded part of the remuneration payable to a worker from being attributed to payment for annual leave without the worker receiving, in that respect, a payment additional to that for work done. The term 'paid annual leave' meant that a worker should be paid his or her normal remuneration for the duration of the annual leave, although the employer will be able to deduct any payments already made provided that these deductions were made in a transparent and comprehensible way.[48] According to the Court, the Working Time Directive treats entitlement to annual leave and to a payment on that account as 'being two aspects of a single right'. Its purpose is to put workers in the position that when they are on leave they are in a comparable position, with regard to remuneration, as when they are working.

Discussion point

What are the advantages for employers in paying for holiday leave before it is taken?

RECORDS

There is an obligation, in Regulation 9, for employers to keep records in respect of those workers who have agreed to opt out of the 48-hour limit, night work and health assessment checks for night-workers. These records must be adequate to show that the relevant time limits are being complied with in the case of each worker employed. Such records must be retained for a period of two years.

THE RIGHT NOT TO SUFFER DETRIMENT

According to section 45A ERA 1996, workers have the right not to be subjected to any detriment by any act, or failure to act, on the part of the employer on the grounds that the worker:

- refused, or proposed to refuse, to comply with any requirement in contravention of the WT Regulations
- refused, or proposed to refuse, to give up a right conferred by the WT Regulations
- failed to sign a workforce agreement (see below) or vary any other agreement with the employer which is provided for by the WT Regulations
- was a workforce representative or a candidate in an election for such representatives
- alleged that the employer had infringed the worker's rights under the WT Regulations
- was bringing proceedings to enforce rights under the WT Regulations.

The worker will be entitled to such compensation as the tribunal considers is just and equitable in all the circumstances, taking into account the default of the employer and the loss suffered by the worker.[49] If the detriment amounts to a dismissal for one of the above reasons, an employee may bring a complaint of unfair dismissal in accordance with Part X ERA 1996.[50] Any compensation awarded to a worker who is not an employee will be limited to that which an employee could claim under the unfair dismissal provisions.[51]

Derogation by agreement

Apart from the individual's ability to opt out of the maximum working week (see above), the WT Regulations allow derogations, in some instances, by agreement between the employer and representatives of the employees. The types of agreement are:

1 *collective agreements*
which, according to Regulation 2, are defined in section 178 TULRCA. They are agreements between employers and independent trade unions recognised for collective bargaining purposes, which allow agreement to be reached on

   - extension of the reference period for averaging the 48-hour week from 17 weeks up to a maximum of 52 weeks[52]
   - modifying or excluding the application of the regulations concerning the length of night work, health assessments, daily and weekly rest periods and daily rest breaks[53]

2 *workforce agreements*
which, according to schedule 1 to the Regulations, are valid if the following conditions are met:

   - the agreement is in writing
   - it has effect for a specified period not exceeding five years
   - it applies to all the relevant members of the workforce or to a particular group within the relevant workforce

- the agreement is signed by representatives of the workforce or group
- before the agreement is signed, the employer provides all the workers concerned with a copy plus any necessary guidance.

If the employer has fewer than 20 workers, a workforce agreement can be reached either by representatives of that workforce or by obtaining the support of the majority of the workforce. Representatives of the workforce are the elected representatives of the workforce concerned. A workforce agreement will allow the same derogations as those for collective agreement.

Regulation 2 also contains a definition of a relevant agreement. It is a workforce agreement or any provision of a collective agreement which forms part of a contract between the worker and the employer, or any other agreement in writing that is legally enforceable as between employer and worker.

REFLECTIVE QUESTION

Are the Working Time Regulations more effective in ensuring that workers get paid annual leave than controlling working hours?

TIME OFF FOR TRADE UNION DUTIES AND ACTIVITIES

No minimum period of service is required before trade unionists can claim time off.

TRADE UNION DUTIES

According to section 168 TULRCA 1992, employers must permit employees who are officials of independent trade unions recognised by them to take reasonable time off with pay during working hours to enable them to:

- carry out their duties which are concerned with negotiations with the employer that are related to or connected with any of the matters specified in section 178(2) TULRCA and in relation to which the employer recognises the union
- carry out any other duties which are concerned with the performance of any functions that are related to or connected with any matters listed in section 178(2) TULRCA 1992 and that the employer has agreed may be performed by the union. This includes accompanying workers, at their request, to disciplinary and grievance hearings[54]
- receive information from the employer and be consulted under section 188 TULRCA 1992 or the Transfer Regulations 2006
- undergo training in aspects of industrial relations which is both relevant to the carrying out of any of the duties mentioned in the first bullet point above and approved by their trade union or the TUC.

An official is defined as someone who is an officer of the union or branch of it, or someone who is elected or appointed in accordance with the rules to be a representative of its members or some of them[55] (see Chapter 18 on the meaning of 'independence' and recognition).

The amount of time off allowed, together with the purpose for which, the occasions on which, and any conditions subject to which, time off may be taken, depends on what is reasonable in all the circumstances having regard to any relevant provisions in the ACAS Code of Practice.[56] The Code does not lay down any fixed amount of time that employers should permit officials to take off. Its main theme is that employers and trade unions should reach agreements on arrangements for handling time off in ways appropriate to their situations.

PAY FOR PERMITTED TIME OFF

Officials who are permitted time off should receive normal remuneration as if they had worked. Where the remuneration varies with the work done, average hourly earnings should be paid.[57] No claim can be made for overtime which would normally have been worked unless that overtime was contractually required, and there is no entitlement to be paid for time spent on trade union duties outside working hours.[58] It follows that an employee on the night shift who attends a works committee meeting during the day will not be entitled to a payment, whereas a day shift worker would. Nevertheless, employees may reasonably require paid time off during working hours to enable them to undertake the relevant duties or training – for example, to travel to or return from a training course.[59] Two further points should be noted. First, the 'set-off formula' applies here.[60] Second, employers who give their part-time employees paid time off only up to the limit of their normal working hours may be discriminating contrary to Article 157 TFEU.

CASE STUDY

DAVIES v NEATH PORT TALBOT BOROUGH COUNCIL

In *Davies v Neath Port Talbot Borough Council*,[61] the employee worked a 22-hour week. The individual was a health and safety representative and was given time off to attend two five-day courses run by the union. The employer agreed to pay for the usual working hours but not the actual time spent on the courses, so the employee made an equal pay claim under (what is now) Article 157 TFEU. The EAT agreed that part-time workers had a right to be paid on the same basis as full-timers when attending such courses and that to do otherwise would amount to indirect sex discrimination.

LEGITIMATE REASONS FOR TIME OFF

The Code of Practice recommends that officials of recognised trade unions should be allowed reasonable time off for duties concerned with negotiations related to or connected with:[62]

- terms and conditions of employment, or the conditions in which employees are required to work – eg pay, hours of work, holiday pay and entitlement, sick pay arrangements, pensions, vocational training, equal opportunities, notice periods, the working environment and the utilisation of machinery and other equipment

- engagement or non-engagement, or termination or suspension of employment or the duties of employment, of one or more workers – eg recruitment and selection policies, human resource planning, redundancy and dismissal arrangements
- allocation of work, or the duties of employment as between workers or groups of workers – eg job grading, job evaluation, job descriptions and flexible working practices
- matters of discipline – eg disciplinary procedures, arrangements for representing trade union members at internal interviews, arrangements for appearing on behalf of trade union members, or as witnesses before agreed outside appeal bodies or employment tribunals
- trade union membership or non-membership – eg representational agreements, any union involvement in the induction of new workers
- facilities for officials of trade unions – eg accommodation, equipment, names of new workers to the union
- machinery for negotiation and consultation and other procedures – eg arrangements for collective bargaining, grievance procedures, joint consultation, communicating with members, communicating with other union officials also concerned with collective bargaining with the employer.

The Code states that where an official is not taking part in industrial action but represents members who are, normal arrangements for time off with pay should apply.[63] Additionally, the Code suggests that management should make available the facilities necessary for officials to perform their duties efficiently and to communicate effectively with members. The items mentioned are accommodation for meetings, access to a telephone, notice-boards and the use of office facilities.

Preparatory and explanatory work by officials may well be in fulfilment of duties concerned with any of the matters listed in section 178(2) TULRCA 1992.[64] What has to be demonstrated is that there is a sufficient connection between the collective bargaining and the duty for which leave is sought.[65] Employment tribunals will have to decide whether the preparatory work is directly relevant to one of the matters specified in section 178(2), and if the employer does not negotiate on the issue, the employer's agreement to the performance of the duty will have to be demonstrated.[66] It also seems that the recognised union must, expressly or impliedly, require the performance of the duty; otherwise, it would be impossible to hold that the individual was 'carrying out those duties … as such an official'.[67] If no agreement on time off is reached in advance of a meeting, a sensible approach might be to determine claims for payment on the basis of what the minutes disclosed. Where only a proportion of the time was spent on section 168 TULRCA 1992 matters, a tribunal will probably find that only a proportion of the time should reasonably be paid for.

As regards industrial relations training, again no fixed amount of time is specified but the Code recommends that officials should be permitted paid time off for initial basic training as soon as possible after their election or appointment. Time off should be allowed for further training where the official has special responsibilities or where it is necessary to meet changed industrial relations circumstances.[68] In determining whether a course meets the requirement of relevance to the specified duties, the description of people attending the course by those responsible for it will be pertinent.[69] Indeed, as a general principle it would seem wise for employers to insist on being shown a copy of course prospectuses.

TRADE UNION ACTIVITIES

An employer must also permit a member of a recognised independent trade union to take reasonable time off during working hours for trade union activities and to represent the union. However, in the absence of any contractual term to the contrary, an employer does not have to pay for such time off. Trade union activities are not statutorily defined, although the Code gives the following examples of the activities of a member:

- attending workplace meetings to discuss and vote on the outcome of negotiations with the employer
- meeting full-time officials to discuss issues relevant to the workplace
- voting in properly conducted ballots on industrial action
- voting in union elections.
- having access to the services of a union learning representative (see below).[70]

Paragraph 38 of the Code gives examples of activities where the member is acting as a representative of a union:

- branch, area or regional meetings of the union where the business of the union is under discussion
- meetings of official policy-making bodies such as the executive committee or annual conference
- meetings with full-time officials to discuss issues relevant to the workplace.

Section 170(2) TULRCA expressly excludes activities which consist of industrial action. Finally, in *Wignall v British Gas*,[71] the EAT rejected the argument that the statute requires each proposed activity on the part of the employee in the service of his or her union to be weighed and tested on its own merits without regard to any other activities or duties on the union's behalf for which the employee might be taking time off. Thus every application for time off under section 170 should be looked at on its merits in the particular circumstances.

Employees wishing to complain of failure to permit time off or to pay the amount required by section 169 TULRCA 1992 must apply to an employment tribunal within three months of the date when the failure occurred.[72] According to the EAT, a complainant must establish on the balance of probabilities that a request for time off was made, that it came to the notice of the employer's appropriate representative, and that he or she refused it, ignored it or failed to respond to it.[73] If the tribunal finds that the claim is well-founded, it must make a declaration to that effect. It may also make an award of compensation, which can include reparation to the official for the wrong done to him or her,[74] of such amount as it considers 'just and equitable in all the circumstances having regard to the employer's default … and to any loss sustained by the employee which is attributable to the matters complained of'.[75]

Time off for union learning representatives

Section 168A(1) TULRCA provides that an employee who is a member of an independent trade union recognised by the employer, must be given time off with pay to perform the duties of being a union learning representative (ULR).[76] The employer has this obligation if notice has been received from the trade union that the employee is a ULR and has undergone (or will undergo) sufficient training for the role.[77] The employee is also to be permitted time off to undergo training for the role.[78]

The functions of a ULR are to:

- analyse learning or training needs
- provide information about learning or training matters
- arrange learning or training, and
- promote the value of learning or training.

This will include consultations with the employer about carrying out these activities and any necessary preparations.[79]

TIME OFF FOR PUBLIC DUTIES

Section 50 ERA 1996 permits employees who are, for example,

- members of a local authority[80]
- members of any statutory tribunal
- members of a health authority, NHS trust or a Health Board
- members of a relevant education body[81]
- members of a police authority[82]
- part of the Service Authority of the National Crime Squad or the National Criminal Intelligence Service
- members of a board of prison visitors or a prison visiting committee[83]
- members of the Environment Agency or the Scottish Environment Protection Agency
- members of Scottish Water Customer Consultation Panel

to take time off during working hours for the purpose of performing any of the duties of their office or as members. Employees are eligible for time off irrespective of their length of service, but are not entitled to a payment from their employer by virtue of this section.

The duties referred to are attendance at meetings of the body (or its committees or sub-committees) and 'the doing of any other thing approved by the body' for the purpose of discharging its functions. The amount of time off which is to be allowed and the occasions on which and conditions subject to which it may be taken are those that are reasonable in the circumstances. No code of practice exists for these purposes but what must be taken into consideration is:[84]

- how much time off is required for the performance of the public duty as a whole and how much is required for the particular duty

- how much time off has already been permitted for trade union duties and activities (see above)
- the circumstances of the employer's business and the effect of the employee's absence on the running of it.

The EAT has commented that an employee who undertakes a variety of public and other duties may have some responsibility to plan the absences from work, and to scale down the level of commitment which such public duties involve, so as to produce a pattern which can be regarded as reasonable in the circumstances.[85] A complaint that an employer has failed to permit time off in accordance with the above provisions must be lodged in the same way as a claim that the employer has not complied with sections 168 or 170 TULRCA 1992, and the remedies available are identical. However, two observations may be helpful at this stage. First, rearranging employees' hours of work but requiring them to perform the same duties does not constitute giving time off. Second, it is not the function of employment tribunals to stipulate what amounts of, or conditions for, time off would be appropriate in the future.[86]

TIME OFF FOR EMPLOYEE REPRESENTATIVES[87] AND EMPLOYEE TRUSTEES OF PENSION FUNDS

A person who is an employee representative for the purposes of consultation over redundancies or the transfer of undertakings (see Chapters 17 and 16 respectively), or a candidate in an election to be such a representative, is entitled to reasonable time off during working hours to perform the functions of such a representative or candidate.[88] Employees who are permitted time off are entitled to be paid at the appropriate rate.[89] Those who feel that their rights have been infringed can use the enforcement mechanisms available in relation to time off for antenatal care.[90]

Section 58(1) ERA 1996 allows employee trustees of a pension fund reasonable time off during working hours for the purpose of performing any of their duties as a trustee or undergoing training relevant to those duties. In ascertaining what is reasonable in all the circumstances, account must be taken of:

- how much time off is required for the performance of the trustee's duties and undergoing relevant training, and how much time off is needed for undertaking the particular duty or training, and
- the circumstances of the employer's business and the effect of the employee's absence on the running of it.[91]

Employees who feel that this right has been infringed must normally complain to an employment tribunal within three months. The remedies available are identical to those that apply to time off for trade union duties (see above).[92]

It should also be noted that employee representatives (or candidates in an election) and trustees of pension funds have the right not to be subjected to any detriment on the ground that they performed (or proposed to perform) their functions or activities.[93] Claims must be lodged within three months of the act (or failure to act) complained of and the remedies available are the same as for the right not to be subject to detriment on trade union grounds (see above).[94]

TIME OFF FOR STUDY OR TRAINING

Section 63A of the ERA 1996 permits certain young employees to have time off for study or training. The employees concerned are those who

- are aged 16 or 17 years, and
- are not receiving full-time or further education, and
- have not attained such standard of achievement as is prescribed by regulations made by the Secretary of State.[95]

These standards of achievement are set out in the Right to Time Off for Study or Training Regulations 200193 (RTOST Regulations). Examples of the standards of achievement are grades A–C in five subjects at GCSE or one intermediate level GNVQ or one GSVQ at level 2.[96]

In addition young employees who

- are aged 18 years
- are undertaking training or study leading to a relevant qualification
- began that study before reaching the age of 18 years

are also entitled to time off during working hours.

The amount of time off permitted must be reasonable, taking into account the requirements of the employee's study or training and the circumstances of the employer's business and the effect of the time taken off on that business.[97] An employee who has the right to take time off for study and training also has the right to be paid remuneration by the employer at the normal hourly rate.[98] If an employee has been unreasonably refused permission for time off or has not been paid correctly for that time off, he or she may make a complaint to an employment tribunal.[99] The complaint must be made within three months, unless not reasonably practicable, beginning with the day that the time off was taken or should have been taken. If the complaint is well-founded, the tribunal may make a declaration to that effect or order the employer to pay compensation equal to the amount of remuneration to which the employee would have been entitled.

Since April 2010 employees in organisations with 250 or more employees have had a new right to request time off to undertake training. This is modelled on the flexible working provisions (see Chapter 9), which means that employers must consider requests seriously but can refuse time off if there is a good reason for doing so.[100]

TIME OFF TO LOOK FOR WORK

A person who has been continuously employed for two years or more and is under notice of dismissal by reason of redundancy is entitled to reasonable time off during working hours to look for new employment or make arrangements for training for future employment.[101] Such an employee should be paid at the appropriate hourly rate for the period of absence. This is one week's pay divided by the number of normal weekly hours, or, where the number of working hours varies, the average of such hours.[102]

A complaint that an employer has unreasonably refused time off or has failed to pay the whole or any part of any amount to which the employee is entitled must be presented to an employment tribunal, if reasonably practicable, within three months of the day on which it is alleged that the time off should have been allowed or paid for.[103] If the complaint is well-founded, the tribunal must make a declaration to that effect and order the employer to pay the amount which it finds due to the employee. Curiously, although the employee is entitled to be paid 'an amount equal to the remuneration to which he would have been entitled if he had been allowed the time off', the maximum that a tribunal can award is two-fifths of a week's pay. In *Dutton v Hawker Siddeley Aviation Ltd*,[104] the EAT rejected the argument that employees had to give details of any appointments or interviews for which they wished to take time off.

KEY LEARNING POINTS

- The WT Regulations implement the WT Directive and parts of the Young Workers Directive.
- The Regulations provide for a maximum 48-hour week during a 17-week reference period and provide rules on night work, rest periods and annual leave.
- The individual is able to agree to opt out of the 48-hour week and there are provisions for determining the rules by collective and workforce agreements.
- No minimum period of service is required before trade unionists can claim time off.
- Employers must permit employees who are officials of independent trade unions recognised by them to take reasonable time off with pay.
- Members of a recognised independent trade union are entitled to reasonable time off during working hours for trade union activities and to represent the union.
- Employees are to be permitted time off, without pay, for a variety of public duties such as being a justice of the peace or a member of a local authority.
- Young employees who are not receiving full-time education are entitled to time off to study and train for certain qualifications.
- A person who has been continuously employed for two years or more and is under notice of dismissal for redundancy is entitled to reasonable time off, during working hours, to look for new work.

REFERENCES

1 SI 1998/1833

2 Directive 93/104 concerning certain aspects of the organisation of working time

3 Directive 94/33 on the protection of young people at work

4 *UK v Council of the European Union* (1997) ICR 443

5 SI 2003/1684

6 (2001) IRLR 838

7 See amended Regulation 18 WT Regulations 1998

8 See Regulations 2 and 24A WT Regulations 1998

9 Regulation 19 WT Regulations 1998

10 Regulation 25A WT Regulations 1998

11 *Bacica v Muir* (2006) IRLR 35

12 (2003) IRLR 211

13 *Byrne Brothers (Formwork) Ltd v Baird* (2002) IRLR 96

14 (2003) IRLR 199

15 See Regulation 2 WT Regulations 1998

16 *Landeshauptstadt Kiel v Jaeger* (2003) IRLR 804

17 *Pfeiffer and others v Deutsches Rotes Kreuz, Kreisverband Waldshut* Case C-397/01 (2005) IRLR 137

18 (1999) IRLR 308

19 Regulation 4(6) WT Regulations 1998

20 Regulation 5A WT Regulations 1998

21 Regulation 27A WT Regulations 1998

22 See *R v Attorney-General for Northern Ireland* (1999) IRLR 315

23 (1999) IRLR 315

24 Regulation 6(7) WT Regulations 1998

25 Regulation 7 WT Regulations 1998

26 Regulation 8 WT Regulations 1998

27 Regulation 6A WT Regulations 1998

28 Regulation 27A(3) WT Regulations 1998

29 Regulation 11 WT Regulations 1998; Regulation 11(7) states that the weekly rest period may not be in addition to the daily rest period 'where this is justified by objective or technical reasons or reasons concerning the organisation of work'.

30 Regulation 11(8) WT Regulations 1998; the rest period may not be less than 36 consecutive hours

31 *Corps of Commissionaires Ltd v Hughes* (2009) IRLR 122

32 *Deakin v Kuehne & Nagel Drinks Logistics Services Ltd* (2012) IRLR 513

33 *Gallagher v Alpha Catering Services Ltd* (2005) IRLR 102

34 Regulation 13 and 13A WT Regulations 1998

35 Regulation 15A WT Regulations 1998

36 *British Airways plc v Williams* (2011) IRLR 948

37 In which case the worker is entitled to a proportionate payment in lieu; see Regulation 14

38 *Federatie Nederlandse Vakbeweging v Staat der Nederlanden* Case C-124/05 (2006) IRLR 561

39 *Dominguez v Centre Informatique du Centre Ouest Atlantique* Case C-282/10 (2012) IRLR 321

40 *Leisure Leagues UK Ltd v Maconnachie* (2002) IRLR 600

41 *Hill v Chapell* (2002) IRLR 19

42 Regulation 15 WT Regulations 1998. See *Fraser v South West London St George's Mental Health Trust* (2012) IRLR 100

43 A week's pay is defined in sections 221–224 ERA 1996. See *Davies v MJ Wyatt (Decorators) Ltd* (2000) IRLR 759, where the EAT held that an employer could not unilaterally reduce an employee's contractual pay in order to provide for holiday pay

44 (2009) IRLR 214

45 *Pereda v Madrid Movilidad SA* (2009) IRLR 959

46 *KHS AG v Schulte* Case C-214/10 (2011) IRLR 156

47 *Robinson-Steele v R.D. Retail Services Ltd* Case C-131/04 (2006) IRLR 386

48 *Lyddon v Englefield Brickwork Ltd* (2008) IRLR 198

49 Regulation 30 WT Regulations 1998

50 Section 101A ERA 1996

51 Section 49(5A) ERA 1996

52 Regulation 23(b) WT Regulations 1998

53 Regulation 23(a) WT Regulations 1998, although Regulation 24 allows for compensatory rest periods and rest breaks

54 Section 10(7) ERel Act 1999

55 Section 119 TULRCA 1992

56 ACAS Code of Practice on Time Off For Trade Union Duties and Activities 2009. For guidance see also ACAS booklet entitled *Trade Union Representation in the Workplace* 2009

57 Section 169(3) TULRCA 1992

58 Working hours are defined in the same way as section 146(2) TULRCA 1992

59 See *Hairsine v Kingston-upon-Hull City Council* (1992) IRLR 211

60 Section 169(4) TULRCA 1992

61 (1999) IRLR 769

62 Paragraph 9

63 Paragraph 62

64 See paragraph 46

65 See *London Ambulance Service v Charlton* (1992) IRLR 510
66 See *British Bakeries v Adlington* (1989) IRLR 218
67 See *Ashley v Ministry of Defence* (1984) IRLR 57
68 Paragraph 26
69 See *Ministry of Defence v Crook* (1982) IRLR 488
70 Paragraph 37
71 (1984) IRLR 493
72 Unless the 'time-lapse escape clause' applies; section 171 TULRCA 1992
73 *Ryford Ltd v Drinkwater* (1995) IRLR 16
74 *Skiggs v South West Trains Ltd* (2005) IRLR 459
75 Section 172 TULRCA 1992
76 The ACAS Code of Practice on Time Off for Trade Union Duties and Activities 2010 includes guidance on time off for union learning representatives. See paragraphs 16–17, 28–35
77 Section 168A(3) TULRCA 1992
78 Section 168A(7) TULRCA 1992
79 Section 168A(2) TULRCA 1992
80 Defined in section 50(5) ERA 1996
81 Defined in section 50(9) ERA 1996
82 Defined in section 50(6) ERA 1996
83 Defined in section 50(7) ERA 1996
84 Section 50(4) ERA 1996
85 *Borders Regional Council v Maule* (1993) IRLR 199
86 See *Corner v Buckinghamshire Council* (1978) IRLR 320
87 Workers must be permitted to take time off during working hours for the purpose of accompanying another worker at a disciplinary or grievance hearing: section 10 ERel Act 1999
88 Section 168(1) TULRCA 1992 and section 61(1) ERA 1996
89 See section 62 ERA 1996
90 Section 63 ERA 1996
91 See section 58(2) ERA 1996
92 Section 60(3)(4) ERA 1996
93 See sections 47 and 46 ERA 1996 respectively. Dismissal on these grounds is unfair (see Chapter 15)
94 Sections 48–49 ERA 1996
95 Section 63A(1)(a)–(c) ERA 1996

96 Regulation 3 RTOST Regulations 2001; the awarding bodies that are recognised for these purposes are listed in the Schedule to the Regulations

97 Section 63A(5) ERA 1996

98 See section 63B(1) ERA 1996

99 Section 63C ERA 1996

100 Part V1A ERA 1996

101 Section 52 ERA 1996

102 Section 53 ERA 1996

103 Section 54 ERA 1996

104 (1978) IRLR 390

EXPLORE FURTHER

Reading

- Davies, A. (2009) *Perspectives on Labour Law.* Oxford University Press, Chapter 6
- Deakin, S. and Morris, G. (2012) *Labour Law.* Hart, Chapter 4
- Smith, I. and Thomas, G. (2010) *Smith & Wood's Employment Law.* Butterworths, Chapter 4

Websites

- Advisory, Conciliation and Arbitration Service www.acas.org.uk
- Chartered Institute of Personnel and Development www.cipd.co.uk
- Department for Business Innovation and Skills www.bis.gov.uk
- DirectGov – Employment www.direct.gov.uk
- Health and Safety Executive www.hse.gov.uk
- HM Revenue and Customs www.hmrc.gov.uk/nmw/
- Trades Union Congress www.tuc.org.uk

CHAPTER 11

Variation, Breach and Termination of the Contract of Employment at Common Law

CHAPTER OVERVIEW

This chapter deals with various issues raised by the common-law approach to the variation and ending of contracts of employment. To begin with we look at the consequences of unilateral variation of the contract by the employer. We then examine the options open when a breach of contract takes place by studying, firstly, the innocent party's choice whether or not to accept the breach, and secondly, the principal remedies for a breach. Issues arising from frustration of the contract and summary dismissal are considered and, finally, we look at the consequences of termination without notice and the remedies for wrongful dismissal.

LEARNING OUTCOMES

After studying this chapter you will be able to:

- understand and explain the common law principles that apply when a contract is varied, breached or terminated
- provide colleagues with practical advice about how to avoid introducing changes unlawfully.

VARIATION

Theoretically, neither employer nor employee can unilaterally alter the terms and conditions of employment because these can only be varied by mutual agreement.[1] It follows that an employer cannot lawfully vary a contract simply by giving 'notice to vary'. Such a notice will have legal effect only if it terminates the existing contract and offers a new contract on revised terms.[2] Consent to change may be obtained through individual or collective negotiation or may be implied from the conduct of the parties. Thus if employees remain at work for a considerable period of time after revised terms have been imposed, they may be deemed to have accepted the changes.[3] However, where the employer purports to change terms unilaterally which do not immediately impact on the employee, the fact that the latter continues to work knowing that the former is asserting that a change has been effected, does not mean that the employee can be taken to have accepted the variation.[4] The relevant test is whether the employee's conduct, by continuing to work, was only referable to having accepted the new terms imposed by the employer.[5]

Where the individual continues in employment but works 'under protest', it is a question of fact whether or not the variation has been accepted. In *WPM Retail v Lang*[6] it was held that the employer's obligation to pay a bonus in accordance with the terms when the employee was promoted remained in force until the employment was terminated three years later, notwithstanding that the bonus had been paid only in the first month after promotion and the employee had carried on working thereafter.

As a general rule, courts and tribunals will be reluctant to find that there has been a consensual variation 'where the employee has been faced with the alternative of dismissal and where the variation has been adverse to his interest'.[7]

A unilateral variation which is not accepted will constitute a breach and could amount to a repudiation of the contract. However, there is no rule of law that any breach which an employee is entitled to treat as repudiatory brings the contract to an end automatically.[8] Where there is repudiatory conduct by the employer, the employee has the choice of affirming the contract (by continuing in employment) or accepting the repudiation as bringing the contract to an end. If the latter option is exercised and the employee resigns within a short period, there will be a **constructive dismissal** for statutory purposes (see Chapter 12). In practice, developments in the law of unfair dismissal make it very difficult for an employee to resist a unilateral variation. Suffice to say at this stage that employers can offer, as a fair reason for dismissal, the fact that there was a sound business reason for insisting on changes being put into effect. So long as a minimum amount of consultation has taken place, it is relatively easy to satisfy a tribunal, particularly where the majority of employees have been prepared to go along with the employer's proposals, that an employer has acted reasonably in treating a refusal to accept a variation as a sufficient reason for dismissing.[9]

REFLECTIVE QUESTION

Does the imbalance of power in the employment relationship mean that in practice it is easy for employers to make unilateral variations to contractual terms?

BREACH OF CONTRACT

The options open to an innocent party will depend on whether the breach is of a minor or serious nature. An innocent party may choose to continue with the contract as if nothing had happened (ie waive the breach), may sue for damages, or, in the case of a serious or fundamental breach, may regard the contract as at an end (ie accept the other party's repudiation of it).[10] Although the employer could sue or possibly dismiss for breach of contract, there are a number of reasons why disciplinary rather than legal action is preferred. First, the potential defendant may be unable to pay any damages awarded. Second, the amount likely to be obtained may not be worth the time and effort involved. Third, taking legal rather than disciplinary action against individual employees is not conducive to harmonious industrial relations.

What options are open to employers when employees refuse to carry out all or part of their contractual obligations? Apart from the measures outlined in the previous paragraph, the employer may withhold pay on the grounds that employees who are not ready and willing to render the services required by their contracts are not entitled to remuneration.[11]

CASE STUDY

WILUSZYNSKI v LONDON BOROUGH OF TOWER HAMLETS

In *Wiluszynski v London Borough of Tower Hamlets*,[12] the employee refused to perform the full range of his duties and had been told by the employer that until he did he would not be required for work or be paid. Although he went to work and performed a substantial part of his duties, the Court of Appeal held that the local authority was entitled to withhold the whole of his remuneration.

Discussion point

From an employee's perspective, is the Court of Appeal's approach to the payment for services rendered a reasonable one?

Clearly, employees are not entitled to pick and choose what work they will do under their contracts. Yet if employers are prepared to accept part-performance, they will be required to pay for such work as is agreed.[13]

The principal remedies for breach of contract are an injunction (an order restraining a particular type of action), a declaration of the rights of the parties, and damages. An account of profits may be ordered in exceptional circumstances.[14] Traditionally, great emphasis was placed on the personal nature of the contract of employment and courts were extremely reluctant to order a party to continue to perform the contract. However, in recent years the courts have been more willing to grant injunctions against employers who act in breach of contract.[15] Nevertheless, they need to be satisfied not only that it would be just to make such an order but also that it would be workable.[16] The mere fact that the employer and employee are in dispute does not mean that mutual confidence has evaporated.[17] Although an employee cannot be compelled to return to work,[18] a tribunal has the power to order the re-employment of someone who has been unfairly dismissed and seeks this remedy (see Chapter 15). Those who seek damages can be compensated for the direct and likely consequences of the breach, although nothing can be recovered for the manner of the breach or for the mental stress, frustration or annoyance caused.[19] However, in *Gogay v*

Hertfordshire County Council [20] the Court of Appeal confirmed that damages could be awarded for a psychological disorder brought on by an unlawful suspension. Compensation will not be recoverable for damage to an existing reputation unless pecuniary loss was sustained as a foreseeable consequence of the breach.[21]

CASE STUDY

JUDGE v CROWN LEISURE LTD

Thomas Judge was one of three special operations managers. When another manager was appointed at a considerably higher salary than others were receiving, they were told that it was the employer's intention to bring the remuneration of all special operations managers roughly into line. After two years Mr Judge resigned because he was still earning substantially less than the new manager. He argued that the employer had failed to fulfil a contractually binding commitment to raise his pay. According to the claimant, during a conversation at the company's Christmas party, the special operations director had expressly promised to put Mr Judge on the same scale as the new manager within two years.

The Court of Appeal upheld the employment tribunal's decision that the statements made at the party did not amount to a contractual promise. For there to be a legally binding and enforceable contractual obligation there must be certainty as to the commitment entered into, or alternatively facts from which certainty can be established. Although a promise to achieve parity within two years might be sufficiently certain, a promise of parity eventually or in due course was too vague.[22]

Discussion point

What are the practical implications of this decision for employees seeking a pay rise?

The jurisdiction of employment tribunals extends to breach of contract claims which have arisen or are outstanding at the end of employment.[23] Under section 3(2) ETA 1996 the claim must be for:

- damages for breach of a contract of employment or any other contract connected with the employment. However, this does not include the loss of an opportunity to claim unfair dismissal through being sacked prior to satisfying the requirement of having one year's service[24]
- a sum owed under such a contract
- the recovery of a sum in pursuance of any enactment relating to the terms or performance of such a contract.

Certain claims are excluded - for example, personal injury, breach of confidence and restrictive covenant cases. Employers can bring proceedings (counterclaims) only if an employee has made a claim first, but the employer's claim can then continue even if the employee is unable to continue with the complaint.[25]

An employee's claim must normally be brought within three months of the effective date of termination,[26] and an employer's counterclaim must be presented within six weeks of receiving a copy of the originating application. A case is heard by a chairperson sitting alone unless it is decided that a full tribunal should hear it. Although ACAS's services are available, the parties can reach their own agreement without any need for a conciliated settlement or compromise agreement.

AUTOMATIC TERMINATION: FRUSTRATION

A contract is said to have been frustrated where events make it physically impossible or unlawful for the contract to be performed, or where there has been a change such as to radically alter its purpose.[27] Once a contract has come to an end by reason of frustration, it cannot be treated by the parties as still subsisting. If the parties come to an arrangement to continue the employment relationship, this may constitute a new contract or some other arrangement. It will not be a continuation of the original contract which has been frustrated.[28] A contract that is still capable of being performed but becomes subject to an unforeseen risk is not frustrated.[29] As long as the frustrating event is not self-induced, there is an automatic termination of the contract – ie there is no dismissal.[30] This being so, it was not uncommon for an employer to resist a claim for unfair dismissal by alleging that the contract had been frustrated – for example, on grounds of sickness. Although the EAT thought that the concept of frustration should normally come into play only where the contract is for a long term and cannot be determined by notice, the Court of Appeal has allowed this doctrine to be applied to contracts of employment that can be terminated by short periods of notice.[31]

FRUSTRATION OF THE CONTRACT THROUGH ILLNESS

The following principles are relevant to the application of the doctrine of frustration in the event of illness.[32] First, the courts must guard against too easy an application of the doctrine. Second, an attempt to decide the date that frustration occurred may help to decide whether it is a true frustration situation. Third, the factors below may help to decide the issue:

- length of previous employment
- how long the employment was expected to continue
- the nature of the job
- the nature, length and effect of the illness or disabling event[33]
- the employer's need for the work to be done and the need for a replacement employee
- whether wages have continued to be paid
- the acts and statements of the employer in relation to the employment. In *Hart v Marshall & Sons* [34] the EAT held that the employer's acceptance of sick notes did not prevent a tribunal from finding that the contract had been frustrated
- whether in all the circumstances a reasonable employer could have been expected to wait any longer
- the terms of the contract as to sick pay, if any
- a consideration of the prospects of recovery.

A prison sentence is a potentially frustrating event. However, the circumstances of each case have to be examined to discover whether such a sentence has in fact operated to frustrate the contract or whether its termination resulted from some other cause.[35]

TERMINATION WITHOUT NOTICE: SUMMARY DISMISSAL

A **summary dismissal** occurs where the employer terminates the contract of employment without notice. It must be distinguished from an **instant dismissal**, which has no legal meaning but normally refers to a dismissal without investigation or inquiry. Whereas an instant dismissal is likely to be procedurally defective in unfair dismissal terms (see Chapter 13), a summary dismissal may be lawful under both common law and statute.

In order to justify summary dismissal the employee must be in breach of an important express or implied term of the contract - ie be guilty of gross misconduct. Although certain terms are always regarded as important - for example, the duty not to steal or damage the employer's property, the duty to obey lawful orders and not to engage in industrial action - the significance of other terms will depend on the nature of the employer's business and the employee's position in it. If an employer feels that a particular act or omission would warrant summary dismissal, this fact should be communicated clearly to all employees.[36]

One consequence of the contractual approach is that everything hinges upon the facts in the particular case and previous decisions usually have little bearing. Nevertheless, a number of general principles can be discerned:

- single acts of misconduct are less likely to give rise to a right of summary dismissal than a persistent pattern
- it is the nature of the act rather than its consequences that is relevant
- an employer is more likely to be entitled to dismiss summarily for misconduct within the workplace than outside it
- a refusal to obey instructions can still amount to repudiation even though the employee has mistakenly proceeded in the *bona fide* belief that the work which he or she had been instructed to do fell outside the scope of the contract.[37]

If employers do not invoke the right to end the contract within a reasonable period, they will be taken to have waived their rights and can only seek damages. What is a reasonable period will depend on the facts of the particular case. In *Allders International v Parkins* [38] it was held that nine days was too long a period to elapse in relation to an allegation of stealing before deciding what to do about the alleged repudiatory conduct. In *Gunton v London Borough of Richmond*,[39] the Court of Appeal decided that the general doctrine that repudiation by one party does not terminate a contract applies to employment law. Thus an unlawful summary dismissal does not terminate a contract of employment until the employee has accepted the employer's repudiation and certain contractual rights and obligations will survive until that time – for example, in relation to a disciplinary procedure (see Chapter 12 on the effective date of termination for statutory purposes). Nevertheless, in the absence of special circumstances, a court will easily infer that the repudiation has been accepted.[40] Finally, at common law an employer is not required to supply a reason for dismissal, although this is now qualified by statute[41] (see Chapter 13).

TERMINATION WITH NOTICE

Usually, either party is entitled to terminate a contract of employment by giving notice,[42] and once notice has been given it cannot be unilaterally withdrawn.[43] (It almost goes without saying that an employer who makes a mistake could offer to re-employ.) The courts have consistently ruled that for notice to be effective it must be possible to ascertain the date of termination and, not infrequently, employees have confused an advanced warning of closure with notice of dismissal.[44] The length of the notice will be determined by the express or implied terms of the contract and, if no term can be identified, both parties are required to give a reasonable period of notice. What is reasonable will depend on the circumstances of the relationship - for example, the employee's position and length of service. Thus in *Hill v CA Parsons & Co. Ltd* [45] a 63-year-old engineer with 35 years' service was held to be entitled to at least six months' notice.

Apart from the situation where individuals are disentitled to notice by reason of their conduct,[46] section 86(1) ERA 1996 provides that certain minimum periods of notice must be given. After a month's service an employee is entitled to a week's notice and this applies until the employment has lasted for two years. At this point two weeks' notice is owed and from then on the employee must receive an extra week's notice for each year of service up to a maximum of 12 weeks. According to section 86(2) ERA 1996, an employee with a month's service or more need give only one week's notice to terminate but there is nothing to prevent the parties from agreeing that both should receive more than the statutory minimum.

Although the ERA 1996 does not prevent an employee from accepting a payment in lieu of notice, strictly speaking an employer must have contractual authority for insisting on such a payment. Without such authority a payment in lieu of notice will be construed as damages for the failure to provide proper notice.[47] Thus a payment in lieu can properly terminate a contract of employment if the contract provides for such a payment or the parties agree that the employee will accept a payment in lieu.[48] The date of termination at common law is the day notice expires or the day wages in lieu are accepted. Except where the notice to be given by the employer is at least one week more than the statutory minimum, an employee is entitled to be paid during the period of notice even if:

- no work is provided by the employer
- the employee is incapable of work because of sickness or injury
- the employee is absent from work wholly or partly because of pregnancy or childbirth
- the employee is absent in accordance with the terms of his or her employment relating to holidays.[49]

Any payments by the employer by way of sick pay, maternity pay, paternity pay, adoption pay, holiday pay or otherwise go towards meeting this liability.[50] If employees take part in a strike after they have been given notice, payment is due for the period when they were not on strike. However, where employees give notice and then go on strike, they do not qualify for any payment under section 88 or 89 ERA 1996.[51]

REMEDIES FOR WRONGFUL DISMISSAL

Basically, a wrongful dismissal is a dismissal without notice or with inadequate notice in circumstances where proper notice should have been given. The expression also covers dismissals which are in breach of agreed procedures. Thus where there is a contractual disciplinary procedure, an employee may be able to obtain an injunction or declaration from the courts so as to prevent a dismissal or declare a dismissal void if the procedure has not been followed.[52] However, an injunction will only be granted if the court is convinced that the employer's repudiation has not been accepted, that the employer has sufficient trust and confidence in the employee, and that damages would not be an adequate remedy.[53]

Judicial review is available where an issue of public law is involved, although employment by a public authority does not by itself inject any element of public law.[54] Indeed, where an alternative remedy is available, judicial review will only be exercised in exceptional circumstances. Factors to be taken into account in considering whether the circumstances are exceptional include the speed of the alternative procedure, whether it was as convenient and whether the matter depended on some particular knowledge available to the appellate body.[55]

For the reason mentioned earlier, the courts are reluctant to enforce a contract of employment, so in the vast majority of cases the employee's remedy will lie in damages for breach of contract. A person who suffers a wrongful dismissal is entitled to be compensated for such loss as arises naturally from the breach and for any loss which was reasonably foreseeable by the parties as being likely to arise from it. Hence an employee will normally recover only the amount of wages lost between the date of the wrongful dismissal and the date when the contract could lawfully have been terminated. According to the Supreme Court, even a breach of an express contractual term relating to disciplinary proceedings will not give rise to damages at large unless the employer's failure precedes and is independent of the dismissal process. This situation gives rise to anomalies, the most obvious of which is that an employee can seek an injunction or declaration for breach of contract but not damages which are the normal remedy![56]

The following are examples of situations in which damages have been awarded:

- An employee was allowed to keep share options, even though the terms of the share option scheme provided that the option to purchase lapsed on termination as a result of disciplinary action.[57]
- A senior employee with a contract that allowed for a 10% per annum salary increase and substantial annual bonuses during a three-year notice period was entitled to the benefit of those payments even though they were at the

discretion of the board; for the board to exercise its discretion to reduce these payments to nil would have been capricious and a breach of contract.[58]

- An employee was entitled to damages in respect of enhanced pension rights which he lost when his employment was terminated without proper notice 12 days before his 55th birthday. For these purposes there is no difference in principle between lost pension rights and lost pay.[59]

Damages are not available for hurt feelings or the manner in which the dismissal took place, even though the manner might have made it more difficult to obtain other employment.[60]

Except where employees have a contractual right to a payment in lieu of notice,[61] or are entitled to their full payments during a contractual notice period,[62] they have a duty to mitigate their loss. In effect, this means that they are obliged to look for another job. Where there is a failure to mitigate, the court will deduct a sum it feels the employee might reasonably have been expected to earn. As regards state benefits, it would appear that any benefit received by the dismissed employee should be deducted only where not to do so would result in a net gain to the employee.[63] Finally, the first £30,000 of damages is to be awarded net of tax but any amount above this figure will be awarded gross because it is taxable in the hands of the recipient.

REFLECTIVE QUESTION

How important is the concept of wrongful dismissal in the twenty-first century?

KEY LEARNING POINTS

- Theoretically, neither employer nor employee can unilaterally alter the terms and conditions of employment.
- A unilateral variation which is not accepted will constitute a breach and, if serious, could amount to a repudiation of the contract.
- An innocent party to a breach may choose to continue the contract, sue for damages or, in serious cases, accept the repudiation and regard the contract as being at an end.
- Frustration of a contract occurs when it is physically impossible or unlawful for the contract to continue to be performed.
- In order to justify summary dismissal the employee must be in breach of an important express or implied term of the contract.
- Once notice to terminate has been given, it cannot be unilaterally withdrawn.
- For notice of termination to be effective, it must be possible to ascertain the date of termination.
- Wrongful dismissal is a dismissal without notice or with inadequate notice in circumstances where proper notice should have been given or where the dismissal has been in breach of an agreed procedure.

REFERENCES

1 See *Adamas Ltd v Cheung* (2011) IRLR 1014
2 *Alexander v STC Ltd* (1991) IRLR 286
3 *Aparau v Iceland Frozen Foods* (1996) IRLR 119. See *Harlow v Artemis Ltd* (2008) IRLR 629
4 See *Khatri v Cooperatieve Centrale Raiffeisen-Boerenleenbank BA* (2010) IRLR 715
5 (1978) IRLR 343
6 See *Sheet Metal Components Ltd v Plumridge* (1979) IRLR 86
7 See *Boyo v Lambeth Borough Council* (1995) IRLR 50
8 See *Hollister v National Farmers Union* (1979) IRLR 238
9 See *Macari v Celtic F.C.* (1999) IRLR 787
10 See *Ticehurst v British Telecom* (1992) IRLR 219; section 14(5) ERA 1996 allows deductions to be made in respect of participation in industrial action
11 (1989) IRLR 279
12 See *Spackman v London Metropolitan University* (2007) IRLR 744
13 See *Attorney-General v Blake* (2001) IRLR 37
14 See *Gryf-Lowczowski v Hinchingbrooke Healthcare NHS Trust* (2006) IRLR 100
15 See *Robb v London Borough of Hammersmith* (1991) IRLR 72
16 See *Hughes v London Borough of Southwark* (1988) IRLR 55
17 Section 236 TULRCA 1992
18 See *Bliss v South East Thames Regional Health Authority* (1988) IRLR 308
19 (2000) IRLR 703
20 See *Malik v BCCI* (1997) IRLR 462 and *BCCI v Ali (No.3)* (1999) IRLR 508
21 *Judge v Crown Leisure Ltd* (2005) IRLR 823
22 See *Fraser v HLMAD Ltd* (2006) IRLR 687 on the problems caused by the financial limit of £25,000
23 See *Harper v Virgin Net Ltd* (2004) IRLR 390
24 See *Patel v RCMS Ltd* (1999) IRLR 161
25 See *Capek v Lincolnshire County Council* (2000) IRLR 590
26 See *Rose v Dodd* (2005) IRLR 977
27 See *G F Sharp & Co. Ltd v McMillan* (1998) IRLR 632
28 See *Converform Ltd v Bell* (1981) IRLR 195
29 Where an employer dies or the business is destroyed, a dismissal is deemed to occur for the purpose of safeguarding an employee's right to a redundancy payment; section 174 ERA 1996.

30 See *Nottcutt v Universal Equipment Ltd* (1986) I WLR 641

31 See *Williams v Watsons Ltd* (1990) IRLR 164

32 Employers must be aware of the possible implications of the DDA 1995 as subsumed in the Equality Act 2010; see Chapter 6

33 (1977) IRLR 61

34 See *Shepherd Ltd v Jerrom* (1986) IRLR 358

35 See ACAS Code of Practice on Disciplinary and Grievance Procedures 2009 paragraph 23

36 See *Blyth v Scottish Liberal Club* (1983) IRLR 245

37 (1981) IRLR 68

38 (1980) IRLR 321

39 See *Boyo v Lambeth Borough Council* (note 8)

40 Section 92 ERA 1996

41 A contract of apprenticeship is for a fixed term and the ordinary law relating to dismissal does not apply; see *Flett v Matheson* (2006) IRLR 277

42 See *Harris & Russell Ltd v Slingsby* (1973) IRLR 221

43 See *ICL v Kennedy* (1981) IRLR 28

44 (1971) 3 WLR 995

45 See section 86(6) ERA 1996

46 See *Cerberus Ltd v Rowley* (2001) IRLR 160

47 On the effect of subsequently discovered misconduct see *Cavenagh v Evans Ltd* (2012) IRLR 679

48 Section 88(1) ERA 1996

49 Section 88(2) ERA 1996

50 Section 91(2) ERA 1996

51 See *Jones v Gwent County Council* (1992) IRLR 521

52 See *Dietman v London Borough of Brent* (1988) IRLR 299 and *Wall v STC* (1990) IRLR 55

53 See *R v East Berkshire Health Authority ex parte Walsh* (1984) IRLR 278 and *McLaren v Home Office* (1990) IRLR 338

54 See *R v Chief Constable of Merseyside Police ex parte Calveley* (1986) 2 WLR 144 and *R v Broxtowe Borough Council ex parte Bradford* (2000) IRLR 329

55 See *Edwards v Chesterfield Royal Hospital NHS Foundation Trust* (2012) IRLR 129

56 See *Lovett v Biotrace International Ltd* (1999) IRLR 375

57 *Clark v BET plc* (1997) IRLR 348; see also *Clark v Nomura plc* (2000) IRLR 766

58 See *Silvey v Pendragon plc* (2001) IRLR 685

59 See *Johnson v Unisys Ltd* (2001) IRLR 716

60 See *Abrahams v Performing Rights Society* (1995) IRLR 486

61 See *Gregory v Wallace* (1998) IRLR 387

62 See *Westwood v Secretary of State* (1984) IRLR 209

EXPLORE FURTHER

Reading

- Deakin, S. and Morris, G. (2012) *Labour Law.* Hart, Chapters 4 and 5
- Smith, I. and Thomas, G. (2010) *Smith & Wood's Employment Law.* Butterworths, Chapters 2 and 6

Websites

- Advisory, Conciliation and Arbitration Service www.acas.org.uk
- Chartered Institute of Personnel and Development www.cipd.co.uk
- Department for Business Innovation and Skills www.bis.gov.uk
- DirectGov - Employment www.direct.gov.uk
- Trades Union Congress www.tuc.org.uk

CHAPTER 12

Unfair Dismissal (1): Exclusions and the Meaning of Dismissal

CHAPTER OVERVIEW

Here we are concerned with the meaning of dismissal for statutory purposes and with the various requirements that must be satisfied before an employee is entitled to protection against unfair dismissal. We start by looking at the hurdles to be overcome, such as the need to have one year's continuous service in order to claim. The ways in which a contract of employment can be ended are considered, such as termination with or without notice, by mutual agreement or by constructive dismissal. We then look at the importance of identifying the effective date of termination.

LEARNING OUTCOMES

After studying this chapter you will be able to:

- understand and explain the importance of identifying a dismissal at law and the principles that are applied by courts and tribunals
- advise colleagues about the practical implications of an employee's being constructively dismissed and lodging a complaint at an employment tribunal.

EXCLUSIONS AND QUALIFICATIONS

Every employee has the right not to be unfairly dismissed, but this generally applies only to those working in Great Britain at the time of dismissal.[1] According to the Supreme Court, where work is performed outside Great Britain 'the employment relationship must have a stronger connection with Great Britain than with the foreign country where the employee works'.[2] There are other general exclusions and qualifications - for example, the need to have two years' service.[3] Although there is no age limit for claiming unfair dismissal, retirement may be a potentially fair reason for dismissal. (The relevant statutory provisions on age discrimination are examined in Chapters 6 and 7.)

CONTINUOUS SERVICE

In order to complain of unfair dismissal, two years' continuous service are required. This qualification does not apply if the reason or principal reason for dismissal was 'inadmissible' (see Chapter 13). Continuity is to be calculated up to the effective date of termination in accordance with sections 210–219 ERA 1996 (see Chapter 16). Employees who are wrongfully deprived of their statutory minimum entitlement to notice or receive a payment in lieu can add on that period of notice in ascertaining their length of service.[4] Longer contractual notice cannot be added, and it should be remembered that employees who are guilty of gross misconduct forfeit their entitlement to notice.[5] Two other exceptions should be borne in mind. First, if an employee is dismissed rather than suspended on medical grounds, only one month's service is required.[6] Second, where unlawful discrimination is being alleged, no minimum period of service is needed because the case will be brought under the relevant anti-discrimination legislation rather than ERA 1996.

CONTRACTING OUT

It is possible to contract out of the unfair dismissal and redundancy payment provisions in the following ways:

- An employee will be excluded if a dismissal procedures agreement has been designated by the Secretary of State as exempting those covered by it. An application must be made jointly by all the parties to the agreement and the Secretary of State must be satisfied about the matters listed in section 110(3) ERA 1996.
- An agreement to refrain from presenting a complaint will be binding if it has been reached after the involvement of a conciliation officer or satisfies the conditions regulating 'compromise agreements' (see Chapter 15).[7]

THE MEANING OF DISMISSAL

Apart from the lay-off and short-time provisions, an employee is to be treated as dismissed if:[8]

- the contract under which he or she is employed is terminated by the employer with or without notice, or
- a limited-term contract terminates by virtue of the limiting event without being renewed under the same contract, or
- the employee terminates the contract with or without notice in circumstances such that he or she is entitled to terminate it without notice by reason of the employer's conduct.

For redundancy purposes section 174 ERA 1996 provides that a contract is terminated by the employer's death unless the business is carried on by the personal representatives of the deceased. Similarly, if the employee dies after being given notice of dismissal, he or she is to be treated as dismissed.[9] Finally, a court order for the compulsory winding up of a company, the appointment of a receiver by a court and a major split in a partnership can all constitute a termination by the employer.

TERMINATION BY THE EMPLOYER WITH OR WITHOUT NOTICE

It is vitally important not to confuse a warning of impending dismissal - for example, through the announcement of a plant closure - with an individual notice to terminate.[10] For the giving of notice to constitute a dismissal at law, the actual date of termination must be ascertainable. Where an employer has given notice to terminate, an employee who gives counter-notice indicating that he or she wishes to leave before the employer's notice has expired is still to be regarded as dismissed.[11] However, in the case of redundancy this counter-notice must be given within the **obligatory period** of the employer's notice. This 'obligatory period' is the minimum period which the employer is required to give by virtue of section 86(1) ERA 1996 (see Chapter 11) or the contract of employment.[12] Before the counter-notice is due to expire, the employer can write to the employee and ask for it to be withdrawn, stating that unless this is done, liability to make a redundancy payment will be contested.[13] If employees do not accede to such a request, a tribunal is empowered to determine whether they should receive the whole or part of the payment to which they would have been entitled. Tribunals decide what is just and equitable 'having regard to the reason for which the employee seeks to leave the employment and those for which the employer requires him to continue in it'.[14] Another possibility is that an employee leaves before the expiry of the employer's notice of termination for reasons of redundancy by mutual consent. This will not affect entitlement to a redundancy payment.[15]

MUTUALLY AGREED TERMINATION

A mutually agreed termination does not amount to a dismissal at law, although as a matter of policy tribunals will not find an agreement to terminate unless it is proved that the employee really did agree with full knowledge of the implications. Thus in *Hellyer Bros v Atkinson* [16] it was held that the employee was merely accepting the fact of his dismissal rather than agreeing to terminate his employment.

Whether a mutual agreement is void because of duress is a matter for the employment tribunal.[17] Moreover, where a provision for automatic termination is introduced by way of a variation to a subsisting contract, it may be declared void if its effect is to exclude or limit the operation of ERA 1996.[18] It is possible to have a mutual determination of a contract in a redundancy situation. Thus in *Birch and Humber v University of Liverpool* [19] the Court of Appeal held that there was no dismissal when the employer accepted the employees' applications for premature retirement. However, where an employer seeks volunteers for redundancy, those who are dismissed will be eligible for a payment despite their willingness to leave.[20]

If people resign of their own volition there is no dismissal at law, but if pressure has been applied the situation is different - for example, where the employee is given the choice of resigning or being dismissed. However, an invitation to resign must not be too imprecise. Hence in *Haseltine Lake & Co. v Dowler* [21] it was held that there was no dismissal when the employee was told that if he did not find a job elsewhere his employment would eventually be terminated. It would also appear that there is no dismissal when an employee resigns on terms offered by an employer's disciplinary subcommittee. In *Staffordshire County Council v Donovan* [22] the EAT stated:

> It seems to us that it would be most unfortunate if, in a situation where the parties are seeking to negotiate in the course of disciplinary proceedings and an agreed form of resignation is worked out by the parties, one of the parties should be able to say subsequently that the fact that the agreement was reached in the course of disciplinary proceedings entitles the employee thereafter to say that there was a dismissal.

THE IMPORTANCE OF THE ACTUAL WORDS USED IN RESIGNING OR DISMISSING

Problems can arise in determining whether the words used by an employee can properly be regarded as amounting to a resignation. Normally, where the words are unequivocal and are understood by the employer as a resignation, it cannot be said that there was no resignation because a reasonable employer would not have so understood the words. However, exceptions may be made in the case of immature employees, or of decisions taken in the heat of the moment or under pressure exerted by an employer.[23] An objective test of whether the employee intended to resign applies only where the language used is ambiguous or where it is not plain how the employer understood the words. In *Sothern v Franks Charlesly* [24] the Court of Appeal decided that the words 'I am resigning' were unambiguous and indicated a present intention of resigning. Equally, doubts can arise in relation to expressions used by an employer. Thus in *Tanner v Kean* [25] it was decided that the words 'You're finished with me' were merely spoken in annoyance and amounted to a reprimand rather than a dismissal. The EAT has advised tribunals that in deciding whether the employer's words constituted a dismissal in law they should consider all the circumstances of the case to determine whether the words were intended to bring the contract to an end.[26]

WHERE A LIMITED-TERM CONTRACT TERMINATES

According to section 235(2A), a **limited-term contract** is one which terminates by virtue of a **limiting event**. There are three categories of limiting event: the expiry of a fixed term (see Chapter 4); the performance of a specific task; or the occurrence of an event or failure of an event to occur.[27]

CONSTRUCTIVE DISMISSAL

The situation in which an employee terminates the contract with or without notice in circumstances such that he or she is entitled to terminate it without notice by reason of the employer's conduct is commonly referred to as a 'constructive' dismissal. In these circumstances the employer's behaviour constitutes a repudiation of the contract and the employee accepts that repudiation by resigning. It should be noted that even though an unaccepted repudiation does not automatically terminate the contract, it will still end the person's status as an employee.[28]

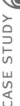

CASE STUDY

TULLETT PREBON PLC v BGC BROKERS LP

In *Tullett Prebon Plc v BGC Brokers LP* [29] the Court of Appeal stated that the legal test is whether, looking at all the circumstances from the perspective of a reasonable person in the position of the innocent party, the contract breaker has clearly displayed an intention to abandon and altogether refuse to perform the contract.

Discussion point

In the light of this decision, can it be said that the circumstances in which an employee can resign and claim constructive dismissal are now entirely clear?

Employees are entitled to treat themselves as constructively dismissed only if the employer is guilty of conduct which is a significant breach going to the root of the contract or which shows that the employer no longer intends to be bound by one or more of its essential terms.[30] Thus a finding that there has been conduct which amounts to a unjustified breach of the implied term of trust and confidence will mean that the employee is entitled to claim constructive dismissal.[31] Whether the repudiatory conduct of a supervisor binds the employer depends on whether the acts were done in the course of the supervisor's employment.[32]

If employees continue for any length of time without leaving, they will be regarded as having elected to affirm the contract and will lose the right to treat themselves as discharged.[33] However, provided that employees make clear their objection to what is being done, they are not to be taken to have affirmed the contract by continuing to work and draw pay for a limited period of time.[34] Where the employer has allowed the employee time to make up his or her mind, there is no need expressly to reserve the right to accept repudiation.[35] It is also important to note that an employer who commits a fundamental breach cannot cure it while the employee is considering whether or not to treat it as a dismissal.[36]

Even though a repudiatory breach of an express term has been waived, it could still form part of a series of acts which cumulatively amounted to a breach of the employer's implied duty to show trust and confidence. If there is merely a threat to repudiate, the employee is not to be treated as constructively dismissed unless there has been unequivocal acceptance of the repudiation before the threat is withdrawn.[37]

CASE STUDY

LONDON BOROUGH OF WALTHAM FOREST v OMILAJU

Folu Omilaju was employed by a local authority and issued five sets of proceedings alleging race discrimination and victimisation. These were heard in July and August 2001 but the employer refused to pay Mr Omilaju his full salary when he was absent without leave in order to attend the employment tribunal. It was the authority's rule that employees in his position were required to apply for special unpaid leave or annual leave. In September 2001 Mr Omilaju resigned and claimed unfair dismissal.

The Court of Appeal upheld the employment tribunal's decision that the refusal to pay for the time attending the tribunal could not be regarded as the 'final straw' in a series of actions which together amounted to a breach of trust and confidence. According to the Appeal Court, a 'final straw' does not have to be of the same character as earlier acts. However, it must contribute something to the breach of the implied term even if what it adds may be relatively trivial.[38]

In *Robins UK v Triggs* [39] the EAT held that the employer's failure to conduct a proper investigation into grievances contributed materially to earlier acts so as to cumulatively amount to a breach of the implied duty of trust and confidence.

BREACH OF CONTRACT IS A QUESTION OF FACT

It is not necessary to show that the employer intended to repudiate the contract. Equally, the mere fact that a party to a contract takes a view of its construction that is ultimately shown to be wrong does not of itself constitute repudiatory conduct. It has to be shown that he or she did not intend to be bound by the contract as properly construed.[40] According to the Court of Appeal, whether or not there is a fundamental breach of contract is a question of fact, so the EAT cannot substitute its decision for that of an employment tribunal unless the latter misdirected itself in law or the decision was one which no reasonable tribunal could reach.[41]

DEMOTION AND CHANGE OF DUTIES

A physical assault, demotion, or significant change in job duties[42] or place of work[43] can amount to a constructive dismissal. In relation to the place of work, it is now established that even an express right to transfer may be subject to an implied right to reasonable notice, because employers must not exercise their discretion in such a way as to prevent employees from being able to carry out their part of the contract.[44] However, this does not mean that an employer repudiates a contract simply by introducing a general rule with which a particular employee is unable to comply.[45]

In *Millbrook Furnishing Ltd v McIntosh* [46] the EAT accepted that 'if an employer, under the stresses of the requirements of his business, directs an employee to transfer to other suitable work on a purely temporary basis and at no diminution in wages, that may, in the ordinary case, not constitute a breach of contract'. Nevertheless, the EAT has also held that for a breach to go to the root of the contract it need not involve a substantial alteration to terms and conditions on a permanent basis. A substantial alteration is sufficient by itself.[47] As regards demotion, even where this is provided for within a disciplinary procedure it may amount to repudiation if it can be said that the punishment was grossly out of proportion to the offence.[48] Similarly, issuing a final written warning in respect of a relatively minor incident could amount to a constructive dismissal.[49]

ISSUES OF PAY

It is clear that an employer is not entitled to alter the formula whereby wages are calculated but whether a unilateral reduction in additional pay or fringe benefits is of sufficient materiality as to entitle the employee to resign is a matter of degree.[50] A failure to pay an employee's salary or wage is likely to constitute a fundamental breach if it is a deliberate act on the part of an employer rather than a mere breakdown in technology.[51]

CASE STUDY

GARDNER LTD v BERESFORD

In *Gardner Ltd v Beresford*,[52] where the employee resigned because she had not received a pay increase for two years while others had, the EAT accepted that in most circumstances it would be reasonable to infer a term that the employer will not treat employees arbitrarily, capriciously or inequitably in the matter of remuneration.

Discussion point

Does this decision cause any practical problems for employers in fixing pay?

However, if a contract makes no reference at all to pay increases, it is impossible to say that there is an implied term that there will always be a pay rise.[53]

Many cases have been decided on the basis that the employer failed to display sufficient trust and confidence in the employee (see Chapter 3).[54] Thus unjustified accusations of theft, foul language or a refusal to act reasonably in dealing with grievances, matters of safety or incidents of harassment could all give rise to claims of constructive dismissal. According to the EAT, whatever the respective actions of employer and employee at the time of termination, the relevant question is: who really terminated the contract? So when an employer falsely inveigled an employee to resign and take another job with the express purpose of avoiding liability for redundancy, it was held that there was a dismissal at law.[55]

Similarly, where an employer unilaterally imposes radically different terms of employment, these will be a dismissal under section 95(l)(a) or section 136(1)(a) ERA 1996 if, on an objective construction of the employer's conduct, there is a removal or withdrawal of the old contract. This was held to be the case in *Alcan Extrusions v Yates*,[56] where the employer imposed a continuous rolling shift system in place of the traditional shifts provided for in contracts of employment.

REFLECTIVE QUESTION

In what circumstances might it be difficult to distinguish a constructive dismissal from an employer termination - and why does it matter?

THE EFFECTIVE AND RELEVANT DATE OF TERMINATION

Whether a person is qualified to complain of unfair dismissal or has presented a claim within the prescribed time period (see Chapter 15) must be answered by reference to the effective date of termination. Similarly, entitlement to a redundancy payment and the computation of it, together with the time-limit for submitting a claim, all depend on ascertaining the 'relevant date' of dismissal. Thus, as a matter of policy, employers should ensure that there is no doubt as to what constitutes the effective or relevant date. Sections 97 and 145 ERA 1996 provide that:

- where the contract is terminated by notice, the effective or relevant date is the date on which the notice expires even though the employee does not work out that notice.[57] Where the employee gives counter-notice, the effective date is when the employee ceased working in accordance with that notice.[58] If the employee has given counter-notice in accordance with section 136(3) ERA 1996, the 'relevant date' is the date the counter-notice expires. However, once an employee has been given notice of redundancy to take effect on a specified date, there is nothing to prevent the employer and employee from altering that date by mutual agreement.[59] According to the EAT, unless there is a contractual provision to the contrary, both oral and written notices start to run the day after they are given[60]
- where the contract is determined without notice, the effective or relevant date is the date on which the termination takes effect.[61] The date of termination of people dismissed with payments in lieu of notice is the date on which they are told they are dismissed.[62] According to the Court of Appeal in *Octavius Atkinson Ltd v Morris*,[63] where an employee is summarily dismissed during the course of a working day, and no question arises as to whether that dismissal constitutes a repudiation which the employee has not accepted, both the contract of employment and the status of employee cease at the moment when the dismissal is communicated to the employee. Where employees are given notice of dismissal and told to work it but the employer subsequently requires them to leave immediately, the effective or relevant date is the date when they stop working[64]

- where a limited-term contract terminates by virtue of the limiting event without being renewed under the same contract, the effective or relevant date is the date on which the termination takes effect
- where under the redundancy provisions a statutory trial period has been served, for the purpose of submitting a claim in time the relevant date is the day that the new or renewed contract terminated. This is to be assessed in accordance with the three points above.

According to the Court of Appeal, the effective date of termination is to be objectively determined and cannot be fixed by agreement between the employer and employee.[65] It is also worth noting that the form P45 has nothing to do with the date on which employment terminates.[66]

Whether in a particular case the words of dismissal evince an intention to terminate the contract at once or an intention to terminate it only at a future date depends on the construction of those words. Such construction should not be technical but reflect what an ordinary, reasonable employee would understand by the language used. Moreover, words should be construed in the light of the facts known to the employee at the time of notification.[67] If the language used is ambiguous, it is likely that tribunals will apply the principle that words should be interpreted most strongly against the person who uses them.[68] It should also be observed that where a dismissal has been communicated by letter, the contract of employment does not terminate until the employee has actually read the letter or had a reasonable opportunity of reading it.[69] What is the effective (or relevant) date where there is an appeal against dismissal? According to the House of Lords, unless there is a contractual provision to the contrary, the date of termination is to be ascertained in accordance with the above formula and is not the date on which the employee was informed that his or her appeal had failed.[70]

Figure 3 Unfair dismissal flowchart

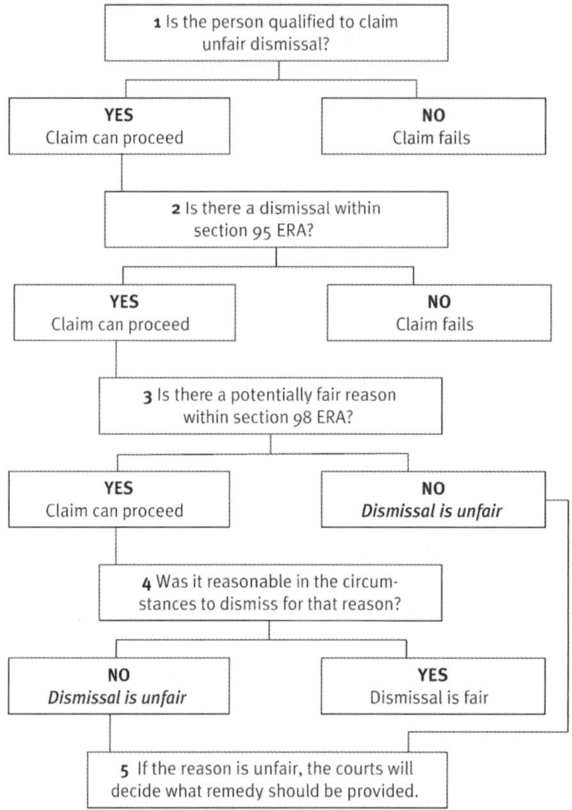
1 Is the person qualified to claim unfair dismissal?
YES
Claim can proceed
NO
Claim fails
2 Is there a dismissal within section 95 ERA?
YES
Claim can proceed
NO
Claim fails
3 Is there a potentially fair reason within section 98 ERA?
YES
Claim can proceed
NO
Dismissal is unfair
4 Was it reasonable in the circumstances to dismiss for that reason?
NO
Dismissal is unfair
YES
Dismissal is fair
5 If the reason is unfair, the courts will decide what remedy should be provided.

KEY LEARNING POINTS

- Employees have the right not to be unfairly dismissed, although there are a number of exclusions and qualifications.
- An employee is to be treated as dismissed if his or her contract of employment is terminated by the employer with or without notice, a limited-term contract expires without renewal, or the employee terminates it as a result of the employer's conduct.
- Employees are entitled to treat themselves as constructively dismissed if the employer is guilty of conduct which is a significant breach going to the root of the contract of employment, or which shows that the employer no longer intends to be bound by one or more of its essential terms.
- In order to complain of unfair dismissal, two years' continuous service is required, unless the dismissal is for an inadmissible reason.
- Whether a person is qualified to complain of unfair dismissal or claim a redundancy payment must be answered by reference to the effective date of termination which, in the case of termination by notice, is the date on which notice expires, or otherwise the date on which termination takes effect.

REFERENCES

1 See Section 94 ERA 1996

2 *Ravat v Halliburton Manufacturing and Services Ltd* (2012) IRLR 315

3 On national security see sections 193 ERA 1996 and *B v BAA* (2005) IRLR 927

4 Sections 97(2) and 213(1) ERA 1996. See *Staffordshire C.C. v Secretary of State* (1989) IRLR 117

5 See *Lanton Leisure v White* (1987) IRLR 119

6 Section 108(2) ERA 1996

7 Section 203(2)(e) and (f) ERA 1996

8 Sections 95 and 136 ERA 1996

9 See section 176 ERA 1996

10 See *Doble v Firestone Tyre and Rubber Co. Ltd* (1981) IRLR 300

11 Section 95(2) ERA 1996 and *Ready Case Ltd v Jackson* (1981) IRLR 312

12 Section 136(4) ERA 1996

13 Section 142(2) ERA 1996

14 Section 142(3) ERA 1996

15 See *CPS Recruitment Ltd v Bowen* (1982) IRLR 54

16 (1994) IRLR 88

17 See *Logan Salton v Durham C.C.* (1989) IRLR 99

18 See *Igbo v Johnson Matthey* (1986) IRLR 215

19 (1985) IRLR 165; see also *Scott v Coalite* (1988) IRLR 131

20 *Lassman v De Vere University Arms Hotel* (2003) ICR 44

21 (1981) IRLR 25

22 (1981) IRLR 108; see also *Logan Salton v Durham C.C.* (note 17 above)

23 See *Kwik-Fit v Lineham* (1992) IRLR 156

24 (1981) IRLR 278

25 (1978) IRLR 110

26 See *Willoughby v CF Capital plc* (2012) IRLR 985

27 Section 235 (2B) ERA 1996

28 *Société Générale (London Branch) v Geys* (2011) IRLR 482

29 (2010) IRLR 648

30 See *Kerry Foods Ltd v Lynch* (2005) IRLR 680

31 See *Morrow v Safeway Stores* (2002) IRLR 9

32 See *Hilton Hotels v Protopapa* (1990) IRLR 316

33 See *Wilton v Cornwall Health Authority* (1993) IRLR 482

34 See *Cantor Fitzgerald v Bird* (2002) IRLR 867
35 See *Bliss v South East Thames Regional Health Authority* (1985) IRLR 308
36 See *Buckland v Bournemouth University* (2010) IRLR 445
37 See *Harrison v Norwest Holst* (1985) IRLR 240
38 *London Borough of Waltham Forest v Omilaju* (2005) IRLR 35
39 *Robins UK v Triggs* (2007) IRLR 857
40 See *Brown v JBD Engineering Ltd* (1993) IRLR 568
41 See *Martin v MBS Fastenings* (1983) IRLR 198
42 See *Land Securities v Thornley* (2005) IRLR 765
43 See *Aparau v Iceland Frozen Foods* (1996) IRLR 119
44 See *White v Reflecting Roadstuds* (1991) IRLR 332
45 See *Dryden v Greater Glasgow Health Board* (1992) IRLR 469
46 (1981) IRLR 309
47 See *McNeil v Crimin Ltd* (1984) IRLR 179
48 See *Cawley v South Wales Electricity Board* (1985) IRLR 89
49 *Cole Ltd v Sheridan* (2003) IRLR 52
50 See *Rigby v Ferodo Ltd* (1987) IRLR 516
51 See *Cantor Fitzgerald International v Callaghan* (1999) IRLR 234
52 (1978) IRLR 63
53 See *Murco Petroleum Ltd v Forge* (1987) IRLR 50
54 See *Morrow v Safeway Stores* (2002) IRLR 9
55 *Caledonian Mining Ltd v Bassett* (1987) IRLR 165; on possible fraudulent misrepresentation, see *Post Office v Sanhotra* (2000) IRLR 866
56 (1996) IRLR 327
57 See *TBA Industrial Products Ltd v Morland* (1982) IRLR 331
58 See *Thompson v GEC Avionics* (1991) IRLR 448
59 See *Mowlem Northern Ltd v Watson* (1990) IRLR 500
60 See *Wang v University of Keele* (2011) IRLR 542
61 See *Kirklees MBC v Radecki* (2009) IRLR 555
62 See *R. Cort & Son Ltd v Charman* (1981) IRLR 437
63 (1989) IRLR 158
64 See *Stapp v Shaftesbury Society* (1982) IRLR 326
65 *Fitzgerald v University of Kent* (2004) IRLR 300
66 See *Leech v Preston B.C.* (1985) IRLR 337
67 See *London Borough of Newham v Ward* (1985) IRLR 509
68 See *Chapman v Letheby & Christopher Ltd* (1981) IRLR 440

69 See *Gisda Cyf v Barratt* (2009) IRLR 933

70 *West Midlands Co-op Ltd v Tipton* (1986) IRLR 112; see also *Drage v Governors of Greenford High School* (2000) IRLR 314

EXPLORE FURTHER

Reading

- Davies, A. (2009) *Perspectives on Labour Law.* Oxford University Press, Chapter 9
- Deakin, S. and Morris, G. (2012) *Labour Law.* Hart, Chapter 5
- Smith, I. and Thomas, G. (2010) *Smith & Wood's Employment Law.* Butterworths, Chapter 7

Websites

- Advisory, Conciliation and Arbitration Service www.acas.org.uk
- Chartered Institute of Personnel and Development www.cipd.co.uk
- Department for Business Innovation and Skills www.bis.gov.uk
- DirectGov - Employment wwwdirect.gov.uk
- Trades Union Congress www.tuc.org.uk

CHAPTER 13

Unfair Dismissal (2): Potentially Fair Reasons and the Concept of Reasonableness

CHAPTER OVERVIEW

We continue our examination of the rules concerning unfair dismissal by looking at the procedures to be followed after an employee has established that he or she qualifies to make a claim. We begin by looking at the burden on employers to show the reason for dismissal and then consider those reasons that are automatically unfair. We study the potentially fair reasons of capability or qualifications, conduct, statutory ban and some other substantial reason. We consider the particular rules that apply to dismissals during industrial action and look at the ACAS Code of Practice on Disciplinary and Grievance Procedures 2009.

LEARNING OUTCOMES

After studying this chapter you will be able to:

- understand when a dismissal will be automatically fair or unfair, and explain and illustrate the potentially fair reasons for dismissal that can be offered to an employment tribunal
- advise colleagues about the impact of the relevant ACAS Code of Practice and participate in the production of rules and procedures to ensure that dismissals are reasonable in all the circumstances.

GIVING A REASON FOR DISMISSAL

Once employees have proved that they were dismissed, the burden shifts to the employer to show the reason, or, if there was more than one, the principal reason, for the dismissal and that it falls within one of the following categories:[1]

- It relates to the capacity or qualifications of the employee for performing work of the kind which he or she was employed to do.
- It relates to the conduct of the employee.
- The employee was redundant.

- The employee could not continue to work in the position held without contravention, either on the employee's part or that of the employer, of a duty or restriction imposed by or under a statute.
- There was some other substantial reason of such a kind as to justify the dismissal of an employee holding the position which the employee held.

Several points must be made at this stage:

- Where no reason is given by the employer, a dismissal will be unfair simply because the statutory burden has not been discharged. Equally, if a reason is engineered in order to effect dismissal because the real reason would not be acceptable, the employer will fail because the underlying principal reason is not within section 98(1) or (2) ERA 1996.[2]
- The fact that an employer has inaccurately described the reason for dismissal is not necessarily fatal, for it is the tribunal's task to discover what reason actually motivated the employer at the time of dismissal.[3] That the correct approach is the subjective one has been confirmed by the Court of Appeal: 'A reason for the dismissal of an employee is a set of facts known to the employer, or it may be of beliefs held by him, which causes him to dismiss the employee.'[4] Subsequently, the Court of Appeal has been prepared to attribute a reason for dismissal even where the employers had argued throughout the case that they had not dismissed but the employee had resigned.[5]
- The reason for dismissal must have existed and been known to the employer at the time of dismissal, which makes it impossible, for example, to rely on subsequently discovered misconduct.[6] The reason itself may be an anticipated event. For example, if an employee is subject to a long period of notice, it is possible to give notice in anticipation of a decision, giving what the employer expects to happen as a reason for the dismissal.[7]
- Section 107 ERA 1996 provides that in determining the reason for dismissal, or whether it was sufficient to dismiss, a tribunal cannot take account of any pressure, in the form of industrial action or a threat of it, which was exercised on the employer to secure the employee's dismissal. It is not necessary that those exerting the pressure explicitly sought the dismissal of the employee: the test is whether it could be foreseen that the pressure would be likely to result in dismissal.[8]

EMPLOYERS' DUTY TO PROVIDE A STATEMENT OF REASONS FOR DISMISSAL

According to section 92 ERA 1996, a person who has been continuously employed for one year[9] and has been dismissed or is under notice of dismissal has the right to be supplied with a written statement giving particulars of the reasons for dismissal. The employer must provide the statement within 14 days of a specific request being made. In *Gilham v Kent County Council* [10] the Court of Appeal held that the Council had responded adequately by referring the employee's legal representative to two previous letters in which the reasons for dismissal were fully set out, enclosing copies of those letters and stating that their contents contained the reasons for dismissal. A claim may be presented to an employment tribunal on the grounds that the employer unreasonably failed to provide such a statement or that the particulars given were inadequate or untrue. However, section 92 merely obliges employers to indicate truthfully the reasons they were relying on when they dismissed. Only if an unfair dismissal claim is brought will a tribunal have to examine whether the reasons given justify dismissal.[11] The same time-limit applies as for unfair dismissal claims (see Chapter 15).

The test for determining the reasonableness of an employer's failure is objective. Thus, where the employer maintains that there was no dismissal in law but the tribunal finds that there was, it must then decide whether there was an unreasonable failure to supply a statement.[12] If the complaint is well-founded, a tribunal may make a declaration as to what it finds the employer's reasons were for dismissing and must order that the employee receive two weeks' pay.[13] Perhaps the most important aspect of this section is that such a statement is admissible in evidence in any proceedings. This means that an employee who detects any inconsistency between the particulars given and the reasons offered as a defence to an unfair dismissal claim can exploit the situation to the full.

REFLECTIVE QUESTION

Should Parliament require written reasons to be supplied whenever there is a dismissal?

AUTOMATICALLY UNFAIR DISMISSAL

A dismissal will be automatically unfair if the reason for it is related to any of the following:

- the assertion of a statutory right (see below)
- trade union membership or activities, or non-union membership
- pregnancy or maternity (see Chapter 8)
- certain health and safety grounds (see below)
- certain shop workers and betting workers who refuse to work on a Sunday[14]
- refusing to comply with a requirement which is in contravention of the WT Regulations 1998 (see Chapter 10)[15]
- the reason, or the principal reason, for the dismissal is that the employee made a protected disclosure (see Chapter 3)[16]
- the employee is dismissed for trying to enforce the national minimum wage[17]
- the proposed or actual performance of any of the functions of an employee trustee of a pension scheme[18]
- the proposed or actual performance of any functions or activities as an employee representative or candidate[19]
- the dismissal of a worker for exercising rights in relation to the statutory recognition of a trade union (see Chapter 18)
- the dismissal of a worker within eight weeks of taking part in protected industrial action (see below)
- the application of the Tax Credits Act 2002[20]

- the exercise of a right to request a contract variation (see Chapter 8 on flexible working)[21]
- the exercise of rights under the Part-Time Workers Regulations 2000 and Fixed-term Employees Regulations 2002[22]
- the exercise of a right in relation to flexible working[23]
- the exercise of a right in relation to pension enrolment[24]
- the exercise of a right in relation to study leave or training[25]
- the existence of a prohibited list under the Blacklists Regulations 2010 (see Chapter 18).[26]

Additionally, if any of the above 'inadmissible' reasons was used to select a person for redundancy, dismissal will also be unfair (see below). Other unfair reasons for dismissal are those connected to transfers of undertakings (see Chapter 16); to the anti-discrimination provisions, which stipulate that it is unlawful to discriminate on the prohibited grounds by way of dismissal (see Chapters 6 and 7); and to the Rehabilitation of Offenders Act 1974, which states that 'a conviction which has become spent ... shall not be a proper ground for dismissing' (see Chapter 4).[27]

ASSERTING STATUTORY RIGHTS

Employees are protected if they have brought proceedings against the employer to enforce one of the following 'relevant' statutory rights:

- any right conferred by ERA 1996 which may be the subject of a complaint to an employment tribunal
- minimum notice rights under section 86 ERA 1996
- certain rights relating to the unlawful deduction of union contributions from pay,[28] action short of dismissal on union membership grounds, time off for union duties and activities and union learning representatives
- rights afforded by the WT Regulations 1998[29]
- rights afforded by TULRCA 1992 in relation to statutory recognition of trade unions
- rights afforded by the TUPE Regulations 2006.

It should be noted that employees are protected irrespective of whether they qualify for the right that has been asserted or whether the right was actually infringed. All that has to be demonstrated is that the employee's claim was made in good faith.[30]

HEALTH AND SAFETY

In relation to health and safety, section 100 ERA 1996 provides that a dismissal is unfair if the reason for it was that the employee:

- carried out, or proposed to carry out, activities designated by the employer in connection with preventing or reducing risks to the health and safety of employees
- performed, or proposed to perform, any of his or her functions as a safety representative or a member of a safety committee

- took part or proposed to take part in consultation with the employer pursuant to the HSCE Regulations 1996 (see Chapter 9) or in an election of representatives of employee safety within the meaning of those Regulations
- where there was no safety representative or committee or it was not reasonably practicable to raise the matter in that way, brought to the employer's attention, by reasonable means, circumstances connected with his or her work which he or she reasonably believed were harmful or potentially harmful to health and safety[31]
- left or proposed to leave, or refused to return to (while the danger persisted), his or her place of work or any dangerous part of the workplace, in circumstances of danger which he or she reasonably believed to be serious and imminent and which he or she could not reasonably have been expected to avert
- took, or proposed to take, appropriate steps to protect himself or herself or other persons, in circumstances of danger which he or she reasonably believed to be serious and imminent. Whether those steps were 'appropriate' must be judged by reference to all the circumstances, including the employee's knowledge and the facilities and advice available at the time. A dismissal will not be regarded as unfair if the employer can show that it was, or would have been, so negligent for the employee to take the steps which he or she took, or proposed to take, that a reasonable employer might have dismissed on these grounds.

POTENTIALLY FAIR REASONS FOR DISMISSAL

CAPABILITY OR QUALIFICATIONS

According to section 98(3) ERA 1996, 'capability' is to be assessed by reference to 'skill, aptitude, health or any other physical or mental quality', and it has been held that an employee's inflexibility or lack of adaptability came within his or her aptitude and mental qualities.[32] 'Qualifications' means 'any degree, diploma, or other academic, technical or professional qualification relevant to the position which the employee held'. In *Blue Star Ltd v Williams* [33] it was held that a mere licence, permit or authorisation is not such a qualification unless it is substantially concerned with the aptitude or ability of the person to do the job.

Poor performance

Paragraph 1 of the ACAS Code of Practice on Disciplinary and Grievance Procedures 2009 observes that poor performance may be regarded as a disciplinary matter and comments that 'If employers have a separate capability procedure, they may prefer to address performance issues under this procedure.'

Dealing with absence

Appendix 4 of the ACAS Guide on Discipline and Grievances at Work discusses how to handle absence problems. It provides information under the following headings:

- How should frequent and persistent short-term absence be handled?

- How should longer-term absence through ill health be handled?
- Specific health problems
- Failure to return from extended leave on the agreed date.

Types of ill health

In cases of intermittent absences owing to ill health, there is no obligation on an employer to call medical evidence.

CASE STUDY

CEREAL PACKAGING LTD v LYNOCK

In *Cereal Packaging Ltd v Lynock*,[34] the EAT affirmed that an employer has to have regard to the whole history of employment and to take into account a range of factors including: the nature of the illness and the likelihood of its recurrence; the lengths of absences compared with the intervals of good health; the employer's need for that particular employee; the impact of the absences on the rest of the workforce; and the extent to which the employee was made aware of his or her position. There is no principle that the mere fact that the employee is fit at the time of dismissal makes that dismissal unfair.

Where there is long-term absence for ill health an employer is usually expected to take reasonable steps to consult the employee, to obtain appropriate medical evidence about the nature and prognosis of the condition and to consider alternative employment. If employers provide an enhanced pension on ill-health retirement, they will also be expected to take reasonable steps to ascertain whether the employee is entitled to benefit from the scheme.[35]

Four further points must be made:

- An employee's incapability need only 'relate to' the performance of contractual duties; there is no requirement to show that the performance of all those duties has been affected.[36]
- Although employees who are sick will hope to remain employed at least until their contractual sick pay entitlement (if any) is exhausted, this does not mean that a person cannot be dismissed before the period of sick pay has elapsed. Equally, it will be unfair to dismiss simply because the sick pay period has expired.
- The fact that the employer caused the employee's incapacity does not prevent a finding of fair dismissal.[37]
- An employee who has become incapable of work may have to be treated as a person with a disability within the meaning of section 6 of the Equality Act 2010 (see Chapter 6).

CONDUCT

It is the function of tribunals to decide not whether misconduct is gross or criminal but whether the employer has, in the circumstances of the case, acted reasonably in dismissing. Thus in *John Lewis plc v Coyne* [38] it was held that the employer had acted unfairly in dismissing the employee for using the company telephone for making personal calls without investigating the seriousness of the offence.

There is no necessary inference that because an employee is guilty of gross misconduct in relation to his or her actual employment, he or she must necessarily be considered unsuitable for any employment whatsoever.[39] Clearly, there will be cases where the misconduct is sufficiently serious that an employee can be dismissed without warning, and paragraph 23 of the ACAS Code of Practice on Disciplinary and Grievance Procedures advocates that employees should be given 'examples of acts which the employer regards as acts of gross misconduct'.

Employers must clarify what conduct leads to summary dismissal

According to the EAT, disciplinary rules which fail to follow the ACAS Code in specifying those offences that constitute gross misconduct and justify dismissal at the first breach will be defective.

CASE STUDY

LOCK v CARDIFF RAILWAY CO. LTD

In *Lock v Cardiff Railway Co. Ltd* [40] a train conductor was dismissed for gross misconduct when he asked a 16-year-old to leave the train because he did not have a valid ticket or sufficient money to pay the excess fare. The employer's disciplinary code did not specify which offences would be regarded as gross misconduct that would result in dismissal for the first offence. As a result the EAT held that no reasonable tribunal properly directing itself could have concluded that the dismissal was fair.

Fighting is an example of an area where it is not necessary to state that such behaviour will be regarded very gravely, because the courts have decided that whether or not to dismiss for this reason is essentially a matter for the employer. The test is what would be the reaction of a reasonable employer in the circumstances. Thus, if without proper inquiry an employer implements a policy of dismissing any employee who struck another, there could be a finding of unfairness.[41] Similarly, false clocking or claims in respect of hours done are serious offences which can justify dismissal without a warning if the employer has had due regard to all the circumstances.[42]

Disobedience: when it is and is not 'reasonable'

As a general rule, if an order is lawful, a refusal to obey it will be a breach of contract and amount to misconduct even when similar refusals have been condoned in the past. Nevertheless, in disobedience cases the primary factor to be considered is whether the employee is acting reasonably in refusing to carry out an instruction.[43] In *Robinson v Tescom Corporation* [44] the employee had agreed to work under the terms of a varied job description while negotiations were ongoing. His subsequent refusal to do so was held to amount to disobedience of a lawful order. Acknowledging that employers are obliged to issue instructions in order to ensure compliance with health and safety legislation, tribunals have readily accepted that non-compliance with safety rules or procedures constitute sufficient grounds for dismissal.

Dismissal arising from issues of competition

The intention to set up in competition with the employer is not in itself a breach of the implied duty of loyalty. Unless the employer has reasonable grounds for believing that the employee has done or is about to do some wrongful act, dismissal will not be justified.[45]

CASE STUDY

MARSHALL v INDUSTRIAL SYSTEMS LTD

In *Marshall v Industrial Systems Ltd*[46] the EAT held that it was reasonable to dismiss a managing director after discovering that (with another manager) he was planning to set up in competition and take away the business of their best client and that he tried to induce another key employee to join them in that venture.

Discussion point

If employers are concerned about employees setting up in competition, is it sufficient to rely on the implied duty of loyalty?

Suspicion of dishonesty

Theft of an employer's property will amount to a fair reason for dismissal; far more difficult to handle are cases of *suspected* dishonesty. According to the Court of Appeal, fairness demands that serious allegations of dishonesty be put with sufficient formality and at an early enough stage to provide a full opportunity for answer.[47]

CASE STUDY

BRITISH HOME STORES v BURCHELL

In *British Home Stores v Burchell*,[48] it was stated that tribunals had to decide whether the employer entertained a reasonable suspicion amounting to a belief in the guilt of the employee at that time. There are three elements to this:

- The employer must establish the fact of that belief.
- The employer must show that there were reasonable grounds upon which to sustain that belief.
- At the stage at which the belief was formed the employer must have carried out as much investigation

into the matter as was reasonable in the circumstances.

Discussion point

What are the consequences for employers if it emerges that an employee reasonably accused of misconduct is wholly innocent?

Thus the question to be determined is not whether, by an objective standard, the employer's belief that the employee was guilty of the misconduct was well-founded but whether the employer believed that the employee was guilty and was entitled so to believe having regard to the investigation conducted.[49] If these requirements are met, it is irrelevant that the employee is acquitted of criminal charges or that they are dropped.

Where there is a reasonable suspicion that one or more employees within a group have acted dishonestly, it is not necessary for the employer to identify which of them acted dishonestly.[50] Thus, provided certain conditions are satisfied, an employer who cannot identify which member of a group was responsible for an act can fairly dismiss the whole group, even where it is probable that not all were guilty of the act. These conditions are:

- The act must be such that if committed by an identified individual it would justify dismissal.
- The employer had made a sufficiently thorough investigation with appropriate procedures.
- As a result of that investigation the employer reasonably believed that more than one person could have committed the act.
- The employer had acted reasonably in identifying the group of employees who could have committed the act and each member of the group was individually capable of doing so.
- Between the members of the group the employer could not reasonably identify the individual perpetrator.

The fact that one or more of the group is not dismissed does not necessarily render the dismissal of the remainder unfair, provided the employer is able to show solid and sensible grounds for differentiating between members of the group.[51]

In certain cases it will be reasonable to rely on the results of extensive police investigation rather than carry out independent inquiries.[52] Similarly, where an employee admits dishonesty there is little scope for the kind of investigation referred to in *Burchell*'s case (above). Where the probability of guilt is less apparent, the safer course may be to suspend until any criminal proceedings have been completed.[53] Whether a conviction forms an adequate basis for dismissal will depend to some extent on the nature of the crime. Clearly, there may be cases where the offence is trivial and dismissal would be unreasonable.[54]

Employers' contact with employees under criminal investigation

The fact that employees have been charged with a criminal offence does not prevent the employer from communicating with them or their representatives to discuss the matter. What must be discussed is not so much the alleged offence as the action the employer is proposing to take. If the employee chooses not to give a statement to the employer, the latter is entitled to consider whether the evidence available is strong enough to justify dismissal.[55] It will not always be wrong to dismiss before a belief in guilt has been established, because involvement in an alleged criminal offence often involves a serious breach of duty or discipline. However, even if they are charged by the police with a criminal offence, failure to give employees an opportunity to explain themselves may render the dismissal unfair.[56]

Offences committed outside the workplace

In the context of unfair dismissal, conduct may mean actions of such a nature, whether done in the course of employment or outside, that reflect in some way on the employer-employee relationship.[57] Thus it may cover the wilful concealment of convictions which are not 'spent', criminal offences outside employment, such as stealing or gross indecency, or even 'moonlighting'. Finally, in an appropriate case it may be unfair to dismiss without first considering whether the employee could be offered some other job.[58]

STATUTORY BAN

Section 98(2)(d) ERA 1996 states that if it would be unlawful to continue to work in the position which the employee held, there is a valid reason for dismissing. In *Bouchaala v Trust House Forte* [59] the EAT held that the absence of the words 'related to' in this section were significant and that a genuine but erroneous belief is insufficient for these purposes. Again, a tribunal must be satisfied that the requirements of section 98(4) ERA 1996 have been met. Thus the loss of a permit or licence may fall within section 98(2)(d) ERA 1996 but, in deciding what is reasonable, attention will focus on whether the legal ban is permanent or temporary. If the former, an employer might be expected to consider the feasibility of redeployment, and if the latter, short-term alternative work might be offered. Whether such measures should be taken will depend on the type of business and the employee's work record. Indeed, in some circumstances it may be possible for employees to continue in their normal job by making special arrangements. For example, a sales representative who has been disqualified from driving may be prepared to hire a driver at his or her own expense in order to remain in employment.

SOME OTHER SUBSTANTIAL REASON

Section 98(1)(b) ERA 1996 was included in the legislative scheme so as to give tribunals the discretion to accept as a fair reason for dismissal something that would not conveniently fit into any of the other categories. It covers such diverse matters as dismissal for having been sentenced to imprisonment,[60] the loss of confidence in a manager because of his manner and management style,[61] being dismissed as manager of a public house because a partner had resigned from jointly holding the position,[62] dismissal for refusing to sign an undertaking not to compete,[63] or dismissal because an important client was unwilling to accept the particular individual.[64] However, in *Wadley v Eager Electrical* [65] the EAT decided that an employee's dismissal on the grounds that there had been breaches of trust by his wife during her employment with the employer did not amount to a substantial reason.

According to the Court of Appeal, tribunals have to decide whether the reason established by the employer falls within the category of reasons which *could* justify the dismissal of an employee holding the position that the employee held.[66] Employers cannot claim that a reason for dismissal is substantial if it is whimsical or capricious. Nevertheless, if they can show that they genuinely believed a reason to be fair and that they had it in mind at the time of dismissal,[67] this would bring the case within section 98(1)(b) ERA 1996. It may be held that the reason was substantial even though more sophisticated opinion can be adduced to demonstrate that the belief had no scientific foundation.[68] The notion of genuine belief has also been invoked to assist employers who are unable to rely on any other reasons for dismissal owing to an error of fact. Thus this subsection was relied on where an employee was dismissed as a result of the employer's mistaken belief that the individual could not continue to work because there had been no valid application to extend leave to remain in the country.[69]

Dismissal for refusing new terms arising from a business reorganisation

'Some other substantial reason' has frequently provided a convenient context in which employees have been dismissed as a result of a reorganisation of the business. In *Hollister v National Farmers Union*, the Court of Appeal indicated that it is not necessary for an employer to show that in the absence of a reorganisation there would be a total business disaster. It is sufficient if there is a sound business reason, which means only that there is a reason which management thinks on reasonable grounds is sound.[70] Thus if the employer can satisfy a tribunal that a certain policy has evolved which was thought to have discernible advantages, dismissal in accordance with that policy can be said to be for 'some other substantial reason'.

Where an employee refuses to agree changes consequent upon a reorganisation, the test to be applied by tribunals is not simply whether the terms offered were those which a reasonable employer could offer. Looking at the employer's offer alone would exclude from scrutiny everything that happened between the time the offer was made and the dismissal. For example, a potentially significant factor is whether other employees accepted the offer.[71] Equally, there is no principle of law that if new contractual terms are much less favourable to an employee than the previous ones, dismissal for refusing to accept them will be unfair unless the business reasons are so pressing that it is vital for the survival of the business that the revised terms are accepted.

CASE STUDY

FARRANT v THE WOODROFFE SCHOOL

In *Farrant v The Woodroffe School*,[72] an employee was dismissed for refusing to accept organisational changes. The employer mistakenly believed that the employee was obliged to accept a new job description and that the dismissal was therefore lawful. The EAT held that dismissal for refusing to obey an unlawful order was not necessarily unfair. Of importance was not the lawfulness or otherwise of the employer's instructions but the overall question of reasonableness. In this case it was not unreasonable for the employer to act on professional advice, even if that advice was wrong.

Discussion point

Would it be fair to conclude that an employer's contractual rights are not particularly important in unfair dismissal cases?

Tribunals will examine an employer's motive for introducing changes in order to ensure that they are not being imposed arbitrarily.[73] The reasonable employer will explore all the alternatives to dismissal but, like consultation with trade unions and the individual concerned, such a consideration is only one of the factors that must be taken into account under section 98(4) ERA 1996 (see below).

INDUSTRIAL ACTION AND LACK OF JURISDICTION

PROTECTED INDUSTRIAL ACTION

Section 238A TULRCA states that a dismissal will be unfair if the reason is that the employee took part in protected industrial action[74] and one of three situations applies:

- The dismissal takes place within a period of twelve weeks from the day on which the employee first took part in the protected industrial action.
- The dismissal takes place after that twelve-week period and the employee had ceased to take part in protected industrial action before the end of that period.
- The dismissal takes place after the end of the period and the employee has not ceased to take part in the protected industrial action before the end of that period but the employer has not taken such procedural steps as would have been reasonable for the purpose of resolving the dispute to which the action relates.

In deciding whether an employer has taken those steps mentioned in the last point above, tribunals will look at whether the employer or union:[75]

- has followed procedures established by a collective agreement
- had offered or agreed to start or resume negotiations after the start of the protected industrial action
- unreasonably refused a request that conciliation services be used
- unreasonably refused a request that mediation services be used.

Where there was an agreement to use conciliation or mediation services, section 238B TULRCA 1992 provides that regard should be had to four matters:

- whether the parties were represented at the meeting by an appropriate person
- whether the parties co-operated in the making of arrangements for meetings to be held
- whether the parties fulfilled any commitment given to take particular action
- whether the parties answered any reasonable question put to them at meetings.

The fact that employees are in breach of their duty to attend work is relevant to the question of whether they are taking part in a strike but it is not an essential ingredient. Thus employees who are off sick or on holiday could be held to be taking part in a strike if they associated themselves with it - for example, by attending a picket line.[76] By way of contrast, if sick employees merely wish their colleagues well, this may be regarded as supportive but would not amount to taking part in industrial action.[77]

UNOFFICIAL ACTION

By virtue of section 237 TULRCA 1992 employees cannot complain of unfair dismissal if at the time of dismissal they were taking part in an unofficial strike or other unofficial industrial action. For these purposes, a strike or other industrial action will be treated as unofficial unless the employee:

- is a union member and the action is authorised or endorsed by that union, or
- is not a union member but there are among those taking part in the industrial action members of a union by which the action has been authorised or endorsed within the meaning of section 20(2) TULRCA 1992 (see Chapter 18).

A strike or other industrial action will not be regarded as unofficial if none of those taking part in it is a union member. However, employees who were union members when they began to take industrial action will continue to be treated as such even if they have subsequently ceased to be union members.[78]

Section 237(4) states that the issue of whether or not the industrial action is unofficial is to be determined by reference to the facts at the time of the dismissal. Nevertheless, where the action is repudiated in accordance with section 21 TULRCA 1992 it is not to be treated as unofficial before the end of the next working day after the repudiation has taken place. According to the EAT, this means midnight on the following working day.[79] On industrial action generally see Chapter 18.

REASONABLENESS IN THE CIRCUMSTANCES

Where the employer has given a valid reason for dismissal, the determination of the question whether the dismissal was fair or unfair depends on whether in the circumstances (including the size and administrative resources of the employer's undertaking) the employer acted reasonably or unreasonably in treating it as a sufficient reason for dismissing the employee. This is to be decided in accordance with equity and the substantial merits of the case.[80] Recently, the Court of Appeal faced the question 'Whose knowledge or state of mind was for this purpose intended to count as the knowledge or state of mind of the employer?' The answer given was 'The person who was deputed to carry out the employer's functions under Section 98.' The knowledge held by other employees cannot be imputed to that person if he or she could not reasonably have acquired that knowledge through the appropriate disciplinary process.[81]

As a matter of law, a reason cannot be treated as sufficient where it has not been established as true or that there were reasonable grounds on which the employer could have concluded that it was true.[82] Under section 98(4) ERA 1996, tribunals must take account of the wider circumstances. In addition to the employer's business needs, attention must be paid to the personal attributes of the employee - for example, seniority and previous work record. Thus when all the relevant facts are considered, a dismissal may be deemed unfair notwithstanding the fact that the disciplinary rules specified that such behaviour would result in immediate dismissal.[83] Conversely, employers may act reasonably in dismissing even though they have breached an employee's contract.[84] In appropriate cases the test of fairness must be interpreted, so far as possible, compatibly with the European Convention on Human Rights.[85]

Employers will be expected to treat employees in similar circumstances in a similar way. The requirement that the employer must act consistently between all employees means that an employer should consider truly comparable cases which were known about or ought to have been known about. Nevertheless, the overriding principle seems to be that each case must be considered on its own facts and with the freedom to consider both aggravating factors and mitigating circumstances.[86] The words 'equity and the substantial merits' also allow tribunals to apply their knowledge of good industrial relations practice and to ensure that there has been procedural fairness (see below).[87]

According to the Court of Appeal, employment tribunals should not ask themselves whether they would have done what the employer did in the circumstances. Their function is merely to assess the employer's decision to dismiss and decide if it falls within a range of responses that a reasonable employer could have adopted.[88] Even so, the 'range of reasonable responses' test does not mean that such a high degree of unreasonableness must be shown so that nothing short of a perverse decision to dismiss can be held unfair.[89] Finally, it would seem that in determining the reasonableness of a dismissal tribunals are not barred from taking into account events which occurred between the giving of notice and its expiry - for example, if alternative work becomes available after redundancy notices have been issued.[90]

CASE STUDY

WILLOW OAK LTD v SILVERWOOD

Willow Oak Ltd specialised in the supply of agency workers for the health and associated services. After a number of attempts by competitors to poach staff and business from them, some of which had been successful, the company sought to impose new restrictive covenants on its employees. Without prior consultation, everyone was presented with a new contract which restricted their post-employment activities and was told to sign and return it within half an hour. When they refused to do so they were given notice of termination, although none of them had been warned that they would be dismissed if they did not accept the new terms.

An employment tribunal decided that the covenants were unreasonably wide and, as a consequence, the employers could not establish that the dismissals were for 'some other substantial reason' (see above). However, the Court of Appeal ruled that it was inappropriate for an ET to decide the validity of a proposed restrictive covenant. The reasonableness of the covenant should have been examined as part of all the circumstances of the case as provided for in section 98(4) ERA 1996. Nevertheless, the appeal was dismissed since the ET had been entitled to hold that the employers had failed to follow a fair procedure.[91]

THE CODE OF PRACTICE AND PROCEDURAL FAIRNESS

The ACAS Code of Practice on Disciplinary and Grievance Procedures 2009 does not have the force of law, so failure to comply with it does not make a dismissal automatically unfair. However, it will weigh heavily against the employer if not followed,[92] and tribunals will be able to adjust any awards made in relevant cases by up to 25% for unreasonable failure to comply with any provision of the Code.[93] In addition, ACAS has produced a guide to good practice which complements its Code.

SITUATIONS IN WHICH THE CODE MAY BE IGNORED

In certain circumstances there may be a good excuse for not following the Code. For example, if the inadequacy of the employee's performance is extreme or the actual or potential consequences of a mistake are grave, warnings may not be necessary.[94] Although it is management's responsibility to ensure that there are adequate disciplinary rules and procedures, the Code mentions the desirability of involving employees and their representatives in the development of rules and procedures.[95] Naturally, tribunals tend to pay greater attention to agreed rather than unilaterally imposed procedures. The rules required will again depend on the nature of the employment but they should be reasonable in themselves, consistently enforced, and reviewed in the light of legal developments and organisational needs. Employees should know and understand the rules and be made aware of the likely consequences of breaking them.

KEYS TO HANDLING DISCIPLINARY PROBLEMS IN THE WORKPLACE

The ACAS Code of Practice suggests the following steps:

- Establish the facts of each case (see paragraphs 5–8, ACAS Guide page 17).
- Inform the employee of the problem (see paragraphs 9–10, ACAS Guide page 18).
- Hold a meeting with the employee to discuss the problem (see paragraphs 11–12, ACAS Guide page 18).
- Allow the employee to be accompanied at the meeting (see paragraphs 13–16, ACAS Guide page 18 and *Employee representation* below).
- Decide on appropriate action (see paragraphs 17–24, ACAS Guide page 26).
- Provide employees with an opportunity to appeal (see paragraphs 25–28, ACAS Guide page 33).

Paragraphs 29–30 of the ACAS Code of Practice suggest that special consideration be given to the way in which disciplinary procedures operate in relation to trade union officials and those charged or convicted of a criminal offence. In addition, page 35 of the ACAS Guide provides further advice about dealing with special cases.

PROCEDURAL FAIRNESS AND NATURAL JUSTICE

According to paragraph 2 of the ACAS Code of Practice, 'rules and procedures for handling disciplinary and grievance situations … should be set down in writing, be clear and specific'. Paragraph 4 identifies the following aspects of fairness: [96]

- Employers and employees should raise and deal with issues promptly and should not unreasonably delay meetings, decisions or confirmation of those decisions.
- Employers and employees should act consistently.
- Employers should carry out any necessary investigations, to establish the facts of the case.
- Employers should inform employees of the basis of the problem and give them an opportunity to put their case in response before any decisions are made.[97]
- Employees should allow employees to be accompanied at any formal disciplinary or grievance meeting.
- Employers should allow an employee to appeal against any formal decision made.

In addition, the Foreword to the ACAS Code of Practice emphasises the desirability of keeping written records.[98] Although it is clear from the above that natural justice is an important element in such procedures, it would seem that legal representation can be excluded unless the proceedings could have the effect of depriving individuals of the right to practise their profession.[99] According to the Court of Appeal, where the employee's reputation or ability to work in his or her chosen field is potentially apposite, it will be particularly important to conduct a fair investigation. However, an employer is not obliged to believe one employee and disbelieve another, and in some cases it might be proper to give an alleged wrongdoer the benefit of the doubt.[100] Employees should only be found guilty of offences with which they have been charged. Such charges should be precisely formulated and evidence confined to the particulars of the charge.[101] If allegations are made by an informant, a careful balance must be maintained between the desirability of protecting informants who are genuinely in fear and providing a fair hearing of the issues for employees who are accused.[102]

EMPLOYEE REPRESENTATION

Section 10 ERel Act 1999 gives workers the right to make a reasonable request to be accompanied during a disciplinary or grievance hearing. For these purposes a disciplinary hearing is one which could result in the administration of a formal warning, the taking of some other action or the confirmation of previous actions.[103] Whether there is a disciplinary hearing depends on the nature of the meeting itself and not on the description the parties attach to it or its possible consequences.[104] Thus there was no disciplinary hearing where the purpose of the meeting was simply to inform the employee about dismissal for redundancy.[105] According to the EAT, a disciplinary warning becomes a 'formal warning' if it becomes part of the employee's disciplinary record.[106] A grievance hearing is one which concerns the performance of an employer's duty in relation to a worker.[107]

A worker may be accompanied by a single companion who is:

- chosen by the worker
- to be permitted to address the hearing
- not to answer questions on behalf of the worker
- to be allowed to confer with the worker during the hearing.

Such a person can be an official of a trade union or another of the employer's workers.[108] A worker may propose an alternative time for the hearing if his or her chosen companion is unavailable at the time proposed by the employer. The employer must postpone the hearing to the time proposed by the worker, provided that the alternative time is reasonable and falls within a period of five working days beginning with the first working day after the day on which the worker was informed of the time by the employer. An employer must permit a worker to take time off during working hours in order to accompany another of the employer's workers. Section 11 ERel Act 1999 provides that an employer who infringes these rights is liable to pay up to two weeks' pay. In addition, section 12 ERel Act 1999 protects workers who are subjected to a detriment on the ground that they have exercised a right under section 10 ERel Act 1999 or sought to accompany another worker pursuant to a request under that section.

'RECTIFIABLE' AND 'FINAL' WARNINGS

Warnings are particularly appropriate in cases of misconduct but may also be useful in dealing with other types of case. Basically, there are two types of warning that must be distinguished: a 'rectifiable' warning means that the employee will be dismissed unless an existing situation is resolved, whereas a 'final' warning indicates that the employee will be dismissed if further unacceptable behaviour occurs. Warnings are dealt with in paragraphs 18–20 of the ACAS Code of Practice, where it is recommended that written warnings should set out the nature of the offence and the likely consequences of its being repeated. Because an ambiguous warning will be construed strictly against the employer who drafted it, the date and time on which a warning is to commence and expire should be clearly specified.[109]

According to the Court of Appeal, provided a formal disciplinary warning has been given on adequate evidence, and not for an oblique or improper motive, it is a relevant consideration to which an employment tribunal should have regard in deciding whether the dismissal was unfair, even where the warning was under appeal and the appeal had not been determined at the time of the dismissal.[110] It follows that systematic records will have to be kept by employers. Although it is suggested in paragraph 20 of the Code of Practice that the employee 'should be told how long the warning will remain current', in *Airbus Ltd v Webb* [111] the Court of Appeal held that an expired warning does not make the earlier misconduct an irrelevant circumstance under section 98(4) ERA 1996.

THE IMPACT OF APPEAL PROCEDURES

In *Rowe v Radio Rentals* [112] the EAT decided that the employer's appeal procedure did not conflict with the rules of natural justice because the person hearing the appeal had been informed of the decision to dismiss before it took place and the person who took that decision was also present throughout the appeal hearing. It was recognised as inevitable that those involved in the original decision to dismiss will be in daily contact with their supervisors who will be responsible for deciding the appeal.

However, if it is not necessary for the same person to act as both witness and judge in the procedure leading to dismissal, there may be a finding of unfairness.[113]

The Supreme Court has confirmed that a dismissal is unfair if the employer unreasonably treats the reason for dismissal as a sufficient one, either when the original decision to dismiss is made or when that decision is maintained at the conclusion of an internal appeal.[114] Indeed, a dismissal may also be unfair if the employer refuses to comply with the full requirements of the appeal procedure.[115] Where two employees are dismissed for the same incident, and one is successful on appeal and the other is not, in determining the fairness of the latter's dismissal the question is whether the appeal panel's decision was so irrational that no employer could reasonably have accepted it.[116] Whether procedural defects can be rectified on appeal will depend on the degree of unfairness at the original hearing.[117]

REFLECTIVE QUESTION

To what extent does the concept of reasonableness in unfair dismissal law enable employment tribunals to ensure that there is justice between the parties?

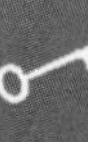

KEY LEARNING POINTS

- Once employees have proved that they were dismissed, the employer must show the reason for the dismissal.
- The employer must demonstrate that the reason for the dismissal relates to capability or qualifications, conduct, a statutory ban or some other substantial reason of a kind to justify the dismissal.
- There are certain reasons which are automatically unfair, such as those relating to trade union membership or activities or to pregnancy and maternity.
- Employees cannot claim unfair dismissal if they are dismissed while taking part in unofficial industrial action.
- Capability is assessed by reference to 'skill, aptitude, health or any other physical or mental ability'.
- Misconduct is a potentially fair reason for dismissal, but the employment tribunal will decide whether dismissal was a reasonable course of action, taking into account all the circumstances.
- 'Some other substantial reason' is a category which gives tribunals the discretion to accept as fair reasons that have not been defined by statute, such as those arising out of the reorganisation of a business.
- An employer must act reasonably in treating a reason as sufficient for dismissal. It should be guided by the ACAS Code of Practice and must follow contractual procedures.

REFERENCES

1 Sections 98(1) and (2) ERA 1996

2 See *ASLEF v Brady* (2006) IRLR 76

3 See *Wilson v Post Office* (2000) IRLR 834

4 See *Abernathy v Mott, Hay and Anderson* (1974) IRLR 213

5 See *Ely v YKK Ltd* (1993) IRLR 500

6 See *Devis & Sons Ltd v Atkins* (1977) IRLR 314

7 See *Parkinson v March Consulting* (1997) IRLR 308

8 See *Ford Motor Co. v Hudson* (1978) IRLR 66

9 No service qualification applies if a dismissal is on the grounds of pregnancy, maternity or adoption; see Chapter 8

10 (1985) IRLR 16

11 See *Harvard Securities v Younghusband* (1990) IRLR 17

12 See *Bromsgrove v Eagle Alexander* (1981) IRLR 127

13 Section 93(2) ERA 1996

14 Section 101 ERA 1996

15 Section 101A ERA 1996

16 Section 103A ERA 1996

17 Section 104A ERA 1996

18 Section 102 ERA 1996

19 Section 103 ERA 1996

20 Section 104B ERA 1996

21 Section 104C ERA 1996

22 Regulation 7 Part-time Workers Regulations 2000 and Regulation 6 Fixed-term Employees Regulations 2002 respectively

23 Section 101C ERA 1996

24 Section 101D ERA 1996

25 Section 101E ERA 1996

26 Section 101F ERA 1996

27 Section 4(3)b Rehabilitation of Offenders Act 1974; see *Wood v Coverage Care Ltd* (1996) IRLR 264

28 See *Elizabeth Claire Ltd v Francis* (2005) IRLR 858

29 See *McClean v Rainbow Homeloans Ltd* (2007) IRLR 15

30 Section 104 ERA 1996; see also *Mennell v Newell & Wright Ltd* (1997) IRLR 519

31 See *Balfour Kilpatrick Ltd v Acheson* (2003) IRLR 683

32 See *Abernathy v Mott, Hay and Anderson* (note 4)

33 (1979) IRLR 16

34 (1998) IRLR 510

35 See *First West Yorkshire Ltd v Haigh* (2008) IRLR 182

36 See *Shook v London Borough of Ealing* (1986) IRLR 46

37 See *McAdie v Royal Bank of Scotland* (2007) IRLR 895

38 (2001) IRLR 139

39 See *Hamilton v Argyll and Clyde Health Authority* (1993) IRLR 99

40 (1998) IRLR 358

41 See *Taylor v Parsons Peebles Ltd* (1981) IRLR 199 where the employee concerned had a good conduct record extending over 20 years

42 See also *United Distillers v Conlin* (1992) IRLR 503

43 See *UCATT v Brain* (1981) IRLR 224

44 (2008) IRLR 408

45 See *Laughton v Bapp Industrial Ltd* (1986) IRLR 245

46 (1992) IRLR 294; see also *Adamson v B&L Cleaning Ltd* (1995) IRLR 193

47 See *Panama v London Borough of Hackney* (2003) IRLR 278

48 (1978) IRLR 379

49 *Scottish Midland Co-op v Cullion* (1991) IRLR 261. See also *Sainsburys Ltd v Hitt* (2003) IRLR 23

50 See *Parr v Whitbread plc* (1990) IRLR 39

51 *Frames Snooker v Boyce* (1992) IRLR 472

52 See *Rhondda Cynon Taf County Borough Council v Close* (2008) IRLR 868

53 On suspension see ACAS Code of Practice on Disciplinary and Grievance Procedures paragraph 8 and page 17 of the Guide

54 See *Secretary of State v Campbell* (1992) IRLR 263

55 See *Harris v Courage Ltd* (1982) IRLR 509

56 *Lovie Ltd v Anderson* (1999) IRLR 164

57 See *Thomson v Alloa Motor Co.* (1983) IRLR 403

58 See *P v Nottingham County Council* (1992) IRLR 362

59 (1980) IRLR 382

60 See *Kingston v British Rail* (1984) IRLR 146

61 *Perkin v St Georges NHS Trust* (2005) IRLR 934

62 *Alboni v Ind Coope Retail Ltd* (1998) IRLR 131

63 *Willow Oak Ltd v Silverwood* (2006) IRLR 607 (see case study below, and note 91)

64 See *Henderson v Connect Ltd* (2010) IRLR 466

65 (1986) IRLR 93

66 See *Dobie v Burns International* (1984) IRLR 329

67 See *Ely v YKK Ltd* (note 5)

68 See *Saunders v National Scottish Camps Association* (1981) IRLR 277

69 See *Hounslow L.B.C. v Klusova* (2008) ICR 396

70 (1979) IRLR 238

71 See *St John of God Ltd v Brooks* (1992) IRLR 546

72 (1998) IRLR 176

73 See *Catamaran Cruisers v Williams* (1994) IRLR 386

74 'Protected industrial action' consists of acts that are not actionable in tort; see section 219 TULRCA 1992

75 Section 238A(6) TULRCA 1992

76 See *Bolton Roadways Ltd v Edwards* (1987) IRLR 392

77 See *Rogers v Chloride Systems* (1992) ICR 198

78 Section 237(6) TULRCA 1992

79 *Balfour Kilpatrick Ltd v Acheson* (2003) IRLR 683

80 Section 98(4) ERA 1996

81 See *Garside & Laycock Ltd v Booth* (2011) IRLR 735

82 See *Smith v City of Glasgow D.C.* (1987) IRLR 326

83 See *Ladbroke Racing v Arnott* (1983) IRLR 154

84 See *Brandon v Murphy Bros* (1983) IRLR 54

85 See *X v Y* (2004) IRLR 625 on Article 8 and respect for private life, and *R v Bradford Teaching Hospital* (2011) IRLR 582 on Article 6 and the right to a 'fair and public hearing within a reasonable time by an independent and impartial tribunal established by law'

86 See *London Borough of Harrow v Cunningham* (1996) IRLR 256

87 See *Whitbread plc v Hall* (2001) IRLR 275

88 See *Anglian Homes Ltd v Kelly* (2004) IRLR 793

89 See *Rentokil Ltd v Mackin* (1989) IRLR 286

90 See *Stacey v Babcock Power Ltd* (1986) IRLR 3

91 *Willow Oak Ltd v Silverwood* (2006) IRLR 607

92 See *Lock v Cardiff Railway Co. Ltd* (1998) IRLR 358

93 Section 207A TULRCA 1992

94 See *Alidair Ltd v Taylor* (1978) IRLR 82

95 See ACAS Code of Practice on Disciplinary and Grievance Procedures paragraph 2

96 Page 11 of the ACAS Guide provides considerable detail about the contents of good disciplinary procedures

97 See *Spence v the Department of Agriculture and Rural Development (DARD)* (2011) IRLR 806

98 See also page 15 of the ACAS Guide

99 See *Kulkarni v Milton Keynes Hospital NHS Trust* (2009) IRLR 829

100 See *Salford Royal NHS Trust v Roldan* (2010) IRLR 721

101 *Strouthos v London Underground Ltd* (2004) IRLR 636

102 Section 13(4) ERel Act 1999

103 *Skiggs v South West Trains* (2005) IRLR 560

104 *Heathmill Ltd v Jones* (2003) IRLR 865

105 See *Harding v London Underground* (2003) IRLR 252

106 See section 13(5) ERel Act 1999

107 Pages 24–26 of the ACAS guide deal with the role of the companion

108 See *Ramsey v Walkers Snack Foods Ltd* (2004) IRLR 754

109 See *Bevan Ashford v Malin* (1995) IRLR 360

110 See *Tower Hamlets Health Authority v Anthony* (1989) IRLR 394

111 (2008) IRLR 309

112 (1982) IRLR 177

113 See *Byrne v BOC Ltd* (1992) IRLR 505

114 See *West Midlands Co-op Ltd v Tipton* (1986) IRLR 112

115 See *Tarbuck v Sainsburys Ltd* (2006) IRLR 664

116 See *Securicor Ltd v Smith* (1989) IRLR 356

117 See *Taylor v OCS Ltd* (2006) IRLR 613

EXPLORE FURTHER

Reading

- Davies, A. (2009) *Perspectives on Labour Law.* Oxford University Press, Chapter 9
- Deakin, S. and Morris, G. (2012) *Labour Law.* Hart, Chapter 5
- Smith, I. and Thomas, G. (2010) *Smith & Wood's Employment Law.* Butterworths, Chapter 7

Websites

- Advisory, Conciliation and Arbitration Service www.acas.org.uk
- Chartered Institute of Personnel and Development www.cipd.co.uk
- Department for Business Innovation and Skills www.bis.gov.uk
- DirectGov - Employment www.direct.gov.uk
- Trades Union Congress www.tuc.org.uk

CHAPTER 14

Redundancy

CHAPTER OVERVIEW

In this chapter we consider dismissals on the grounds of redundancy. We begin by looking at the statutory definition and then consider the rules concerning offers of alternative employment and the opportunity for the employee to make a decision about them. Finally, there is an examination of possible unfairness in the redundancy process.

LEARNING OUTCOMES

After studying this chapter you will be able to:

- understand and explain the statutory definition of redundancy and the circumstances in which a claim for a payment can be made
- advise colleagues about the need for both individual and collective consultation
- help to devise a procedure that is designed to avoid the unfair treatment of workers in a redundancy situation.

QUALIFICATIONS AND EXCLUSIONS

In order to qualify for a redundancy payment an employee must have been continuously employed for two years at the relevant date.[1] Only employees have a right to a redundancy payment and there are a number of situations in which this can be lost:

- employees who are dismissed with or without notice for reasons connected to their conduct[2]
- employees who give notice to the employer terminating the employment with effect from a date prior to the date upon which the employer's notice of redundancy is due to expire. In such a case employees may lose their right to a redundancy payment, although if they leave early by mutual consent this payment will not be affected[3]
- an employee whose contract of employment is renewed, or who is re-engaged under a new contract of employment, provided that the renewal or re-engagement takes place within four weeks of the ending of the employment[4]

- an employee who takes part in strike action after receiving notice of termination. In such a case the employer is entitled to issue a notice of extension. This notice, which must be in writing and indicate the employer's reasons, may request the employee to extend their contract beyond the termination date by a period equivalent to the number of days lost through strike action. Failure by the employee to agree to this extension, unless he or she has good reasons such as sickness or injury, may enable the employer to challenge the right to a redundancy payment[5]
- certain specifically excluded categories of employee, such as public-office-holders and civil servants.[6]

The ending of a limited-term contract is a dismissal and may be for reasons of redundancy. Thus in *Pfaffinger v City of Liverpool Community College* [7] college lecturers who were employed during each academic year only were held to be dismissed for redundancy at the end of each academic term.

THE DEFINITION OF REDUNDANCY

According to 139(1) ERA 1996, employees[8] are to be regarded as being redundant if their dismissals are attributable wholly or mainly to:

- the fact that the employer has ceased, or intends to cease, to carry on the business[9] for the purposes the employees were employed, or
- the fact that the employer has ceased, or intends to cease, to carry on that business in the place where the employees were so employed, or
- the fact that the requirement of that business for employees to carry out work of a particular kind, or for employees to carry out work of a particular kind in the place where they were so employed, has ceased or diminished or is expected to cease or diminish.

In this context 'cease' or 'diminish' mean either permanently or temporarily and from whatever cause.[10]

CASE STUDY

MURRAY v FOYLE MEATS LTD

In *Murray v Foyle Meats Ltd*,[11] the Supreme Court held that the definition of redundancy requires two questions of fact to be answered:

- Have the requirements of the employer's business for employees to carry out work of a particular kind ceased or diminished, or were they expected to cease or diminish?
- Was the dismissal of the employee attributable, wholly or mainly, to this state of affairs?

Discussion point

What would be the consequences if employment tribunals investigated how a redundancy situation came to arise?

This means looking at the employer's overall requirements to decide whether there has been a diminution of the need for employees irrespective of the terms of the individual's contract or of the function that each performed. In *Murray*'s case, the Supreme Court approved the approach of the EAT[12] in deciding that 'bumping' could give rise to a redundancy payment. 'Bumping' is where an individual's job may continue but there is a reduction in requirement for the same number of people to carry out the work and that individual is made redundant.

DETERMINING WHAT CONSTITUTES THE PLACE OF EMPLOYMENT

For these purposes, the place where an employee was employed does not extend to any place where he or she could contractually be required to work. The question of what is the place of employment concerns the extent or area of a single place, not the transfer from one place to another.[13] If there is no express term relating to mobility, a tribunal will have to examine all the evidence to see if a term should be inferred.[14] However, even though an employee may be contractually justified in declining to move, a request to do so may have to be considered as an offer of suitable alternative employment (see below).

DETERMINING WHAT CONSTITUTES 'WORK OF A PARTICULAR KIND'

One of the most onerous tasks of tribunals is to determine what constitutes 'work of a particular kind'. It is clear that a change in the time when the work is to be performed will not give rise to a redundancy payment,[15] nor will a reduction of overtime if the work to be done remains the same. Thus in *Lesney Products Ltd v Nolan* [16] the Court of Appeal held that the company's reorganisation, by which one long day shift plus overtime was changed into two day shifts, was done in the interests of efficiency and was not the result of any diminution in the employer's requirements for employees to carry out work of a particular kind.[17]

However, both the work that the employee actually carried out and the work that the employee was contractually required to do will be considerations when an employment tribunal decides this issue.[18]

Three further points must be made:

- Employees will be entitled to a payment notwithstanding that it could be seen from the commencement of the contract that they would be dismissed for redundancy. The fact that the contract was temporary and short-term makes no difference in this respect.[19]
- The statutory definition of redundancy focuses on the employer's requirements rather than needs. Thus - even where there is still a need for the work to be done – if, owing to lack of funds, the requirement for the employee's service has ceased, the employee is redundant.[20]
- Section 163(2) ERA 1996 states that an employee who is dismissed is presumed to have been dismissed by reason of redundancy unless the contrary is proved.[21]

OFFERS OF ALTERNATIVE EMPLOYMENT

If, before the ending of a person's employment, the employer or an associated employer makes an offer, in writing or not, to renew the contract or to re-engage under a new contract which is to take effect either on the ending of the old one or within four weeks, then section 141 ERA 1996 has the following effect:

- if the provisions of the new or renewed contract as to the capacity and place in which the person would be employed, together with the other terms and conditions, do not differ from the corresponding terms of the previous contract, or
- if the terms and conditions differ, wholly or in part, but the offer constitutes an offer of suitable employment, and
- if in either case the employee unreasonably refuses that offer,

then he or she will not be entitled to a redundancy payment.

The burden is on an employer to prove both the suitability of the offer and the unreasonableness of the employee's refusal.[22] Offers do not have to be formal, nor do they have to contain all the conditions which are ultimately agreed.[23] However, supplying details of vacancies is not the same as an offer of employment[24] and sufficient information must be provided to enable the employee to take a realistic decision.[25]

The suitability of the alternative work must be assessed objectively by comparing the terms on offer with those previously enjoyed. A convenient test has been whether the proposed employment will be 'substantially equivalent' to that which has ceased.[26] Merely offering the same salary will not be sufficient[27] but the fact that the employment will be at a different location does not necessarily mean that it will be regarded as unsuitable.

'REASONABLE' REFUSAL BY EMPLOYEES OF ALTERNATIVE EMPLOYMENT

By way of contrast, in adjudicating upon the reasonableness of an employee's refusal, subjective considerations can be taken into account - for example, domestic responsibilities. In *Spencer v Gloucestershire County Council* [28] the employees had refused offers of suitable employment on the grounds that they would not be able to do their work to a satisfactory standard in the reduced hours and with lower staffing levels. The Court of Appeal held that it was for employers to set the standard of work they wanted carried out but it was a different question whether it was reasonable for a particular employee, in all the circumstances, to refuse to work to the standard set. This is a question of fact for the tribunal.

Similarly, it might be reasonable for an employee to refuse an offer of employment which, although suitable, involved loss of status.[29]

REFLECTIVE QUESTION

Does the reasonable refusal test create too much uncertainty for both employers and employees?

TRIAL PERIODS FOR NEW OR RENEWED CONTRACTS

To allow an employee to make a rational decision about any alternative employment offered, section 138(3) ERA 1996 states that if the terms and conditions differ, wholly or in part, from those of the previous contract, a trial period may be invoked. Such a period commences when the employee starts work under the new or renewed contract and ends four calendar weeks later,[30] unless a longer period has been agreed for the purpose of retraining. Any such agreement must be made before the employee starts work under the new or renewed contract; it must be in writing, and specify the date the trial period ends, and the terms and conditions which will apply afterwards.[31] In order to have an agreement, an employee must do something to indicate acceptance. However, it is not necessary for the employer to provide all the information required by section 1 ERA 1996; the agreement need embody only important matters such as remuneration, status and job description.[32] If, during the trial period, the employee for any reason terminates or gives notice to terminate the contract, or the employer terminates or gives notice to terminate it for any reason connected with or arising out of the change, the employee is to be treated, for redundancy payment purposes, as having been dismissed on the date the previous contract ended. It should be noted that the employee's contract may be renewed again, or he or she may be re-engaged under a new contract in circumstances which give rise to another trial period.[33] Indeed, the termination of a trial period could lead to a finding of unfair dismissal.[34]

UNFAIR REDUNDANCY

It is possible for a dismissed employee to claim both a redundancy payment and unfair dismissal, although double compensation cannot be obtained.[35] For unfair dismissal purposes the statutory presumption of redundancy does not apply, so it is up to the employer to establish this as the reason, or principal reason, for dismissal. However, tribunals will not investigate the background which led to the redundancy or require the employer to justify redundancies in economic terms. According to the EAT, employers do not have to show that their requirements for employees to carry out work of a particular kind have diminished in relation to *any* work that the employees could have been asked to do under their contracts. Thus where an employee is hired to perform a particular trade, it is that basic obligation which has to be looked at when deciding whether the employer's requirements have ceased or diminished, rather than any work that the employee could be required to carry out in accordance with a contractual flexibility clause.[36]

A dismissal on grounds of redundancy will be unfair if it is shown that 'the circumstances constituting the redundancy applied equally to one or more other employees in the same undertaking who held positions similar' and either the reason, or principal reason, for which the employee was selected was inadmissible (see Chapter 13).[37] A situation where a number of employees at a similar level are made to apply for a reduced number of jobs at that level may still result in a dismissal on the grounds of redundancy which is fair, even though the work of that particular employee still continues to be done.[38]

THE INVOLVEMENT OF TRADE UNIONS

Because section 105 ERA 1996 is concerned purely with selection on grounds that are not permissible, a failure to comply with a procedural requirement to consult trade unions and to consider volunteers will not automatically be unfair.[39] Nevertheless, section 98(4) ERA 1996 can still have a considerable impact on dismissals for redundancy.

CASE STUDY

WILLIAMS v COMPAIR MAXAM LTD

In *Williams v Compair Maxam Ltd*[40] it was held that it is not enough to show that it was reasonable to dismiss *an* employee – a tribunal must be satisfied that the employer acted reasonably in treating redundancy as 'sufficient reason for dismissing the employee'. According to the EAT, where employees are represented by a recognised independent trade union, reasonable employers will seek to act in accordance with the following principles:

- The employer will seek to give as much warning as possible of impending redundancies so as to enable the union and employees who may be affected to take early steps to inform themselves of the relevant facts, consider possible alternative solutions, and, if necessary, find alternative employment in the undertaking or elsewhere.
- The employer will consult the union as to the best means by which the desired management result can be achieved fairly and with as little hardship to the employees as possible.[41] In particular, the employer will seek to agree with the union the criteria to be applied in selecting the employees to be made redundant.[42] When a selection has been made, the employer will consider with the union whether the selection has been made in accordance with those criteria.[43]
- Whether or not an agreement as to the criteria to be adopted has been reached with the union, the employer will seek to establish criteria for selection which so far as possible do not depend solely upon the opinion of the person making the selection but can be checked objectively against such things as attendance record, efficiency at the job or length of service.
- The employer will seek to ensure that the selection is made fairly in accordance with these criteria and will consider any representations the union may make as to such selection.
- The employer will seek to see whether instead of dismissing, an employee could be offered alternative employment.

FAIR APPLICATION OF SELECTION CRITERIA

In selecting employees for redundancy, a senior manager is entitled to rely on the assessments of employees made by those who have direct knowledge of their work. However, employers may need to show that their method of selection was fair and applied reasonably.[44] An absence of adequate consultation with the employees concerned or their representatives might affect their ability to do this[45] (consultation issues are considered below). It will not always be possible to call evidence subsequently to show that adequate consultation would have made no difference to the decision about those selected for redundancy. If the flaws in the process were procedural, it might be possible to reconstruct what might have happened if the correct procedures had been followed. However, where the tribunal decides that the flaws were more substantive, such a reconstruction may not be possible.[46] In practice, many employers have established redundancy appeal procedures to deal with complaints that selection criteria have been unfairly applied.

ALTERNATIVES TO COMPULSORY REDUNDANCY

It is now well established that employers have a duty to consider the alternatives to compulsory redundancy. According to ACAS, the measures for minimising or avoiding compulsory redundancies may include:

- natural wastage
- restrictions on recruitment
- reduction or elimination of overtime
- the introduction of short-time working or temporary lay-off (where this is provided for in the contract of employment or by an agreed variation of its terms)
- retraining and redeployment to other parts of the organisation
- termination of the employment of temporary or contract staff
- seeking applicants for early retirement or voluntary redundancy.[47]

'Last in, first out' is still used as a criterion for selection and it is assumed to be based on periods of continuous rather than cumulative service.[48] Arguably, this form of selection indirectly discriminates on the grounds of both sex and age and therefore needs to be objectively justified (see Chapter 6). Selecting employees on part-time and/or fixed-term contracts may also be potentially discriminatory. In *Whiffen v Milham Ford Girls School* [49] those employees not employed under a permanent contract of employment were the first to be selected in a redundancy exercise. This was held to be indirectly discriminatory because a smaller proportion of women than comparable men were able to satisfy this condition.

As regards alternative employment, 'the size and administrative resources' of the employer will be a relevant consideration here. However, if a vacancy exists, an employer would be advised to offer it rather than speculate about the likelihood of the employee accepting it. This is so even if the new job entails demotion or other radical changes in the terms and conditions of employment. Nevertheless, only in very rare cases will a tribunal accept that a reasonable employer would have created a job by dismissing someone else. Finally, employers should consider establishing both redundancy counselling services - which would provide information on alternative employment, training, occupational and state benefits – and hardship committees, which would seek to alleviate 'undue hardship'.[50]

CONSULTATION

An important requirement in redundancy situations is the need for consultation (see Chapter 17 for specific requirements in relation to collective redundancies). Consultation may be directly with the employees concerned or with their representatives.

CASE STUDY

MUGFORD v MIDLAND BANK PLC

In *Mugford v Midland Bank plc*[51] the EAT held that a dismissal on the grounds of redundancy was not unfair because no consultation had taken place with the employee individually, only with the recognised trade union. The EAT described the position with regard to consultation as follows:

- Where no consultation about redundancy has taken place with either the trade union or the employee, the dismissal will normally be unfair, unless the reasonable employer would have concluded that the consultation would be an 'utterly futile' exercise.
- Consultation with the trade union over the selection criteria does not of itself release the employer from considering with the employee individually the fact that he or she has been identified for redundancy.
- It will be a question of fact and degree for the tribunal to consider whether the consultation with the individual and/or the trade union was so inadequate as to render the dismissal unfair.

For the tribunal to decide whether or not the employer acted reasonably, the overall picture must be viewed at the time of termination. The consultation must be fair and proper, which means that there must be:

- consultation when the proposals are still at a formative stage
- adequate information and adequate time to respond[52]
- a conscientious consideration by the employer of the response to consultation.[53]

Although proper consultation may be regarded as a procedural matter, it might have a direct bearing on the substantive decision to select a particular employee, since a different employee might have been selected if, following proper consultation, different criteria had been adopted. It is not normally permissible for an employer to argue that a failure to consult or warn would have made no difference to the outcome in the particular case. It is what the employer did that is to be judged, not what might have been done. While the size of an undertaking might affect the nature or formality of the consultation, it cannot excuse lack of any consultation at all.[54] Finally, it should be noted that the EAT has taken the view that warning and consultation are part of the same single process of consultation, which should commence with a warning that the employee is at risk.[55]

REFLECTIVE QUESTION

Given the broad legal definition of redundancy, is it fair to conclude that the only real protection for employees is that employers are required to consult?

CASE STUDY

ELKOUIL v CONEY ISLAND LTD

Mr Elkouil was a credit controller at a night club. He was made redundant with immediate effect, although at no time was he warned that his job was at risk. The EAT held that the employment tribunal was wrong to limit the compensatory award to two weeks' pay on the basis that if the employer had consulted with him properly, he would have been employed for a further two weeks.

The EAT ruled that this was not an appropriate measure of the claimant's loss when the employer knew at least ten weeks before the dismissal that Mr Elkouil was going to be made redundant. The ET should have considered what would have been the likely outcome if the employer had done what it ought to have done. Here the consequence of the failure to consult was that the employee was disadvantaged in seeking another job, and ten weeks' pay was awarded.[56]

Discussion point

Is it fair to conclude from this case that unfair dismissal law requires employers to consult with individual employees about their possible redundancy at the earliest opportunity?

KEY LEARNING POINTS

- Employees are to be regarded as redundant if the employer has ceased or intends to cease carrying on the business for the purposes for which the employees were employed, or in the place where they are employed there has been, or will be, a diminution in the need for work of a particular kind.
- If there is no express term relating to mobility in the contract of employment, the tribunal will have to consider whether one should be inferred.
- The burden of proof is on the employer to show that any offer of alternative employment was suitable and that any refusal by the employee was unreasonable.
- A trial period may be invoked to consider offers of alternative employment if there is likely to be a difference in terms and conditions of employment.
- The employer should give as much warning as possible of impending redundancies to enable the union and the affected employees to take early steps to consider alternative solutions or possibly find alternative work in the undertaking or elsewhere.

Figure 4 Redundancy payment flowchart

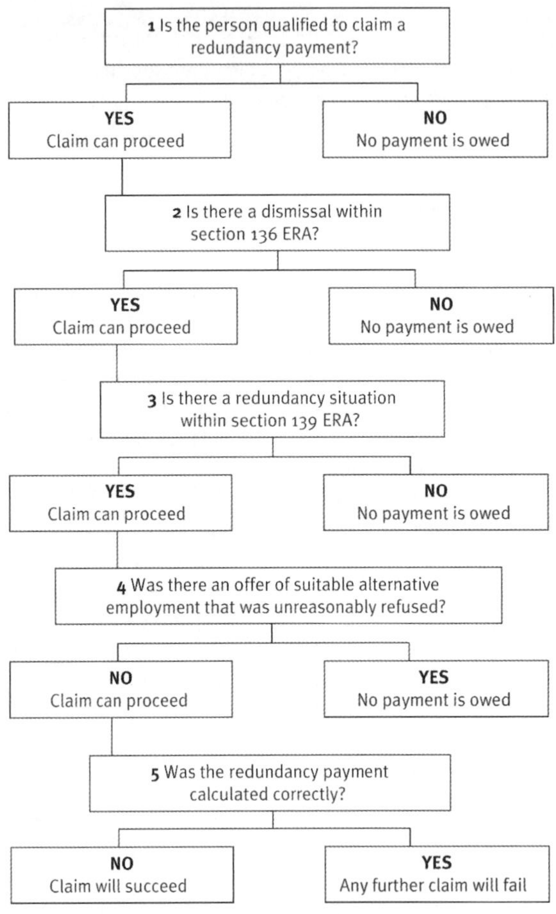

REFERENCES

1 Section 155 ERA 1996
2 See Section 140 ERA 1996
3 See *CPS Recruitment Ltd v Bowen* (1982) IRLR 54
4 Section 138(1) ERA 1996
5 Sections 143–4 ERA 1996
6 See sections 159 and 191 ERA 1996
7 (1996) IRLR 508
8 It is for the tribunal to decide if a person is an employee by considering the facts and concluding that there is a genuine contract of employment; see *Secretary of State for Trade and Industry v Bottrill* (1999) IRLR 326
9 'Business' is defined in section 235(1) ERA 1996
10 Section 139(6) ERA 1996

11 (1999) IRLR 562

12 *Safeway Stores v Burrell* (1997) IRLR 200

13 See *Bass Leisure v Thomas* (1994) IRLR 104; also *High Table Ltd v Horst* (1997) IRLR 514

14 See *Aparau v Iceland Frozen Foods* (1996) IRLR 119

15 See *Johnson v Nottingham Police Authority* (1974) ICR 170

16 (1977) IRLR 77

17 See also *Shawkat v Nottingham City Hospital NHS Trust (No. 2)* (2001) IRLR 555

18 See *Shawkat v Nottingham City Hospital NHS Trust (No. 2)* (note 17)

19 See *Pfaffinger v City of Liverpool Community College* (1996) IRLR 508

20 See *AUT v Newcastle University* (1987) ICR 317

21 See *Wilcox v Hastings* (1987) IRLR 299

22 See *Jones v Aston Cabinet Co. Ltd* (1973) ICR 292

23 See *Singer Co. v Ferrier* (1980) IRLR 300

24 See *Curling v Securicor Ltd* (1992) IRLR 549

25 See *Modern Injection Moulds Ltd v Price* (1976) IRLR 172

26 See *Hindes v Supersine Ltd* (1979) IRLR 343

27 See *Taylor v Kent County Council.* (1969) 2 QB 560

28 (1985) IRLR 393

29 See *Cambridge and District Co-op v Ruse* (1993) IRLR 156

30 See *Benton v Sanderson Kayser* (1989) IRLR 299

31 Section 138(6) ERA 1996

32 See *McKindley v W Hill Ltd* (1985) IRLR 492

33 Section 138(5) ERA 1996

34 See *Hempell v W H Smith & Sons Ltd* (1986) IRLR 95

35 Section 122(4) ERA 1996

36 See *Johnson v Peabody Trust* (1996) IRLR 387

37 Section 105 ERA 1996. 'Undertaking' is not defined in this context; 'position' is defined in section 235(1) ERA 1996 as meaning the following matters taken as a whole: status, the nature of the work, and the terms and conditions of employment; on 'position similar' see *Powers and Villiers v A Clarke & Co.* (1981) IRLR 483

38 See *Safeway Stores v Burrell* (1997) IRLR 200 (note 12)

39 See *McDowell v Eastern BRS Ltd* (1981) IRLR 482

40 (1982) IRLR 83

41 See *Hough v Leyland DAF Ltd* (1991) IRLR 194

42 See *Rolls-Royce Ltd v Price* (1993) IRLR 203. There is no legal requirement that a redundancy pool should be restricted to employees doing similar work: **Capital Hartshead Ltd v Byard (2012) IRLR 814**

43 See *John Brown Engineering Ltd v Brown* (1997) IRLR 90

44 In *Northgate HR Ltd v Mercy* (2008) IRLR 222 the Court of Appeal ruled that a tribunal was entitled to conclude that a glaring inconsistency produced in good faith could amount to unfairness in the administration of a selection procedure

45 See *King v Eaton Ltd* (1996) IRLR 199

46 See *King v Eaton Ltd (No. 2)* (1998) IRLR 686

47 Advisory booklet on redundancy-handling (2009). It should be noted that paragraph 1 of the ACAS Code of Practice on Disciplinary and Grievance Procedures states that it 'does not apply to redundancy dismissals or the non-renewal of fixed-term contracts on their expiry'

48 See *International Paint Co. v Cameron* (1979) IRLR 62

49 (2001) IRLR 468

50 See generally ACAS advisory booklet on redundancy-handling (2009)

51 (1997) IRLR 208

52 See *Pinewood Repro Ltd v Page* (2011) ICR 508

53 *King v Eaton Ltd* (1996) (note 45)

54 See *De Grasse v Stockwell Tools* (1992) IRLR 269

55 See *Elkouil v Coney Island Ltd* (2002) IRLR 174

56 *Elkouil v Coney Island Ltd* (note 55)

EXPLORE FURTHER

Reading

- Davies, A. (2009) *Perspectives on Labour Law.* Oxford University Press, Chapter 9
- Deakin, S. and Morris, G. (2012) *Labour Law.* Hart, Chapter 5
- Smith, I. and Thomas, G. (2010) *Smith & Wood's Employment Law.* Butterworths, Chapters 7 and 8

Websites

- Advisory, Conciliation and Arbitration Service www.acas.org.uk
- Chartered Institute of Personnel and Development www.cipd.co.uk
- Department for Business Innovation and Skills www.bis.gov.uk
- DirectGov – Employment wwwdirect.gov.uk
- Trades Union Congress www.tuc.org.uk

CHAPTER 15

Unfair Dismissal and Redundancy Claims

CHAPTER OVERVIEW

This chapter looks at the rules about claiming unfair dismissal or a redundancy payment. We begin by discussing the time-limits for making a complaint to an employment tribunal and then look at the making of conciliation and compromise agreements or using arbitration as an alternative to presenting a complaint. We go on to examine the remedies for unfair dismissal, which consist of reinstatement, re-engagement or compensation. There is then a consideration of how awards of compensation are arrived at and the method for calculating redundancy payments. The chapter concludes by outlining the rights of employees if the employer becomes insolvent.

LEARNING OUTCOMES

After studying this chapter you will be able to:

- understand and explain the legal principles that apply when a claim for unfair dismissal or a redundancy payment is lodged
- advise colleagues about the types of award likely to be made by employment tribunals and the desirability of settling claims via conciliation, arbitration or compromise agreements.

MAKING A CLAIM

UNFAIR DISMISSAL

Unless the 'time-limit escape clause' applies,[1] claims must normally arrive at an employment tribunal within three months of the effective date of termination. However, where employees dismissed for taking part in industrial action allege that they should have been offered re-engagement, a complaint must be lodged within six months of the date of dismissal.[2] A time-limit expires at midnight on the last day of the stipulated period even when that is a non-working day.[3] A complaint can also be presented before the effective date of termination provided it is lodged after notice has been given. This includes notice given by an employee who is alleging constructive dismissal.[4] What is or is not reasonably practicable is a question of fact and the onus is on the employee to prove that it was not reasonably practicable to claim in time. The meaning of 'reasonably practicable' lies somewhere between reasonable and reasonably capable of physically being done.[5] The tribunal will look at this issue of reasonableness against all the surrounding circumstances. Sickness may be taken into account but will be more important if it falls within the critical latter part of the three-month period rather than at the beginning.[6]

The courts have dealt with this jurisdictional point on many occasions and have taken the view that because the unfair dismissal provisions have been in force for many years, tribunals should be fairly strict in enforcing the time-limit.[7] Nevertheless, the issue of reasonable practicability depends upon the awareness of specific grounds for complaint, not upon the right to complain at all. Thus there is nothing to prevent an employee who is time-barred from claiming on one ground from proceeding with a second complaint on another ground if it is raised within a reasonable period. According to the Court of Appeal, if employers want to protect themselves from late claims presented on the basis of newly discovered facts they should ensure that the fullest information is made available to the employee at the time of dismissal.[8]

Delaying an application through ignorance or mistaken belief

The fact that an internal appeal or criminal action is pending does not by itself provide a sufficient excuse for delaying an application.[9] The correct procedure is for employees to submit their applications and request that they be held in abeyance. It is a general principle of English law that ignorance does not afford an excuse. Nevertheless, in *Wall's Meat Co. Ltd v Khan* [10] it was decided that ignorance or mistaken belief can be grounds for holding that it was not reasonably practicable if it could be shown that the ignorance or mistaken belief was itself reasonable.

CASE STUDY

CHURCHILL v YEATES LTD

In *Churchill v Yeates Ltd*[11] the EAT held that it was not reasonably practicable for an employee to bring a complaint until he or she had knowledge of a fundamental fact which rendered the dismissal unfair. In this case, after the three-month period had elapsed an employee who had been dismissed on the grounds of redundancy discovered that he had been replaced.

Discussion point

Would it be sensible for employers to inform employees that normally they need to complain about unfair dismissal within three months?

Ignorance or mistaken belief will not be reasonable if it arises from the fault of complainants in not making such inquiries as they reasonably should have in the circumstances. However, the failure by an adviser – such as a trade union official, Citizen's Advice Bureau worker or solicitor – to give correct advice about a time-limit will not necessarily prevent an employee from arguing that it was not reasonably practicable to claim in time.[12]

The correct way to calculate the period of three months beginning with the effective date of termination is to take the day before the effective date and go forward three months. If there is no corresponding date (31st or 30th) in that month, the last day of the month is taken.[13] Where an application is posted within three months but arrives after the period has expired, the question to be determined is whether the claimant could reasonably have expected the application to be delivered in time in the ordinary course of the post.[14] In relation to electronic communications, the EAT has accepted that an application is presented when it is successfully submitted online at the Employment Tribunal Service website.[15] Finally, it should be noted that the unexplained failure of an application to reach the tribunal is insufficient to satisfy the statutory test unless all reasonable steps were taken to confirm that the application was duly received.[16]

REFLECTIVE QUESTION

Should late claims for unfair dismissal be accepted by tribunals if it is thought just and equitable to do so?

REDUNDANCY

Employees who have not received a redundancy payment will normally be entitled to make a claim only if within six months of the relevant date they have:

- given written notice to the employer that they want a payment, or
- referred a question as to their right to a payment, or its amount, to a tribunal, or
- presented a complaint of unfair dismissal to a tribunal.[17]

The written notice to the employer does not have to be in a particular form. The test is whether it is of such a character that the recipient would reasonably understand in all the circumstances that it was the employee's intention to seek a payment.[18] In this context the words 'presented' and 'referred' seem to have the same meaning – ie an application must have been received by the employment tribunal within the six-month period.[19] Nevertheless, if any of the above steps are taken outside this period but within 12 months of the relevant date, a tribunal has the discretion to award a payment if it thinks that it would be just and equitable to do so. In such a case a tribunal must have regard to the employee's reasons for failing to take any of the steps within the normal time-limit.[20]

CONCILIATION AND COMPROMISE AGREEMENTS

Copies of unfair dismissal applications and redundancy claims and subsequent correspondence are sent to an ACAS conciliation officer who has the duty to promote a settlement of the complaint:

- if requested to do so by the complainant and the employer (known as the respondent), or
- if, in the absence of any such request, the conciliation officer considers that he or she could act with a reasonable prospect of success.

In *Moore v Duport Furniture* [21] the Supreme Court decided that the expression 'promote a settlement' should be given a liberal construction capable of covering whatever action by way of such promotion is appropriate in the circumstances. Where the complainant has ceased to be employed, the conciliation officer must seek to promote that person's re-employment (ie reinstatement or re-engagement) on terms that appear to be equitable. If the complainant does not wish to be re-employed, or this is not practicable, the conciliation officer must seek to promote agreement on compensation.[22] In addition, section 18(3) ETA 1996 allows conciliation officers to make their services available before a complaint has been presented if requested to do so by either a potential applicant or a respondent. However, conciliation officers have no duty to explain to employees what their statutory rights are.[23]

Where appropriate, a conciliation officer is to 'have regard to the desirability of encouraging the use of other procedures available for the settlement of grievances' and anything communicated to a conciliation officer in connection with the performance of the above functions is not admissible in evidence in any proceedings before a tribunal except with the consent of the person who communicated it.[24] It should be noted that an agreement to refrain from lodging a tribunal complaint is subject to all the qualifications by which an agreement can be avoided at common law – for example, on grounds of economic duress.[25] Where a representative holds himself or herself out as having authority to reach a settlement, in the absence of any notice to the contrary, the other party is entitled to assume that the representative does in fact have that authority. In such circumstances the agreement is binding on the client whether or not the adviser had any authority to enter into it.[26] A conciliated settlement will be binding even though it is not in writing[27] and the employee will be prevented from bringing the case before a tribunal.[28]

Additionally, an agreement to refrain from bringing certain tribunal proceedings will not be void if it satisfies the conditions governing 'compromise agreements'. These conditions are that:

- the agreement must be in writing and must relate to the particular complaint
- the employee must have received independent legal advice from a relevant independent adviser[29] as to the terms and effect of the proposed agreement and, in particular, its effect on the employee's ability to pursue his or her rights before a tribunal

- at the time the adviser gives the advice there must be in force an insurance policy covering the risk of a claim by the employee in respect of loss arising in consequence of the advice
- the agreement must identify the adviser and state that the conditions regulating compromise agreements under ERA 1996 are satisfied.[30]

According to the EAT, an employment tribunal has jurisdiction to enforce a compromise agreement relating to the terms on which employment is to terminate.[31] It can also consider whether such an agreement was unenforceable on the grounds of misrepresentation.[32]

CASE STUDY

HINTON v UNIVERSITY OF EAST LONDON

David Hinton took early retirement under an agreement which included a provision purporting to compromise all claims against his employer and satisfy the conditions laid down in section 203 ERA 1996 (above). However, the Court of Appeal upheld the ET's decision that Dr Hinton was not precluded from pursuing his complaint under section 47B ERA 1996 since it had not been itemised in the agreement.

According to the Appeal Court, the requirement that in order to constitute a valid compromise an agreement must 'relate to the particular proceedings' should be construed as requiring those proceedings to be clearly identified. Although one document can be used to compromise all the proceedings, it is insufficient to use the expression 'all statutory rights'. Thus the claims to be covered by an agreement must be identified either by a generic description (for example, 'unfair dismissal') or by reference to the relevant section of the statute.[33]

ARBITRATION

ACAS has produced an arbitration scheme as an alternative to an employment tribunal hearing for the resolution of unfair dismissal claims. The central feature of the scheme is that it is 'designed to be free of legalism'.[34] The arbitrator will decide on procedural and evidential matters and appeals will be allowed against awards only where EU law or the Human Rights Act 1998 are relevant. Hearings will be conducted in an inquisitorial manner, rather than an adversarial one, and the parties must comply with any instruction given by the arbitrator. Entry to the scheme is to be entirely voluntary but the parties will opt for arbitration on the understanding that they accept the arbitrator's decision as final. The arbitrator will decide whether the dismissal was fair or unfair and, in doing so, will have regard to the ACAS Code of Practice on Disciplinary and Grievance Procedures and the ACAS Guide. Where the dismissal is found to be unfair, the arbitrator may award reinstatement, re-engagement or compensation. Hearings will take place in a location convenient to all the parties and they will be responsible for their own expenses.

THE REMEDIES FOR UNFAIR DISMISSAL

RE-EMPLOYMENT

When applicants are found to have been unfairly dismissed, tribunals must explain their power to order reinstatement or re-engagement and ask employees if they wish such an order to be made.[35] Only if such a wish is expressed can an order be made, and if no order is made, the tribunal must turn to the question of compensation.[36] Where re-employment is sought, a tribunal must first consider whether reinstatement is appropriate and, in so doing, must take into account the following matters:

- whether the complainant wishes to be reinstated
- whether it is practicable for the employer to comply with an order for reinstatement
- where the complainant caused or contributed to some extent to the dismissal, whether it would be just to order reinstatement.[37]

If reinstatement is not ordered, the tribunal must then decide whether to make an order for re-engagement, and if so, on what terms. At this stage the tribunal must take into account the following considerations:

- any wish expressed by the complainant as to the nature of the order to be made
- whether it is practicable for the employer or, as the case may be, a successor or associated employer to comply with an order for re-engagement
- where the complainant caused or contributed to some extent to the dismissal, whether it would be just to order re-engagement, and if so, on what terms.

Except in a case where the tribunal takes into account contributory fault under the last point above, if it orders re-engagement it will do so in terms that are, so far as is reasonably practicable, as favourable as an order for reinstatement.[38] However, it would seem that tribunals cannot order that employees be re-engaged on significantly more favourable terms than they would have enjoyed had they been reinstated in their former jobs.[39]

CASE STUDY

PORT OF LONDON AUTHORITY v PAYNE

In *Port of London Authority v Payne*,[40] the Court of Appeal suggested that a tribunal could approach the question of whether it would be practicable to order re-employment in two stages. The first stage would be before any order had been made, when a provisional decision could be taken. The second stage would arise if such an order was made but not complied with.

Discussion point

How important is it that employers think about the practicability of re-employment as soon as a complaint of unfair dismissal is received?

If at least seven days before the hearing the employee has expressed a wish to be re-employed but it becomes necessary to postpone or adjourn the hearing because the employer does not, without special reason, adduce reasonable evidence about the availability of the job from which the employee was dismissed, the employer will be required to pay the costs of the adjournment or postponement.[41] In addition, section 116(5) ERA 1996 states that where an employer has taken on a permanent replacement, this shall not be taken into account unless the employer shows either:

- that it was not practicable to arrange for the dismissed employee's work to be done without engaging a permanent replacement, or
- that a replacement was engaged after the lapse of a reasonable period without having heard from the dismissed employee that he or she wished to be reinstated or re-engaged, and that when the employer engaged the replacement it was no longer reasonable to arrange for the dismissed employee's work to be done except by a permanent replacement.

The practicability of reinstating employees

Practicability is a question of fact for each tribunal. In *Boots plc v Lees* [42] the EAT agreed that it was practicable to reinstate notwithstanding that the employee's ultimate superior remained convinced that he was guilty of theft. By way of contrast, in *Wood Group Heavy Industrial Turbines Ltd v Crossan*,[43] the EAT held that an employer's genuine belief that an employee was dealing in drugs made re-engagement impracticable.

In addition, the following arguments have been used to prevent an order being made: that the employee was unable to perform the work; that a redundancy situation arose subsequent to the dismissal; and that other employees were hostile to the complainant's return to work. It has also been suggested by the EAT that in a small concern where a close personal relationship exists reinstatement will be appropriate only in exceptional circumstances.[44]

For these purposes reinstatement is defined as treating the complainant 'in all respects as if he had not been dismissed', and on making an order the tribunal must specify:

- any amount payable by the employer in respect of any benefit which the complainant might reasonably be expected to have had but for the dismissal, including arrears of pay, for the period between the date of termination and the date of reinstatement
- any rights and privileges, including seniority and pension rights, which must be restored to the employee
- the date by which the order must be complied with.[45]

The complainant also benefits from any improvements that have been made to the terms and conditions of employment since dismissal.[46]

The terms that a tribunal must set out for re-engagement

An order for re-engagement may be on such terms as the tribunal decides and the complainant may be re-engaged by the employer, a successor or an associated employer in comparable or suitable employment. On making such an order the tribunal must set out the terms, including: the identity of the employer, the nature of the employment and the remuneration payable, together with the matters listed above in relation to reinstatement.[47]

Redress for non-compliance with a tribunal order to re-engage

Where a person is reinstated or re-engaged as the result of a tribunal order but the terms are not fully complied with,[48] a tribunal must make an additional award of compensation of such amount as it thinks fit, having regard to the loss sustained by the complainant in consequence of the failure to comply fully with the terms of the order.[49] It is a matter for speculation how long re-employment must last for it to be said that an order has been complied with. If a complainant is not re-employed in accordance with a tribunal order, he or she is entitled to enforce the monetary element at the employment tribunal.[50] Compensation will be awarded together with an additional award unless the employer satisfies the tribunal that it was not practicable to comply with the order.[51] However, according to the Court of Appeal, a re-engagement order does not place a duty on an employer to search for a job for the dismissed employee irrespective of the vacancies that arise.[52]

The additional award will be of between 26 and 52 weeks' pay.[53] The employment tribunal has discretion as to where, within this range, the additional compensation should fall, but it must be exercised on the basis of a proper assessment of the factors involved. One factor would ordinarily be the view taken of the employer's conduct in refusing to comply with the order.[54] Conversely, employees who unreasonably prevent an order being complied with will be regarded as having failed to mitigate their loss.

AWARDS OF COMPENSATION

Compensation for unfair dismissal will usually consist of a basic award and a compensatory award. It should be noted that if an award is not paid within 42 days of the tribunal's decision being recorded, it will attract interest.

BASIC AWARD

Normally, this will be calculated in the same way as a redundancy payment and will be reduced by the amount of any redundancy payment received.[55] Where the reason or principal reason for dismissal is related to union membership or the employee's health and safety responsibilities, there is a minimum award of £5,300 in 2012 (subject to any deduction on the grounds stated below).[56] The basic award can be reduced by such proportion as the tribunal considers just and equitable on two grounds:[57]

- the complainant unreasonably refused an offer of reinstatement. Such an offer could have been made before any finding of unfairness
- any conduct of the complainant before the dismissal, or before notice was given.[58] This does not apply where the reason for dismissal was redundancy unless the dismissal was regarded as unfair by virtue of section 100(1)(a) or (b),

101A(d), 102(1) or 103 ERA 1996. In that event the reduction will apply only to that part of the award payable because of section 120 ERA 1996.

An award of two weeks' pay will be made to employees who were redundant but unable to obtain a redundancy payment in either of the following circumstances:

- they are not to be treated as dismissed by virtue of section 138 ERA 1996, which deals with the renewal of a contract or re-engagement under a new one, or
- they are not entitled to a payment because of the operation of section 141 ERA 1996, which is concerned with offers of alternative employment.[59]

COMPENSATORY AWARD

The amount of this award is that which a tribunal 'considers just and equitable in all the circumstances having regard to the loss sustained by the complainant in consequence of the dismissal insofar as that loss is attributable to action taken by the employer'.[60] This may include losses resulting from subsequent employment or unemployment if those losses can be attributed to the dismissal. In *Dench v Flynn & Partners* [61] an assistant solicitor was able to claim compensation for unemployment after a subsequent short-term job because it was attributable to the original dismissal. However, the mere fact that the employer could have dismissed fairly on another ground arising out of the same factual situation does not render it unjust or inequitable to award compensation.[62]

Section 123(3) ERA 1996 specifically mentions that an individual whose redundancy entitlement would have exceeded the basic award can be compensated for the difference, while a redundancy payment received in excess of the basic award payable goes to reduce the compensatory award. The compensatory award can be reduced in two other circumstances: where the employee's action caused or contributed to the dismissal, and where the employee failed to mitigate his or her loss. Before reducing an award on the ground that the complainant caused or contributed to the dismissal, a tribunal must be satisfied that the employee's conduct was culpable or blameworthy – ie foolish, perverse or unreasonable in the circumstances.[63] Thus there could be a finding of contributory fault in a case of constructive dismissal on the basis that there was a causal link between the employee's conduct and the employer's repudiatory breach of contract.[64] However, compensation in respect of discriminatory non-re-engagement following dismissal while taking part in industrial action will not normally be reduced on the grounds of contributory conduct.[65]

Reductions to compensatory awards

In determining whether to reduce compensation the tribunal must take into account the conduct of the complainant and not what happened to some other employee – for example, one who was treated more leniently.[66] Not all unreasonable conduct will necessarily be culpable or blameworthy: it will depend on the degree of unreasonableness. Although ill-health cases will rarely give rise to a reduction in compensation on grounds of contributory fault, it is clear that an award may be reduced under the overriding 'just and equitable' provisions.[67]

Having found that an employee was to blame, a tribunal must reduce the award to some extent, although the proportion of culpability is a matter for the tribunal.[68] According to the Court of Appeal, tribunals should first assess the amount which it is just and equitable to award because this may have a very significant bearing on what reduction to make for contributory conduct.[69] The percentage amount of reduction is to be taken from the total awarded to the employee before other deductions, such as offsetting what has already been paid by the employer, because this would be fairer to the employer.[70]

Complainants are obliged to look for work. According to *Savage v Saxena*,[71] the tribunal must go through the following three stages before it can decide what amount to deduct for an employee's failure to find work:

- identify what steps should have been taken by the applicant to mitigate loss
- find the date on which such steps would have produced an alternative income
- thereafter, reduce the amount of compensation by the amount of income which would have been earned.

The onus is on the employer to prove that there was such a failure. While acknowledging that the employee has a duty to act reasonably, the EAT has concluded that this standard is not high in view of the fact that the employer is the wrongdoer.[72]

No account is to be taken of any pressure that was exercised on the employer to dismiss the employee[73] and, according to section 155 TULRCA 1992, compensation cannot be reduced on the grounds that the complainant:

- was in breach of (or proposed to breach) a requirement that he or she: must be, or become, a member of a particular trade union or one of a number of trade unions; ceases to be, or refrains from becoming a member of any trade union or of a particular trade union or of one of a number of particular trade unions; would not take part in the activities of any trade union, of a particular trade union or of one of a number of particular trade unions; would not make use of union services
- refused, or proposed to refuse, to comply with a requirement of a kind mentioned in section 152(3)(a) TULRCA 1992
- objected, or proposed to object, to the operation of a provision of a kind mentioned in section 152(3)(b) TULRCA 1992
- accepted or failed to accept an offer made in contravention of section 145A or 145B TULRCA 1992.

Nevertheless, this section permits a distinction to be drawn between what was done by the complainant and the way in which it was done.[74]

The maximum compensatory award is £72,300 in 2012, but it should be noted that this figure is linked to the retail price index. The limit applies only after credit has been given for any payments made by the employer and any deductions have been made.[75] However, any 'excess' payments made by the employer over that which is required are deducted after the amount of the compensatory award has been fixed.[76] As regards deductions, normally an employer is to be given credit for all payments made to an employee in respect of claims for wages and other benefits (apart from pension payments received).[77] Where an employee has suffered discrimination as well as unfair dismissal, section 126 ERA 1996 prevents double compensation for the same loss.

It is the duty of tribunals to inquire into the various grounds for damages but it is the responsibility of the aggrieved person to prove the loss. The legislation aims to reimburse the employee rather than to punish the employer.[78] Hence employees who appear to have lost nothing – for example, where it can be said that irrespective of the procedural unfairness which occurred, they would have been dismissed anyway – do not qualify for a compensatory award. However, if the employee puts forward an arguable case that dismissal was not inevitable, the evidential burden shifts to the employer to show that dismissal was likely to have occurred in any event.[79] Additionally, a nil or nominal award may be thought just and equitable in a case where misconduct was discovered subsequently to the dismissal.[80]

The possible heads of loss have been divided into the following categories:

1 *Loss incurred up to the date of the hearing*
Here attention focuses on the employee's actual loss of income, which makes it necessary to ascertain the employee's take-home pay. Thus, tax and National Insurance contributions are to be deducted, but overtime earnings and tips can be taken into account. Similarly, any sickness or incapacity benefits received may be taken into account.[81] It should also be noted that the loss sustained should be based on what the employee was entitled to, whether or not he or she was receiving it at the time of dismissal.[82] As well as lost wages, section 123(2) ERA 1996 enables an individual to claim compensation for the loss of other benefits – for example, a company car or other perks. Additionally, 'expenses reasonably incurred' are mentioned in the statute so employees will be able to recover the cost of looking for a new job or setting up their own business. However, complainants cannot be reimbursed for the cost of pursuing their unfair dismissal claims.

2 *Loss flowing from the manner of dismissal*
Compensation can be awarded only if the manner of dismissal has made the individual less acceptable to potential employers. Nothing is available for non-economic loss – for example, hurt feelings.

CASE STUDY

DUNNACHIE v HULL CITY COUNCIL

In *Dunnachie v Hull City Council*[83] it was noted that economic loss may arise where the person is not fit to take up alternative employment as early as he or she would otherwise have done (or ever); or where by virtue of stigma damage, loss of reputation or embarrassment no suitable employer was prepared to engage him or her, at any rate on terms that would not cause continuing loss.

Discussion point

Should employment tribunals have the power to compensate for non-economic losses incurred as a result of unfair dismissal?

3 *Loss of accrued rights*
This head of loss is intended to compensate the employee for the loss of rights dependent on a period of continuous service, but because the basic award reflects lost redundancy entitlement, sums awarded on these grounds have tended to be nominal. Nevertheless, tribunals should include a sum to reflect the fact that dismissed employees lose the statutory minimum notice protection that they have built up.[84]

4 *Loss of pension rights*
Undoubtedly this presents the most complex problems of computation. Basically, there are two types of loss: the loss of the present pension position and the loss of the opportunity to improve one's pension position with the dismissing employer. When an employee is close to retirement, the cost of an annuity which will provide a sum equal to the likely pension can be calculated. In other cases the starting-point will be the contributions already paid into the scheme, and in addition to having their own contributions returned, employees can claim an interest in their employer's contributions, except in cases of transferred or deferred pensions. However, in assessing future loss the tribunal must take into account a number of possibilities – for example, future dismissal or resignation, early death, and the fact that a capital sum is being paid sooner than would have been expected. Although employment tribunals have been given actuarial guidelines on loss of pension rights, in each case the factors must be evaluated to see what adjustment should be made or whether the guidelines are safe to use at all.[85]

5 *Future loss*
Where no further employment has been secured, tribunals will have to speculate how long the employee will remain unemployed. Here the tribunal must utilise its knowledge of local market conditions as well as considering personal circumstances in order to identify when the employee is likely to obtain an equivalent job.[86] According to the EAT, employees who have become unfit for work wholly or partly as a result of unfair dismissal are entitled to compensation for loss of earnings, at least for a reasonable period following the dismissal, until they might reasonably have been expected to find other employment.[87] In *Tradewind Airways Ltd v Fletcher* [88] it was ruled that if another job has been obtained, tribunals must compare the employee's salary prospects for the future in each job and see as best they can how long it will take the employee to reach in the new position the salary equivalent to that which would have been attained had he or she remained with the original employer. Where the employee is earning a higher rate of pay at the time compensation is being assessed, the tribunal should decide whether the new

employment is permanent, and if so, should calculate the loss as between the date of dismissal and the date the new job was secured.[89]

REFLECTIVE QUESTIONS

What is the justification for putting a limit on compensation for unfair dismissal?

Does the cap on unfair dismissal compensation make common law actions for breach of contract more likely?

Awards and the Jobseeker's Allowance

Finally, mention must be made of Employment Protection (Recoupment of Jobseeker's Allowance and Income Support) Regulations 1996,[90] which were designed to remove the state subsidy to employers who dismiss unfairly. Such benefits had the effect of reducing the losses suffered by dismissed persons. These Regulations provide that a tribunal must not deduct from the compensation awarded any sum which represents Jobseeker's Allowance received, and the employer is instructed not to pay immediately the amount of compensation which represents loss of income up to the hearing (known as the 'prescribed element'). The National Insurance Fund can then serve the employer with a recoupment notice which will require him or her to pay the Fund from the prescribed element the amount which represents the Jobseeker's Allowance paid to the employee prior to the hearing.[91] When the amount has been refunded by the employer, the remainder of the prescribed element becomes the employee's property. It is important to note that private settlements do not fall within the scope of these Regulations.

CALCULATING A REDUNDANCY PAYMENT

The size of a redundancy payment depends on the employee's length of continuous service, his or her age and the amount of a week's pay. A week's pay is calculated in accordance with sections 220–9 ERA 1996 (see Chapter 16) and in this context means gross pay.[92] However, it does not take into account increased wage rates agreed subsequently to the employee's dismissal but backdated to a date prior to the dismissal.[93] Unless the contrary is shown, employment is presumed to have been continuous (see Chapter 16), but this only applies in relation to the dismissing employer (except when a business or undertaking has been transferred[94] or an employee has been taken into employment by an associated employer). If continuity is not preserved on a transfer, an assurance given by one employer that the obligations of another will be met will not confer jurisdiction on a tribunal to award a payment based on overall service. However, an employee may be able to show that there was a contract to the effect that he or she would retain the benefit of previous employment.[95]

Redundancy payments are calculated according to the following formula, with a maximum of 20 years' service being taken into account. Starting at the end of the employee's period of service and calculating backwards:

- one and a half weeks' pay is allowed for each year of employment in which the individual was 41 and over
- a week's pay for each year of employment in which the individual was between the ages of 22 and 40
- half a week's pay for each year of employment between the ages of 18 and 21.[96]

Thus the maximum statutory redundancy payment is £12,900 in 2012 (ie 30 x £430). However, where a tribunal decides that an employee is entitled to such a payment it can provide compensation for financial losses which are attributable to the employer's non-payment.[97] On making a payment the employer must give the employee a written statement indicating how the amount has been calculated. An employer who, without reasonable excuse, fails to do so can receive a fine not exceeding level 3 on the standard scale.[98]

EMPLOYEE RIGHTS ON INSOLVENCY

If an employer becomes insolvent or bankrupt, an employee's wages in respect of the four months beforehand, up to a maximum of £800, become a preferential debt.[99] In addition, Schedule 6 of the Insolvency Act 1986 provides that the following shall be treated as wages for these purposes: a guarantee payment; remuneration payable under suspension on medical or maternity grounds; remuneration payable during a protective award; and a payment for time off for union duties, antenatal care, or to look for work or make arrangements for training in a redundancy situation.

Section 182 ERA 1996 gives employees the right to make a written request to the Secretary of State for a payment out of the National Insurance Fund to meet certain other debts which arise out of the employer's insolvency.[100] These debts are:

- arrears of pay up to a maximum of eight weeks; this includes any of the matters treated as wages for the purposes of the Insolvency Act 1986
- wages payable during the statutory notice period. It should be noted that employees are still required to mitigate their loss
- holiday pay up to a maximum of six weeks, provided the entitlement accrued during the preceding 12 months
- a basic award of compensation for unfair dismissal
- any reasonable sum by way of reimbursement of the whole or part of any fee or premium paid by an apprentice or articled clerk.

A financial limit is imposed on the amount that can be recovered in respect of any one week[101] (£430 per week in 2012).

Before reimbursing the employee the Secretary of State must be satisfied both that the employer has become insolvent[102] and that the employee is entitled to be paid the whole or part of the debt claimed.[103] The Secretary of State is liable only to the extent to which the employee is legally entitled to make a claim against the employer. Also, a payment cannot be made unless a 'relevant officer' appointed in connection with the insolvency – for example, a liquidator, receiver or trustee in bankruptcy – has supplied a statement of the amount owed to the employee.

However, this requirement may be waived if the Secretary of State is satisfied that the statement is not necessary to determine the amount owing.[104] If the Secretary of State fails to make a payment or if it is less than the amount which the employee thinks should have been made,[105] a complaint may be presented to an employment tribunal within three months of the Secretary of State's decision being communicated.[106] Where a tribunal finds that a payment ought to have been made under section 182 ERA 1996, it must make a declaration to that effect and state the amount that ought to be paid. Finally, it should be noted that when the Secretary of State makes a payment to the employee, the rights and remedies of the latter in relation to the employer's insolvency are transferred to the Secretary of State.[107]

KEY LEARNING POINTS

- Complaints of unfair dismissal must normally arrive at an employment tribunal within three months of the effective date of termination.
- Employees who have not received a redundancy payment will normally be entitled to make a claim within six months of the relevant date.
- ACAS will assist the employee and the employer to try to reach an agreement to settle the complaint.
- Remedies for unfair dismissal include reinstatement, re-engagement or compensation.
- Compensation for unfair dismissal will consist of a basic award and a compensatory award.
- The maximum compensatory award is £72,300 in 2012 and is linked to the retail price index.
- The size of a redundancy payment depends upon the employee's age, length of service and the amount of a week's pay.
- If an employer becomes insolvent, some liabilities will pass to the Secretary of State for payment out of the National Insurance Fund.

REFERENCES

1 Section 111(2) ERA 1996

2 Section 239(2) TULRCA 1992

3 See *Swainston v Hetton Victory Club* (1983) IRLR 164

4 Section 111(4) ERA 1996; see *Patel v Nagesan* (1995) IRLR 370

5 See *Palmer v Southend B.C.* (1984) IRLR 119

6 See *Schultz v Esso Petroleum Co. Ltd* (1999) IRLR 488

7 See *London Underground v Noel* (1999) IRLR 621

8 See *Marley Ltd v Anderson* (1996) IRLR 163

9 See *Palmer v Southend B.C.* (note 5 above)

10 (1978) IRLR 499

11 (1983) IRLR 187. See also *Cambridge and Peterborough NHS Trust v Crouchman* (2009) ICR 306

12 See *Northamptonshire County Council v Entwhistle* (2010) IRLR 740
13 See *Pruden v Cunard Ltd* (1993) IRLR 317
14 See *Consignia plc v Sealy* (2002) IRLR 624 where detailed guidance is provided
15 *Tyne & Wear Autistic Society v Smith* (2005) IRLR 336
16 See *Camden and Islington NHS Trust v Kennedy* (1996) IRLR 381
17 Section 164(1) ERA 1996
18 See *Price v Smithfield Group Ltd* (1978) IRLR 80
19 See *Secretary of State v Banks* (1983) ICR 48 and *Swainston v Hetton Victory Club* (note 3 above)
20 Section 164(2) ERA 1996
21 (1982) IRLR 31
22 Section 18(4) ETA 1996
23 See *Clarke v Redcar and Cleveland Borough Council* (2006) IRLR 324
24 Section 18(6) and (7) ETA 1996
25 See *Hennessy v Craigmyle Ltd* (1985) IRLR 446
26 See *Freeman v Sovereign Chicken Ltd* (1991) IRLR 408
27 See *Gilbert v Kembridge Fibres Ltd* (1984) IRLR 52
28 Section 203(2)(e) ERA 1996. See *Alma Ltd v Bonner* (2011) IRLR 204
29 Section 203(3A) ERA 1996 defines 'relevant independent adviser' as a qualified lawyer; an officer, official, member or employee of a trade union who has been certified to give advice by the union; an authorised advice centre worker; or others specified by the Secretary of State
30 Section 203(2)(f) and 203(3) ERA 1996
31 See *Rock-It Cargo Ltd v Green* (1997) IRLR 582 and *Sutherland v Network Appliance* (2001) IRLR 12
32 See *Industrious Ltd v Horizon Ltd* (2010) IRLR 204
33 *Hinton v University of East London* (2005) IRLR 552
34 See ACAS Arbitration Scheme (Great Britain) Order 2004, SI No.753
35 See *Constantine v Cory Ltd* (2000) IRLR 939
36 Section 112 ERA 1996
37 Section 116(1) ERA 1996
38 Section 116(4) ERA 1996
39 See *Rank Xerox v Stryczek* (1995) IRLR 568
40 (1994) IRLR 9
41 Section 13(2) ETA 1996
42 (1986) IRLR 485

43 (1998) IRLR 680

44 See *Enessy Co. v Minoprio* (1978) IRLR 489

45 Section 114(2) ERA 1996

46 Section 114(3) ERA 1996

47 Section 115(2) ERA 1996

48 See *Artisan Press v Strawley* (1986) IRLR 126 on the difference between not re-employing and not fully complying with an order.

49 Section 117(2) ERA 1996. See *Parry v National Westminster Bank* (2005) IRLR 193

50 See section 124(4) ERA 1996

51 Section 117(3) and (4) ERA 1996. See *Awotana v South Tyneside NHS Trust* (2005) IRLR 958

52 See *Port of London Authority v Payne* (note 40 above)

53 Section 117(3)(b) ERA 1996

54 See *Motherwell Railway Club v McQueen* (1989) ICR 419

55 Section 122(4) ERA 1996; see *Boorman v Allmakes Ltd* (1995) IRLR 553

56 Section 120 ERA 1996

57 Section 122(1) and (2) ERA 1996

58 See *RSPCA v Cruden* (1986) IRLR 83

59 Section 121 ERA 1996

60 Section 123 ERA 1996

61 (1998) IRLR 653

62 See *Devonshire v Trico-Folberth* (1989) IRLR 397

63 See *Nelson v BBC (No.2)* (1979) IRLR 304; *Morrison v ATGWU* (1989) IRLR 361

64 See *Polentarutti v Autokraft Ltd* (1991) IRLR 457

65 See *Crosville Wales Ltd v Tracey and another (No.2)* (1996) IRLR 691

66 See *Parker Foundry Ltd v Slack* (1992) IRLR 11

67 See *Slaughter v Brewer Ltd* (1990) IRLR 426

68 See *Warrilow v Walker Ltd* (1984) IRLR 304

69 See *Rao v Civil Aviation Authority* (1994) IRLR 240

70 See *Heggie v Uniroyal Englebert Tyres Ltd* (1998) IRLR 425

71 (1998) IRLR 182

72 See *Fyfe v Scientific Furnishings Ltd* (1989) IRLR 331. On unreasonable refusal of an offer of re-employment and the failure to mitigate loss see *Wilding v BT plc* (2002) IRLR 524

73 Section 123(5) ERA 1996

74 See *TGWU v Howard* (1992) IRLR 170

75 Section 124(5) ERA 1996; see *Braund Ltd v Murray* (1991) IRLR 100

76 See *Digital Equipment Co Ltd v Clements (No.2)* (1998) ICR 258

77 See *Knapton v ECC Clothing Ltd* (2006) ICR 1084

78 See *Burlo v Langley* (2007) IRLR 145

79 See *Britool Ltd v Roberts* (1993) IRLR 481

80 See *Tele-trading Ltd v Jenkins* (1990) IRLR 430

81 See *Morgans v Alpha Plus Ltd* (2005) IRLR 234

82 For example, the national minimum wage: see *Paggetti v Cobb* (2002) IRLR 861

83 (2004) IRLR 727

84 See *Guinness Ltd v Green* (1989) IRLR 289

85 See *Port of Tilbury v Birch* (2005) IRLR 92

86 See *Wardle v Credit Agricole Bank* (2011) IRLR 604

87 On compensating for career-long loss see *Kingston upon Hull City Council v Dunnachie (No.3)* (2003) IRLR 843

88 (1981) IRLR 272

89 See *Fentiman v Fluid Engineering Ltd* (1991) IRLR 150

90 SI 1996/2439; see also sections 16 and 17 ETA 1996

91 See *Homan v A1 Bacon Ltd* (1996) ICR 846

92 See *Secretary of State v Woodrow* (1983) IRLR 11; the maximum amount of a week's pay is £430 in 2012

93 See *Leyland Vehicles Ltd v Reston* (1981) IRLR 19

94 See *Lassman v Secretary of State* (1999) ICR 416 where continuity was preserved by the Transfer Regulations 1981, even though, at the time of the transfer, the employees received statutory redundancy payments

95 *Secretary of State v Globe Elastic Thread Co Ltd* (1979) IRLR 327

96 Section 162(1) and (2) ERA 1996. On age discrimination see Chapter 6

97 Section 163(5) ERA 1996

98 Section 165 ERA 1996; see *Barnsley M.B.C. v Prest* (1996) ICR 85

99 Section 386 Insolvency Act 1986

100 Insolvency is defined in section 183 ERA 1996; see *Secretary of State v Stone* (1994) ICR 761

101 See *Benson v Secretary of State* (2003) IRLR 748

102 See *Morris v Secretary of State* (1985) IRLR 297

103 See *Secretary of State v Walden* (2001) IRLR 168

104 Section 187(2) ERA 1996

105 See *Potter v Secretary of State for Employment* (1997) IRLR 21 on the ability of the Secretary of State to set off protective awards against the claims of the employees

106 Section 188 ERA 1996; the 'time-limit escape clause' applies here

107 Section 189 ERA 1996

EXPLORE FURTHER

Reading

- Davies, A. (2009) *Perspectives on Labour Law.* Oxford University Press, Chapter 9
- Deakin, S. and Morris, G. (2012) *Labour Law.* Hart, Chapter 5
- Smith, I. and Thomas, G. (2010) *Smith & Wood's Employment Law.* Butterworths, Chapters 7 and 8

Websites

- Advisory, Conciliation and Arbitration Service www.acas.org.uk
- Chartered Institute of Personnel and Development www.cipd.co.uk
- Department for Business Innovation and Skills www.bis.gov.uk
- DirectGov – Employment wwwdirect.gov.uk
- Trades Union Congress www.tuc.org.uk

CHAPTER 16

Continuity of Employment and Transfers of Undertakings

CHAPTER OVERVIEW

In this chapter we are concerned with the concepts of continuity of service, including the effect of the Transfer of Undertakings (Protection of Employment) Regulations 2006 (TUPE), normal working hours and a week's pay. They are important because many statutory rights are dependent upon minimum length of service, and payments are related to statutory concepts of normal working hours and a week's pay. We begin by looking at continuity of employment and what impact different types of gaps in service have on these statutory rights. We then look briefly at normal working hours (aspects of the regulation of working time are dealt with in Chapter 10). We then examine the concept of a week's pay which is used for computing many payments under ERA 1996, such as redundancy payments and compensation for unfair dismissal. Finally we consider the TUPE Regulations 2006.

LEARNING OUTCOMES

After studying this chapter[1] you will be able to:

- understand and explain the legal principles that apply in relation to the issues of continuity of employment and transfers of undertakings, including how to decide whether there has been a transfer
- advise colleagues about the importance of protecting employees' contractual rights and job security in negotiations with a possible buyer in a business transfer situation, and how employees' security of employment and other statutory rights are affected by a break in their continuity of employment.

CONTINUITY OF EMPLOYMENT

Continuous employment is an important concept because many statutory rights are dependent on a minimum service qualification and certain benefits – for example, redundancy payments and basic awards – are calculated by reference to length of service. Continuity of employment is a statutory concept[2] in accordance with sections 210–19 ERA 1996, and the courts will look to see whether there has been a break in service.

In *Morris v Walsh Western UK Ltd*,[3] the employer agreed to ignore a month's break in employment and treat the employee as having been continuously employed. Despite this, the EAT held that the month's gap had constituted a break in service because the arrangement was not entered into prior to the break. However, in *London Probation Board v Kirkpatrick* the EAT did not follow *Morris* and held that such an arrangement could be made retrospectively.[4]

Section 210(5) ERA 1996 states that employment is presumed to have been continuous unless the contrary is shown, although this is not so where there is a succession of employers.[5] Apart from redundancy payment purposes, these provisions also apply to periods of employment wholly or mainly outside Great Britain.[6] Continuity is normally assessed in relation to the particular contract on which a claim is based. However, it may be possible for an employer to deliberately subject employees to a combination of separate contracts which amount to a series of fixed-term contracts with a break in between. In the case outlined below, the EAT concluded that any anomalies or avoidance of the legislation is a matter for Parliament rather than the courts.

CASE STUDY

BOOTH v UNITED STATES OF AMERICA[7]

Three maintenance workers worked for the US army in the UK on a succession of fixed-term contracts. In total, they had all worked over two years (two years was the minimum qualifying service period for unfair dismissal, as well as redundancy claims, at that time) but no single contract was of that length. The employer always insisted on a gap of around two weeks between the contracts. The employees had to fill in application forms for each new contract. However, when the employees came back to start work under the new contract they were given the same employee number as before, the same tools and clothing and even the same locker. The EAT nevertheless held that the effect of the two-week gap between each contract was to break continuity of employment so that the men could not claim for unfair dismissal or redundancy when their contracts were not renewed. The employers were entitled to exploit this loophole in the law and it was for Parliament to close the loophole if necessary.

Discussion point

Should employers be free to avoid the creation of continuous employment as was done in the *Booth* case?

(For the effect of the Fixed-term Employees/Prevention of Less Favourable Treatment Regulations 2002 on continuity of employment, see Chapter 4.)

A period of continuous employment, which begins with the day on which the employee 'starts work'[8] is to be computed in months, and except in so far as is otherwise provided, a week which does not count breaks the period of continuous employment.[9] A person accrues a period of continuous service only if he or she is employed under a legal contract of employment. Thus, if for a period of time the contract is illegal, then for that period the contract cannot be relied on.[10] Where there is a dispute over continuity, employees have to establish that there was a week which counted, but in respect of subsequent weeks they can rely on the presumption contained in section 210(5) ERA 1996 that employment is continuous (unless there is evidence to the contrary).[11]

WEEKS THAT COUNT

According to section 212(1) ERA 1996, any week[12] during the whole or part of which a person has a contract of employment will count.

CASE STUDY

SWEENEY v J & S HENDERSON LTD

Mr Sweeney was originally employed on 19 June 1995. He resigned on Saturday 15 February 1997 and immediately took up employment with another employer. Within a few days he regretted his decision and applied for, and received, re-employment with his old employer, from Friday 21 February 1997. This employment lasted until 12 March 1998 when he was dismissed.

At the time there was a two-year qualification period to be entitled to make a claim for unfair dismissal. The issue was whether he had this length of service. Was the gap in his employment between 15 and 21 February 1997 enough to mean that he did not have two years' continuous employment prior to 12 March 1998?

The EAT held that the employment was continuous, in accordance with section 212(1) ERA 1996. This section, according to the Court, clearly contemplates that continuous employment can have gaps, provided that during the relevant weeks there is at least one day governed by the contract of employment. This was so in this case, and it was not relevant how the gap was created nor what the employee did during the gap.[13]

A week counts if one of the following applies for the whole or part of that week:

- The employee is incapable of work as a consequence of sickness or injury.[14] Not more than 26 consecutive weeks can be counted under this head.[15] In this context the expression 'incapable of work' does not mean incapable of work generally, nor does it always refer to the particular work provided for in the contract which has ended. According to the Court of Appeal, where the work on offer by the employer differs from that for which the employee was previously employed, the tribunal must consider whether the work offered was of a kind which the employee was willing to accept or, even if the employee was unwilling, was suited to his or her particular circumstances.[16]
- The employee is absent from work on account of a temporary **cessation of work.**[17] In this context the phrase 'absent from work' does not necessarily mean

physical absence but means not performing in substance the contract that previously existed between the parties.[18] The words 'on account of' refer to the reason when the employer dismissed, and the fact that the unavailability of work was foreseen and the employee took another job will not prevent a tribunal holding that this provision applies. 'Cessation of work' denotes that a quantity of work has for the time being ceased to exist and was therefore no longer available to be given to the employee. Thus, when a member of a pool of casual cleaners was not allocated work under a pool arrangement, that absence was not on account of a temporary cessation of work.[19]

According to the House of Lords, 'temporary' means lasting a relatively short time and whether an interval can be so characterised is a question of fact for the employment tribunal. Where there is a succession of fixed-term contracts with intervals between them, continuity is not broken unless 'looking backwards from the date of expiry of the fixed-term contract on which the claim is based, there is to be found between one fixed-term contract and its immediate predecessor an interval that cannot be characterised as short relative to the combined duration of the two fixed-term contracts'.[20] In *Flack v Kodak Ltd* [21] the Court of Appeal held that where an employee has worked intermittently over a period of years in an irregular pattern, tribunals ought to have regard to all the circumstances and should not confine themselves to the mathematical approach of looking at each gap and immediately adjoining periods of employment. The fact that cessation is not permanent does not mean that it must be temporary for these purposes.[22]

CASE STUDY

CORNWALL COUNTY COUNCIL v PRATER

Over a period of ten years Mrs Prater was employed under a succession of individual contracts to teach children who were, for a variety of reasons, unable to attend school. Work was offered to her by way of care for an individual pupil, whom she would teach at the pupil's home. There was no obligation by the Council to offer her work and she was under no contractual obligation to accept further pupils. Once she had taken on a pupil, however, she was obliged to complete the particular assignment. During the whole of the period Mrs Prater never refused any offers of work.

She became a permanent employee of the Council, but there was a dispute about whether her employment status during the period was continuous and included the previous ten years.

The EAT held that she had been employed throughout the ten-year period and that she had worked under a number of successive engagements. During each of those engagements there was a mutuality of obligation, particularly as she was obliged to complete each one, which made it a contract of employment. The gaps in between could be viewed as temporary cessations of work.[23]

- The employee is absent from work in circumstances such that by arrangement or custom he or she is regarded as continuing in the employment of the employer for all or any purposes.[24] Although an arrangement must normally exist at the time the absence began, as seen above the EAT has held in *London Probation Board v Kirkpatrick* [25] that such an arrangement could be made retrospectively – that is, after the gap in service has appeared. For section 212(3)(c) ERA to preserve continuity of employment by arrangement or custom there must be a mutual recognition, by the employer and the employee, that although the employee is absent from work, he or she continues to be employed by the employer. A recognition that there is some other kind of continuing relationship is not enough. Thus in *Curr v Marks & Spencer plc* [26] a child break scheme which guaranteed the employee a post similar to that which she had previously held and which had arrangements for keeping the parties in contact during the absence was held not to be an arrangement preserving continuity because the employee was required to resign from her employment at the beginning of the scheme.
  It would appear that the cause of the absence is immaterial. Thus employees who have been loaned to a third party may be protected as well as those given leave of absence for personal reasons. In *Colley v Corkindale* [27] the EAT held that employees who worked alternate weeks were to be regarded as being absent by arrangement on their weeks off.

It should be noted that continuity of employment where employees are absent from work for family reasons is now dealt with under the Maternity and Parental Leave Regulations 1999 and the Paternity and Adoptions Leave Regulations 2002 (see Chapter 8).

REFLECTIVE QUESTION

Should the employer and employee have greater freedom to agree that employment should be treated as continuous?

STRIKES AND LOCK-OUTS

Days on which an employee is on strike neither count towards nor break the employee's period of continuous service.[28] By virtue of section 235(5) ERA 1996 for this purpose 'strike' means:

a) the cessation of work by a body of persons employed acting in combination, or

b) a concerted refusal or a refusal under a common understanding of any number of persons employed to continue to work for an employer in consequence of a dispute, done as a means of compelling their employer or any person or body of persons employed, or to aid other employees in compelling their employer or any person or body of persons employed, to accept or not to accept terms and conditions of or affecting employment.

Where an employee is absent from work because of a lock-out, again continuity is not broken and if the contract of employment subsists, the period of absence could be counted under section 212(1) ERA 1996.[29] 'Lock-out' means:[30]

a) the closing of a place of employment
b) the suspension of work
c) the refusal by an employer to continue to employ any number of persons employed by him in consequence of a dispute, done with a view to compelling those persons, or to aid another employer in compelling persons employed by him, to accept terms or conditions of or affecting employment.

It makes no difference that employees were dismissed during a strike or lock-out; as long as they were subsequently re-engaged, their period of continuous employment will be preserved. Any attempt to provide otherwise – for example, by introducing a specific term relating to previous employment – will be construed as an attempt to exclude or limit the operation of this paragraph and will be ineffective as a result of section 203 ERA 1996.[31]

CHANGE OF EMPLOYER

Usually when an employee leaves one employer and starts working for another, his or her period of continuous service will be broken. However, in certain circumstances a person will be regarded as having been employed by the new employer as from the date his or her previous employment commenced. Apart from the situation where an employer voluntarily agrees to give credit for service with a previous employer (which does not bind the Secretary of State),[32] there are six main types of case in which employment is deemed to be continuous despite a change of employer:

- if there is a transfer of a trade, undertaking, business or part of a business.[33] The words 'trade' and 'undertaking' are not defined in ERA 1996, but 'business' includes a trade or profession and any activity carried on by a body of persons, whether corporate or unincorporated.[34] In relation to business transfers the critical question is whether there has been the transfer of a 'going concern' which could be carried on without interruption or merely the disposal of assets. If the latter, continuity of employment is not maintained.
  If the transfer is a relevant transfer for the purposes of the Transfer Regulations 2006 (see below), the fact that the employees were dismissed and given redundancy payments at the time of the transfer will not necessarily affect continuity of employment.[35]
- if an Act of Parliament results in one corporate body replacing another as employer[36]
- if the employer dies and the employee is then re-employed by the personal representatives or trustees of the deceased[37]
- if there is a change in the partners, personal representatives or trustees who employ the individual[38]
- if the individual is taken into the employment of an associated employer.[39] 'Associated employer' is defined in section 231 ERA 1996 as follows: 'Any two employers are to be treated as associated if (a) one is a company of which the

other (directly or indirectly) has control; or (b) both are companies of which a third person (directly or indirectly) has control.' The expression 'has control' is used in the company-law sense of controlling 51% or more of the shares. However, the register of shares does not conclusively establish the identity of the possessor of control because the person registered as owner might be a nominee.[40] According to the EAT, tribunals should look at the way in which control had in fact been exercised.[41] While there must not be a gap between the employments (unless it is covered by the statute), it is not necessary that the move to an associated employer be made with the acquiescence of either employer.

- if the employee is employed by the governors of a school maintained by a local education authority or by the authority itself and he or she is transferred to another school or local education authority.[42]

A WEEK'S PAY

This concept is used for computing many payments under ERA 1996 – for example, redundancy payments and the basic award of compensation for unfair dismissal. The maximum week's pay for the purpose of calculating a redundancy payment and other awards is £430 in 2012.

Where there are normal working hours:

- if remuneration does not vary with the amount of work done, a week's pay is the gross amount payable for a week's work under the contract of employment in force on the calculation date.[43] Calculation dates are laid down in section 225 ERA 1996 and vary according to the particular statutory rights being enforced
- if the remuneration varies with the amount of work done, a week's pay is the remuneration for the number of normal working hours payable at the average hourly rate.[44] The average hourly rate is ascertained by calculating the total number of hours actually worked in the 12 calendar weeks preceding the calculation date, the total amount of remuneration paid for these hours, and then deducing the average hourly payment. The 12 calendar weeks preceding the calculation date consist of weeks during which the employee actually worked even though for some of this time he or she might have earned less than usual. However, a week in which no remuneration was required to be paid must be disregarded.[45] In *British Coal v Cheesebrough* [46] the average hourly rate was calculated by taking into account all remuneration paid in respect of all hours worked, including overtime, except that the premium element in respect of overtime was disregarded
- and they are worked at varying times and in varying amounts in different weeks – for example, in the case of shift-workers – both the average rate of remuneration and the number of hours worked in a week will have to be computed in the 12 calendar weeks preceding the calculation date. In these circumstances, a week's pay is the average weekly number of normal working hours payable at the average hourly rate of remuneration.[47]

Where there are no normal working hours, a week's pay is the average weekly remuneration received over the period of 12 calendar weeks preceding the calculation date.[48]

If an employee has not been employed for a sufficient period to enable a calculation to be made under any of the above provisions, a tribunal must decide what amount 'fairly represents a week's pay'. Section 228(2)–(3) ERA 1996 sets out some matters for consideration in this respect. Where an individual's actual rate of pay is less than the national minimum wage (see Chapter 5) the tribunal will use the higher figure when computing basic and compensatory awards for unfair dismissal.[49]

Annualised hours contracts can present a problem here.

CASE STUDY

ALI v CHRISTIAN SALVESEN FOOD SERVICES LTD

In *Ali v Christian Salvesen Food Services Ltd* the employees agreed a total number of hours per annum as part of a collective agreement. Overtime would be paid only once that total figure of *annual hours* had been exceeded. The arrangement, however, did not deal with the situation where employees left during the year, after they had worked in excess of the notional 40 hours per week on which their standard rate of pay was based but before reaching the required annual total. The Court of Appeal refused to fill the gap in the agreement so that the employees could claim for the hours actually worked.[50]

Discussion point

Could the court not have implied a term (see Chapter 2) into the contract that the employees would be entitled to overtime in this situation? See the EAT decision in this case.[51]

Finally, the word 'remuneration' has not been statutorily defined for these purposes but it has been held to include any payments made on a regular basis – eg commission, bonuses and attendance allowances. The payment of commission does not, however, override the need for the amount of remuneration to vary with the amount of actual work done in order for it to be taken into account where normal hours are worked. Thus, if commission is earned as a result of successful sales during normal working hours, it may not necessarily be taken into account when working out the average hourly rate. The Court of Appeal held in *Evans v Malley Organisation Ltd*,[52] that time spent attempting unsuccessfully to sell to a client was as much work as that spent successfully selling. Remuneration did not, therefore, vary with the amount of work done, so only the basic pay was to be used in the calculation (in this case holiday entitlement under the Working Time Regulations 1998 – see Chapter 10). Payments in kind are excluded – eg free accommodation – as are payments received from a third party, such as tips. However, gratuities added to cheques and credit card vouchers are paid to the employer, who then pays an equivalent amount to the employee, and so these gratuities may be treated as remuneration for these purposes.[53] Where such gratuities were paid into a 'tronc' fund administered by the employees, the Court of Appeal held in *Annabel's (Berkeley Square) Ltd v HM Revenue and Customs Commissioners* [54] that they did not count towards the national minimum wage.

TRANSFERS OF UNDERTAKINGS

The Transfer of Undertakings (Protection of Employment) Regulations 2006[55] replaced the 1981 Regulations[56] and implement the Directive 2001/23/EC relating to the safeguarding of employees' rights in the event of transfers of undertakings, businesses or parts of undertakings or businesses, which had in turn amended a previous Directive on the subject. The intention of the Directive and the TUPE Regulations is to protect the contract of employment and the employment relationship of employees who are transferred from one employer to another. The employer *from whom* the business employees move is the *transferor*, the one *to whom* they move is called the *transferee*. When a transfer takes place, it is as if the employee's contract of employment was initially agreed with the transferee employer. All rights contained in the contract of employment, except pension benefits,[57] are transferred, as are all outstanding claims and liabilities of the employer to the employees.[58] This may include non-contractual obligations such as in *DJM International Ltd v Nicholas*.[59] In this case the EAT held that liability for an alleged act of sex discrimination transferred from the transferor company to the transferee employer.

THE MEANING OF A TRANSFER OF AN UNDERTAKING

In the seminal case on the application of the original Directive the Court of Justice, in *Spijkers*,[60] defined a transfer of an undertaking as 'the transfer of an **economic entity** that retained its identity'. Put very simply, this means that one reviews the organisation before and after the transfer and determines whether there are enough common features that identify it as the same organisation. The Court of Justice looked at the purpose of the Directive and concluded that its aim was to ensure the continuity of existing employment relationships. Thus, if the operation that is transferred is an identifiable entity before and after the transfer, then a relevant transfer is likely to have taken place. One needs to look at the situation before the transfer and identify an economic entity, then after the transfer to consider whether the economic entity has retained its identity.

The Court of Justice then gave further guidance on factors which would help in the decision as to whether a transfer had taken place. It was necessary to take all the factual circumstances of the transaction into account, including

- the type of undertaking or business in question
- the transfer or otherwise of tangible assets such as buildings and stocks
- the value of intangible assets at the date of transfer
- whether the majority of staff are taken over by the new employer
- the transfer or otherwise of customers
- the degree of similarity between activities before and after the transfer

- the duration of any interruption in those activities.

The Court stated that each of these factors was only part of the assessment. One had to examine what existed before the transfer and then examine the entity after the change in order to decide whether the operation was continued, but these factors might help that consideration.

This approach was further emphasised by the case of *Schmidt*,[61] which concerned the contracting out of a small cleaning operation at a bank. Mrs Schmidt complained about her dismissal and eventually her claim ended up in the national court, which then referred the issue – of whether the transfer of a single person to an outside contractor could be a transfer of an undertaking – to the European Court of Justice. The bank, as well as the German and UK governments, argued that the answer should be in the negative because the cleaning operation was neither a main function nor an ancillary function of the bank and that there was not a transfer of an economic entity. The fact that it was a small operation was not held to be relevant. What mattered was that there was a stable operation which retained its identity. This was indicated by the fact that before the transfer there was a cleaning operation and, again, after the transfer this continued or was resumed.[62]

In the United Kingdom this approach by the European Court of Justice resulted in decisions in which the court held that contracting out of services, or outsourcing, could amount to a relevant transfer for the purposes of the Transfer Regulations.

CASE STUDY

KENNY v SOUTH MANCHESTER COLLEGE

The case concerned the provision of education services at a young offenders' institution. After a tendering exercise the contract was won by South Manchester College.

The question was whether the undertaking had retained its identity.

The High Court stated that 'the prisoners and young offenders who attend, say, a carpentry class next Thursday will, save those released from the institution, be likely in the main to be the same as those who attended the same class in the same classroom the day before and will doubtless be using exactly the same tools and machinery.' Thus a relevant transfer of an entity that retained its identity had taken place.[63]

This was followed by other cases such as where the outsourcing of a local authority refuse collection contract,[64] and the moving of a hospital cleaning contract from one contractor to another,[65] were held to be relevant transfers.

It was then that the Court of Justice appeared to have second thoughts about its approach. In *Süzen*,[66] the Court distinguished between the transfer of an entity and the transfer of an activity. As in the case of *Schmidt*, before the transfer there was a cleaning operation and after the transfer there was a cleaning operation. On the face of it, there was relevant transfer because the entity appeared to retain its identity, as evidenced by its continuation and resumption. The Court of Justice, however, then stated that an entity could not be reduced to the activity entrusted to it. Thus the Court distinguished between an entity that transferred and an activity that transferred. An entity, according to the Court, was

> an organised grouping of persons or assets facilitating the exercise of an economic activity which pursues a specific objective.

There has, therefore, to be something else, other than the activity taking place, which needs to transfer, such as assets or 'an organised grouping' of people. Without these, there appeared to be only the transfer of an activity. This was not enough to provide the protection of the Directive.

It is from this point that many of the problems concerning the applicability of the Directive and the Regulations arose. *Süzen* set limits on the applicability of the Directive, but there has been confusion as to where these limits apply and the real difference between an entity and an activity. Both the *Schmidt* and the *Süzen* cases concerned the transfer of cleaning contracts, but in one the Court held that an entity transferred, and in the second held that the cleaning contract only amounted to an activity and was therefore not protected by the Directive.

TUPE REGULATIONS 2006

The UK Government decided to try to remove this uncertainty with the introduction of the 2006 TUPE Regulations. The different types of transfers of an undertaking, and the legal consequences of a transfer are summarised in Figure 5 below and explained in the remainder of this section of the chapter.

Figure 5 Transfer of an undertaking flowchart

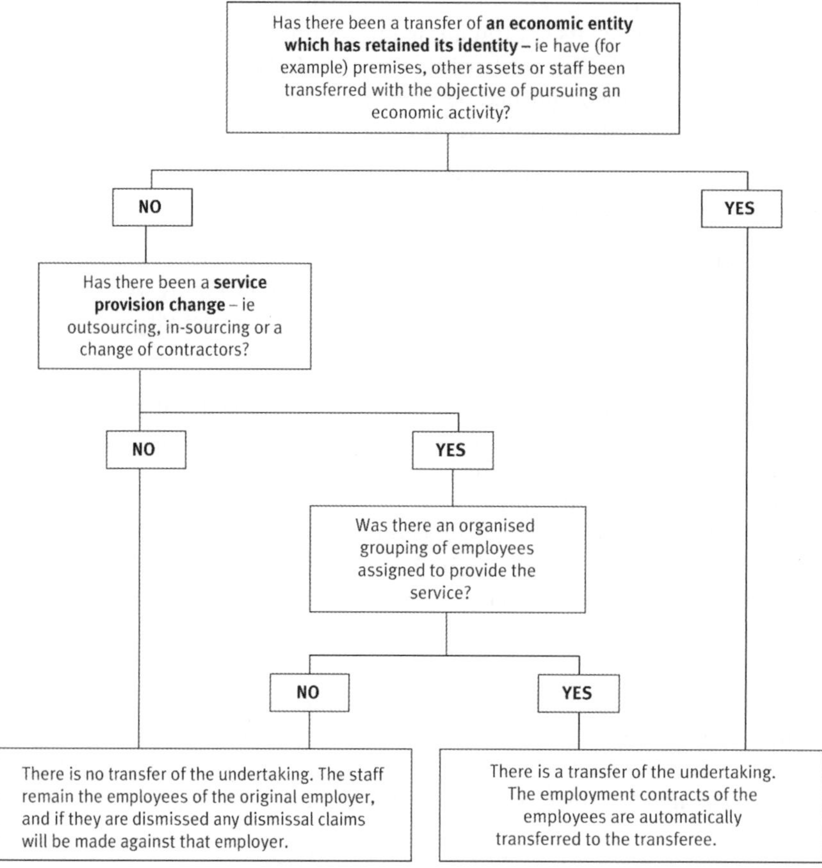

Regulation 3(1) of the 2006 TUPE Regulations states that the Regulations apply, firstly, under 3(1)(a), to a transfer of an undertaking, business or part of an undertaking or business situated immediately before the transfer in the United Kingdom where there is a transfer of an economic entity that retains its identity (the *Spijkers* test), and, secondly, under 3(1)(b), to a service provision change. An economic entity is defined in Regulation 3(2) as 'an organised grouping of resources which has the objective of pursuing an economic activity, whether or not that activity is central or ancillary' (the *Süzen* test).

Regulation 3(1)(b) provides that the Regulations also apply to a **service provision change**. These are relevant to outsourcing situations and are meant to ensure a wide coverage of the Regulations. A service provision change takes place:

- when a person (client) first contracts out some part of its activities to a contractor
- when such a contract is taken over by another contractor (so-called second-generation transfers), and
- when the client takes back the activity in-house from a contractor. Whereas, however, a relevant transfer consists of an 'organised grouping of resources', a

service provision change requires there to be 'an organised grouping of employees, which has, as its principal purpose, the carrying out of activities concerned'.[67] In *Metropolitan Resources Ltd v Churchill Dulwich Ltd*,[68] the EAT made clear that the service provision change is a new statutory concept and a tribunal should ask itself simply whether on the facts one of the above three situations in regulation 3(1)(b) existed. There is no need for a tribunal to consider a formal list of factors such as those mentioned in *Spijkers* (above).

REFLECTIVE QUESTION

Do you think Regulation 3(1)(b) is fair to employers – should such situations come under the Transfer of Undertakings at all?

The issue of where the business or undertaking is situated is important, especially with cross-border transfers. The Regulations were held to apply, for example, when a company transferred part of its business from the UK to Israel.[69]

WHO IS TO BE TRANSFERRED?

Regulation 4(1) of the 2006 Regulations provides that except where an objection is made, a relevant transfer shall not operate to terminate any contract of employment of any person employed by the transferor and assigned to the 'organised grouping of resources or employees that is subject to the relevant transfer'. Although Regulation 2(1) states that temporary assignments are excluded, the European Court of Justice has held that the Directive can apply to the transfer of a temporary agency workforce from one agency to another.[70]

One problem that has occurred is in deciding who is assigned to the part transferred, when only part of an organisation is transferred to a new employer. If, for example, a business decides to contract out its non-core activities and only retain those parts of the business that are concerned with its primary activities, or if only a part of the business is sold off, there are likely to be a number of employees, such as those in Human Resources, who work in the parts remaining, but whose jobs consisted of servicing those parts transferred. This may be the entire content of their jobs or only a part. If such staff remain with the transferor organisation, they may be faced with the loss of their jobs or, at the very least, a significant change in their job activities. The question then is whether these support staff have the right to transfer also.

It was in the case of *Botzen* [71] that the European Court of Justice first devised the assignment test to deal with such situations. The Advocate General in the case proposed a test for deciding who should be transferred if only a part of a business was sold off:

> A basic working test, it seems to me, is to ask whether, if that part of the business had been separately owned before the transfer, the worker would

have been employed by the owners of that part or the owners of the remaining part.

The Advocate General did admit that employees could be involved in work other than for the part transferred, but only on a *de minimis* basis.

Some people, of course, would not have been employed in either part if they were separately owned. It may have been because the whole was a certain size that they were employed. This may be especially true of HR departments in that bigger organisations may perhaps have the capacity to employ more specialists whereas a smaller organisation might demand more generalist abilities.

CASE STUDY

KIMBERLEY GROUP HOUSING LTD v HAMBLEY

This case concerned a contract from the Home Office to provide accommodation and other services for asylum-seekers while their asylum applications were being processed. The contractor lost the contract and it was taken over by two new contractors, both of whom denied that the TUPE Regulations applied. Some of the employees of the original contractor had lost their jobs and they claimed unfair dismissal.

The EAT agreed that a service provision had taken place within the provisions of the 2006 TUPE Regulations. The issue then was to which of the two new contractors the dismissed employees should have transferred. The employment tribunal had held that the liabilities under the contracts of employment should be split between the two contractors.

The EAT did not agree. It held that the principle was that if the employee was assigned to the part transferred, then the contract of employment passes to the transferee. There is no exhaustive list of factors which can conclusively determine this issue and it would have to be resolved as a matter of fact. In this case the great majority of the activities of the employees had passed to one contractor, Kimberley Housing, so the contracts of employment were transferred to them solely.[72]

Regulation 4(3) also provides that it is only persons employed by the transferor and assigned to an organised grouping who are so employed immediately before the transfer, or who would have been had they not been unfairly dismissed, who are protected.[73]

CONTRACT VARIATIONS

An important aspect of the 2006 Regulations is added flexibility, perhaps mostly for employers. This is true when the issue of the ability to vary contracts of employment during or after the transfer is considered. The whole issue of making changes and reorganising the business either before or after a transfer is one that is important to many employers. Quite apart from the issue of bringing in a workforce with different terms and conditions, there is often a need to reorganise the business to cope with any such transfers. The 2006 TUPE Regulations provide that it is not possible to vary a contract of employment if the sole or main reason was the transfer or any other reason that was not an *economic, technical or organisational* (ETO) reason entailing changes in the workforce (Regulation 4(4)). The employer and employee *are* able, therefore, to agree a variation if it *is* changed for an ETO reason or 'a reason unconnected to the transfer'.

AUTOMATICALLY UNFAIR DISMISSAL

Under Regulation 7, if an employee of either the transferor or transferee is dismissed by reason of the transfer, then the general rule is that this is automatically unfair dismissal – although we should note now that the usual two-year qualifying period applies. There are exceptions if the dismissal is due to an ETO reason entailing changes in the workforce of either the transferor or the transferee. This would cover, for example, a genuine redundancy situation.

CASE STUDY

HYND v ARMSTRONG

In *Hynd v Armstrong* it was held that this must be an ETO reason of the business which dismisses. Mr Hynd was a solicitor in the Glasgow office of a law firm which also had an office in Edinburgh. He specialised in corporate and education law. The firm was dissolved and the Glasgow partners set up a new practice in which there was no need for a corporate lawyer. Mr Hynd was dismissed for redundancy just before the transfer. It was held by the Court of Session that there was no ETO defence in this case. To be an ETO reason it must be a dismissal by an employer relating to the future conduct of its own business, entailing a change in its own workforce. This was a dismissal by the transferor in the light of the future needs of the transferee. Accordingly, Mr Hynd had been unfairly dismissed.[74]

For an ETO reason to be available there must be an intention to change the workforce and to continue to conduct the business, rather than to sell it. It is not available – as in the case of *Spaceright Europe Ltd v Baillavoine* – when an administrator dismisses an employee in order to make the business a more attractive proposition for potential transferees of a going concern.

EMPLOYEE CHOICE

The original Directive was silent on the subject of whether an individual employee can decide that he or she does not wish to transfer. Initially it was left to the European Court of Justice to decide. In *Daddy's Dance Hall*[75] the Court suggested that employees had no choice in the matter. Whether the individuals wished it or not, there was a public policy reason for not allowing employees to opt out, because the alternative would normally be that they would be worse off by opting out. This position was considerably softened in *Katsikas*[76] when the Court of Justice held that to stop someone objecting to the transfer of his or her employment would undermine the fundamental rights of the employee, who must be free to choose his employer and cannot be obliged to work for an employer whom he or she has not freely chosen to do. It followed, therefore, that the Directive does not oblige employees to transfer provided that they choose freely not to continue the employment relationship. It was then left to the Member State to 'decide the fate of the contract of employment or employment relationship with the transferor'.

The problem for such an employee in the UK is that he or she is left in a sort of employment nether region with no claims against the transferor or the transferee. Regulation 4(7) of the 2006 Regulations repeats the current position that an employee is not transferred if he or she objects to being so transferred. The outcome is contained in Regulation 4(8) where the employee is then in a 'no man's land'; he or she has not been transferred, but the transferor cannot be treated as having dismissed the employee.

CASE STUDY

CAPITA HEALTH SOLUTIONS LTD v McLEAN

Capita Health Solutions Ltd v McLean [77] concerned an occupational health nurse working for the BBC. Her function was transferred to a contractor and she intimated that she was unhappy with the prospect of being transferred. In the event she agreed to continue working for the contractor for six weeks after the transfer date, although her pay etc was provided by the BBC. At the end of this secondment the question was whether or not the contract of employment had transferred, even though she was unhappy at the prospect. The EAT held that the effect of an objection to being transferred is that the existing contract terminates, no matter what agreements have been reached. If Mrs McLean had objected, then at best she would have been working under a new temporary contract with either the BBC or Capita. On the facts of the case, though unhappy with the transfer, she had not objected, but had, in effect, agreed to transfer for six weeks. The result was that her contract of employment was transferred under the regulations to Capita.

REFLECTIVE QUESTION

Is there any other solution to the problem of 'no man's land' which is the result of Regulation 4(7)? Should the potential/unwilling transferee be entitled to claim compensation for a dismissal due to redundancy? (See Chapter 15.)

Nevertheless, it is sometimes possible to object to a transfer after it has taken place. In *New ISG Ltd v Vernon* [78] employees did not know the identity of the transferee until after the transfer had taken place. They then objected and the

High Court held that these objections were valid because of a fundamental principle that allows an employee to choose his or her own employer.

INSOLVENCY

Measures to deal with insolvency situations were absent from the original Directive and the problems resulting from this were recognised by the European Court of Justice at an early stage. The main problem perceived was that the obligation, imposed by the original Directive, for the transferee enterprise to take over all the debts in relation to the insolvent organisation's employees and, indeed, to transfer all those employees on their current terms and conditions, would act as an disincentive to the 'rescue' of such enterprises.

The 2001 Directive incorporated much greater flexibility and in Article 5(1) excluded any transfers where the transfer is the subject of bankruptcy proceedings with a view to liquidation of the assets of the transferor. Article 5(2) of the Directive also gives Member States the option of excluding transfers of liabilities in other types of insolvency proceedings as well as giving them the option of agreed changes to terms and conditions of employees which are 'designed to safeguard employment opportunities by ensuring the survival of the undertaking, business or part of the undertaking or business'.

The TUPE Regulations 2006 take advantage of both of these options in Regulations 8 and 9. Relevant insolvency proceedings for this purpose in the Regulations repeat the definition stated in the Directive – namely, that they are 'insolvency proceedings which have been opened in relation to the transferor not with a view to the liquidation of the assets of the transferor and which are under the supervision of an insolvency practitioner' (Regulation 8(6)). Effectively, the government is subsidising the transferee by taking on some of the debts of the transferor in order to help the transfer and prevent a loss of jobs which might follow a liquidation. The outcome is that those elements which the government would normally be responsible for under its statutory obligations towards the employees of insolvent employers do not transfer. The debts owed to employees by the transferor, to the limits of its statutory obligations, will be guaranteed by the Secretary of State. This includes some arrears of pay, notice pay, holiday pay and any basic award for unfair dismissal compensation.[79] The liability is only for debts at the time of the transfer, so if an employee were subsequently dismissed, the government would not be liable for any part of the monies owed to that employee.[80] Other debts owed to employees will transfer.

In addition to this subsidy there is provision in Regulation 9 for the employer and employee representatives to agreeing 'permitted variations' to their contracts of employment. Permitted variations are those which are not due to ETO reasons entailing a change in the workforce and are designed to safeguard employment opportunities by ensuring the survival of the undertaking (Regulation 9(7)). It is interesting that the phrase 'employment opportunities' is used, rather than just 'employment'. This suggests that the justification for any variations can be argued widely on the basis that the business is rescued or safeguarded and this will safeguard employment opportunities in the future.

INFORMATION AND CONSULTATION

Regulations 13 to 16 TUPE Regulations 2006 contain the obligations to inform and consult employees (see Chapter 17).

Regulations 11 and 12 of the TUPE Regulations 2006 concern the notification of employee liability information and now provide a statutory duty for the transferor to pass on to the transferee certain information. This includes the identity and age of the employee; his or her terms and conditions of employment (as required by section 1 of the Employment Rights Act 1996); disciplinary or grievance action over the previous two years; and any details of any claims, cases or action brought in the last two years and any future actions that the transferor might have reasonable grounds to believe are possible. The 2006 Regulations provide for compensation to be paid to the transferee, with a normal minimum of £500 per employee.

COLLECTIVE AGREEMENTS

An interesting issue that has arisen from time to time is the question of whether the transferee employer is bound by a collective agreement which covered transferred employees with the transferor employer. If the employees' contracts of employment included a provision that their terms and conditions of employment were to be in accordance with a collective agreement of which the transferor employer is part, what happens when those contracts of employment are transferred to a transferee employer who is not party to the collective agreement? This can happen, for example, in the public sector when outsourcing takes place. In *Parkwood Leisure Ltd v Alemo-Herron* [81] some local government employees were outsourced to the private sector. Their terms and conditions had been set by a national agreement for local government workers. This was an agreement between employers and employees in the public sector. The transferee employer was not in the public sector. The question is whether a 'dynamic' interpretation of the Directive was the correct one – whether the new employer was bound by changes in the collective agreement even though it was not in the public sector. In the event the Supreme Court has referred this question to the Court of Justice of the European Union for an answer.

REFLECTIVE QUESTION

How do you think that this issue should be resolved? You need to think about this from both the employees' and the employers' perspectives.

PENSIONS

The 2006 Regulations repeat the provisions of the Directive in Regulation 10(1) by excluding occupational pension schemes from being transferred, but state that any other provisions which do not relate to old age, invalidity or survivors' pensions should not be treated as part of the scheme (Regulation 10(2)). But although the existing pension is not transferred, the transferee is under an obligation to provide access to a pension with provisions on employer contributions at a required minimum level.[82] In the public sector, the objective, as set out in an annex to the government's Statement of Practice on Staff Transfers in the Public Sector (as revised November 2007), is to offer 'broadly comparable' pensions.[83]

KEY LEARNING POINTS

- Continuous employment is an important concept because important statutory rights are dependent upon the length of continuous service.
- Any week during which a person has a contract of employment counts for the purpose of calculating continuous service.
- There is a statutory definition of a week's pay which sets a maximum amount for use in defining amounts due in such situations as calculating redundancy payments.
- The TUPE Regulations 2006 provide for the transfer of contracts when there has been a transfer of an economic entity that retains its identity.
- The TUPE Regulations 2006 also provide for a transfer of contracts when there has been a service provision change.

REFERENCES

1 **This chapter contains extracts from or close paraphrasing of legislation, which is on the opsi.gov.uk website (and its successor) and is subject to crown copyright. It also contains other public sector information. The reproduction of this material here is licensed under the open government licence v1.0**

2 See *Collison v BBC* (1998) IRLR 239

3 (1997) IRLR 562

4 (2005) IRLR 443

5 See *Secretary of State v Cohen* (1987) IRLR 169

6 See section 215 ERA 1996 and *Weston v Vega Space Ltd* (1989) IRLR 509

7 (1999) IRLR 16

8 *General of the Salvation Army v Dewsbury* (1984) IRLR 222

9 Section 210(4) ERA 1996

10 See *Hyland v J. Barker Ltd* (1985) IRLR 403

11 See *Nicoll v Nocorrode Ltd* (1981) IRLR 163

12 'Week' means a week ending with Saturday; see section 235(1) ERA 1996

13 (1999) IRLR 306

14 Section 212(3)(a) ERA 1996

15 Section 212(4) ERA 1996
16 See *Pearson v Kent County Council* (1993) IRLR 165
17 Section 212(3)(b) ERA 1996
18 See *Stephens & Son v Fish* (1989) ICR 324
19 *Byrne v City of Birmingham D.C.* (1987) IRLR 191
20 *Ford v Warwickshire County Council* (1983) IRLR 126
21 (1986) IRLR 255
22 See *Sillars v Charrington Ltd* (1989) IRLR 152 on seasonal work
23 (2006) IRLR 362
24 Section 212(3)(c) ERA 1996
25 (2005) IRLR 443 (note 4)
26 (2003) IRLR 75
27 (1995) ICR 965
28 Section 216(1) and (2) ERA 1996
29 Section 216(3) ERA 1996
30 Section 235(4) ERA 1996
31 See *Hanson v Fashion Industries* (1980) IRLR 393
32 See *Secretary of State v Globe Elastic Thread Co. Ltd* (1979) IRLR 327
33 Section 218(2) ERA 1996
34 Section 235(1) ERA 1996
35 See *Secretary of State v Lassman* (2000) IRLR 411
36 Section 218(3) ERA 1996
37 Section 218(4) ERA 1996
38 Section 218(5) ERA 1996; see *Jeetle v Elster* (1985) IRLR 227
39 Section 218(6) ERA 1996
40 See *Payne v Secretary of State* (1989) IRLR 352
41 *Tice v Cartwright* (1999) ICR 769
42 Section 218(7) ERA 1996; see also section 218(8)–(10) on certain types of employment in the health service
43 Section 221(2) ERA 1996; see *Keywest Club v Choudhury* (1988) IRLR 51
44 Section 221(3) ERA 1996
45 Section 225 ERA 1996; see *Secretary of State v Crane* (1988) IRLR 238
46 (1990) IRLR 148
47 Section 221 ERA 1996
48 Section 224 ERA 1996
49 *Paggetti v Cobb* (2002) IRLR 861

50 (1997) IRLR 17

51 (1995) IRLR 624

52 (2003) IRLR 156

53 See *Nerva v UK* (2002) IRLR 815

54 *Annabel's (Berkeley Square) Ltd v HM Revenue and Customs* (2009) ICR 1123

55 SI 2006/246

56 SI 1981/1796

57 See *Adams v Lancashire County Council.* (1996) IRLR 154

58 Regulation 5(1) Transfer Regulations 1981

59 (1996) IRLR 76

60 Case 24/85 *JMA Spijkers v Gebroeders Benedik Abbatoir CV* (1986) ECR 1119

61 Case 392/92 *Schmidt v Spar- und Leihkasse der Früheren Ämter Bordesholm, Kiel und Cronshagen* (1994) IRLR 30262 See also *Dudley Bower Building Services Ltd v Lowe* (2003) IRLR 260

62 (1993) IRLR 265

63 *Wren v Eastbourne Borough Council* (1993) IRLR 425 *Dines v Initial Health Care Services and Pall Mall Services Group Ltd* (1994) IRLR 336

64 Case 13/95 *Süzen v Zehnacker Gebäudereinigung* (1997) IRLR 255 67 Regulation 2(1) provides that references to an 'organised grouping of employees' includes a single employee; nor does it apply to single specific events or tasks of a short-term duration, Regulation 3(3)(ii)

65 (2009) IRLR 700

66 *Holis Metal Industries Ltd v GMB* (2008) IRLR 187

67 Case C-458/05 *Jouini v Princess Personal Service GmbH* (2007) IRLR 1005

68 *Botzen and others v Rotterdamsche Droogdok Maatschappij BV* Case 186/83 (1986) 2 CMLR 50 ECJ

69 (2008) IRLR 682

70 *Litster v Forth Dry Dock and Engineering Ltd* (1989) IRLR 161

71 (2007) IRLR 338

72 Case 324/86 *Foreningen af Arbejdsledere i Danmark v Daddy's Dance Hall A/S* (1985) IRLR 315

73 Case 132/91 *Katsikas v Konstantidis* (1993) IRLR 179

74 *Capita Health Solutions Ltd v McLean* (2008) IRLR 595

75 (2008) IRLR 115

76 See, for example, Part XII of the Employment Rights Act 1996

77 *Pressure Coolers Ltd v Molloy s* (2011) IRLR 630

78 (2011) IRLR 696

79 The Transfer of Employment (Pension Protection) Regulations 2005, SI 2005/649

80 *Staff Transfers from Central Government: A fair deal for staff pensions*, HM Treasury, 1999

EXPLORE FURTHER

Reading

- Deakin, S. and Morris, G. (2012) *Labour Law.* Hart, Chapter 3
- Smith, I. and Thomas, G. (2010) *Smith & Wood's Employment Law.* Butterworths, Chapters 2 and 8

Websites

- Advisory, Conciliation and Arbitration Service www.acas.org.uk
- Chartered Institute of Personnel and Development www.cipd.co.uk
- Department for Business Innovation and Skills www.bis.gov.uk
- DirectGov – Employment www.direct.gov.uk
- Trades Union Congress www.tuc.org.uk

CHAPTER 17

Information and Consultation

CHAPTER OVERVIEW

This chapter deals with the rights of employees to be *informed* and *consulted* by their employers. Many of these rights have come from laws made by the European Union (EU), which has pursued a policy over many years to require this. We will see that there are requirements for a) on-going consultation of employees on the functioning of the undertaking for which they work, both at the EU level (for larger undertakings) and at the national level; and b) consultation of employees when particular events occur, such as when there are collective redundancies or there is a transfer of the undertaking for which they work. Finally, we examine information and consultation in relation to health and safety matters. We begin by looking at information and consultation at the EU level and go on to consider it at UK level.

LEARNING OUTCOMES

After studying this chapter[1] you will be able to:

- advise on how to go about establishing information and consultation procedures either on a one-off basis (to deal with a particular situation) or on a more permanent basis; advise on the importance of providing safety representatives with information and consulting with them when, for example, a measure is introduced that may substantially affect the health and safety of the employees represented; and advise on the various legal rights that safety representatives are given – and on the risk of legal penalties for failing to comply with informing and consulting duties
- advise colleagues on when, for example, it is necessary to set up an information and consultation procedure within the organisation, and when information and consultation is required in relation to, for instance, collective redundancies and a transfer of an undertaking.

INTRODUCTION: DUTIES TO INFORM AND CONSULT

Suppose a car manufacturer is planning to close down a plant, with the loss of 2,000 jobs. What are the employees' rights, if any, as regards the closure? Can they do anything to stop or delay it, or, indeed, is the employer obliged to take their interests into account at all? This is a typical situation in which, as we shall see in this chapter, there is a duty on the employer to *inform and consult* representatives of the affected employees.

What might a duty to inform and consult involve? Essentially, it means exactly what it what it says – an employer is obliged, in situations like the example above, to provide its workforce with *information* on what it is planning to do, and to listen to what the employees' representatives have to say about it (*consultation*). But management in the UK retains the full right to manage – the most that the courts have said is that a duty to inform and consult might sometimes mean that the employer has an obligation to *negotiate* with the employees.[2] The employees cannot prevent any planned action from taking place – in our example the employees have no legal right to stop or even delay the closure of the plant, even if the employer failed totally to provide them with information and consultation.

TRANSNATIONAL INFORMATION AND CONSULTATION

The first measures we shall examine apply to companies and businesses with a transnational presence within the EU – ie operating in more than one Member State within the EU. We consider here laws relating to the establishment of European Works Councils (EWCs) and those dealing with the information and consultation requirements in a European Company (SE).

THE TRANSNATIONAL INFORMATION AND CONSULTATION OF EMPLOYEES REGULATIONS 1999

Works councils are committees or councils of employee representatives within companies and businesses which have been a feature of industrial relations in a number of European countries, such as Germany and France, for many years. The powers and functions of works councils vary greatly from country to country, but typically a works council has the right to be informed and consulted by the employer on matters such as employment and human resources issues, and on developments within the business affecting the workforce. In the United Kingdom there is no tradition of works councils – instead, it has generally been trade unions who have represented workers' interests within the business or industry: see Chapter 18.

At the European Union level, momentum developed from the 1980s onwards for a law requiring the setting up of works councils in the Member States for businesses of a certain size. The European Works Council (EWC) Directive was finally adopted by the EU in 1994 after some 14 years of debate, but due to an opt-out by the British Government the Directive did not originally apply to the United Kingdom. After the 1997 General Election there was a change of policy by the new Government, and as a result the EWC Directive became applicable to the UK as well. The EWC Directive was implemented in the UK by the Transnational Information and Consultation of Employees Regulations 1999 (TICE Regulations), which came into effect on 15 January 2000.[3]

In December 2008 a 'recast' Directive on EWCs was agreed by the Council of Ministers and the European Parliament.[4] It was implemented into UK law by the Transnational Information and Consultation of Employees (Amendment) Regulations 2010 (TICE Regulations 2010), which came into effect on 6 June 2011.

The purpose of the Directive (and consequently the TICE Regulations) is to improve the right to information and to consultation of employees in Community-scale undertakings and Community-scale groups of undertakings.[5] This law was therefore aimed at bringing about the informing and consulting of employees within large business organisations with a multinational presence within the EU. As we will see later in this chapter, the EU subsequently extended the requirement of informing and consulting to smaller organisations operating at a national level only.

Measures concerning informing and consulting employees within the Transnational Information and Consultation of Employees Regulations 1999 include:

- The Regulations apply to undertakings with at least 1,000 employees within the EU Member States and at least 150 employees in each of at least two Member States.
- Central management may start the process towards establishing informing and consulting procedures, or it can be started with a request from 100 employees, or their representatives, in two undertakings in two Member States.
- A 'special negotiating body' (SNB) of employee representatives is established, which endeavours to negotiate with central management a written agreement to put in place *either* an EWC *or* some other informing and consulting procedure.
- The two sides are to negotiate in 'a spirit of co-operation with a view to reaching an agreement'.
- If no agreement is reached, the 'default agreement' will apply.
- Under the default agreement an EWC is set up with between three and 30 members, and must meet at least once a year.

For an illustrative case study of an EWC in practice, see the example of British Airways listed in *Explore further* at the end of this chapter.

The Regulations in more detail

A 'Community-scale undertaking' is one that has at least 1,000 employees within the European Union Member States and at least 150 employees in each of at least two Member States. A 'Community-scale group of undertakings' is a group of undertakings that has at least 1,000 employees within the Member States and at least two group undertakings in different Member States employing at least 150 employees[6] each.

The central management of the organisation may take the initiative to kick-start the procedure, but if it does not do so, the process of establishing an EWC can be started with a request from 100 employees, or their representatives, in two undertakings in two Member States. If there is a dispute as to whether a valid request has been made, this can be referred in the UK to the Central Arbitration Committee (CAC – see Chapter 1) for a decision.

The first stage is the establishment of the 'special negotiating body' (SNB) for the employees. The SNB's task is to negotiate with central management a written agreement which, essentially, will

- either lay down a constitution for an EWC within the organisation
- or set out the arrangements for implementing an alternative information and consultation procedure. It is important to note, therefore, that there is flexibility under the regulations – information and consultation must be provided, but it does not have to be via an EWC.

The SNB must consist of at least one representative from each Member State in which there is a group undertaking, the UK representatives being elected by a ballot of the UK employees.

The employer and the SNB are to negotiate in 'a spirit of co-operation with a view to reaching an agreement'. Consultation is defined in the TICE Regulations as meaning the exchange of views and the establishment of a dialogue in the context of an EWC or in the context of an information and consultation procedure.[7] They may negotiate an agreement to set up an EWC or to establish an information and consultation procedure. If the agreement is to set up an EWC, this must include consensus on

- the undertakings covered by the agreement
- the composition of the EWC
- the functions and procedures for informing and consulting
- the venue, frequency and duration of meetings
- the financial and material resources to be allocated to the EWC
- the duration of the agreement and the procedure for re-negotiation.

If the parties decide to establish an information and consultation procedure instead of an EWC, the agreement must specify a method by which the information and consultation representatives[8] 'are to enjoy the right to meet and discuss the information conveyed to them'.

The information conveyed to the representatives must relate in particular to 'transnational questions which significantly affect the interests of employees'.

If negotiations do not start within six months of a valid request by employees or fail to finish within three years from the date of that request, the Regulations provide for a default agreement, which is contained in the Schedule. This stipulates an EWC of between three and 30 members, with at least one member from each Member State in which there is a group undertaking. This representation is weighted numerically according to the relative size of the undertakings in different States. The rules cover the election or appointment of UK delegates and provide that the EWC should meet at least once per annum.

REFLECTIVE QUESTION

Do you think that an obligation to meet once a year is of any real value?

Complaints about the failure of the negotiating process – either because of lack of agreement or a failure to start the process, or because of a failure to keep to the agreement – are (in the UK) to be referred directly to the CAC. The CAC may order the employer to remedy the failure and impose a fine of up to £100,000. Central management will have a defence if it is able to show that the failure resulted 'from a reason beyond the central management's control or that it has some other reasonable excuse for its failure'.

One concern related to statutory rights to information is the revealing by management of 'confidential' information. Regulation 24 TICE Regulations provides that central management is not required to disclose any information or document which, 'according to objective criteria', would seriously prejudice or harm the functioning of the undertaking concerned. It is interesting to speculate as to what this actually means. Would the sale of a subsidiary undertaking in one Member State be such information, if it would prejudice the price received, even though it might have important effects for employees? There is an obligation for a representative, or an adviser to a representative, not to disclose confidential information unless it is a protected disclosure under section 43A ERA 1996 (whistleblowing). In the UK the CAC has the responsibility of settling disputes about confidentiality and can order information to be disclosed by management or order a representative not to disclose information.

Information and consultation representatives, members of EWCs, SNBs and candidates for relevant elections have certain rights in respect of these responsibilities. They are:

- the right to reasonable time off with pay during working hours
- protection against unfair dismissal – dismissal as a result of performing any of the functions or duties related to any of these bodies will make the dismissal automatically unfair
- the right not to be subject to detriment as a result of performing any of the duties or functions related to the bodies.

Complaints about any infringement of these rights are (in the UK) to be made to an employment tribunal.

REFLECTIVE QUESTION

Do you think the CAC should have the power to decide on the confidentiality of information?

THE COMPANY STATUTE

The European Company Statute gives a company operating in more than one Member State the option of establishing itself as a 'European company' (*Societas Europaea* or SE) operating under EU rules rather than under a variety of national rules as at present. An SE can be established by the merger or formation of companies with a presence in at least two different Member States.

One concern in establishing this procedure was that companies previously based in countries with strong requirements for information and consultation might be able to avoid these requirements by establishing themselves as an SE, especially if they were merging with companies from countries with weak consultation requirements. As part of this agreement, therefore, there is a Directive[9] establishing rules for information, consultation and, possibly, the participation of workers employed by the SE. This has been implemented in the UK by the impressively titled European Public Limited-Liability Company (Employee Involvement) (Great Britain) Regulations 2009.[10]

In 2003 the European Co-operative Society Statute (SCE) was also adopted.[11] This provided similar rules for dialogue and consultation for any newly formed SCEs.

INFORMATION AND CONSULTATION REQUIREMENTS IN THE UNITED KINGDOM

So far we have been looking at information and consultation required of large businesses with a transnational presence within the EU. We now examine information and consultation requirements on businesses which operate only in the UK. We start by looking at the general on-going duties to inform and consult under the Information and Consultation Regulations 2004, which apply in all undertakings employing 50 or more employees in the UK. After that we consider specific information and consultation duties which apply in situations of collective redundancies and transfers of undertakings. Finally, we examine informing and consulting in relation to health and safety matters.

THE INFORMATION AND CONSULTATION REGULATIONS 2004

These regulations implemented in the UK another EU Directive (the Directive on Informing and Consulting Employees). This was the first EU Directive to introduce a general on-going requirement on businesses operating in a single Member State of the EU (eg in the UK) to provide information and consultation for their employees.[12]

Measures concerning informing and consulting employees within the Information and Consultation Regulations 2004[13] include:

- The Regulations apply to undertakings with at least 50 employees in the UK.
- The employer may start the process towards establishing information and consultation, or it can be triggered by a request from 10% of the employees.
- If the business already has a valid pre-existing agreement for informing and consulting, the employer need not take steps to set up new informing and consulting arrangements unless a sufficient proportion of the employees endorse this request (see below).
- The first step in setting up new informing and consulting arrangements is for the employees to elect or appoint negotiating representatives who try to negotiate with the employer an informing and consulting agreement.
- The requirements for what must be in an informing and consulting agreement are extremely flexible. Information and consultation may be provided either for elected information and consultation representatives of the employees or it may be provided for the employees directly.

- If no agreement is reached, the 'standard' informing and consulting provisions will apply.
- The two sides are under a duty to work in a spirit of co-operation in negotiating and implementing informing and consulting.

CASE STUDY

COORS BREWERS LTD[14]

Note: *The following case study was published in 2007 by the then Department of Trade and Industry. The name of the company was changed to Molson Coors Brewing Company (UK) Ltd in 2009. Information in the 'Background' introductory paragraph of the case study may no longer be accurate.*

Background

Based in Burton-upon-Trent, Coors Brewers Ltd (previously Bass Brewers Ltd) produces some of the UK's top beer brands, including Carling, Grolsch, Coors Fine Light Beer and Worthington's. The company employs 2,500 people in the UK across eight locations. Around 600 employees are covered by recognition agreements with the Transport & General Workers Union.

Informing and consulting practices

Coors had several years' experience of employee consultation on a number of issues when it decided in late 2004 to create the Coors Brewers Employee Forum. Up until then, consultation had been *ad hoc*, on specific issues as the need arose. The new Employee Forum was to be a permanent body covering a broader range of business issues. The company publicised the creation of the Forum internally in early 2005 and advertised for 16 employee representatives to be drawn from constituencies across the business and representing both negotiated and non-negotiated employees. Constituencies were based on a combination of geography and function, and averaged around 170 employees. Nominees had to be supported by two colleagues, and elections were held where there was more than one nomination.

The first meeting was held in March 2005. The agreed constitution envisages two meetings a year, held to coincide with full and half-year company results, plus special meetings as the need arises. In practice, there have been so many issues on which to consult that 15 meetings were called in the first eighteen months. Coors agreed with the Forum that it would *inform* all representatives about issues affecting a part of the company, but only *consult* representatives from the affected area.

Representatives serve for a three-year term. They are not obliged to attend all meetings, but in practice most do. The Forum's bi-annual meetings are chaired by the company's CEO, with the Business Services Director also attending, and a third board director on a rotating basis – every board member will have attended at least one regular meeting over the course of three years. The special meetings tend to be chaired by senior leaders from the HR function, with business leaders invited to present on issues being discussed. A dedicated intranet is used to support the work of the Forum, with presentations, notes and action points from meetings posted on the site. Communications arising from meetings are agreed with the representatives, and circulated by them, adding their own 'gloss' if they wish.

Business benefits

The Forum has proved very valuable because its existence has coincided with a period of significant change at Coors. A substantial downsizing project started in April 2005 and the company engaged in a long period of consultation with the Forum which resulted in the initial proposals being changed. In addition the Forum agreed some key principles for redundancy selection. Since then there has been a further process of change in the supply chain with a reduction in the manufacturing operation, on which the Forum has been consulted and agreed that the same redundancy arrangements should apply.

It has now become established practice that any issue that has to be communicated to all employees which concerns terms and conditions or organisational change is taken to the Forum first for feedback and to help identify problems and concerns that may arise. Subjects that have been dealt with include: two significant organisational change projects, training on TUPE regulations, proposed changes to the company car policy, changes to several policies required as a consequence of the new age discrimination legislation, and proposals for introducing a smoking ban in 2007. Another important subject that has been discussed is a new employee incentive plan. Coors consulted the Forum about a draft communication to employees explaining the new plan and how it was to be introduced. Many employees found the original communication difficult to understand, which resulted in a meeting of the Forum with the CEO, and the decision to rewrite and re-communicate the incentive plan invitation. As a result, a lot more information was given to employees who felt they were more informed about the decision they were being asked to take.

What makes it work?

Coors is in no doubt that what makes their Employee Forum work is a genuine willingness on the part of the company and the representatives to work together and to openly discuss issues and concerns and seek appropriate solutions to business issues. They will do this quite early in the process, even before they have formal proposals to make, giving a 'heads-up' that an issue is coming over the horizon. At first, there was some anxiety on the part of management about sharing confidential information, but experience has shown this not to be a problem – the Forum has reached a high level of maturity in a relatively short period of time, and the company feels it can have absolute trust in the representatives.

Ideas for the future

In 2007 there is an intention to revisit the constitution to ensure that it remains fit for purpose and to arrange training for employee representatives on diversity awareness and pensions. In addition, Coors will continue to work with Forum representatives to ensure that they are informed about company performance and business issues and are consulted about issues that might affect employees or terms and conditions of employment.

The Regulations in more detail

The Regulations apply only to undertakings with at least 50 employees in the UK. We may note that the result of this minimum requirement was that fewer than 3% of UK businesses were bound by the Regulations! However, the proportion of UK *employees* employed by those businesses is considerably higher.

The employer may start the process towards establishing informing and consulting, or it can be triggered by a request from 10% of the employees (subject to a maximum figure of 2,500 employees).

The Regulations aim for a high degree of flexibility in how informing and consulting takes place, leaving it as far as possible to the two sides to agree. The agreement must set out the circumstances in which informing and consulting will take place, but it is up to the two sides to agree when this will be, and also *how* it will take place. Information and consultation may be provided for representatives of the employees or it may instead be provided for employees directly. It might be possible therefore for valid informing and consulting simply to be made available in electronic form to all staff.

The flexibility in the regulations is also evident in that the employer will often be allowed to continue with existing informing and consulting arrangements rather than putting new informing and consulting measures in place. If the business already has valid existing information and consultation arrangements covering all the employees, the employer will not need to set up new arrangements unless it is insisted upon by quite a high proportion of the employees. The slightly complicated majority proportion required is made up as follows:

- where a valid request is made by less than 40 per cent of the employees and
- there are already valid existing informing and consulting agreements, then
- instead of starting negotiations, the employer may hold a ballot to seek the endorsement of employees for the request. In order for it to be endorsed, at least 40% of all the employees employed must have voted for it and also a majority of those who actually vote in the ballot (Regulations 8–9). Unless both these majorities are obtained, the employer can keep the existing informing and consulting arrangements.

CASE STUDY

STEWART v MORAY COUNCIL[15]

Mr Stewart, an employee of Moray Council, submitted a request to the Council on behalf of 500 employees, asking for negotiations on an information and consultation agreement. The Council had a number of agreements with trade unions and took the view that these were valid existing informing and consulting agreements and that it would therefore hold a ballot to see if there was employee endorsement of the request for new informing and consulting.

The rules in Regulation 8(1) provide that to be valid, the pre-existing agreement must (a) be in writing; (b) cover all employees; (c) have been approved by the employees; and (d) set out how the employer is to give information to the employees or their representatives and seek their views on such information.

Mr Stewart claimed that the agreements did not cover all employees, only those in trade unions; similarly, he argued that the existing agreements had been approved only by those employees who were trade union members.

The Employment Appeal Tribunal approved the approach of the Central Arbitration Committee. The CAC had held that the existing agreements *did* cover all employees and that it could not be accepted that the agreements only covered those who were members of the trade unions. The agreements related to negotiation and consultation for all employees. Nor, according to the CAC, could it be held that the agreements had not been approved by the employees. The CAC did, however, hold that one of the conditions in Regulation 8(1) was not met. This related to the setting out of how the employer was going to give information and seek the views of representatives.

A provision that stated that the joint negotiating committee would be a forum for discussion and/or consultation on a range of matters not subject to national bargaining was not sufficiently detailed. As a result the EAT held in favour of Mr Stewart that the collective agreements did *not* fulfil the criteria for pre-existing agreements and the Council was ordered to initiate negotiations for a new informing and consulting agreement.

STANDARD INFORMATION AND CONSULTATION PROVISIONS

Where the employer fails to initiate negotiations within the necessary time-limits, or if no agreement is reached in time, the standard informing and consulting provisions will apply.

The time-limit is

- either six months from when the original employee request was made
- or when the information and consultation representatives are elected (whichever is the sooner) (Regulation 18(1)).

Where there are negotiations but no agreement is reached within six months, the standard provisions will apply from that date. There is therefore significant pressure upon employers to take action and come to an agreement if they wish any sort of arrangement other than the standard provisions to be agreed. Furthermore, an employer who fails to take the necessary steps to negotiate an informing and consulting procedure risks incurring a fine – see below.

Under the standard provisions the employer must provide the information and consultation representatives with information under the following three categories, and consultation on the latter two headings:

- the recent and probable development of the undertaking's activities and economic situation
- the situation, structure and probable development of employment within the undertaking and any anticipatory measures envisaged – in particular, where there is a threat to employment within the undertaking, and
- decisions which are likely to lead to substantial changes in work organisation or contractual relations, including those concerned with collective redundancies and transfers of undertakings (where there are specific requirements to inform and consult – see below) (Regulation 20(1)).

If you look again at the case study on *Coors Brewers* above, you will see that most or all the matters on which information and consultation were provided for the

Employee Forum would very probably have had to be conveyed under the standard provisions as well.

The information must be given in good time, so that the representatives have time to carry out a study and prepare for the consultation, which must be carried out on the basis of the information supplied by the employer. The employer must ensure that the representatives are able to meet and consult with the relevant level of management. Management must provide a reasoned response (Regulation 20(4)). All parties have a duty 'to work in a spirit of co-operation' (Regulation 21).

CONFIDENTIALITY

In complying with a duty to provide its employees or their representatives with information, what account may an employer take of confidential information – for example, sensitive commercial data? This has always been an important concern of employers, and the question of what is confidential and what is not is an interesting one. We saw above the provisions in the TICE Regulations dealing with this issue, and the treatment of it in the informing and consulting Regulations is much the same. Again, there are two aspects to confidentiality dealt with in the Regulations. One imposes an obligation upon the parties to maintain a confidence. The second is the decision over what material is so confidential that it cannot be revealed at all.

In dealing with the first of these, Regulation 25 provides that a person who reveals information entrusted in confidence to him or her by the employer (unless it is done as a whistleblower under section 43A ERA 1996 – see Chapter 3) commits a breach of a statutory duty owed to the employer, giving the employer a possible claim for damages. The second aspect is that the employer may also withhold information that he or she believes is 'such that, according to objective criteria, the disclosure of the information or document would seriously harm the functioning of, or be prejudicial to, the undertaking' (Regulation 26). Any dispute on the confidentiality of the information will be settled by the CAC.

PENALTIES AND PROTECTION

Failure to follow the procedures can result in significant fines, such as the penalty of £55,000 imposed on Macmillan Publishers where the employer, according to the EAT, ignored the provisions of the Regulations at almost every stage.[16] The maximum fine that can be imposed under the Regulations is £75,000. In this case the employer had argued that they had an existing consultation agreement in place. This argument failed because the agreement did not cover all employees and because the employer did not follow the necessary procedures.[17]

REFLECTIVE QUESTION

Is a fine of £75,000 a sufficient deterrent for a large company that does not wish to comply with the provisions?

Part VIII of the Regulations provides for protection against detriment and dismissal and the right to time off for information and consultation representatives.

It is likely that HRM practitioners would have played a central role in introducing and administering the information and consultation procedures under the Regulations. The CIPD supported the principle of legislation on the subject, but called for the Regulations to be as flexible as possible so that organisations might develop arrangements that are best suited to their circumstances.[18]

COLLECTIVE REDUNDANCIES

When a number of employees are going to lose their jobs at the same time or within a certain period due to redundancy (as defined below), there is a specific duty on the employer to provide information and consultation. This duty is found in Chapter 2 of the Trade Union and Labour Relations Consolidation Act 1992 (TULRCA), originating from an EU Directive, the Collective Redundancies Directive. Employers proposing to dismiss as redundant 20 or more employees at one establishment within a period of 90 days or less must consult 'appropriate representatives' of the relevant employees.[19] Those volunteering to take redundancy in a redundancy situation can count towards this total, so, as in *Optare Group plc v TGWU*,[20] when there were 17 people made compulsorily redundant together with a further three who took voluntary redundancy, that was enough to trigger the process. The consultation must begin 'in good time' and in any event:

- where the employer is proposing to dismiss 100 or more employees, at least 90 days, and
- otherwise, at least 30 days before the first of the dismissals takes effect.[21]

Who are the 'appropriate representatives' who must be consulted?

- If the employer has recognised a trade union – ie there is a trade union representing the employees with which the employer bargains (see Chapter 18) – representatives from that union will represent the employees.
- If there are no such representatives, the employer may choose to consult either employee representatives who have been specifically elected or appointed by the affected employees for the purpose of this consultation or existing employee representatives who may have been elected or appointed by the employees for another purpose.[22]

Employers have a responsibility for ensuring that elections for employee representatives are fair and may determine the number of representatives to be elected.[23] If the affected employees fail to elect or appoint representatives, employers may fulfil their obligations by giving the employees themselves the appropriate information.[24]

REDUNDANCY WHERE NO JOBS ARE ACTUALLY LOST

In this context, redundancy is defined in section 195 of TULRCA as 'dismissal for a reason not related to the individual concerned or for a number of reasons all of which are not so related'.[25] By stating that it is for a reason 'not related to the individual' it is intended to deal only with situations in which jobs are being lost due to the economic position of the employer as opposed to, for example, a dismissal due to an individual employee's misconduct. But that said, it is nevertheless a much broader definition of a redundancy than the one we have seen in the context of an individual redundancy dismissal (see Chapter 14). It might include, for example, collective dismissals resulting from a refusal to accept a change in terms and conditions of employment:

CASE STUDY

GMB v MAN TRUCK AND BUS UK LTD

In *GMB v Man Truck and Bus UK Ltd*[26] a new company was formed by the merger of two independent businesses. In order to harmonise the terms and conditions of the employees of the two businesses, the company wrote to all the employees terminating their contracts of employment on a particular day. They also wrote to all the employees offering to re-employ them from the same day, but on the new harmonised terms and conditions. All the employees accepted the altered terms and were re-employed. The EAT held that the blanket dismissals of all the employees in this case – even though the intention was to change the terms of their contracts rather than for jobs to be lost – came within the broad definition of 'redundancy' dismissals in section 195. The employer therefore had a duty to inform and consult in this case.

Discussion point

Do you think the EAT's interpretation of the statute was correct – was this a case in which the employer was 'proposing to dismiss employees as redundant'?

Similarly, if an employer is proposing to redeploy staff and put them on what is in reality a different contract of employment, this may amount to a proposal to terminate the existing contracts.[27]

It is important to note that the employees covered need not be employed for any minimum number of hours per week. However, those who work under a contract for a fixed term of three months or less will be excluded unless the employment lasted for more than three months.[28]

Defining 'establishment'

We mentioned above that the duty to inform and consult arises only if 20 or more employees at one establishment are facing dismissal. 'Establishment' is not defined by the statute and the EAT has ruled that this is a question for the employment tribunal to decide, using its common sense on the particular facts of the case. In *Bakers' Union v Clark's of Hove Ltd*,[29] it was accepted that separate premises could be regarded as one establishment if there was common management and accounting. The ECJ has indicated that the word 'establishment' must be understood as designating the unit to which the workers made redundant are assigned to carry out their duties. It is not essential for that unit to be endowed with a management that can independently effect collective dismissals.[30]

THE CONSULTATION PROCEDURE

The consultation required must include consultation about ways of:

- avoiding the dismissals,
- reducing the numbers to be dismissed, and
- mitigating the consequences of the dismissals,

and must be undertaken 'with a view to reaching agreement with the appropriate representatives'.

REFLECTIVE QUESTION

Should the duty to consult be strengthened so that the redundancies cannot go ahead if agreement is not reached?

An employer is required to consult on each of the above three aspects individually. It is not enough just to consult on ways of reducing the numbers of employees to be dismissed and mitigating the consequences of dismissals, without consulting on ways of avoiding the dismissals. In such a case the employer would not have met the statutory requirements.[31] The obligation to consult over avoiding redundancies almost inevitably means consulting over the reasons for the dismissals.[32]

It is important to note that Article 2 of the Collective Redundancies Directive,[33] from which the UK law on this subject originates, requires consultation at the stage when an employer is 'contemplating' collective redundancies. May an employer send out notices of dismissal at this stage – ie at the beginning of, or during, the consultation process? After all, the notices of dismissal could be withdrawn if the consultation finds a way to avoid the dismissals. In a major decision, the European Court of Justice in *Junk v Kühnel*[34] held that an employer was *not* permitted to send out dismissal notices until consultation had finished. The reasoning was simple and logical. The stage at which an employer was 'contemplating' redundancies – when the duty to consult arises – meant by definition a stage where no decision had yet been taken on whether there would be redundancies. Sending out a notice of dismissal is a clear indication that an employer has made up its mind – 'the expression of a decision to sever the employment relationship', as the court put it. Thus sending out a notice of dismissal was incompatible with the consultation process. The court stated that consultation under the Directive effectively requires the employer to *negotiate* – and to allow the termination of the contracts of employment before that negotiation takes place would be to compromise those negotiations.

CASE STUDY

LEICESTERSHIRE COUNTY COUNCIL v UNISON[35]

In accordance with a national agreement, the Council had carried out a job evaluation exercise covering about 9,000 jobs. As a result of the exercise there were a number of jobs which were due to be downgraded and some others which would have various payments lowered or removed. The Officers decided that the best way to deal with this was to give notice terminating the contracts of those affected and then simultaneously offer new contracts on the new terms.

On 18 November an Officer of the Council presented a report to the councillors on the Employment Committee with this recommendation. The formal decision to proceed was taken by the Committee on 12 December. On 18 December a notice was sent to the local Branch Secretary of UNISON and, thereafter, there was total failure to consult with these staff.

The EAT held that the 'proposal' on the part of the Officers of the Council to dismiss employees as redundant came into existence in mid-November, even though it was a month later that the decision was taken by the politicians on the Employment Committee. Thus the obligation to consult was triggered in mid-November. 'Proposing to dismiss' was less than a decision that dismissals are to be made, though more than just a 'possibility' that they might occur. This view of things was consistent with the decision in *Junk*. There had, consequently, been a total failure to consult according to the statutory requirements.

What employers must disclose in writing

The employer must disclose in writing the following matters at the beginning of the consultation period, although a lack of information should not be allowed to delay the start of consultation:[36]

a) the reason for the proposals
b) the number and description of employees whom it is proposed to dismiss
c) the total number of employees of any such description employed by the employer at that establishment
d) the proposed method of selecting the employees who may be dismissed

e) the proposed method of carrying out the dismissals, with due regard to any agreed procedure, including the period over which the dismissals are to take effect

f) the proposed method of calculating the redundancy payment if this differs from the statutory sum.

This information must be delivered to each of the appropriate representatives, or sent by post to an address notified by them or, in the case of union representatives, to the union head office. In *Lancaster University v University and College Union* [37] it was the employer's practice to send the union a periodic list of individuals on fixed-term contracts whose contracts would not be renewed when their term ended. This process was accepted by the union for many years. When a new union representative was appointed she took the view that the sending of a list did not fulfil the employer's consultation obligations. Eventually, after a complaint to the employment tribunal a protective award of 60 days' pay was made because the employer's practice was a significant breach of its statutory obligations.

'Special circumstances' permitting employers to depart from consultation requirements

If there are 'special circumstances' which render it not reasonably practicable for the employer to comply with the above-mentioned provisions, an employer must take 'all such steps towards compliance' as are reasonably practicable in the circumstances. 'Special circumstances' mean circumstances which are uncommon or out of the ordinary, so insolvency by itself will not provide an excuse, because it may well be foreseeable.[38] However, that the employer has continued trading in the face of adverse economic pointers in the genuine and reasonable expectation that redundancies would be avoided can justify non-compliance.[39] Additionally, a pending application for government financial aid, the withdrawal of a prospective purchaser from negotiations combined with a bank's immediate appointment of a receiver, and the need for confidentiality in negotiating a sale, have all constituted 'special circumstances'. By way of contrast, the following have *not* been accepted as being 'special circumstances':

- the alarm and chaos which would be caused by the disclosure of information about the proposed redundancies
- a genuine belief that the union had not been recognised: in *Wilson & Bros Ltd v USDAW* [40] it was held that such a belief must be reasonable
- the fact that the employer had been informed by the relevant government department that there was no duty to consult in the particular case.[41]

Section 188(7) TULRCA 1992 also states that where the decision leading to the proposed dismissals is that of a person controlling the employer, a failure on the part of that person to provide the employer with information will not constitute 'special circumstances'. If the employer has invited any of the employees who may be dismissed to elect employee representatives, and this invitation was issued long enough before the time when consultation must begin to allow them to elect representatives by that time, the employer is not in breach of the statute if he or she complies with the consultation requirements as soon as reasonably practicable after the election of the representatives.[42]

PROTECTIVE AWARDS

Where the employer has failed to comply with any of the above requirements under TULRCA 1992, the employee representatives can complain to an employment tribunal in respect of any failure relating to them (except failures relating to their election), and a trade union can complain where there is a failure relating to its representatives. In any other case, employees who have been or may be dismissed as redundant can complain. It will therefore usually be the union or the employee representatives who will have to bring the initial tribunal claim about a failure to inform and consult under TULRCA. Claims can be made to an employment tribunal before the proposed dismissal takes effect or within three months of its doing so.[43] Employers wishing to argue that there were 'special circumstances' justifying non-compliance must prove that these circumstances existed and that they took all such steps towards compliance as were reasonably practicable. If a complaint is well-founded, the tribunal must make a declaration to that effect and may also make a protective award. A protective award refers to the wages payable for the protected period to employees who have been dismissed or whom it is proposed to dismiss. This is a maximum 90-day period[44] – how long it is depends on the tribunal's view of what is 'just and equitable' having regard to the seriousness of the employer's failure.[45] The rate of pay under a protective award is a week's pay for each week of the protected period (or pro rata for part of a week).[46]

What is the purpose of the protective award? Is it to provide compensation for the employees, or is punitive – to punish the employers for failing to inform and consult? There was some uncertainty about this for a number of years but in *Susie Radin v GMB* [47] (see the case study below) the Court of Appeal emphatically decided that the purpose of the protective award is punitive.

CASE STUDY

SUSIE RADIN v GMB

Susie Radin Ltd was a clothing manufacturer employing 108 workers. The company got into financial difficulties and sent out letters of dismissal to all its employees. The company closed down three months later. It failed totally to provide information and consultation as required by TULRCA. The employment tribunal awarded a maximum protective award of 90 days' wages for each employee, totalling £250,000, even though it found as a fact that any consultation would have been 'futile' – the company would have had to close down anyway. The company appealed against this decision in the Court of Appeal. The purpose of a protective award, argued the company, was to compensate the employees for their financial losses arising out of the employer's failure to inform and consult. Since the tribunal had found that the company would have had to close down even if there had been proper consultation, it could not be said that the employees had incurred any financial losses due to the employer's failure to consult. The Court of Appeal rejected this argument. The purpose of the protective award, said the court, was punitive – to deter employers from ignoring their obligations to inform and consult. Therefore whether or not the employees had suffered any financial losses due to the employer's failure to consult was irrelevant, a protective award would still be made. The size of the award would depend on how bad the employer's failure had been – where, as in this case, there was a total failure to inform and consult, a maximum award of 90 days was appropriate.

Discussion point

Do you think that even substantial compensation is a sufficient deterrent? Can you suggest any other remedy that the law could provide?

If during the protected period employees are fairly dismissed for a reason other than redundancy, or if they unreasonably resign, then their entitlement to remuneration under the protective award ceases on the day the contract is terminated. Similarly, employees who unreasonably refuse an offer of employment on the previous terms and conditions or an offer of suitable alternative employment will not be entitled to any remuneration under a protective award in respect of any period during which, but for that refusal, they would have been employed.[48]

What remedy is there for the employee if the employer does not pay a protective award? An employee covered by the award may bring a further claim to a tribunal that their employer has failed, wholly or in part, to pay the award. This claim must be made within three months, unless the tribunal allows a late claim on the basis that it was 'not reasonably practicable' to bring the claim within that time. If the complaint is well-founded, the employer will be ordered to pay the amount due to the employee.[49] The three-month time limit to bring the claim runs from the last day of the protected period to which the award relates.[50]

Finally, section 198 TULRCA 1992 enables the parties to a collective agreement to apply to the Secretary of State for an exemption order in respect of the consultation provisions.

DUTY ON THE EMPLOYER TO NOTIFY THE DEPARTMENT FOR BUSINESS

An employer proposing to dismiss as redundant 100 or more employees at one establishment within a period of 90 days, or 20 or more employees within 30 days, must notify the Department for Business, Innovation and Skills in writing of the proposal within 90 or 30 days respectively.[51] There is thus no obligation to notify if fewer than 20 employees are to be dismissed.

If there are special circumstances rendering it not reasonably practicable for an employer to comply with this requirement, the employer must take all such steps as are reasonably practicable in the circumstances. Again, where the decision leading to the proposed dismissals is that of a person controlling the employer, a failure on the part of that person to provide the employer with information will not constitute 'special circumstances'.[52] Employers who fail to give notice in accordance with this section may be prosecuted and pay a fine not exceeding level 5 on the standard scale.

TRANSFERS OF UNDERTAKINGS

We looked at the Transfer of Undertakings Regulations[53] in Chapter 16 and we saw that the effect of the Regulations is as if the contract of employment was originally made between the transferee and the employee.

Regulations 13 and 14 of the Transfer Regulations are concerned with the duty to inform and consult employee representatives, and Regulation 15 with the consequences of failing to do so. Information should be provided 'long enough before a relevant transfer to enable the employer of any affected employees to consult all the persons who are appropriate representatives of any of those affected employees'. The High Court, in *Institution of Professional Civil Servants v Secretary of State for Defence*,[54] decided that the words 'long enough before' a transfer to enable consultation to take place meant as soon as measures are envisaged and *if possible* long enough before the transfer to enable consultation.[55] This case concerned the introduction of private management into the Royal Dockyards at Rosyth and Devonport – a measure that was opposed by the trade unions. Unless 'measures' were envisaged – which meant some definite plans or proposals by the employer – there was no obligation to inform and consult.

The information to be provided should consist of:

- the fact that a relevant transfer is to take place
- approximately when it is to take place
- the reasons for it
- the legal, economic and social implications for the affected employees
- the measures that are envisaged to take place in connection with the transfer, in relation to the affected employees or the fact that there are no such measures envisaged.

REFLECTIVE QUESTION

Should the employee representatives have a say in whether the transfer should take place at all, rather than just a right to be informed of the fact of the transfer?

The duty to inform applies even where the obligation to consult does not arise. However, an employer is not in breach of its duty to inform employee representatives if it forms a genuine belief after consideration that no relevant transfer is to take place.[56] There is no duty, either under the Directive or under the Transfer Regulations, to consult *after* the transfer.[57]

The rules concerning the election of employee representatives are contained in Regulation 14 of the Transfer Regulations. These are identical to those rules concerning the appointment of appropriate representatives for the purposes of consultation in collective redundancies (see above). That is to say, if the employer has recognised a trade union, representatives from that union will represent the employees. If there is no such trade union, then the employer may choose to consult either employee representatives who have been specifically elected or appointed for this consultation or existing employee representatives.

Both the transferor and the transferee must consult, and there is an obligation upon the transferee to provide the transferor with information about its (the transferee's) plans, so that the transferor can carry out its duty to consult. The 2006 version of the Transfer Regulations introduced joint liability between the transferor and the transferee for any compensation awarded as a result of a failure to inform or consult (Regulations 15(8) and 15(9)). This is because if the transferor did not retain some liability, there would be no incentive for him or her to inform or consult at all. An example of this – before joint liability was introduced – occurred in *Alamo Group (Europe) Ltd v Tucker*.[58] Here the transferor, which was a company in administration, failed to inform or consult employees about the transfer. The EAT held that the liability to consult transferred and that the transferee was therefore liable to pay compensation for the transferor's failure. The transferee, according to the court, could protect itself by providing for warranties and indemnities in the contract of transfer.

Where the employer actually envisages taking measures in relation to any of the affected employees, the employer must consult the appropriate representatives 'with a view to seeking their agreement to the measures to be taken'. In the course of these consultations the employer will consider the representations made by the appropriate representatives, and if any of those representations are rejected, the employer must state the reasons for so doing.

As with collective redundancies, there is a 'special circumstances' defence for the employer if it renders it not reasonably practicable to perform the duty to inform or consult. In such a case the employer must take all such steps as are reasonable in the circumstances. There is also a defence for the employer if the employees fail to elect representatives. In such a case the duty to consult is fulfilled if the employer gives each employee the necessary information.

Complaints to an employment tribunal may be made for a breach of the rules concerning consultation. If the complaint is well-founded, the employment tribunal may make an award of up to a maximum of 13 weeks' pay to each affected employee. In *Zaman v Kozee Sleep Products Ltd (trading as Dorlux Beds UK)*,[59] the employment tribunal awarded claimants compensation but applied the statutory cap (£430 per week in 2012), thus limiting the amount of payment due. The EAT changed this and stated that a week's pay in this case is not subject to the statutory cap.

As with protective awards for failure to consult in collective redundancy situations, awards for failure to inform and consult here should contain a punitive element designed to punish the employer as well as to compensate the employee.[60]

HEALTH AND SAFETY

CASE STUDY

THE STAFF NURSE SAFETY REPRESENTATIVE

Note: *The following is from one of a number of case studies produced by the Royal College of Nursing to illustrate the work of its safety representatives. The study describes the work as a safety representative carried out by a Staff Nurse in a nursing home.*[61]

Developing the role in a nursing home

At my interview the director of the Trust saw that I was an RCN safety representative and her response was 'Yippee!' Both she and the manager were very pleased for me to continue with my role which I did not begin to develop until after I had settled into life at the Nursing Home.

I started by having discussions with the nominated health and safety person who looked after all four of the units within the Trust. When she emigrated, it was decided that health and safety (H&S) responsibility would be better dealt with within each individual unit.

I spend one or two days a month working on a variety of issues. I've developed an annual visual checklist for all the rooms in the building, written policies and procedures, delivered training sessions and participate in the monthly checks which are performed throughout the building.

The role is quite different in a nursing home from that of a hospital ward, in that the whole building is covered, including the kitchen, boilers, bathrooms, inside and outside – not just one area. A lot of this work isn't very exciting but it is important and necessary for the safe and smooth operation of our service.

I meet with the H&S forum (which covers the four units) every three months and have raised awareness of various issues such as security, criminal records bureau checks, staffing, building security. For example, when a visitor comes, there are various health and safety issues – we have a door answering system with intercom, but someone needs to meet the visitor, make sure that they sign in as they enter, and that they know the fire drill. We also need to be aware of the client response to the visitor to ensure that they are welcome. I have also highlighted nursing to the overweight and obese patients to raise awareness of the limitations we could be faced with in the future.

I look at the risk assessments to see that they are updated every month. I look at things like the alarm system, personal safety alarms, check that the H&S policy is on the notice-board, and H&S inductions have been carried out for new staff. I do H&S training every month at one or other of the units. I plan to develop a second stage of training to update staff.

We're lucky in that health and safety is well supported throughout the organisation. We have very good staffing levels and high standards of care which our Commission for Social Care Inspection report reflects. Also, because there is a good regular workforce, it means we can develop relationships with people, and gradually build up their knowledge base.

I attend the RCN regional health and safety representative meetings in Cambridge regularly and find them a very useful tool. At these meetings participants are able to 'network', share good practice and come away having learned something useful.

Risk assessments and monthly check

We undertake a risk assessment throughout the entire premises, and perform monthly supervised checks. It's extremely well supported. Everyone's encouraged to get involved; nurses, assistants and kitchen staff also take part. Staff carry out the safety checks. Each month a new person does it, so that gradually everyone becomes more aware of the H&S issues. If I tried to get the same thing across sitting in a classroom, people would get bored. Getting them involved is a good learning experience and helps to make people more aware of H&S in general.

At the end of the day if everyone on the premises is aware of health and safety issues we will all be working in an environment where staff, residents, visitors, contractors, etc, feel safe and secure. What better surroundings to work in! This in turn leads to a happy and productive workforce.

The law on information and consultation in regard to health and safety originated, as with the other duties in this chapter, from an EU law – in this case the European Council Directive on the introduction of measures to encourage improvements in the safety and health of workers.[62] This Directive has specific requirements both for

- providing workers with information, and for
- the consultation and participation of workers.

Article 10 of the Directive ensures that workers receive information from the employer about the safety and health risks of their jobs, or their workplaces, as well as information about what protective and preventive measures are to be taken. Article 11 of the Directive provides that employers shall consult workers and/or their representatives 'and allow them to take part in discussions' on all questions relating to safety and health at work. Protection is also offered to the workers or workers' representatives who take part in this process, including the right to time off work with pay for the purpose of carrying out their duties.

The Safety Representatives and Safety Committee Regulations 1977 (SRSC Regulations) implemented the Directive in the UK but provided for the appointment of safety representatives only when there was a trade union recognised by the employer for collective bargaining purposes. Accordingly, the Health and Safety (Consultation with Employees) Regulations 1996 (HSCE Regulations) were introduced to ensure that the information and consultation requirements of the SRSC Regulations were extended to those workplaces where there was no recognised trade union. In such workplaces the employers must either consult the employees directly or 'representatives of employee safety' who have been elected by employees. In the remainder of this section, therefore, the term 'safety representatives' refers to those appointed or elected by a trade union, and 'representatives of employee safety' refers to non-union representatives.

Regulation 5 requires employers to make available to those employees or representatives such information as is necessary to enable them to participate fully and effectively in the consultation. Representatives of employee safety must also be given information to enable them to carry out their functions.[63] In addition, 'inspectors' are obliged, in circumstances in which it is necessary to do so for the purpose of assisting in keeping employees adequately informed about health, safety and welfare matters, to give employees or their representatives factual information relating to an employer's premises, as well as information with respect to any action they have taken or propose to take in connection with those premises. Such information must be conveyed to the employer, and inspectors can also give a written statement of their observations to anyone likely to be a party to any civil proceedings arising out of any accident, etc.[64]

Regulation 13 of the MHSW Regulations (see Chapter 9) stipulates that in entrusting tasks to their employees, employers must take into account their capabilities in relation to health and safety. In particular, employers have a duty to ensure that their employees are provided with adequate health and safety training when recruited or if they are exposed to new or increased risks. As regards supervision, it would seem to follow that if the employer's efforts do not persuade an employee to adopt safe working practices, disciplinary or other action may have to be taken.

SAFETY REPRESENTATIVES

Section 2(4) HASAWA 1974 provides for the appointment by recognised trade unions of safety representatives from among the employees.[65] Where such representatives are appointed, employers have a duty under section 2(6) (see above) to consult them with a view to the making and maintenance of arrangements that will enable the employer and employees to co-operate effectively in promoting and developing measures to ensure the health and safety at work of the employees, and in checking the effectiveness of such measures.[66] In particular, employers must consult union safety representatives in good time with regard to:

- the introduction of any measure which may substantially affect the health and safety of the employees represented
- the arrangements for appointing or nominating competent persons in accordance with Regulations 7(1) and 8(1)b of the MHSW Regulations
- any health and safety information that the employer must provide the employees represented with
- the planning and organisation of any health and safety training the employer is required to provide for the employees represented
- the health and safety consequences for the employees represented of the planning and introduction of new technologies.[67]

Employers' duty to consult

Union safety representatives may be elected or appointed. If there are employees who are not covered by union safety representatives, the employers must as we have seen either consult the employees directly or the 'representatives of employee safety' about the matters listed above. In either case employers must make available such information within their knowledge as is necessary to enable full and effective participation in the consultation.[68] Where employers consult representatives of employee safety, they must inform the employees represented of the names of the representatives and the groups they represent.[69] Similarly, if employers discontinue consultation with a representative of employee safety, they must inform the employees in the group concerned of that fact.[70]

Trade union safety representatives

The SRSC Regulations stipulate that if an employer has received written notification from a recognised independent trade union of the names of the people appointed as union safety representatives, such persons have the functions set out in Regulation 4 of the SRSC Regulations (below). So far as is reasonably practicable, union safety representatives will either have been employed by their employer throughout the preceding two years or have had at least two years' experience in similar employment.[71] Employees cease to be union safety representatives for the purpose of these regulations when:

- the trade union which appointed them notifies the employer in writing that their appointment has been terminated
- they cease to be employed at the workplace[72]
- they resign.

Functions of union safety representatives

Apart from representing all employees (not only trade union members) in consultation with the employer under section 2(6) HASAWA 1974, union safety representatives are given the following functions by Regulation 4(1) SRSC Regulations:

- to investigate potential hazards and dangerous occurrences at the workplace (whether or not they are drawn to their attention by the employees they represent) and to examine the causes of accidents at the workplace
- to investigate complaints by any employee they represent relating to that employee's health, safety or welfare at work
- to make representations to the employer on general matters affecting the health, safety or welfare at work of the employees at the workplace
- to carry out inspections in accordance with Regulations 5, 6 and 7 SRSC Regulations
- to represent the employees they are appointed to represent in consultation at the workplace with inspectors from the enforcing authorities
- to receive information from inspectors in accordance with section 28(8) of HASAWA 1974
- to attend meetings of safety committees where they attend in their capacity as safety representatives in connection with any of the above functions.

Functions of representatives of employee safety

By way of contrast, representatives of employee safety have only the following functions:[73]

- to make representations to the employer on potential hazards and dangerous occurrences at the workplace which affect, or could affect, the group of employees represented
- to make representations to the employer on general matters affecting the health and safety at work of the group represented and, in particular, on such matters as he or she is consulted about by the employer under Regulation 3 of the HSCE Regulations 1996, and
- to represent the group of employees in consultations at the workplace with inspectors appointed under section 19 HASAWA 1974.

REFLECTIVE QUESTION

Should the representatives of employee safety have the same powers as the union safety representatives?

Further points to note are:

- None of these functions imposes a duty on safety representatives, although they will be liable for the actions they take as ordinary employees.
- Employers who consult representatives of employee safety have a duty to ensure that those representatives are provided with such training in respect of their functions as is reasonable in all the circumstances. The employer must also meet any reasonable costs associated with such training, including travel and subsistence costs.[74]

Regulation 5 SRSC Regulations entitles safety representatives to inspect the workplace at least every three months, but they must give reasonable notice in writing of their intention to do so. Of course, inspections may take place more frequently if the employer agrees. Additional inspections may be made if there has been a substantial change in the conditions of work or new information has been published by the Health and Safety Executive (HSE) relevant to the hazards of the workplace. Inspections may also be conducted where there has been a notifiable accident or dangerous occurrence or a notifiable disease[75] contracted, for the purpose of determining the cause. The employer must provide reasonable facilities and assistance for the purpose of carrying out an inspection, including facilities for independent investigation by the union representatives and private discussion with the employees. However, there is nothing to prevent the employers or their representatives from being present during an inspection.

Time off for safety representatives

According to Regulation 4(2) of the SRSC Regulations and Regulation 7(1)(b) of the HSCE Regulations a trade union safety representative or a representative of employee safety is entitled to time off, with normal or average pay,[76] during working hours to perform his or her functions and to undergo such training as may be reasonable in the circumstances. In relation to trade union safety representatives elected or appointed under the SSRC Regulations, regard has to be had for the provisions of an approved code of practice. In *White v Pressed Steel Fisher*[77] the EAT held that if employers provide an adequate in-house course, it is not necessarily reasonable for them to be required to grant paid time off for safety representatives to attend a union course. The approved Code of Practice produced by the HSE recommends that as soon as possible after their appointment union safety representatives should be permitted time off with pay for basic training approved by the TUC or the independent union which appointed the representatives. Further training, similarly approved, should be undertaken where the safety representative has special responsibilities or where such training is necessary to meet changes in circumstances or relevant legislation. Aggrieved safety representatives or representatives of employee safety can complain to an employment tribunal that their employer has failed to permit them to take time off or that they have not been paid in accordance with the Regulations. If the complaint is well-founded, the tribunal must make a declaration and may make an award of compensation.[78]

SAFETY COMMITTEES

Where at least two union safety representatives submit a written request, employers must establish a safety committee – but before doing so they must consult the union safety representatives who made the request and the representatives of recognised trade unions. Such a committee must be formed within three months of the request being made, and a notice must be posted stating the composition of the committee and the workplaces covered.[79] Under section 2(7) HASAWA 1974, the function of safety committees is to keep under review the measures taken to ensure the health and safety at work of employees.

PROTECTION AGAINST DETRIMENT OR DISMISSAL

It should be noted that the Code of Practice advises employers, recognised unions and union safety representatives to make full and proper use of existing industrial relations machinery to reach the degree of agreement necessary to achieve the purpose of the SRSC Regulations and to resolve any differences. However, where an employee suffers a detriment short of dismissal as a result of certain health and safety activities, he or she may bring a claim under section 44 of the Employment Rights Act 1996. The remedies available for infringement of section 44 mirror those available for detriment on trade union grounds (see Chapter 18). If the employee is dismissed because of these activities, the dismissal is automatically unfair under section 100 ERA.

CASE STUDY

SHILLITO v VAN LEER

In *Shillito v Van Leer*,[80] an employee who was a safety representative for one production line became involved, in a belligerent way, in safety issues affecting another production line, for which the employee was not a representative. The employee was disciplined and given a formal warning. A complaint to the tribunal about suffering a detriment failed because the person involved was not a safety representative in the area concerned.

GOODWIN v CABLETEL

In *Goodwin v Cabletel*,[81] Mr Goodwin was a construction manager who had responsibility for health and safety matters on site. He was unhappy with one subcontractor and took an aggressive approach. The manager's employer, however, wished to be more conciliatory. After a number of acrimonious meetings Mr Goodwin was demoted, upon which he resigned and claimed constructive dismissal. The employment tribunal held that his claim failed because section 100 gave protection against dismissal only when carrying out health and safety duties – not a dismissal arising from the way in which a person carried them out. But the EAT held that this was the wrong approach and that protection under section 100 could also extend to a dismissal because of the way the duties were carried out. That was not to say that 'every act, however malicious or irrelevant' would be protected!

REFLECTIVE QUESTION

Does the duty to inform and consult seen throughout this chapter have any real substance? Should employees be given more power in relation to major decisions affecting their jobs?

KEY LEARNING POINTS

- Community-scale undertakings with at least 1,000 employees within the EU and at least 150 employees in two Member States must establish a European works council.
- A company that establishes itself as a *Societas Europaea* is required to negotiate an information and consultation procedure with representatives of employees.
- The Information and Consultation Regulations 2004 require the establishment of information and consultation procedures on an on-going basis in all UK organisations employing 50 or more people.
- Mandatory requirements to consult, in the United Kingdom, in specific circumstances include matters in relation to health and safety, transfers of undertakings and collective redundancies.

REFERENCES

1. **This chapter contains extracts from or close paraphrasing of legislation, and explanatory memoranda to that legislation, which is on the opsi.gov.uk website (and its successor) and is subject to crown copyright. It also contains other public sector information. The reproduction of this material here is licensed under the open government licence v1.0.**
2. See *Junk v Kühnel* Case C-188/03 (2005) IRLR 310
3. SI 1999/3323; the Regulations are very lengthy, so what follows can only be regarded as a summary of the main points
4. Directive 2009/38/EC
5. Article 1(1) EWC Directive
6. Article 2(a) and (c) EWC Directive
7. Regulation 2 TICE Regulations 1999
8. Defined in Regulation 2 TICE Regulations as a person who represents employees in the context of an information and consultation procedure
9. Directive 2001/86/EC
10. SI 2009/2401
11. Directive 2003/72/EC
12. OJ L80/29 23.3.02
13. SI 2004/3426
14. Case study published by DTI March 2007, subject to Crown Copyright, reproduced here under the Open Government Licence v.1.0: http://webarchive.nationalarchives. gov.uk/+/http://www.berr.gov.uk/employment/employment-legislation/ice/ information-consultation/page37920.html [accessed 17 October 2010]
15. (2006) IRLR 592
16. *Amicus v Macmillan Publishers Ltd* (2007) IRLR 885
17. *Amicus v Macmillan Publishers Ltd* (2007) IRLR 378
18. CIPD (2001). Response of the CIPD to the government's consultation on implementation of the EU Directive on information and consultation
19. Section 188(1) TULRCA 1992 as amended by the Collective Redundancies and Transfers of Undertakings (Protection of Employment) (Amendment) Regulations 1999, SI 1999/1925
20. (2007) IRLR 931
21. Section 188(1A) TULRCA 1992
22. Section 188(1B) TULRCA 1992
23. Section 188A TULRCA 1992
24. Section 188(7B) TULRCA 1992
25. Section 195 TULRCA 1992

26 (2000) IRLR 636

27 *Hardy v Tourism South East* (2005) IRLR 243

28 Section 282(1) TULRCA 1992

29 (1978) IRLR 366

30 *Rockfon A/S v Specialarbejderforbundet i Danmark acting for Nielsen and others* (1996) IRLR 168

31 See *Middlesbrough B.C. v TGWU* (2002) IRLR 332

32 *UK Coal Mining Ltd v National Union of Mineworkers* (2008) IRLR 4

33 Directive 98/59

34 (2005) IRLR 310

35 (2005) IRLR 920

36 Section 188(4) TULRCA 1992 and *GMB and AMICUS v Beloit Walmsley Ltd* (2004) IRLR 18

37 (2011) IRLR 4

38 See *GMB v Rankin* (1992) IRLR 514

39 See *APAC v Kirwin* (1978) IRLR 318

40 (1978) IRLR 20

41 See *UCATT v Rooke & Son Ltd* (1978) IRLR 204

42 Section 188(7A) TULRCA 1992

43 Section 189(1) and (5) TULRCA 1992

44 Section 189(4) TULRCA 1992 as amended by the CRTUPEA Regulations 1999

45 The period runs from the proposed date of the first dismissals: see *E Green Ltd v ASTMS and AUEW* (1984) IRLR 135

46 Section 190(2) TULRCA 1992

47 (2004) IRLR 400, applied by the EAT in *Smith v Cherry Lewis Ltd* (2005) IRLR 86

48 Section 191(1–3) TULRCA 1992

49 Section 192 TULRCA 1992

50 See *Howlett Marine Services Ltd v Bowlam* (2001) IRLR 201; the original award is often made long after the protected period has expired, so in such cases the tribunal must always allow a late claim

51 Section 193 TULRCA 1992

52 See section 193(7) TULRCA 1992

53 Transfer of Undertakings (Protection of Employment) Regulations 2006

54 (1987) IRLR 373

55 Rather than 'as soon as measures are envisaged and *in any event* long enough before the transfer'

56 *Royal Mail Group v Communication Workers Union* (2009) IRLR 1046
57 *Amicus v City Building* (2009) IRLR 253
58 (2003) IRLR 266
59 (2011) IRLR 196
60 *Sweetin v Coral Racing* (2006) IRLR 252
61 http://www.rcn.org.uk/support/the_working_environment/health_and_safety/ ?a=195436 [accessed 17 October 2010]. This material is subject to copyright held by the RCN, whose permission to reproduce here a slightly amended version of the case study is gratefully acknowledged
62 Directive 89/391/EC
63 For exceptions see Regulation 5(3) HSCE Regulations 1996
64 Section 28(8)(b) HASAWA 1974
65 In this context 'recognition' means recognition for the purposes of collective bargaining. See Regulation 2 SRSC Regulations and *Cleveland County Council v Springett* (1985) IRLR 131
66 Section 2(6) HASAWA 1974
67 Regulation 4A SRSC Regulations
68 Regulation 5(2) of HSCE 1996. 'Representatives of employee safety' are defined in Regulation 4(1)(b) HSCE Regulations 1996
69 Regulation 4(2) HSCE Regulations 1996
70 Regulation 4(3) HSCE Regulations 1996
71 Regulation 3(4) HSCE Regulations 1996
72 Defined by Regulation 2(1) SRSC Regulations
73 Regulation 6 HSCE Regulations 1996
74 See Regulation 7(1)(a) HSCE Regulations 1996
75 For definitions see Regulations 6(3) SRSC Regulations
76 See the Schedule to the SRSC Regulations 1977 and the HSCE Regulations 1996
77 (1980) IRLR 176
78 Regulation 11 SRSC Regulations and Schedule 2 HSCE Regulations 1996
79 Regulation 9 SRSC Regulations. See also the Guidance notes on safety committees
80 (1997) IRLR 495
81 (1997) IRLR 665

EXPLORE FURTHER

Reading

- Davies, A. (2009) *Perspectives on Labour Law.* Oxford University Press, Chapter 10
- Deakin, S. and Morris, G. (2012) *Labour Law.* Hart, Chapter 9
- Smith, I. and Baker, A. (2010) *Smith & Wood's Employment Law.* Butterworths, Chapters 8 and 9

Websites

- Advisory, Conciliation and Arbitration Service www.acas.org.uk
- Chartered Institute of Personnel and Development www.cipd.co.uk
- Department for Business Innovation and Skills www.bis.gov.uk
- DirectGov – Employment www.direct.gov.uk
- Trades Union Congress www.tuc.org.uk

Online case studies

- On transnational EWC consultation, see the study on British Airways, EWC Case Studies published by the European Foundation for the Improvement of Living and Working Conditions, July 2003: http://www.eurofound.europa.eu/ pubdocs/ 2005/711/en/1/ef05711en.pdf
- On national information and consultation, in addition to the case study for Coors Brewers which appears in the chapter, there are a number of other short case studies relating to other companies: see http://webarchive. nationalarchives.gov.uk/+/http://www.berr.gov.uk/employment/employment-legislation/ice/information-consultation/page37920.html
- On safety representatives, in addition to the RCN case study which appears in the chapter, there are a number of other studies of RCN safety representatives: see http://www.rcn.org.uk/support/the_working_ environment/health_and_safety/ safety_representatives

CHAPTER 18

Trade Unions and Collective Bargaining

CHAPTER OVERVIEW

In this chapter we first consider the legal definition of a trade union, and describe the mechanism by which a union can obtain a certificate of independence. We also consider the question of recognition, including the statutory right to recognition of trade unions, and the duty placed upon employers to disclose information for the purpose of collective bargaining. We consider what protection trade unionists receive to stop them being discriminated against by employers. We then go on to consider the law on industrial action. An individual who takes part in a strike is likely to be acting in breach of his or her contract of employment because it is a basic contractual obligation of the employee to be willing to serve. Participating in other forms of industrial action short of a strike, such as a 'work to rule' or a 'go slow', will also often constitute a breach of the employment contract. But in this chapter we shall be concentrating on the liability more of those who organise industrial action than of those who participate in it.

LEARNING OUTCOMES

After studying this chapter[1] you will be able to:

- understand and explain the legal principles that apply in respect of the law relating to trade unions, such as the rights of individual trade unionists not to experience discrimination and collective trade union freedoms such as the freedom to take industrial action
- advise colleagues about such matters as a trade union's right to seek recognition from an employer if it has sufficient workforce support and the risk of compulsory recognition if negotiations are not successful; about how industrial action may easily become unlawful, and the remedies that may be sought against a union if this occurs.

TRADE UNIONS AND CERTIFICATES OF INDEPENDENCE

What are trade unions and what do they do? Trade unions are organised groups of workers which represent their members' interests in negotiations or situations of conflict with their employers. The trade union movement developed in the nineteenth century to try to obtain better pay and working conditions for the union members. Unions faced fierce opposition from employers and generally hostility from the legal system but managed to survive and grow. By the 1960s and 1970s unions had become a powerful industrial and political force, which no government could afford to ignore. Trade unions in the UK are now much less powerful and important players than they once were, and their freedom to organise industrial action (see below) has been significantly restricted in recent years. But unions are still seen as having a key part to play in making the employment relationship a more equal one.

The legal definition of a trade union is found in section 1 of the Trade Union and Labour Relations (Consolidation) Act (TULRCA) 1992. According to this definition a trade union means an organisation, whether permanent or temporary, which consists either:

- wholly or mainly of workers whose principal purposes include the regulation of relations between workers and employers (or employers' associations), or
- wholly or mainly of constituent or affiliated organisations with those purposes, or representatives of such organisations,

and in either case is an organisation whose principal purposes include the regulation of relations between workers and employers (or employers' associations) or include the regulation of relations between its constituent or affiliated organisations.

This definition covers not only individual and confederated unions and the TUC, but also the union side of a joint negotiating committee. Section 10 TULRCA 1992 states that a trade union 'shall not be, or be treated as if it were, a body corporate' – ie a trade union is not a company – yet it is capable of making contracts, suing and being sued in its own name, and being prosecuted. However, in *EETPU v Times Newspapers* [2] it was held that the union could not sue for libel because it did not have the necessary legal personality to be protected by an action for defamation. All property belonging to a trade union must be vested in trustees, and any judgment, order or award is enforceable against the property held in trust.[3]

'LISTED' TRADE UNIONS

Trade unions still have a significant role in industrial relations and in society at large and therefore employment law gives important rights to trade unions and their members.

Many, though not all, of these rights are given only to unions and members of unions which have been given a Certificate of Independence by the Certification Officer. 'Independence' in this context means being independent of the employer – ie a union which exists to represent the interests of its members, not one that is in a cosy relationship with the employer.

Before a union can be certified as independent it must first be 'listed' by the Certification Officer. The Certification Officer maintains a list of trade unions, and a trade union which submits the appropriate fee, a copy of its rules, a list of officers, the address of its head office and the name under which it is known may apply for inclusion on this list.[4] A listed union is entitled to a certificate stating that its name is included on the list, and such listing is a prerequisite for obtaining a Certificate of Independence. The Certification Officer makes copies of the lists of trade unions and employers' associations available for public inspection and must remove the name of an organisation if requested to do so by that organisation or if he or she is satisfied that the organisation has ceased to exist.[5] Any organisation that is aggrieved by the refusal of the Certification Officer to enter its name on the relevant list, or by a decision to remove its name, may appeal to the EAT on a question of fact or law.[6]

CERTIFICATION OF INDEPENDENCE FOR UNIONS

A trade union whose name is on the relevant list can apply to the Certification Officer for a certificate that it is independent. The Certification Officer is responsible for keeping a record of all applications and must decide whether the applicant union is independent or not.[7] Section 5 TULRCA 1992 deems a trade union to be independent if:

- it is not under the domination or control of an employer or a group of employers or of one or more employers' associations, and
- it is not liable to interference by an employer or any such group or association, arising out of the provision of financial or material support or by any other means whatsoever, tending towards such control.

A certificate constitutes conclusive evidence for all purposes that the union is independent. If a question arises in any proceedings as to whether a trade union is independent and there is no certificate in force and no refusal, withdrawal or cancellation of a certificate recorded, the body before whom the issue arose cannot decide the matter but may refer it to the Certification Officer.[8]

Employer control of or domination over a union

Over the years, certain criteria have evolved for assessing whether a union is under the domination or control of an employer.

CASE STUDY

MONK STAFF ASSOCIATION v CO AND ASTMS[9]

This staff association applied for a Certificate of Independence. The application, and two subsequent ones, were rejected because the Certification Officer concluded that it was not independent. Factors that influenced the decision were that all the association's officers and members were employed by the company, and because the company still decided individual salaries, it had the power to influence officers of the association; the association was also dependent upon company facilities.

The staff association appealed against this refusal to the EAT. In the EAT it was confirmed that the following matters should be considered:

- the union's history (was it originally the employer's creation?)
- its organisation and structure (is it likely to be controlled by senior members of management?)
- its finances (to what extent is it subsidised by the employer?)

- the extent of employer-provided facilities (are there free premises, etc?)
- its collective bargaining record.

Here there had been significant changes since the Certification Officer investigated the matter, including the appointment of an independent consultant/negotiator. The question of independence should be decided on all the evidence available and not confined to the material that was before the Certification Officer. The EAT allowed the appeal and held that the staff association was entitled to a Certificate of Independence.

Discussion point

Why is so much importance placed on independence? Should the same legal rights not be given to all trade unions and their members?

As regards 'liable to interference', the Court of Appeal ruled in *Certification Officer v Squibb UK Staff Association* [10] that the Certification Officer is not required to assess the likelihood of interference by the employer. The Certification Officer's interpretation of the words as meaning 'vulnerable to interference' was the correct one – ie the degree of risk is irrelevant so long as it is recognisable and not insignificant. This interpretation was applied by the EAT in *GCSF v Certification Officer* [11] where the Government Communications Staff Federation was denied a certificate because its continued existence depended on the approval of the GCHQ director. The EAT held that the Certification Officer had been correct to deny the Staff Federation a certificate.

Finally, it is worth documenting the major advantages that accrue to independent trade unions:

- If recognised, they have the right to appoint safety representatives (see Chapter 17).
- If recognised, their representatives are entitled to receive information for collective bargaining purposes (see below).
- If recognised, their representatives may be consulted in respect of redundancies and transfers of undertakings (see Chapter 17).
- If recognised, their officials can take time off for union activities (see Chapter 10).
- Employees cannot have action taken against them because they seek to join, have joined, or have taken part in the activities of such a union. Interim relief is available to members who have been dismissed.

RECOGNITION

An independent trade union must be recognised by the employer in order to enjoy a number of statutory rights. When an employer is said to recognise a union for collective bargaining purposes, this means that the employer agrees to bargain with a union on various matters such as pay rates and hours of work. By agreeing to bargain with the union on such matters, the employer is recognising the union as the representative of its members. The legal definition of recognition in TULRCA[12] is

> Recognition in relation to a trade union means the recognition of the union by an employer, or two or more associated employers, to any extent for the purpose of collective bargaining.

Collective bargaining means negotiations relating to or connected with one or more of the matters specified in section 178(2) TULRCA 1992.[13] These matters cover, for example, terms and conditions of employment and the engagement of workers or termination of their employment.

The court or tribunal may find that the employer has *expressly* agreed to recognition, or it may find that there has been an *implied* recognition agreement between the union and the employer (but see statutory rights to recognition below) to negotiate on one or more of the matters listed in section 178(2) TULRCA 1992. For agreement to be implied there must be clear and unequivocal conduct over a period of time.[14] Thus although recognition has been inferred from consultations on discipline and facilities for union representatives despite the absence of formal agreement,[15] a discussion on wages which took place on a particular occasion was held to be insufficient to establish recognition, particularly when the employer's attitude was one of refusing to bargain.[16] Neither the fact that the union has a right of representation on a national body responsible for negotiating pay[17] nor the fact that the employers' association to which the employer belongs recognises the union will, by itself, constitute recognition by the employer.[18]

STATUTORY RECOGNITION PROCEDURES

Historically, recognition was a matter for negotiation between unions and employers, apart from a period in the 1970s when there were statutory provisions. So if an employer refused to give recognition, there was no legal recourse available to the union.

Under the Employment Relations Act 1999 the government restored a legal right to trade union recognition for collective bargaining purposes if the necessary conditions are fulfilled. This is now found in Schedule A1 to TULRCA 1992. The procedures are aimed at getting employers and trade unions to agree a recognition arrangement. A recognition order which compels an employer to recognise a union is intended to be the last resort.

The key points of the statutory procedure are:

- The procedure is only available to an independent union (see above).
- It only applies where an employer employs at least 21 workers.
- Statutory recognition covers only pay, hours and holidays, unless the two sides agree to extend the coverage.
- The union first makes a request for recognition to the employer. If the employer agrees, that is the end of the procedure.

- If the employer and the union do not reach agreement, the union may apply to the CAC (Central Arbitration Committee) for a declaration (an order) for recognition.
- The CAC will only admit the application by the union for consideration if it decides that
  - at least 10% of the 'bargaining unit' (the group of workers which the union will be representing) are members of the union, *and*
  - a majority of the relevant group of workers would be likely to be in favour of recognition.
- The CAC will help the parties to agree on the appropriate 'bargaining unit', or if necessary, will decide this itself.
- The CAC will make a declaration in favour of recognition – ie order the employer to recognise the union – if
  - *either* a majority of workers already belong to the trade union (unless one of three situations applies)
  - *or*, on the holding of a secret ballot, a majority of those actually voting, who must also constitute at least 40% of all those entitled to vote, vote in favour of recognition.
- If the CAC orders recognition, the employer and the union are given time to agree their bargaining method – ie the procedure to be followed. For example, when will negotiations take place? Who will represent both sides? What will happen if no agreement can be reached in the negotiations?
- If the employer and union cannot agree a bargaining method, the CAC will impose one, enforceable in court as a legally binding contract.
- Recognition under the statute cannot be ended ('derecognition') for three years; after that period it is possible for derecognition to take place.

REFLECTIVE QUESTION

Do you think that the approach in the statutory procedure of compulsion only as a last resort is the best approach?

CASE STUDY

R v CENTRAL ARBITRATION COMMITTEE[19]

Two trade unions sought recognition on behalf of a group of workers working for one employer. The employer refused the request, and so the unions made an application under the statutory recognition procedure.

The CAC arranged a secret ballot and appointed a qualified independent person to conduct it. The result of the ballot was that a majority of those voting supported recognition, but the numbers in favour fell short of the 40% total by four votes.

The unions complained that not all workers had received ballot papers. After an enquiry by the CAC it was concluded that five workers who would have voted in favour of recognition had not been given sufficient opportunity to vote. The CAC ordered the ballot to be re-run.

The employer challenged this and stated that the CAC did not have the power to go behind the result of the ballot. The Court of Appeal, however, concluded that the CAC did have jurisdiction to investigate and, if necessary, to annul the result. The CAC had control over all the other stages and Parliament could not have intended that the CAC would be deprived of the power to investigate, and act upon, a ballot that might have been unreliable.

The CAC will not accept an application if it is satisfied that there is already a union recognised on behalf of any of the workers in the bargaining unit.

CASE STUDY

R v CENTRAL ARBITRATION COMMITTEE[20]

The National Union of Journalists (NUJ) had a significant number of members amongst the sports division of Mirror Group Newspapers. The union had a meeting with the management to discuss recognition and became hopeful that an agreement could be reached whereby they could show that they had the support of the majority of the journalists concerned.

In the meantime the employers were also approached by a breakaway union called the British Association of Journalists (BAJ), which had, at most, just one member working in the sports division. The BAJ was an independent union, but was not affiliated to the TUC. The result was that the employers recognised the BAJ's exclusive bargaining rights to represent its journalists in the sports division.

The NUJ submitted an application to the CAC for statutory recognition. The employer opposed the application on the grounds that there was another trade union already recognised for collective bargaining purposes, even though at that stage there had been no negotiations on pay or conditions. The union argued that because this negotiation had not taken place, the collective agreement was 'not yet in force'.

The Court of Appeal held that the agreement was in force, within the natural meaning of those words. Thus the NUJ was unable to progress its claim for recognition.

DISCLOSURE OF INFORMATION FOR COLLECTIVE BARGAINING

In order to help a trade union to bargain more effectively with the employer, the law provides that the employer must disclose certain information to an independent union which it recognises. Section 181 of TULRCA 1992 states that for the purposes of all the stages of collective bargaining between employers and representatives of recognised independent trade unions, employers have a duty to disclose to those representatives, on request, all such information relating to their undertakings as is in their possession or that of any associated employer which is both:[21]

- information without which the union representatives would be to a material extent impeded in carrying on such collective bargaining, and
- information which it would be in accordance with good industrial relations practice that they should disclose.

The phrase 'of all the stages' means that information can be sought in order to prepare a claim, although it must relate to matters in respect of which the union is recognised. In *R v CAC ex parte BTP Tioxide* [22] the High Court held that the CAC had misdirected itself in concluding that the union was entitled to information relating to a job evaluation scheme in respect of which it had no bargaining rights but only the right to represent its members in re-evaluation appeals.

In essence, for information to be disclosed under these provisions it must be both relevant and important. Although each case must be judged on its merits, unions may be entitled to information about groups not covered for collective bargaining purposes. Thus in Award 80/40 the CAC held that information about a productivity scheme for management not covered by the union was relevant and important to negotiations over a scheme for technical staff because of the similarity of the work of some employees within both groups.

'GOOD PRACTICE' AND THE ACAS CODE

In determining what constitutes 'good industrial relations practice' in section 181, attention must be paid to the ACAS Code of Practice,[23] although other evidence is not to be excluded.[24] Thus unions may seek to demonstrate good practice by referring to the approaches taken by comparable employers. To decide what information is relevant, negotiators are advised to take account of the subject matter of the negotiations and the issues raised during them, the level at which negotiations take place, the size of the company and its type of business.[25] There is no list of items that should be disclosed in all circumstances, but the following examples of information which could be relevant in certain situations are given as a guide:[26]

- pay and benefits
- conditions of service
- manpower
- performance
- finance.

This is not an exhaustive list and other items may be relevant in particular negotiations. The underlying philosophy of the Code is that employers and unions should endeavour to reach a joint understanding on how the disclosure provisions can be implemented most effectively: 'In particular, the parties should endeavour to reach an understanding on what information could most appropriately be provided on a regular basis.'[27]

The duty to disclose is subject to the exceptions detailed in section 182 TULRCA 1992. Employers are not required to disclose:

a) any information the disclosure of which would be against the interests of national security
b) any information which could not be disclosed without contravening other legislation
c) any information which has been communicated to the employer in confidence
d) any information relating specifically to an individual unless he or she has consented to its disclosure
e) any information the disclosure of which would cause substantial injury to the employer's undertaking for reasons other than its effect on collective bargaining
f) information obtained by the employer for the purpose of bringing or defending any legal proceedings.

As regards **(e)**, paragraph 14 of the Code offers some examples of information which, if disclosed in particular circumstances, might cause substantial injury. This would cover such matters as cost information on individual products, detailed analysis of proposed investment, marketing or pricing policies, price quotas and the make-up of tender prices. Further guidance is offered in paragraph 15:

> Substantial injury may occur if, for example, certain customers would be lost to competitors, or suppliers would refuse to supply necessary materials, or the ability to raise funds to finance the company would be seriously impaired as a result of disclosing certain information. The burden of establishing a claim that disclosure of certain information would cause substantial injury lies with the employer.

REMEDY FOR FAILURE TO DISCLOSE

A union which feels that its representatives have not received the information to which they are entitled can complain in writing to the CAC, and if the CAC is of the opinion that the complaint is 'reasonably likely to be settled by conciliation', it must refer it to ACAS. Where no reference to ACAS is made or no settlement or withdrawal is achieved, the CAC must hear the complaint, make a declaration stating whether it is well-founded, wholly or in part, and give reasons for its finding. If the complaint is upheld, the declaration will specify the information in respect of which the CAC believed the complaint to be well-founded, the date on which the employer refused or failed to disclose information, and the period within which the employer ought to disclose the information specified.[28]

If the employer still fails to disclose the information when the time-limit is reached, a further complaint may be made and the union may also make a specific claim for better terms and conditions – eg a pay rise. If the CAC decides that the employer is in breach of the order to disclose, it may make an award – eg order the pay rise to be granted. These new terms and conditions are then incorporated into the employees' individual employment contracts (see Chapter 2) and can be enforced in the ordinary courts like any other term of the contract. But we should note that the CAC is not given the power to force the employer to disclose the information!

REFLECTIVE QUESTION

Should the CAC have the power to compel the employer to disclose the requested information?

THE LEGAL ENFORCEABILITY OF COLLECTIVE AGREEMENTS

In this section we are concerned with the legal enforceability of collective agreements between employers and trade unions and not the effect of such agreements on individual contracts of employment. It is important to remember that the legal status of the arrangements made between the employer and the union has no bearing on the relationship between the employer and his or her workers. The mechanisms by which the terms of a collective agreement may be enforced between the parties to a contract of employment have been described in Chapter 2.

A collective agreement is statutorily defined as any agreement or arrangement made by or on behalf of one or more trade unions[29] and one or more employers, or employers' associations, which relates to one or more of the matters mentioned in section 178(2) TULRCA 1992.[30] A collective agreement is conclusively presumed not to have been intended by the parties to be a legally enforceable contract unless the agreement is in writing and contains a provision which states that the parties intend the agreement to be a legally enforceable contract,[31] or the agreement has been specified by the CAC as a result of the statutory recognition procedures. Equally, the parties may declare that one or more parts only of an agreement are intended to be legally enforceable.[32] Nevertheless, it should not be assumed that a collective agreement which declares the parties' intention to create legal relations is necessarily legally binding, because the agreement's wording might mean that it is too vague or uncertain to be enforced as a contract.

REFLECTIVE QUESTION

Why is it the UK approach that collective agreements should not generally be legally binding?

DISCRIMINATION ON THE GROUNDS OF TRADE UNION MEMBERSHIP OR ACTIVITIES

We saw in Chapter 6 that in relation to discrimination law under the Equality Act 2010 a person is protected against discrimination because of a protected characteristic at the hiring stage, during employment, at the termination of employment, and even sometimes once employment has ended. Similarly, trade unionists, or those who wish to join a union, are given protection under TULRCA 1992 at the hiring and termination stages as well as during employment. 'Blacklisting' individuals in relation to trade union membership or activities is also unlawful.

UNLAWFUL REFUSAL OF EMPLOYMENT ON GROUNDS RELATED TO UNION MEMBERSHIP

Section 137(1) of TULRCA 1992 makes it unlawful to refuse employment to people because

- they are or are not members of a trade union
- they refuse to accept a requirement that they become members or cease to be members, or a requirement that they make payments as an alternative to joining.[33]

As we see, the section gives protection equally to those who wish to belong to a union and to those who do not wish to belong. The protection for those who do not wish to belong is also given by sections 146 and 152 – see below.

REFLECTIVE QUESTION

When might a person need protection against discrimination because he or she does not wish to join a trade union?

Section 138 makes it unlawful for an agency which finds employment for workers, or supplies employers with workers, to refuse its services to people because they are or are not union members or are unwilling to accept a condition or requirement of the type mentioned in section 137(1)(b).

Complaints about unlawful refusal of employment

A person wishing to make a claim under the above sections must normally present the claim to an employment tribunal within three months of the date of the refusal of employment/services. If the claim is upheld, the tribunal must make a declaration and may

- order compensation, which may include damages for injury to feelings
- make a recommendation that the respondent (the would-be employer or agency) takes such action as the tribunal thinks practicable to obviate or reduce the effect on the complainant of the conduct to which the claim relates. If the recommendation is not complied with, any award of compensation can be increased, although the total award cannot be more than the compensatory award for unfair dismissal (see Chapter 15: this is £72,300 in 2012).

SUBJECTING TO DETRIMENT SHORT OF DISMISSAL

Section 146 TULRCA 1992 gives employees the right not to be subjected to any detriment as an individual by any act, or any deliberate failure to act, by an employer if the act or failure takes place for the sole or main purpose of:

- preventing or deterring them from being or seeking to become members of an independent trade union or penalising them for doing so
- preventing or deterring them from taking part in the activities of an independent trade union or from making use of trade union services at any appropriate time, or penalising them for doing so
- compelling them to become members of any trade union or of a particular trade union or of one of a number of particular trade unions
- enforcing a requirement that in the event of their failure to become, or their ceasing to remain, members of any trade union or a particular trade union or one of a number of particular trade unions, they must make one or more payments. For this purpose, any deduction from remuneration which is attributable to the employee's failure to become, or his or her ceasing to be, a trade union member will be treated as a detriment.

As regards the requirement that the action must be taken against an employee as an individual, the Court of Appeal has offered the following guidance:[34]

> If an employee is selected for discrimination because of some characteristic which he shares with others, such as membership of a particular trade union, then the action is … taken against him as an individual.

Thus derecognition of an individual shop steward by an employer can be action taken against the shop steward as an individual, rather than action taken against the trade union.[35]

The word 'purpose' connotes an object that the employer seeks to achieve, and the purpose of an action must not be confused with its effect. So when a full-time union official was turned down for promotion, the Court of Appeal accepted that section 146 had not been infringed because the employer's purpose had been to ensure that only those with sufficient managerial experience were promoted.[36] By way of contrast, when a full-time branch secretary was offered promotion without the usual salary increase, it was held that the employer's purpose was to deter the individual from engaging in union activities.[37] It is clear that employees have the right to join any independent trade union of their choice.[38] Thus in *Carlson*'s case[39] the EAT decided that the denial of a car-park permit to a member of a non-recognised independent trade union constituted a form of penalising outlawed by the section. In this context 'penalising' was held to mean 'subjecting to a disadvantage'. For the purposes of this section and section 152 (see below), 'trade union services' are those made available by virtue of union membership, and 'making use' includes consenting to the raising of a matter by the union on the member's behalf.[40]

DISMISSALS RELATING TO TRADE UNION MEMBERSHIP

According to section 152(1) TULRCA 1992 a dismissal is unfair if the reason for it (or if more than one, the principal reason) was that the employee:

- was or proposed to become a member of an independent trade union
- had taken (or proposed to take) part in the activities of an independent trade union or had used (or proposed to use) union services at an appropriate time
- was not a member of any trade union or of a particular trade union, or had refused or proposed to refuse to become or to remain a member
- had failed to accept an offer in contravention of section 145A or B (see above).

Section 152(3) TULRCA 1992 states that dismissals are to be treated as falling within the third bullet-point above if one of the reasons for them was that employees:

- refused (or proposed to refuse) to comply with a requirement that in the event of their failure to become, or their ceasing to remain, a trade union member they must make some kind of payment
- objected, or proposed to object, to the operation of a provision under which their employer was entitled to deduct sums from their remuneration if they failed to become or remain a trade union member.

It would seem that if an employee is dismissed because of her or his proposal to leave an independent trade union, that will be unfair, even though the proposal is conditional on something occurring or not occurring.[41]

The usual qualifying period for claiming unfair dismissal does not apply if the reason, or principal reason, for dismissal was one of those specified in section 152 TULRCA 1992.[42] This being so, the burden is on employees to prove that their dismissal related to trade union membership. However, where the question of jurisdiction does not arise, the only burden on the employee is to produce some evidence that casts doubt upon the employer's reason.[43]

Where employees allege that their dismissals were unfair by virtue of section 152 TULRCA 1992, they can seek interim relief.[44] This is a remedy which puts the employee back in employment with the employer on a temporary basis until the full hearing of the section 152 claim. It is available where employees present their claims within seven days of the effective date of termination and, where the claim is that the dismissal was for union membership or activities, they submit written certificates signed by an authorised union official which state that there appears to be reasonable grounds for supposing that the reason for dismissal was the one alleged in the complaints. The tribunal must hear such an application as soon as practicable,[45] and if it thinks it 'likely' (ie there is 'a pretty good chance'[46]) that the complainant will be found to have been unfairly dismissed by virtue of section 152 TULRCA 1992, it must ask whether the employer is willing to re-employ[47] the employee until the hearing. If the employer is willing to re-employ the employee, the tribunal should make an order to that effect. Where the employer fails to attend the hearing or is unwilling to re-employ, the tribunal must make an order for the continuation of the employee's contract of employment. In essence, this order amounts to suspension on full pay.[48]

REFLECTIVE QUESTION

Why is interim relief a valuable temporary remedy – and should it be available more widely in claims of unfair dismissal?

Where there has been pressure on the employer by a third party (usually a trade union) to dismiss an employee for non-membership of a trade union, section 160 TULRCA 1992 enables either the employer or the dismissed employee to request from the tribunal that the party who applied the pressure be 'joined' – ie be brought in as a party with either the employer or the employee to the unfair dismissal proceedings. This request must be granted by the tribunal if it is made before the hearing but can be refused if it is made after that time. No such request can be entertained after a remedy has been awarded. If a third party is joined, and the unfair dismissal claim succeeds, the tribunal may

- *either* order the third party to pay all the compensation
- *or* order that it be paid partly by the employer and partly by the third party, as the tribunal considers just and equitable.

BLACKLISTING

Blacklisting of trade unionists is where information is compiled on people relating to their union membership or activities which is then used to discriminate against them. For instance, in recent years such lists were widely used by companies in the construction industry where around 3,000 individuals were so listed.[49]

Under the Employment Relations Act 1999 (Blacklists) Regulations 2010[50] it is unlawful:

- to compile, disseminate and use a 'prohibited list'
- to refuse employment, dismiss an employee or cause detriment to a worker for a reason related to a prohibited list
- for an employment agency to refuse a service to a worker for a reason related to a prohibited list.

A claim for a breach of the Regulations may be brought in an employment tribunal or the courts.

INDUSTRIAL ACTION

THE ECONOMIC TORTS

Trade unions and their members and officials would be likely, in the course of taking industrial action, to commit a number of torts, particularly the economic torts. A 'tort' is a common-law wrong which is neither a crime nor a breach of contract. Examples of torts are negligence and trespass. What are called economic torts are those torts which interfere with someone's trade or business. They are:[51]

- inducing a breach of contract

- causing economic loss by unlawful means
- conspiracy.

The definitions of the economic torts are complex and discussion of them is beyond the scope of this book,[52] but it will be seen, for example, that when a trade union calls on members to come out on strike, and so break their individual contracts of employment, it is likely to be committing the tort of inducing a breach of contract.

The possible legal consequences of industrial action are summarised in Figure 6 and are explained in the remainder of the chapter.

Figure 6 The liability of a trade union for economic torts committed during industrial action

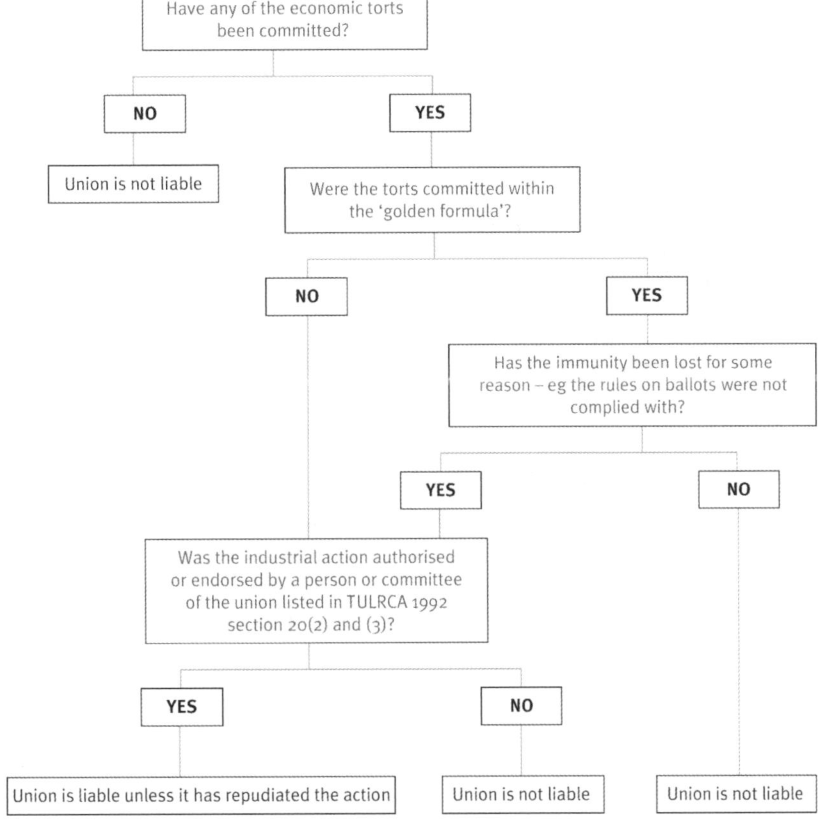

THE GOLDEN FORMULA

In order to preserve the fundamental freedom of workers to take industrial action, the legislation provides that a person will not be legally liable for committing the economic torts mentioned above if these torts were committed 'in contemplation or furtherance of a **trade dispute**'.[53] These words – 'in contemplation or furtherance of a trade dispute' – have become known as the 'golden formula'. This immunity from liability applies to a trade union as well as to individual officers and members of the union. If the industrial action is not within the 'golden formula', it will be relatively easy for an employer to show that one of the economic torts is being committed, and to succeed in its claim against the union.

The meaning of 'trade dispute'

The definition of 'trade dispute' is found in section 244 of TULRCA. It must be a dispute between 'workers' and their employer which relates wholly or mainly to one of a number of listed matters, such as the workers' terms and conditions of employment and the engagement and suspension or termination of workers.

CASE STUDY

UNIVERSITY COLLEGE HOSPITAL NHS TRUST v UNISON

In *University College London Hospital NHS Trust v Unison*[54] the union gained an overwhelming majority in favour of strike action in support of a demand for employment guarantees associated with the building of a new hospital under the Private Finance Initiative. This would have involved the transfer of some workers to a new employer. The Court of Appeal held that the dispute was about terms and conditions which would apply to workers not currently employed by the NHS Trust and that such a dispute about future employment with a new employer was outside the provisions of section 244. Subsequently, the European Court of Human Rights ruled that in these circumstances the UK did not exceed the margin of appreciation accorded to it in regulating trade union action.[55]

The meaning of 'contemplation or furtherance'

The word 'contemplation' suggests something being thought of as likely to occur, so the 'golden formula' cannot be invoked if the action was taken too far in advance of any dispute. 'Furtherance' assumes the existence of a dispute and an act will not be protected if it is not for the purpose of promoting the interests of a party to the dispute (for example, if it is in pursuit of a personal vendetta) or occurs after its conclusion.[56]

CASE STUDY

MacSHANE AND ASHTON v EXPRESS NEWSPAPERS

In *MacShane and Ashton v Express Newspapers*[57] the Supreme Court held that while the existence of a trade dispute had to be determined objectively, the test for deciding whether an act is in furtherance of such a dispute is a subjective one: 'If the person doing the act honestly thinks at the time he does it that it may help one of the parties to the dispute to achieve their objective and does it for that reason, he is protected.'

Discussion point

Would an *objective* test for 'contemplation or furtherance' be fairer, so that the immunity would be lost if the action was not reasonably capable of achieving the aim?

INDUSTRIAL ACTION WHICH IS UNLAWFUL EVEN THOUGH WITHIN THE GOLDEN FORMULA

Even if the industrial action *is* in contemplation or furtherance of a trade dispute, there will still be legal liability in a number of situations. We here briefly discuss three such situations in which the union may be sued, namely:

- unlawful secondary action
- action taken without a ballot
- action taken without an industrial action notice to the employer.

Unlawful secondary action: section 224 TULRCA 1992

Secondary industrial action is action taken against an employer who is not a party to the trade dispute. A good illustration of secondary action is represented by the facts of *Duport Steels v Sirs*.[58]

CASE STUDY

DUPORT STEELS v SIRS

In this case the ISTC trade union which represented workers in the state-owned British Steel Corporation (BSC) was in dispute over wages with BSC. Steel was also manufactured by a number of private companies with whom the union was not in dispute. The ISTC wished to put pressure on the government by closing down steel production entirely, and so organised industrial action at the private steel companies as well. Under the law which applied at the time of this case the Supreme Court held that this secondary action was lawful. However, today such action would be unlawful under section 224.

Discussion point

Do you think secondary action should be permitted if other unions wish to support the action of the union in dispute?

Action taken without a ballot

In order to be lawful, industrial action – even if it is within the golden formula – may take place only after the union has gained majority support in a postal ballot of the members concerned. If no ballot is held or any of the requirements are not complied with, the union will be liable.[59] There are numerous requirements, some of which are complex, relating to the industrial action ballots. These requirements include:

- The ballot must take place not more than four weeks before the start of the action, or eight weeks if agreed between the union and employer.[60]
- All union members who it is reasonable for the union to believe will be induced to take part in the industrial action must be entitled to vote.[61]If some such members are not allowed to vote, with the exception of small accidental failures,[62] the ballot will be invalid. *London Underground Ltd v ASLEF* [63] concerned a ballot of London Underground train drivers to take industrial action on Boxing Day. The employer argued that the ballot should have been limited to those who would take part in the action – ie those drivers who had been rostered to work on Boxing Day. The Union argued successfully that all the drivers would have been induced by them and so should be included in the ballot. In contrast to this, in *Metroline Travel v UNITE the Union* [64] the employer argued successfully that there was a lack of clarity in knowing who was to be balloted and an interim injunction was granted stopping bus drivers taking industrial action during the London Olympics.
- The content of the voting paper has detailed requirements,[65] relating to information that must be stated and the wording of the question whether the member is prepared to participate in the industrial action.
- The ballot must be fully postal – ie members must be sent a voting paper and return their vote by post.[66]
- The ballot must be overseen by an independent scrutineer (such as a solicitor, accountant or the Electoral Reform Society) who must provide a report on the ballot as to whether, for example, it has complied with all the necessary requirements.[67]

CASE STUDY

BRITISH AIRWAYS v UNITE THE UNION (NO.2)[68]

This very well-publicised case concerned a dispute between the union and the airline. In a strike ballot called by the union the members voted overwhelmingly in favour of industrial action. Under TULRCA section 231 the union was obliged to provide certain information about the ballot result to all those entitled to vote. The required information was: a) the number of votes cast, b) the number of 'Yes' votes, c) the number of 'No' votes, and d) the number of spoiled ballot papers. The union posted all the required information on its websites, on union notice-boards and in other places. It also sent text messages and emails to members who had signed up for this service, but these messages did not contain all the information required under section 231. British Airways claimed that i) posting the information on the websites was 'passive' communication which did not comply with section 231, because it relied on members going online to look for the information, and ii) the text messages were also invalid because they did not contain all the required information. The High Court held in favour of the employers and ordered that the strike could not go ahead – but the Court of Appeal allowed the union's appeal against this decision. The Court of Appeal held that i) minor failures to give all the information stated in section 231 were not a problem, and ii) communication via websites was a valid way in modern times of communicating the necessary information. The strike could therefore go ahead.

Discussion point

Do you think section 231 is a valuable democratic right for union members, or is it an excessive and unnecessary burden on trade unions?

Action taken without an industrial action notice

The union must give the employer at least seven days' notice of official industrial action.[69] Again there are detailed requirements for the information that must appear in the notice. If no notice is given, or it does not comply with the requirements, the employer will be able to sue the union.

REFLECTIVE QUESTION

Are the compulsory strike ballots likely to be popular with unions and members? Do you think there are any changes that should be made?

PICKETING

Industrial action pickets carry out the function during the industrial action of trying to persuade others, such as workers or members of the public, not to go into the workplace. It can be an important way by which the union can strengthen its position in the dispute. You will probably have seen pickets during the course of high-profile industrial action campaigns, such as that undertaken by the Fire Brigades Union in 2002/3 or by the RMT union in their disputes with London Underground in recent years.

Picketing can sometimes become violent, criminal acts such as assault and criminal damage taking place. But even if picketing remains completely peaceful it could involve the commission of crimes such as obstruction of the highway or torts such as nuisance. TULRCA gives a limited immunity from liability for such torts or crimes to industrial action pickets. According to section 220 TULRCA 1992, it is lawful for a person in contemplation or furtherance of a trade dispute to attend:

- at or near their own place of work, or
- if they are an official of a trade union, at or near the place of work of a member of that union whom they are accompanying and whom they represent,

for the purpose only of peacefully obtaining or communicating information, or peacefully persuading any person to work or abstain from working.

Thus, to be lawful, not only must picketing be within the golden formula (see above), but the identity, location and purposes of the pickets must be within the narrow limitations of the section. So a person cannot lawfully picket if he or she does not work for, or represent someone who works for, the employer in dispute. Nor may picket lines be stationed anywhere apart from at or near the place of work of those in dispute.

If section 220 is not complied with by the pickets, they (and the union) will not only be liable for the relatively minor torts and crimes which peaceful picketing might involve such as nuisance and obstructing the highway. There will also be liability for any economic torts which are committed as a result of the picketing – eg inducing breaches of the employment contracts of those people persuaded by the pickets not to go into work.

REFLECTIVE QUESTION

Should people other than those mentioned in the section be permitted to take part in picketing?

HOW MANY PICKETS MAY THERE BE?

There is no limit mentioned in section 220 to the number of people who may picket, but in *Thomas v NUM (South Wales)* [70] it was said that in a situation where feelings were running high, substantial numbers of pickets were almost bound to have an intimidatory effect on those going to work, and therefore such mass picketing would not be permitted by the section. The Code of Practice on Picketing, which is issued by the Secretary of State for Work and Pensions, exhorts pickets and their organisers to ensure that 'in general the number of pickets does not exceed six at any entrance to, or exit from, a workplace;

frequently a smaller number will be appropriate'. Although the Code is not legally binding, it has been taken into account by the courts in decisions in picketing cases.

UNION RESPONSIBILITY FOR THE ACTS OF ITS MEMBERS AND OFFICIALS

A trade union has the same immunity from liability for lawful industrial action as its members and officers, and, like them, it can be sued if it is responsible for unlawful industrial action. However, a union will be held liable for the torts mentioned in section 20(1) TULRCA 1992 only if the acts in question were authorised or endorsed by the union.[71]

Irrespective of union rules, acts are to be regarded as authorised or endorsed if there was authorisation or endorsement by:[72]

- any person empowered by the rules to do, authorise or endorse acts of the kind in question
- the principal executive committee or the president or general secretary, or
- any other committee of the union or any other official of the union (whether employed by it or not).

So, for instance, if a a part-time union official who is not employed by the union calls members out on strike without first holding a strike ballot, the strike therefore being unlawful, the union will face liability for the action in the form of an order for damages or an injunction against it (see below). But the union may avoid this liability by 'repudiating' (ie disowning) the action.

HOW A UNION MAY REPUDIATE ACTS OF ITS COMMITTEES AND OFFICIALS

A union can avoid liability for the actions of union committees and officials (the third bullet point above) only if those actions are repudiated by the principal executive committee or the president or general secretary 'as soon as reasonably practicable after coming to the knowledge of any of them'. However, a repudiation will even then be effective only if:

- written notice of the repudiation is given to the official or committee in question without delay, and
- the union has done its best to give individual written notice of the fact and date of repudiation without delay to every member who the union has reason to believe is taking part, or might otherwise take part, in the industrial action. The notice to members must contain the following statement: 'Your union has repudiated any call for industrial action to which this notice relates and will give no support to such action. If you are dismissed while taking unofficial industrial action, you will have no right to complain of unfair dismissal.' This notice must also be given to the employer of every such member.[73]

An act will not be treated as repudiated if the union's principal executive committee, president or general secretary subsequently behaves in a manner inconsistent with that repudiation.

REMEDIES

If an employer brings a legal action against the union and the court decides that the industrial action is unlawful, there are two remedies which the court may grant the employer – namely, damages and an injunction.

DAMAGES

Section 22(2) TULRCA 1992 limits the amount of damages that can be awarded 'in any proceedings in tort' against a trade union which is deemed liable for industrial action.[74] The words 'in any proceedings' are crucial, since separate proceedings may be brought by all those who have suffered from the industrial action. The limits set are:

- £10,000, if the union has fewer than 5,000 members
- £50,000, if the union has 5,000 or more members but fewer than 25,000
- £125,000 if the union has 25,000 or more members but fewer than 100,000
- £250,000 if the union has 100,000 or more members.

It should be noted that interest on such damages may be available.[75] Finally, it should be noted that damages, costs or expenses cannot be recovered from certain 'protected property'. This includes union provident funds and political funds, which cannot be used for financing industrial action.[76]

INJUNCTIONS

Of greater interest to the employer will be the remedy of an injunction, which is a court order, and usually negative – ie an order *not* to do something. In this context the injunction would be an order to the trade union to stop the industrial action.

There are two basic types of injunction that should be mentioned:

- If the industrial action is continuing, the employer's priority is to get it stopped as soon as possible. The employer will usually seek an 'interim injunction', which can be obtained very quickly if the necessary conditions are met – see below. This injunction is a temporary one, granted by a judge after a short hearing, and it orders the union to cease the industrial action temporarily until the full trial takes place to decide if the action is lawful.
- A permanent injunction is one which is granted at the end of the full trial.

Before granting an interim injunction, a judge will have to consider a number of questions. These include

- Is there is a 'serious question to be tried'? That is, the employer must show that there is at least an arguable case that the industrial action is unlawful.
- Does the 'balance of convenience' lie with the employer? That is, the employer will suffer more harm if the injunction is not granted than the union will suffer if it is granted.
- If the union is claiming that the industrial action was within the golden formula (see above), what is the likelihood of it being able to show this was so?[77]

Failure by the union to comply with an injunction may amount to a contempt of court for which a substantial fine may be imposed.

CASE STUDY

GATE GOURMET LTD v TGWU

Gate Gourmet supply in-flight catering to airlines and recognised the Transport and General Workers Union (TGWU) for the majority of non-manual employees at its Heathrow South premises. The company agreed a package of staff reductions and changes in working practices with the union, but this was rejected in a membership ballot. Before mediation talks started, employees stopped work and held a sit-in without a ballot. This was alleged to be a response to the hiring of seasonal workers. Following the dismissal of 622 workers, there was picketing at two of the company's sites, and the employer maintained that there was intimidation and harassment of the remaining employees.

The High Court granted an interim injunction on the basis that there was a good arguable case that torts contrary to section 20 TULRCA 1992 had occurred which had been authorised or endorsed by the union. Because the TGWU had not repudiated the unlawful activity, it was right that the injunction should be directed at the union. Despite the right to peaceful assembly being guaranteed by Article 11 of the European Convention on Human Rights, the balance of convenience lay firmly in favour of expressly prohibiting any activity which went beyond peaceful approaches being made to the employees.[78]

Union members' right to apply for an injunction

It is not only employers who may apply to the court for an injunction to stop unlawful industrial action. Under section 62 TULRCA 1992 a union member may apply to the court for an injunction to stop authorising or endorsing industrial action which has been called without the support of a ballot, or a ballot not fulfilling all the necessary requirements (see above).

INDUSTRIAL ACTION THAT AFFECTS THE SUPPLY OF GOODS OR SERVICES TO AN INDIVIDUAL

Under section 235A of TULRCA 1992 where unlawful industrial action affects the supply of goods and services to an individual, he or she may apply for an injunction against the union. So, for instance, if a council's refuse collectors go on strike without holding a ballot, a householder affected by this could apply to court for an injunction to halt the strike.

REFLECTIVE QUESTION

Do you think that the current law adopts the right balance between trade unions and employers?

KEY LEARNING POINTS

- The Certification Officer decides if a trade union is entitled to a Certificate of Independence.
- An independent trade union must be recognised by an employer in order to enjoy a number of statutory rights, such as the right to the disclosure of information for collective bargaining purposes.
- The statutory recognition procedures apply to firms with 21 or more employees on the day an independent trade union requests recognition.
- Employers have a duty to disclose to trade unions recognised for collective bargaining purposes such information without which the union representatives would be to a material extent impeded in carrying on collective bargaining with them.
- A collective agreement is conclusively presumed not to be a legally enforceable contract unless it is in writing and contains a provision that the parties intend it to be a legally enforceable contract.
- It is unlawful to refuse employment to a person because he or she is or is not a member of a trade union.
- Employees have the right not to be dismissed or subjected to a detriment for the purposes of preventing them from becoming a member or taking part in the activities of or using the services of a trade union or, conversely, for not wanting to be a member or take part in union activities.
- Blacklisting of trade unionists is also now unlawful.
- Trade unions taking industrial action are likely to commit the economic torts of inducing a breach of contract, causing an economic loss by unlawful means and conspiracy.
- Statutory immunity from these torts depends on the action's taking place in contemplation or furtherance of a trade dispute. This is known as the 'golden formula'.
- Immunity will be lost where the industrial action has not been supported by a majority of members voting in a secret ballot before the action is undertaken.
- Immunity will also be lost in cases of secondary industrial action and where an industrial action notice has not been given to the employer.
- A union will be held liable for the unlawful actions of its committees and officials unless those actions are repudiated by the principal executive committee, the president or the general secretary, and the union has done its best to inform the officials, and those taking part in the industrial action, of its repudiation.
- Trade unions must take all reasonably necessary steps to ensure that the employer of those to be called upon to take part in industrial action receives written notice of both a ballot and any proposed action. The union must also provide information about the number and categories of employees concerned and their workplaces.
- Remedies available for unlawful action are damages, and interim and permanent injunctions.
- Picketing is lawful in contemplation or furtherance of a trade dispute if it takes place near the employee's own place of work, or if the picket is an official of the union accompanying a member, with the intention of peacefully persuading someone to work or abstain from working.

REFERENCES

1. **This chapter contains extracts from or close paraphrasing of legislation, and *Explanatory Memoranda* to that legislation, which is on the opsi.gov.uk website (and its successor) and is subject to crown copyright. It also contains other public sector information from the acas.org.uk website [accessed august 2010]. The reproduction of this material here is licensed under the open government licence v1.0.**
2. (1980) 1 All ER 1097
3. Sections 12 and 13 TULRCA 1992
4. Section 3 TULRCA 1992
5. Section 4 TULRCA 1992
6. Section 9(1) TULRCA 1992
7. Section 6(2) and (5) TULRCA 1992
8. Section 8 TULRCA 1992
9. (1980) IRLR 431
10. (1979) IRLR 75
11. (1993) IRLR 260
12. Section 178(3) TULRCA 1992
13. Section 178(1) TULRCA 1992
14. See *NUGSAT v Albury Bros* (1978) IRLR 504
15. See *J Wilson and Albury Bros v USDAW* (1978) IRLR 20
16. See *NUGSAT v Albury Bros* (note 14)
17. See *Cleveland County Council v Springett* (1985) IRLR 131
18. See *NUGSAT v Albury Bros* (note 14)
19. *R (on the application of Ultraframe) v Central Arbitration Committee* (2005) IRLR 641
20. (2006) IRLR 53
21. Section 181(1) and (2) TULRCA 1992
22. (1982) IRLR 61
23. Disclosure of Information to Trade Unions for Collective Bargaining Purposes, ACAS, 2003
24. Section 181(4) TULRCA 1992
25. Code of Practice paragraph 10
26. Code of Practice paragraph 11
27. Code of Practice paragraph 22
28. Section 183 TULRCA 1992

29 See *Edinburgh Council v Brown* (1999) IRLR 208, where an agreement between the employer and the joint consultative committee constituted a collective agreement

30 Section 178(1) TULRCA 1992

31 Section 179(1) TULRCA 1992

32 Section 179(3) TULRCA 199

33 According to section 285 TULRCA 1992, these provisions do not apply if the prospective employee would ordinarily work outside Great Britain

34 *Ridgway v NCB* (1987) IRLR 80

35 See *Farnsworth Ltd v McCoid* (1999) IRLR 626

36 *Gallacher v Department of Transport* (1994) IRLR 231

37 *Southwark London Borough Council v Whillier* (2001) ICR 142

38 See *Ridgway v NCB* (note 34)

39 *Carlson v Post Office* (1981) IRLR 158

40 Sections 146 (2A) and 152*(2A) TULRCA 1992

41 See *Crosville Motor Services Ltd v Ashfield* (1986) IRLR 475

42 Section 154(1) TULRCA 1992. An employee wishing to complain must first submit a statement of grievance to the employer

43 See *Maund v Penwith District Council* (1984) IRLR 24

44 Section 161 TULRCA 1992

45 Section 162 TULRCA 1992

46 See *Taplin v C. Shippam Ltd* (1978) IRLR 450

47 Either reinstatement or re-engagement, see Chapter 15

48 See section 164 TULRCA 1992

49 *Explanatory Memorandum* to the Employment Relations Act 1999 (Blacklists) Regulations 2010, January 2010

50 SI 2010/493

51 As re-defined in *OBG Ltd v Allan* (2007) IRLR 608

52 For an analysis of these torts, see *Smith & Wood's Employment Law* pp 670–81

53 Section 219 TULRCA 1992

54 (1999) IRLR 31

55 See *Unison v UK* (2002) IRLR 497

56 See *Huntley v Thornton* (1957) 1 WLR 321; also *Stratford v Lindley* (1965) AC 307

57 (1980) IRLR 35

58 (1980) IRLR 116

59 Section 226(1) TULRCA 1992

60 Section 234(1) TULRCA 1992
61 Section 227 TULRCA 1992; see *RMT v Midland Mainline Ltd* (2001) IRLR 813
62 Section 232B TULRCA 1992; see *NURMTW v Serco Ltd* (2011) IRLR 399
63 *London Underground Ltd v Associated Society of Locomotive Engineers and Firemen* (2012) IRLR 196
64 *Metroline Travel and others v UNITE the Union* (2012) IRLR 749
65 Section 229 TULRCA 1992
66 Section 230 TULRCA 1992
67 Sections 226B and 231B 1992
68 (2010) IRLR 809
69 Section 234A 1992
70 (1985) IRLR 136
71 See *Gate Gourmet Ltd v TGWU* (2005) IRLR 881
72 Section 20(2) TULRCA 1992
73 Sections 21(1)–(3) TULRCA 1992. See *Balfour Kilpatrick v Acheson* (2003) IRLR 683
74 For exceptions see section 22(1) TULRCA 1992
75 See *Boxfoldia Ltd v NGA* (1988) IRLR 38376 Section 23 TULRCA 1992
76 See section 221 TULRCA 1992
77 *Gate Gourmet Ltd v TGWU* (note 71)

EXPLORE FURTHER

Reading

- Davies, A. (2009) *Perspectives on Labour Law*. Oxford University Press, Chapters 10, 11 and 12
- Deakin, S. and Morris, G. (2012) *Labour Law*. Hart, Chapters 7, 8, 9 and 11
- Smith, I. and Baker, A. (2010) *Smith & Wood's Employment Law*. Butterworths, Chapters 9 and 10

Websites

- Advisory, Conciliation and Arbitration Service www.acas.org.uk
- Chartered Institute of Personnel and Development www.cipd.co.uk
- Department for Business Innovation and Skills www.bis.gov.uk
- DirectGov – Employment wwwdirect.gov.uk
- Trades Union Congress www.tuc.org.uk

Glossary

Additional maternity leave This commences on the day after the last day of the ordinary maternity leave period and continues for 26 weeks from the day on which it commenced.

Certification Officer Nominal head of the official organisation that holds the list of*independent trade unions* and adjudicates as to their independence or not.

Cessation of work Temporary stoppage or interruption in work, especially when there is no work to do; the date of the cessation may be significant in redundancy situations.

Collective agreement Any agreement or arrangement made by or on behalf of one or more trade unions and one or more employers, or employers' associations, which relates to one or more of the matters mentioned in section 178(2) TULRCA.

Comparator The person to whom a claimant in a discrimination claim compares himself or herself.

Compulsory maternity leave This is not to be less than two weeks in length, commencing with the day on which childbirth occurs, and it is included in the ordinary maternity leave period.

Constructive dismissal This is where an employee terminates the contract with or without notice in circumstances such that he or she is entitled to terminate it without notice by reason of the employer's conduct.

Contract of employment A contract of service or apprenticeship, whether express or implied, and (if it is express) whether oral or in writing.

Default retirement age The age of 65 years.

Economic entity 'An organised grouping of resources which has the objective of pursuing an economic activity, whether or not that activity is central or ancillary' (Regulation 3(2) TUPE).

Employee An individual who has entered into or works under (or, where the employment has ceased, worked under) a *contract of employment.*

Expected week of childbirth The week, beginning with midnight between Saturday and Sunday, in which it is expected that childbirth will occur.

Express terms Those terms which are expressly stated to form part of the *contract of employment.*

Flexible working Permitted variability in hours worked and/or duties performed; it particularly concerns the right of some employees to vary their hours of work for the purposes of caring for certain dependants.

Gender reassignment A process undertaken under medical supervision for the purpose of reassigning a person's sex by changing physiological or other characteristics of sex, that includes any part of such a process.

Implied term of fact Where there is a gap in the *contract of employment* it is possible to imply a term if a court can be persuaded that it is necessary to do so in the circumstances of the particular case.

Implied terms of law Terms regarded by the courts as being inherent in all *contracts of employment* although not formally expressed.

Independent trade union A trade union judged not to be under the domination or control of an employer or a group of employers and not liable to interference by an employer, arising out of the provision of financial or material support or by any other means whatsoever, tending towards such control.

Instant dismissal This has no legal definition but refers to a dismissal on the spot, without investigation or inquiry.

Limited-term contract A contract which terminates by virtue of a *limiting event.*

Limiting event Something that signifies the completion and termination of a contract. There are three categories: the expiry of a fixed term; the performance of a specific task; or the occurrence of an event or the failure of an event to occur.

Night time A period which is not less than seven hours in length and includes the hours of midnight to 5am.

Night worker A worker who, as a normal course, works at least three hours of working time during '*night time*' or is a worker who is likely, during 'night time', to work a certain proportion of his or her annual working time as defined by a collective or workforce agreement.

Obligatory period The minimum period of notice (of redundancy, retirement, dismissal, etc) which the employer is required to give by virtue of section 86(1) ERA 1996 or the *contract of employment.*

Relevant agreement A workforce agreement, a provision of a collective agreement which forms part of a contract between the worker and the employer, or any other agreement in writing that is legally enforceable as between employer and worker.

Restrictive covenant An express clause in the *contract of employment* which restrains competition by ex-employees after they have left.

Service provision change A transfer that takes place when an undertaking contracts out some part of its activities to a contractor, or when such a contract is taken over by another contractor, or when the client takes back the activity in-house from a contractor.

Service-related pay and benefits Forms of reward for service that may include salary, holidays, etc, all or some of which may be related to length of service.

Statutory retirement procedure Legal responsibility of an employer to consider a request from an employee to work beyond the *default retirement age*, and the procedure by which this request is considered.

Summary dismissal Where the employer terminates the contract of employment abruptly and without notice.

Trade dispute A dispute between workers and their employer which relates wholly or mainly to terms and conditions of employment; an engagement or non-engagement or termination or suspension of employment; the allocation of work or the duties of employment as between workers or groups of workers; matters of discipline; membership or non-membership of a trade union; facilities for officials of trade unions; and the machinery for negotiation or consultation about these matters.

Transferee employer The employer to whom staff are transferred in a TUPE transfer.

Transferor employer The employer from whom staff are transferred in a TUPE transfer.

Vicarious liability The responsibility of employers to third parties for the civil wrongs committed by their employees in the course of their employment.

Worker An individual who has entered into, or works under, a *contract of employment*or 'any other contract, whether express or implied and (if it is express) whether oral or in writing, whereby the individual undertakes to do or perform personally any work or services for another party to the contract whose status is not by virtue of the contract that of a client or customer of any profession or business undertaking carried on by the individual'.

Workforce agreement An agreement which a) is in writing, b) has effect for a specified period not exceeding five years, c) applies to all the relevant members of a workforce or all the relevant members who belong to a particular group, and d) is signed by the representatives of the group; copies of the agreement are readily available for reading prior to the signing.

Working time Any period during which the worker is working, at the employer's disposal and carrying out the worker's activity or duties; any period during which the worker is receiving relevant training; any additional period which is to be treated as working time for the purpose of the Working Time Regulations under a relevant agreement.

Young worker An individual who is paid for working, is at least 15 years of age, is over the compulsory school-leaving age, and has not yet attained the age of 18 years.

Index

Absence
  unfair dismissal, 253–254
ACAS
  see also **ACAS Codes of Practice**
  advice, 9
  arbitration, 10
  conciliation, 9–10
  generally, 9
  inquiries, 10
  other duties, 11
ACAS Codes of Practice
  collective bargaining, 366–367
  disciplinary and grievance procedures
    appeal procedures, 266
    cases where procedure may be ignored, 263
    employee representation, 265
    handling disciplinary problems, 264
    introduction, 263
    natural justice, 264–265
    protection of informants, 265
    warnings, 265–266
Acts of Parliament
  sources of law, 2
Additional adoption leave
  generally, 165
Additional maternity leave
  generally, 150–151
Adjustments
  disability discrimination, 109
Adoption leave
  additional adoption leave, 165
  generally, 164
  miscellaneous issues, 166
  ordinary adoption leave, 164–165
  premature ending, 165
Advertisements
  discrimination, 112–113
Advisory, Conciliation and Arbitration Service
  see **ACAS**
Age discrimination
  see **Discrimination**
Agency workers
  control, 63–65
  generally, 62–63
  mutuality of obligation, 63–65
  regulation of agencies, 65–67
Alternative employment
  pregnant/breastfeeding women, 171–172
  redundancy
    generally, 276
    reasonableness of refusal, 276
    trial periods, 277
Amendment of employment contracts
  business reorganisations, 258–260
  generally, 223–224
  transfer of undertakings, 318–319
Annual leave
  working time, 207–209
Antenatal care
  time off work, 149–150
Appeals
  court structure, 4–5
  disciplinary procedures, 266
Appropriate bargaining units
  trade union recognition, 364
Arbitration
  ACAS, 10
  unfair dismissal, 289
Attendance
  see also **Illness**
  unfair dismissal, 253–254
Automatically unfair dismissal
  assertion of statutory rights, 252
  generally, 251–252
  health and safety, 252–253
  maternity leave, 154–155
  parental leave, 160
  paternity leave, 163–164
  transfer of undertakings, 319
Average hours calculations
  generally, 194
  night workers, 195
Ballots
  industrial action, 376
  trade union recognition, 364
Bank holidays
  annual leave, 207–209
Bargaining units
  trade union recognition, 364
Basic awards
  unfair dismissal, 292–293
Blacklisting
  trade unions, 372
Breach of contract
  constructive dismissal, 240
  employers' remedies, 224–227
  wrongful dismissal, 230–231

Breaks
working time, 205
Burden of proof
discrimination, 130–131
Capability
absence, 253–254
illness, 254
introduction, 253
poor performance, 253
Central Arbitration Committee (CAC)
generally, 11
implied terms, 26
trade union recognition
appropriate bargaining units, 364
ballots, 364
derecognition, 364
generally, 362–363
requests for recognition, 363–364
statutory procedures, 363–365
Certification of trade unions
see **Trade unions**
Certification Officer
generally, 11–12
Change of duties
constructive dismissal, 240–241
Change of employer
continuous employment, 310–311
Civil law
sources of law, 1–2
Codes of practice
see also **ACAS Codes of Practice**
health and safety, 178–179
sources of law, 2–3
Colleagues
competence, 37
Collective agreements
discrimination, 210
enforcement, 368
generally, 22–23
no-strike clauses, 23–24
statements of particulars, 20
transfer of undertakings, 322
working time, 210
Collective bargaining
see also **Trade unions**
definition, 363
disclosure of information
ACAS Code of Practice, 366–367
failure to disclose, 367–368
good practice, 366–367
introduction, 365–366
substantial injury, 367
unions' rights, 366–367
Collective redundancies
see also **Redundancy**
appropriate representatives, 338
consultation procedure, 340–343
definition, 339
establishment, definition of, 340
introduction, 338–339
matters to be disclosed, 341–342
no jobs lost, 339
notification, 344–345
protective awards, 343–344
special circumstances allowing non-consultation, 342–343
Common law
sources of law, 3–4
Compensation
age discrimination, 123–124
discrimination, 132–133
industrial action, 380
redundancy payments
amount, 297–298
compromise agreements, 288–289
conciliation, 288–289
time limits for claims, 285–287
week's pay, 311–313
unfair dismissal
basic awards, 292–293
compensatory awards, 293–297
future loss of income, 296–297
introduction, 292
jobseekers' allowance, 297
loss flowing from manner of dismissal, 295
loss of accrued rights, 296
loss of income up to hearing date, 295
loss of pension rights, 296
reduction of compensatory awards, 293–295
week's pay, 311–313
Competent colleagues
employers' duties, 37
Competent persons
health and safety, 185
Competition with employer
dismissal, 256
employees' duties, 40–41
Compromise agreements
unfair dismissal, 288–289
Conciliation
ACAS, 9–10
unfair dismissal, 288–289
Confidentiality
employees' duties, 42–43
information and consultation, 337
Constructive dismissal
breach of contract, 240
breach of duty of trust and confidence, 239–240
change of duties, 240–241
demotion, 240–241
generally, 238–240
pay issues, 241–242

Consultation
see also **Information and consultation**
collective redundancies, 340–343
Continuous employment
change of employer, 310–311
generally, 305–307
redundancy, 273
strikes and lock-outs, 309–310
weeks that count, 307–309
Contract workers
see **Fixed-term contracts**
Contracting out
recruitment, 57
transfer of undertakings, 317
unfair dismissal, 236
Contracts of employment
see **Employment contracts**
Control of substances hazardous to health
health and safety, 186–187
Convictions
recruitment, 68
Co-operation
employees' duties, 39–40
employers' duties, 32–34
Copyright
employee works, 46–47
COSHH Regulations
health and safety, 186–187
Court structure
sources of law, 4–5
Criminal law
sources of law, 1–2
Custom and practice
implied terms, 26
Damages
industrial action, 380
Dangerous occurrences
reporting, 188–189
Deductions from pay
generally, 73–74, 75
Delegated legislation
sources of law, 2
Demotion
constructive dismissal, 240–241
Dependants
time off work, 166–167
Derecognition
trade unions, 364
Detriment
see also **Discrimination**
discrimination, 370
maternity leave, 154–155
parental leave, 160
part-time workers, 61
paternity leave, 163–164
trade union membership, 370
working time, 210–211
Directives
see also under specific subjects
sources of law, 5–6
Disability discrimination
see **Discrimination**
Disciplinary procedures
ACAS Code of Practice
appeal procedures, 266
cases where procedure may be ignored, 263
employee representation, 265
handling disciplinary problems, 264
introduction, 263
natural justice, 264–265
protection of informants, 265
warnings, 265–266
breach of contract, 224–227
statements of particulars, 20
Disclosure of information
see also **Information and consultation**
collective bargaining
ACAS Code of Practice, 366–367
failure to disclose, 367–368
good practice, 366–367
introduction, 365–366
substantial injury, 367
unions' rights, 366–367
public interest disclosure, 43–46
Discrimination
see also **Equality of terms**
advertisements, 112–113
age
child care, 124–125
enhanced redundancy payments, 123–124
length of service benefits, 121–122
life assurance cover for retired workers, 124
national minimum wage, 123
personal pensions, 125
protected characteristics, 93
retirement, 120–121
burden of proof, 130–131
comparators, 111–112
detriment, 370
direct discrimination, 101–104
disability
conditions treated as disabilities, 93–94, 95
definition, 93
discrimination arising from disability, 104–105
normal day-to-day activities, 94
reasonable adjustments, 109
substantial and long-term adverse effect, 94
dismissal, 371–372
employers' liability
generally, 127–129
harassment by third parties, 129
employment, 112–113
enforcement, 132–133

Equality and Human Rights Commission, 133
exceptions
armed forces, 120
child care, 124–125
enhanced redundancy payments, 123–124
ethos relating to religion or belief, 120
generally, 117–118
insurance contracts, 125
length of service benefits, 121–122
life assurance cover for retired workers, 124
national minimum wage, 123
national security, 118
occupational requirements, 118–119
personal pensions, 125
positive action, 125–126
pregnancy and maternity, 125
public services, 125
religious requirements, 119–120
retirement, 120–121
sexual orientation, 125
statutory authority, 118
gender reassignment
absence from work, 105
protected characteristics, 95–96
harassment
employers' liability, 129
generally, 109–111
health-related enquiries, 113
indirect discrimination, 106–108
introduction, 91–92
job advertisements, 112–113
job offers, 112–113
justification, 103–104
'like for like' comparison, 111–112
marriage and civil partnership, 96
obtaining information procedure, 131–132
positive discrimination/action, 125–126
post-termination discrimination, 113
pregnancy and maternity
prohibited conduct, 105–106
protected characteristics, 96
prohibited conduct
direct discrimination, 101–104
disability discrimination, 104–105
failure to make reasonable adjustments, 109
gender reassignment discrimination, 105
generally, 93
harassment, 109–111
indirect discrimination, 106–108
pregnancy and maternity discrimination, 105–106
victimisation, 111
promotion, 112–113
protected characteristics
age, 93
disability, 93–95
gender reassignment, 95–96
generally, 92–93
marriage and civil partnership, 96
pregnancy and maternity, 96
race, 97–98
religion or belief, 98–99
sex, 100
sexual orientation, 101
public sector equality duty, 134
race, 97–98
religion or belief, 98–99
remedies, 132–133
self-employed persons, 112
sex, 100
sexual orientation, 101
sources of law, 91–92
time limits, 132
trade union membership
blacklisting, 372
detriment, 370
dismissal, 371–372
introduction, 368–369
refusal of employment, 369
vicarious liability
generally, 127–129
harassment by third parties, 129
victimisation, 111
Diseases
reporting, 188–189
Dishonesty
dismissal, 256–257
Dismissal
see also **Redundancy; Unfair dismissal**
breach of contract by employee, 224–227
discrimination, 371–372
effective date of termination, 242–243
frustration, 227–228
introduction, 236
limited-term contracts, 238
mutual agreement, 237–238
notice, 229–230
part-time workers, 61
public interest disclosure, 46
resignation, 237–238
summary dismissal, 228–229
trade union membership, 371–372
with or without notice, 237
words used, 238
wrongful dismissal, 230–231
Disobedience
dismissal, 255–256
Display screen equipment
health and safety, 186
Duty of care
see also **Health and safety**
employees' duties, 43
Economic torts

action taken without a ballot, 376
action taken without an industrial action notice, 377
introduction, 372–373
unlawful actions, 375
unlawful secondary action, 375

Effective date of termination
unfair dismissal, 242–243

Employee consultation
see **Information and consultation**

Employee representatives
time off work, 216–217

Employees' duties
co-operation with employer, 39–40
fidelity
confidentiality, 42–43
garden leave, 41–42
generally, 40
non-competition, 40–41
restrictive covenants, 41
health and safety, 182
reasonable skill and care, 43

Employers' associations
generally, 360–361

Employers' duties
see also **Information and consultation**
co-operation with employees, 32–34
health and safety
competent/safe colleagues, 38
delegation, 181–182
duty of care, 35–36
generally, 34–35, 181
safe plant, equipment and tools, 36
safe premises, 36, 182
safe systems of work, 36–37
information and consultation, 327–328
payment of wages, 31, 73–76
provision of references, 38–39
provision of work, 31–32

Employment agencies
see **Agency workers**

Employment Appeal Tribunal
generally, 8

Employment contracts
see also **Termination of employment**
breach of contract
constructive dismissal, 240
employers' remedies, 224–227
wrongful dismissal, 230–231
collective agreements
generally, 22–23
no-strike clauses, 23–24
copyright, 46–47
custom and practice, 26
employees' duties
confidentiality, 42–43
co-operation with employer, 39–40
fidelity, 40–43
garden leave, 41–42
non-competition, 40–41
reasonable skill and care, 43
restrictive covenants, 41
employers' duties
co-operation with employees, 32–34
payment of wages, 31, 73–76
provision of references, 38–39
provision of work, 31–32
reasonable care of employees, 34–38
express terms, 17
fixed-term contracts
continuous employment, 306, 308
discrimination, 105
dismissal, 238
recruitment, 57–59
redundancy, 279
health and safety
competent/safe colleagues, 38
duty of care, 35–36
employers' duties, 34–35
safe plant, equipment and tools, 36
safe premises, 36
safe systems of work, 36–37
illegal contracts, 16–17
implied terms
common law, 27
copyright, 46–47
employees' duties, 39–43
employers' duties, 31–39
inventions, 46–47
public interest disclosure, 42–46
sick pay, 82
statutory provisions, 26–27
introduction, 15–16
inventions, 46–47
no-strike clauses, 23–24
policy guidance, 25
public interest disclosure, 42–46
statements of particulars
contents, 17–21
duty to supply, 17
mandatory/non-mandatory terms, 21–22
status, 21
variation
business reorganisations, 258–260
generally, 223–224
transfer of undertakings, 318–319
whistleblowing, 42–46
workforce agreements, 24–25
works rules, 25

Employment status
generally, 53–56

Employment tribunals
breach of contract claims, 224–227
challenges to decisions, 8

costs and fees, 7–8
generally, 7
representation at hearings, 7
Enhanced redundancy payments
age discrimination, 123–124
Equal pay
see **Equality of terms**
Equality and Human Rights Commission (EHRC)
generally, 133
Equality of terms
see also **Discrimination**
comparators, 135–137
discussions with colleagues, 143–144
enforcement, 142
'gagging clauses', 143–144
generally, 134–135
implied terms, 26, 134–135
material factor defence, 140–142
maternity equality clause, 142–143
red-circling, 142
sex equality clause, 135
work like comparator's work, 138
work of equal value, 140
work rated as equivalent, 138–139
Equipment
health and safety, 35, 186
European companies
information and consultation, 331–332
European co-operative societies
information and consultation, 332
European law
sources of law, 5–6
European Works Councils
information and consultation, 328–331
Fidelity
confidentiality, 42–43
garden leave, 41–42
generally, 40
non-competition, 40–41
restrictive covenants, 41
Final warnings
disciplinary procedures, 265–266
Fixed-term contracts
continuous employment, 306, 308
discrimination, 105
dismissal, 238
recruitment, 57–59
redundancy, 279
Flexible working
generally, 168–169
grounds for refusal, 170–171
procedure, 170
Formation of employment contracts
see **Employment contracts**
Frustration
employment contracts, 227–228
'Gagging clauses'
equality of terms, 143–144
Garden leave
employees' duties, 41–42
Gender reassignment
discrimination
absence from work, 105
protected characteristics, 95–96
Genuine occupational requirements
discrimination, 118–119
'Golden formula'
see **Industrial action**
Gross misconduct
competition, 256
dishonesty, 256–257
disobedience, 255–256
employer contact pending investigation, 258
establishing gross misconduct, 255
generally, 254–255
offences outside the workplace, 258
summary dismissal, 228–229
Guarantee payments
calculation, 81–82
generally, 80–81
Harassment
see also **Discrimination**
employers' liability, 129
generally, 109–111
Hazardous substances
health and safety, 186–187
Health and safety
codes of practice, 178–179
competent persons, 185
Control of Substances Hazardous to Health (COSHH) Regulations, 186–187
Directives, 185
discrimination, 118
display screen equipment, 186
employee involvement, 180
employees' duties, 182
employers' duties
competent/safe colleagues, 38
delegation, 181–182
duty of care, 35–36
generally, 181
safe plant, equipment and tools, 36
safe premises, 36, 182
safe systems of work, 36–37
enforcement
improvement notices, 191–192
inspectors' powers, 189–191
prohibition notices, 191–192
guidance, 178
Health and Safety at Work Act 1974, 179–182
Health and Safety (Display Screen Equipment) Regulations, 186
Health and Safety Executive, 178

implied terms
competent/safe colleagues, 38
duty of care, 35–36
safe plant, equipment and tools, 36
safe premises, 36
safe systems of work, 36–37
improvement notices, 191–192
information and consultation
detriment and dismissal, 352
generally, 180, 347–349
safety committees, 352
safety representatives, 349–352
unfair dismissal, 352
injury prevention/compensation, 177–178
Management of Health and Safety at Work Regulations
competent persons, 185
generally, 182–183
risk assessment, 183–185
Manual Handling Operations Regulations, 185
offences, 192–193
Personal Protective Equipment at Work Regulations, 186
prohibition notices, 191–192
Provision and Use of Work Equipment Regulations, 186
regulations
Control of Substances Hazardous to Health (COSHH) Regulations, 186–187
Health and Safety (Display Screen Equipment) Regulations, 186
introduction, 182
Management of Health and Safety at Work Regulations, 182–185
Manual Handling Operations Regulations, 185
Personal Protective Equipment at Work, 186
Provision and Use of Work Equipment Regulations, 186
Reporting of Injuries, Diseases and Dangerous Occurrences Regulations (RIDDOR), 188–189
subsidiary Directives, 185
Workplace (Health, Safety and Welfare) Regulations, 186
risk assessment, 183–185
safe colleagues, 37
safe plant, equipment and tools, 35
safe premises, 35, 182
safe systems of work, 35–37
safety committees, 352
safety policies, 180–181
safety representatives
duty to consult, 349–350
functions, 350–351
introduction, 349
time off work, 351–352
trade union safety representatives, 350
scope of legislation, 178–179
self-employed persons' duties, 181
unfair dismissal, 252–253
work equipment, 186
Workplace (Health, Safety and Welfare) Regulations, 186
Holidays
annual leave, 207–209
statements of particulars, 19
Illegal contracts
generally, 16–17
Illness
dismissal, 254
frustration of employment contract, 227–228
sick pay
common law entitlement, 82
contractual entitlement, 82–83
statutory sick pay, 84–85
suspension on medical grounds, 85–86
Immigration control
recruitment, 68
Implied terms
common law, 27
copyright, 46–47
employees' duties
confidentiality, 42–43
co-operation with employer, 39–40
fidelity, 40–43
garden leave, 41–42
non-competition, 40–41
reasonable skill and care, 43
restrictive covenants, 41
employers' duties
co-operation with employees, 32–34
payment of wages, 31, 73–76
provision of references, 38–39
provision of work, 31–32
reasonable care of employees, 34–38
inventions, 46–47
public interest disclosure, 42–46
sick pay, 82
statutory provisions, 26–27
Improvement notices
health and safety, 191–192
Incapability
absence, 253–254
illness, 254
introduction, 253
poor performance, 253
Independent contractors
employment status, 53–56
Indirect discrimination
generally, 106–108
Industrial action

ballots, 376
damages, 380
economic torts
action taken without a ballot, 376
action taken without an industrial action notice, 377
introduction, 372–373
unlawful actions, 375
unlawful secondary action, 375
'golden formula'
contemplation or furtherance of trade dispute, 374
introduction, 373–374
trade disputes, definition of, 374
injunctions, 380–381
notice, 377
picketing
generally, 377–378
limitation of numbers, 378–379
redundancy, 274
remedies
damages, 380
injunctions, 380–381
secondary action, 375
supply of goods/services to individuals, action affecting, 381
trade disputes, 374
trade union responsibility, 379
unfair dismissal
protected industrial action, 260–261
unofficial action, 261

Informants
protection, 265

Information and consultation
collective redundancies
appropriate representatives, 338
consultation procedure, 340–343
definition, 339
establishment, definition of, 340
introduction, 338–339
matters to be disclosed, 341–342
no jobs lost, 339
notification, 344–345
protective awards, 343–344
special circumstances allowing non-consultation, 342–343
confidentiality, 337
employers' duties, 327–328
European companies, 331–332
European co-operative societies, 332
European Works Councils, 328–331
failure to consult, 337–338
health and safety
detriment and dismissal, 352
generally, 180, 347–349
safety committees, 352
safety representatives, 349–352
unfair dismissal, 352
Information and Consultation Directive, 332
Information and Consultation Regulations
generally, 332–335
standard provisions, 336–337
introduction, 327–328
redundancy consultation, 280
safety committees, 352
safety representatives
duty to consult, 349–350
functions, 350–351
introduction, 349
time off work, 351–352
trade union safety representatives, 350
Societas Europaea, 331–332
special negotiating bodies
European companies, 331–332
European Works Councils, 328–331
standard provisions, 336–337
transfer of undertakings, 322, 345–347
transnational information and consultation
European companies, 331–332
European Works Councils, 328–331
introduction, 328

Information Commissioner
generally, 12

Injunctions
breach of contract, 225
industrial action, 380–381
wrongful dismissal, 230–231

Injuries
reporting, 188–189

Inquiries
ACAS, 10

Insolvency
redundancy, 298–299
transfer of undertakings, 321

Institutions
ACAS
advice, 9
arbitration, 10
conciliation, 9–10
generally, 9
inquiries, 10
other duties, 11
Central Arbitration Committee, 11
Certification Officer, 11–12
Employment Appeal Tribunal, 8
employment tribunals
challenges to decisions, 8
costs and fees, 7–8
generally, 7
representation at hearings, 7
Information Commissioner, 12

Insubordination
dismissal, 255–256

Intellectual property

employee inventions/copyright works, 46–47

Interim injunctions
industrial action, 380–381

Inventions
employee inventions, 46–47

Itemised pay statements
generally, 80

Job description
statements of particulars, 19

Jobseekers' allowance
unfair dismissal, 297

Judicial review
wrongful dismissal, 230–231

'Keeping in touch' days
maternity leave, 153

'Last in, first out'
redundancy selection, 279

Leave
see also **Parental rights; Time off work**
annual leave, 207–209
statements of particulars, 19

Legislation
sources of law, 2–3

Length of service benefits
age discrimination, 121–122

Less favourable treatment
see **Discrimination**

Limited-term contracts
see also **Fixed-term contracts**
dismissal, 238

Lock-outs
see **Industrial action**

Looking for work
time off work, 217–218

Loss of income/rights on unfair dismissal
accrued rights, 296
future loss of income, 296–297
loss flowing from manner of dismissal, 295
loss up to hearing date, 295
pension rights, 296

Manual handling
health and safety, 185

Marital status
see **Discrimination**

Material factor defence
equality of terms, 140–142

Maternity allowance
parental rights, 155–156

Maternity leave
additional maternity leave, 150–151
compulsory maternity leave period, 152
detriment and dismissal, 154–155
generally, 150
'keeping in touch' days, 153
maternity allowance, 155–156
notification to employer, 151–152
ordinary maternity leave, 150–151
return to work, 153
right to return to work, 154
statutory maternity pay, 155–156
terms and conditions of employment, 153–154
transfer to father, 155

Maximum working week
see **Working time**

Migrant workers
recruitment, 68

Minimum wage
see **National minimum wage**

Misconduct
competition, 256
dishonesty, 256–257
disobedience, 255–256
employer contact pending investigation, 258
establishing gross misconduct, 255
generally, 254–255
offences outside the workplace, 258

Mobile workers
working time, 199–200

Mutual agreement
termination of employment, 237–238

National minimum wage
age discrimination, 123
calculation
hours, 78–79
pay, 78
excluded persons, 77
generally, 76–77
implied terms, 26
output work, 79
rates, 76
salaried hours work, 78–79
time work, 79
underpayment, 79–80
unmeasured work, 79
working, definition of, 77

National security
discrimination, 118

Natural justice
disciplinary procedures, 264–265

Night workers
working time, 203–205

Non-competition
employees' duties, 40–41

No-strike clauses
collective agreements, 23–24

Notice
collective redundancies, 344–345
industrial action, 377
statements of particulars, 19
termination of employment
dismissal, 237
generally, 229–230
wrongful dismissal, 230–231

Occupational pensions
discrimination, 125
loss of rights on unfair dismissal, 296
time off work for trustees, 216–217
transfer of undertakings, 322–323
Occupational requirements
discrimination, 118–119
Offences
dismissal
dishonesty, 256–257
employer contact pending investigation, 258
establishing gross misconduct, 255
generally, 254–255
offences outside the workplace, 258
harassment, 109–111
health and safety, 192–193
picketing
generally, 377–378
limitation of numbers, 378–379
Offenders
recruitment, 68
Offers of alternative employment
pregnant/breastfeeding women, 171–172
redundancy
generally, 276
reasonableness of refusal, 276
trial periods, 277
On-call workers
working time, 202
Output work
national minimum wage, 79
Outsourcing
recruitment, 57
transfer of undertakings, 314–316
Overpayments
recovery by employer, 76
Overseas work
statements of particulars, 20
Parental rights
adoption leave
additional adoption leave, 165
generally, 164
miscellaneous issues, 166
ordinary adoption leave, 164–165
premature ending, 165
flexible working
generally, 168–169
grounds for refusal, 170–171
procedure, 170
maternity leave
additional maternity leave, 150–151
compulsory maternity leave period, 152
detriment and dismissal, 154–155
generally, 150
'keeping in touch' days, 153
maternity allowance, 155–156
notification to employer, 151–152
ordinary maternity leave, 150–151
return to work, 153
right to return to work, 154
statutory maternity pay, 155–156
terms and conditions of employment, 153–154
transfer to father, 155
parental leave
default provisions, 158
detriment and dismissal, 160
generally, 157
notice, 158–159
postponement, 159
right to return to work, 160
terms and conditions of employment, 159–160
paternity leave
additional paternity leave, 162–163
detriment and dismissal, 163–164
ordinary paternity leave, 160–162
risk assessment, 171–172
statutory maternity pay, 155–156
time off work
antenatal care, 149–150
dependants, 166–167
unfair dismissal
maternity leave, 154–155
parental leave, 160
paternity leave, 163–164
Particulars of employment
contents, 17–21
duty to supply, 17
mandatory/non-mandatory terms, 21–22
status, 21
Part-time workers
comparable full-time workers, 59–61
complaints to tribunals, 62
detriment and dismissal, 61–62
generally, 59
less favourable treatment, 61
Patents
employee inventions, 46–47
Paternity leave
additional paternity leave, 162–163
detriment and dismissal, 163–164
ordinary paternity leave, 160–162
Pay
see also **Equality of terms; National minimum wage**
constructive dismissal, 241–242
deductions, 73–74, 75
employers' duties, 31, 73–76
guarantee payments
calculation, 81–82
generally, 80–81
itemised pay statements, 80

national minimum wage
calculation of hours, 78–79
calculation of pay, 78
excluded persons, 77
generally, 76–77
rates, 76
underpayment, 79–80
working, definition of, 77
overpayments, 76
pay statements, 80
payments in lieu of notice, 74–75
sick pay
common law entitlement, 82
contractual entitlement, 82–84
statutory sick pay, 84–85
statements of particulars, 18–19
suspension on medical grounds, 85–86
time off work for trade union duties/activities, 212
wages, definition of, 74
withholding for breach of contract, 225
Payments in lieu of notice
generally, 74–75
wrongful dismissal, 230–231
Pensions
discrimination, 125
loss of rights on unfair dismissal, 296
time off work for trustees, 216–217
transfer of undertakings, 322–323
Performance
dismissal, 253
Personal protective equipment
health and safety, 186
Picketing
generally, 377–378
limitation of numbers, 378–379
Piecework
national minimum wage, 79
Place of work
redundancy, 275
statements of particulars, 20
Plant
health and safety, 36
Policy guidance
employment contract terms, 25
Poor performance
dismissal, 253
Positive action
discrimination, 125–126
Precedent
sources of law, 3–4
Pregnancy
see also **Maternity leave; Parental rights**
sex discrimination, 96, 105–106
unfair dismissal, 154–155
Premises
health and safety, 35, 182
Probationary periods
recruitment, 67
Prohibition notices
health and safety, 191–192
Prohibitions on working
dismissal, 258
Protective awards
collective redundancies, 343–344
'Provision, criterion or practice'
discrimination, 107
Provision of work
employers' duties, 31–32
Public duties
time off work, 215–216
Public holidays
annual leave, 207–209
Public interest disclosure
implied terms, 43–46
Public sector
public sector equality duty, 134
transfer of undertakings, 322
Qualifications
dismissal for lack of, 253
genuine occupational qualifications, 118–119
Race discrimination
see **Discrimination**
Reasonable adjustments
disability discrimination, 109
Reasonable care
see also **Health and safety**
employees' duties, 43
Reasonableness
unfair dismissal, 261–262
Reasons for dismissal
duty to provide statement, 250–251
generally, 249–250
Recognition of trade unions
see **Trade unions**
Recruitment and selection
agency workers
control, 63–65
generally, 62–63
mutuality of obligation, 63–65
regulation of agencies, 65–67
discrimination, 112–113
employment status, 53–56
ex-offenders, 68
fixed-term workers, 57–59
indefinite contracts, 57–59
migrant workers, 68
outsourcing, 57
part-time workers
comparable full-time workers, 59–61
complaints to tribunals, 62
detriment and dismissal, 61–62
generally, 59
less favourable treatment, 61

probationary periods, 67
regulatory constraints
introduction, 67
migrant workers, 68
rehabilitation of offenders, 68
vetting and barring scheme, 67
temporary workers
control, 63–65
generally, 62–63
mutuality of obligation, 63–65
Rectifiable warnings
disciplinary procedures, 265–266
Red-circling
equality of terms, 142
Redundancy
age discrimination, 123–124
alternatives, 279
collective redundancies
appropriate representatives, 338
consultation procedure, 340–343
definition, 339
establishment, definition of, 340
introduction, 338–339
matters to be disclosed, 341–342
no jobs lost, 339
notification, 344–345
protective awards, 343–344
special circumstances allowing non-consultation, 342–343
compensation for unfair dismissal
basic awards, 292–293
compensatory awards, 293–297
future loss of income, 296–297
introduction, 292
jobseekers' allowance, 297
loss flowing from manner of dismissal, 295
loss of accrued rights, 296
loss of income up to hearing date, 295
loss of pension rights, 296
reduction of compensatory awards, 293–295
consultation, 280
continuous employment, 273
definition, 274–275
enhanced redundancy payments, 123–124
exclusions, 273–274
fixed-term contracts, 279
industrial action, 274
insolvency, 298–299
'last in, first out', 279
offers of alternative employment
generally, 276
reasonableness of refusal, 276
trial periods, 277
place of employment, 275
qualifying persons, 273–274
redundancy payments
amount, 297–298
compromise agreements, 288–289
conciliation, 288–289
time limits for claims, 285–287
week's pay, 311–313
re-employment
generally, 290–291
practicability, 291
remedies for refusal to re-employ, 292
terms, 291–292
selection, 278–279
unfair dismissal
alternatives to redundancy, 279
arbitration, 289
compensation, 292–297
compromise agreements, 288–289
conciliation, 288–289
fair application of selection criteria, 278–279
introduction, 277
making claims, 285–287
re-employment, 290–292
time limits for claims, 285–287
trade union involvement, 278
work of a particular kind, 275
Re-employment
see **Redundancy**
References
duty to provide, 38–39
failure to provide, 113
Refusal of employment
trade union membership, 369
Regulations
see also under specific subjects
European law, 6–7
statutory instruments, 2
Rehabilitation of offenders
recruitment, 68
Religious discrimination
see **Discrimination**
Remuneration
see **National minimum wage; Pay**
Reporting of injuries, diseases and dangerous occurrences
health and safety, 188–189
Representation
disciplinary hearings, 265
employment tribunal hearings, 7
Repudiation
constructive dismissal, 238–240
employment contracts
breach by employee, 224–227
unlawful summary dismissal, 228–229
trade union members'/officials' acts, 379
Resignation
dismissal, 237–238
Rest periods

working time, 205
Restrictive covenants
employees' duties, 41
Retirement
age discrimination, 120–121
Return to work
see **Parental rights**
RIDDOR Regulations
health and safety, 188–189
Risk assessment
health and safety, 183–185
pregnant/breastfeeding women, 171–172
Safety
see **Health and safety**
Safety committees
information and consultation, 352
Safety representatives
duty to consult, 349–350
functions, 350–351
introduction, 349
time off work, 351–352
trade union safety representatives, 350
Salaried hours work
national minimum wage, 78–79
Salary
see **Pay**
Secondary action
industrial action, 375
Selection
see **Recruitment and selection; Redundancy**
Self-employed persons
employment status, 53–56
health and safety, 181
Service provision changes
transfer of undertakings, 316–317
Sex discrimination
see **Discrimination; Equality of terms**
Sexual orientation discrimination
see **Discrimination**
Sick pay
common law entitlement, 82
contractual entitlement, 82–83
statutory sick pay, 84–85
Skill and care
see also **Health and safety**
employees' duties, 43
Societas Europaea
information and consultation, 331–332
Some other substantial reason
unfair dismissal, 258–260
Sources of law
civil law, 1–2
codes of practice, 2–3
common law, 3–4
court structure, 4–5
criminal law, 1–2
European law, 5–6
legislation, 2–3
Special negotiating bodies
European companies, 331–332
European Works Councils, 328–331
Spent convictions
recruitment, 68
Statements of particulars
contents, 17–21
duty to supply, 17
mandatory/non-mandatory terms, 21–22
status, 21
Statements of reasons for dismissal
duty to give, 250–251
Statutes
sources of law, 2
Statutory instruments
sources of law, 2
Statutory maternity pay
generally, 155–156
Statutory prohibitions on working
dismissal, 258
Statutory sick pay
generally, 84–85
statements of particulars, 19
Strikes
see **Industrial action**
Study or training
time off work, 217
Subordinate legislation
sources of law, 2
Summary dismissal
generally, 228–229
Suspension on medical grounds
pay, 85–86
Systems of work
health and safety, 35–37
Temporary workers
control, 63–65
generally, 62–63
mutuality of obligation, 63–65
Termination of employment
see also **Redundancy; Unfair dismissal**
breach of contract by employee, 224–227
discrimination, 112–113
dismissal
introduction, 236
mutually agreed termination, 237–238
resignation, 237–238
termination of limited-term contracts, 238
termination with or without notice, 237
words used, 238
effective date of termination, 242–243
frustration, 227–228
notice, 229–230
part-time workers, 61
public interest disclosure, 46
summary dismissal, 228–229

trade union membership, 371–372
wrongful dismissal, 230–231
Theft
gross misconduct, 256–257
Time off work
see also **Parental rights**
antenatal care, 149–150
dependants, 166–167
employee representatives, 216–217
looking for work, 217–218
pension trustees, 216–217
public duties, 215–216
safety representatives, 351–352
study or training, 217
trade union duties and activities
activities, 214–215
duties, 211–212
legitimate reasons for time off, 212–214
pay, 212
union learning representatives, 215
Time work
national minimum wage, 79
Tools
health and safety, 36
Torts
see **Economic torts**
Trade associations
employers' associations, 360–361
Trade disputes
see **Industrial action**
Trade secrets
employees' duty of confidentiality, 42–43
Trade unions
see also **Industrial action**
blacklisting, 372
certificates of independence
certification, 361
employer control over union, 361–362
introduction, 359–360
listed trade unions, 360–361
collective agreements, enforcement of, 368
definition, 360
detriment, 370
disclosure of information
ACAS Code of Practice, 366–367
failure to disclose, 367–368
good practice, 366–367
introduction, 365–366
substantial injury, 367
unions' rights, 366–367
discrimination
blacklisting, 372
detriment, 370
dismissal, 371–372
introduction, 368–369
refusal of employment, 369
dismissal relating to membership, 371–372
employer control, 361–362
employers' associations, 360–361
listed trade unions, 360–361
recognition
appropriate bargaining units, 364
ballots, 364
derecognition, 364
generally, 362–363
requests for recognition, 363–364
statutory procedures, 363–365
redundancy consultation, 280
refusal of employment on grounds of membership, 369
safety representatives, 349–352
time off work for union duties and activities
activities, 214–215
duties, 211–212
legitimate reasons for time off, 212–214
pay, 212
union learning representatives, 215
Training
time off work, 217
Transfer of undertakings
automatically unfair dismissal, 319
collective agreements, 322
contract variations, 318–319
definition, 313–315
employee choice, 319–321
information and consultation, 322, 345–347
insolvency, 321
introduction, 313
pensions, 322–323
persons to be transferred, 317–318
public sector, 322
service provision changes, 316–317
TUPE Regulations, 315–317
Transsexuals
discrimination
absence from work, 105
protected characteristics, 95–96
Trial periods
offers of alternative employment, 277
Tribunal awards
see **Compensation**
Trust and confidence
constructive dismissal, 239–240
TUPE
see **Transfer of undertakings**
Underperformance
dismissal, 253
Unequal treatment
see **Discrimination**
Unfair dismissal
automatically unfair dismissal
assertion of statutory rights, 252
generally, 251–252
health and safety, 252–253